Great Insights

on

Human Creativity

Transforming the Way We Live, Work, Educate, Lead, and Relate

Volume I

Compiled and Synthesized

by

Efiong Etuk, Ph.D.

Foreword by Sid Parnes, Ph.D.
Professor Emeritus, Buffalo State College
Lifetime Trustee, Creative Education Foundation

"… so that we may exist more fully and realize more of our human potential."
— Henry David Thoreau

Great Insights on Human Creativity: Transforming the Way We Live, Work, Educate, Lead, and Relate. Volume I.
Compiled and Synthesized by Efiong Etuk, Ph.D.

First printing 2002
© 2002 by Efiong Etuk.
Mailing Address:
      Unity Scholars, Inc.
      P.O. Box 11226
      Blacksburg
      Virginia 24060
Gift 11-05 USA

ISBN: 0 9717382-0-3

Library of Congress Control Number: 2002090478

Printed in the United States by Morris Publishing
3212 East Highway 30   Kearney, NE 68847
1-800-650-7888

To my mother, Mma Nwa.
Her belief in the intrinsic worth of every human being
and her personal philosophy of making people feel
important inspired this project.

Contents

Preface

Each of us has a piece of the puzzle of solving the great world problems of our time and creating a more just, humane, and beautiful world. ... If everyone who loved to create beauty did so, we would live in a beautiful world. If everyone who loved cleanliness and order, cleaned up, we would live in a clean and orderly world. If everyone who yearned to heal the sick did so, we would live in a healthier world. If everyone who cared about world hunger shared his creative ideas and acted to alleviate the problem, people would all be fed.

– Carol Pearson

A commentator on current events and trends, Eknath Easwaran, correctly observed that lasting change occurs when people themselves discover that a different way of life, a different pattern of existence, is more fulfilling than the current one.

Few periods in recorded human history have so perfectly reflected that observation as the second half of the twentieth century and the beginning of this new millennium. One of the most significant changes in the past fifty years has been the rapidly growing number of people who feel that they and many of the people with whom they relate are not reaching their full potential and who, therefore, are trying to make their individual and our collective existence more meaningful, more productive, and more fulfilling.

It goes by different names and descriptions: identity, human fulfillment, self-actualization, creative selfhood, beyond-survival goals, and more. This is the growing realization that we, humans, are not just economic, but social, emotional, and spiritual beings as well; that our needs are not only food, shelter, clothing, and possessions, but also relatedness, mutual support, sense of participation, compassion, self-esteem, self-transcendence, and the actualization of our innate potentialities; that, for greater balance in our lives, our economic, as well as our social, emotional, and spiritual needs would have to be satisfied or, at least, continuously addressed; that we are not just consumers of other people's creative products but potential creators ourselves – every one of us with something unique and important to contribute for the benefit of our species and

vii

the planet, plus the urge, the desire, a ceaseless yearning to make one's contribution; and, finally, that our personal sense of worth, our productivity as employees, our humaneness toward fellow human beings, our compassion for the rest of creation and, indeed, our collective survival as a species, critically depend on the extent to which we, *each of us,* are able to realize our creative potentialities and contribute them for the common good.

More than ever before, people of all nationalities, racial and ethnic origins, socioeconomic and sociopolitical circumstances are *consciously* struggling to find meaning and fulfillment in their lives and to help those for whom they are responsible to do the same. Practical illustrations of this transformation are:

- The growing popularity of such values as creativity, identity, life purpose, and self-actualization in both academic and popular discourse. The rapidly increasing number of people who are beginning to define themselves primarily in terms of their ability to realize their creative potential and contribute to the common good, and only secondarily in terms of their possessions, power, prestige, and the pleasures that those things give.

- The small but increasing number of schools that are shifting from "educating for diplomas and certificates" to "educating for living and personal fulfillment" – helping each learner (or student) to discover his or her special abilities, and then providing him or her with relevant experiences and resources (including academic skills) to develop those abilities and eventually to engage them in things that he or she is naturally good at or passionate about. The growing number of teachers who are redefining their role as facilitators of learning rather than as dispensers of knowledge: (i) recognizing and assisting their students as people with different but equally valid abilities, aptitudes, goals, and styles of learning; and (ii) organizing their classrooms as a collaborative community of learners (each helping the others to expand their understanding and to succeed in their various ways) rather than as a group of rivals trying to see who is smarter.

- The growing popularity of self-employment with its self-fulfillment component. The increasing number of job seekers who are looking not for just any job that pays a salary, but for something that they really care about, an opportunity to collaborate with fellow human beings in activities they perceive as important and worthy, a chance to actualize their talents and, therefore, to find meaning in their lives.

- The growing number of organizations that are redesigning and organizing their tasks in ways that allow (even require!) their workers to use their ingenuity as much as their skills, their hearts as much as their hands, their passions as much as their intellect. The growing number of "bosses" who are beginning to regard themselves as resource persons to be consulted, rather than old-style masters to be pleased or feared.

* The growing popularity of "win-win thinking" in management circles. The increasing number of management consultants who are advising their clients that the best guarantee for a disciplined, motivated, committed, and productive workforce is activities that workers see not only as paying a salary, but also as nourishing their creative potential and harmonizing their material, emotional, mental, and spiritual needs.

- The increasing number of leaders who are acknowledging the creative potential and, therefore, the incalculable worth, of every one of their constituents. Paradoxically, the growing number of leaders who are beginning to define their responsibilities as producing more leaders rather than more followers: (i) helping their constituents to discover and to actualize their own leadership abilities in areas of their individual potential; and (ii) presenting problems and challenges in ways that call forth the creativity and ingenuity of their constituents as well as their individual ability to lead.

- The growing number of families who are making the unfolding of each child's unique potentialities the guiding principle of every parental action. Shifting values from shaping and molding a child into what parents want him or her to be, to watching the way that each child chooses to act and listening to the things the child likes to talk about for clues to the child's aptitudes, needs, and interests. The growing emphasis on a child's emotional, social, and moral integration – not just his or her material success.

- The growing body of credible evidence suggesting possible association between the fulfillment of human potential and such things as mental health, self-worth, and responsible behavior. The growing number of psychiatrists, medical practitioners, counselors, therapists, and clergymen telling us that the only way that people are going to be happy with themselves, productive as employees, and responsible as citizens is if they are enabled to recognize, to develop, and to express their natural abilities in important and socially beneficial ways.

- Women who are demanding not only equality with their male counterparts, but also respect, mutuality, identity and, above all, opportunity to use their talents and make a difference.

- Ethnic minorities and former colonials who are asserting the integrity of their indigenous cultures as well as their right to develop in their own ways and to contribute their insights both to their nations' political, economic, cultural development and to the urgent task of global civilization building.

These and related trends give indications of the way the world is going. This project is designed to facilitate that transformation.

Great Insights on Human Creativity is a collection of some of the most astonishing interpretations of human nature and the human condition, indicating the centrality of creativity in human life and its absolute necessity for emotional and mental well-being, for high labor productivity, for social and ecological responsibility, and for personal fulfillment. Arranged and synthesized thematically, this treasury of wit and wisdom provides the tools we need to handle some of the most pressing challenges of our time and restore meaning to our lives.

The intended readership of *Great Insights on Human Creativity* includes parents, educators, students, employees, corporate executives, counselors, therapists, management consultants, and the political leadership. The aim is to provide a resource to help us make the most of our lives both as individuals and in our relationships with other people, the larger society, and the natural environment. In this and subsequent volumes, you will find thousands of soul-stirring and memorable ideas to help you:

- raise creative, self-confident children; help your children to recognize, and appreciate the integrity of, their special abilities and, therefore, to develop strong feelings of self-worth.

- teach so that your students can find learning exciting, meaningful, satisfying, and fulfilling; help your students to integrate what they learn with what they see as their goals in life.

- create and maintain a "win-win" organization in which employees can find meaning, purpose, and personal fulfillment in the work they do and, therefore, increase their productivity and commitment.

- energize your subordinates' and constituents' capacities, particularly their leadership potential, for increased participation, loyalty, and sense of responsibility.

- assist economically, socially, and psychologically vulnerable members of society to recognize and more deliberately tap their creative potential for a more meaningful, more productive, and more fulfilling existence.

- participate ever more effectively in building more creativity-friendly families, neighborhoods, schools, workplaces and, therefore, in making our world a more fulfilling place to live.

Several practical concerns prompted this project. The principal ones are:

- the urgent task of building a more humane and more fulfilling human civilization that requires everyone's creative participation.

- the abundance of creative ideas that already exist (albeit scattered) and only need to be brought together and focused on the challenges currently facing humanity.

- the many disparate groups and organizations that are working to make our world a more humane and more fulfilling place to live, but appear to lack a unifying framework within which to coordinate their efforts.

- the large number of psychological and social problems that humanistic psychologists attribute to unfulfilled human potential.

- the growing pressures of modern life (e.g., rapid change that is still accelerating, uncertainties that are deepening, and competition that is unrelenting) that require every bit of one's creativity to thrive or even to cope.

- the many myths about human creativity that must be dispelled, including, for example:
  - creativity as a mysterious and exclusive ("you-have-it-or-you-don't") attribute of a few gifted and talented individuals.
  - creativity as achievable only in selected areas of human activity.
  - creativity as expressible only as tangible products and ideas.

- creativity as following a uniform, step-by-step process.
- creativity as a unidimensional attribute that is measurable by currently available techniques.
- vast reservoirs of, as yet, undiscovered and underutilized human potential that need to be recognized, more fully developed, and channeled to human and environmental ends.
- the ultimate unsustainability of the present consumption-driven world civilization that, visionary thinkers warn, will require fundamental shifts in thinking and action to avert otherwise-inevitable disaster.

To these ends, I have brought together some of the most insightful interpretations of human nature that, collectively: (a) indicate the inherence of creativity in human nature, its primacy among the forces driving human behavior and its significance in every sphere of human activity; (b) affirm the right of every human being to be creative – to discover one's special abilities and to develop and express them in things that one perceives as important and beneficial to oneself, one's society, and the rest of nature; and (c) call attention to the psychological, economic, and social implications of unused or underused human capacity.

My overall purposes in compiling and synthesizing this anthology are these: (i) make creative thinking a subject of interest not only to professionals and academic specialists, but to the general public as well; (ii) encourage more people to take an active interest in exploring their creative potential and engaging them for the common good; (iii) provide a critical resource for parents, educators, corporate executives, consultants, counselors, therapists, and other professionals who are responsible for facilitating the growth and development of other people; (iv) call attention to some of the myths, assumptions, and social practices that tend to constrain the development and actualization of our most important and most distinctive attribute as a species; (v) broaden the framework for understanding and promoting creativity across activities, across social strata, and across the life-span; and (vii) underscore our individual and collective responsibility to try to realize our innate (creative) potential and to help others to do the same.

Six main criteria were applied in selecting insights for this project: wit, evocativeness, relevance, precision, appeal, and memorability. First and foremost, I wanted statements that would significantly expand or deepen our understanding of human nature and the human condition. Second, I was interested in statements that are likely to stimulate readers' minds and possibly inspire a rethinking of some of the things we have always believed or taken for granted. Third, I was looking for statements that are of practical and immediate relevance to our times and circumstances – particularly those that provide guidance for meeting the challenges currently facing humanity. Fourth, in order to meet the needs of today's very busy people, I preferred statements that convey a lot of meaning in a few words and require no technical knowledge to comprehend. Fifth, I wanted statements that are interesting, persuasive and, at the same time, provocative. Sixth, and finally, I wanted ideas that "we already know" but which are stated in a way we may never forget. The result is a compendium of smart, crisp, and witty ideas for a wide range of personal, professional, business, and social situations, including speeches, reports, term-papers, presentations, meetings, personal reflection, mentoring, counseling, and much more.

Several options are available for organizing a collection of this type. The most common practice is simply to list the ideas, often alphabetically and by subject. The problem with that option is that, other than the subject heading, it does little to enlighten the user or to relate the ideas to the daily circumstances of his or her life. In this project, I have chosen to arrange the insights by theme, each of which begins with an introductory synopsis, followed by the relevant statements. The synopses are deliberately kept short in order to give prominence to the insights which, in any case, speak for themselves. I chose this format so as to make it easy for the reader to identify appropriate insights to suit his or her particular purpose, or to convey a particular idea.

I should emphasize that *Great Insights on Human Creativity* is not a substitute for the sources from which the statements were selected. For more detailed discussion of specific issues, the reader is advised to consult the original sources that, as far as possible, are fully referenced.

Certain elements of arbitrariness could not be avoided and must be recognized. The first of these is the necessarily haphazard and incomplete search of the literature. The second is my personal judgment of what is quotable. The third is where to begin and end a quote. The fourth is the theme under which a particular statement is placed. Some "redundancies" will also be observed, both in the statements and in the introductory syntheses. This aspect is due to the unity of the focal construct (creativity) and, therefore, the inevitable overlap of the themes under which it is being presented.

Notwithstanding these limitations, I am confident that this anthology will stimulate fresh new discussions about human capacities and their development, about human life and its purpose, about human existence and its fulfillment. Whatever your reason for opening these pages, I am convinced that you will find *Great Insights on Human Creativity* an invaluable resource: witty, instructive, provocative, and refreshing – something to return to again and again.

Efiong Etuk, Ph.D.
August 2001.

Acknowledgments

Michel de Montaigne characterized one of his many great works as a collection of other men's flowers for which he had merely provided the binding thread. That's exactly how I feel about *Great Insights on Human Creativity*. The 7,000 (still increasing) statements upon which the five-volume anthology is based are *all* other people's ideas. All I have done is merely synthesize them for the guidance they provide for meeting some of the most pressing challenges of our time and, in particular, for restoring meaning and purpose to our lives.

In the course of identifying and selecting statements for this project, I have consulted a few thousand books and published articles. I am deeply indebted to the authors of those publications and, in particular, to the great thinkers whose ideas I am featuring in the collection. I also wish to acknowledge my indebtedness to the editors, compilers, and publishing houses that are preserving these gems of wisdom for posterity. They are individually acknowledged both in the introductory synopses and in the selected remarks for each section and, as far as possible, are fully referenced.

More people than I can ever acknowledge have helped in various ways to bring this project to this stage. The following is a very short list of those individuals:

Professor Sidney Parnes, founding director and professor emeritus, Center for Studies in Creativity, State University of New York at Buffalo and lifetime trustee, Creative Education Foundation, has been a role model for my work in creative thinking. Reading one of his (with Harold F. Harding) publications, entitled *A Sourcebook of Creative Thinking,* changed my professional interest from action research to creative thinking. Professor Parnes' lifetime interest in promoting creative thinking across activities and across social strata has been a great source of inspiration for me.

Part of this project was completed under very difficult circumstances and might have been abandoned without the support of Unity Scholars, Inc., Maine and Vermont, USA, and Forum Foundation, Seattle, Washington State, USA.

Mr. August Jaccaci, president, Unity Scholars, and **Joanne Jaccaci** have literally been the project's moving spirit. Since reviewing the project proposal and reading a few sample chapters of *Great Insights* two years ago, the Jaccacis have consistently played the triple roles of financial angel, mentor, and advocate – sourcing and providing financial and material support and, also, promoting the project as part of the emerging global renaissance. Thank you, Gus and Joanne, for your inestimable assistance and personal sacrifice. Thanks also for your organization's work toward a "conscious, creative, compassionate, collaborative [global] community (C4 community)" within which we, each, can fulfill our destiny.

Dr. Richard Spady, president, Forum Foundation, has been one of this project's greatest promoters. First, he funded the critical final phase of this volume. Second, and coincidentally, his foundation's work toward "a civilization that we and our posterity can love throughout our future history" happens to address the same goal that *Great Insights* is advocating. Third, also coincidentally, the foundation's rapidly spreading Fast Forum® technique for "enhancing communication in organizations and society" is proving itself a powerful tool for tapping the vast reservoir of latent, hitherto hardly recognized, public creativity.

Professor Richard Zody, director, Institute for Public Management, Department of Urban Affairs and Planning, Virginia Polytechnic Institute and State University, recognized the need for this project very early in its inception. Since then, Professor Zody has been a great resource person, providing not only the needed financial and material support, but also quality friendship and professional encouragement.

The Department of Urban Affairs and Planning, Virginia Polytechnic Institute and State University, successively chaired by **Professors Jim Bohland and John Randolph**, graciously hosted me while I was working on parts of this project.

Professors John Dickey, **Robert Dyck**, and **Jan Howard**, Department of Urban Affairs and Planning, Virginia Polytechnic Institute and State University, were very generous with their books. As a matter of fact, there were times when my bookshelves held more of Professor Dickey's books than my own.

Professor Ted Koebel, director, Virginia Center for Housing Research, provided every support I needed: intellectual, professional, administrative, financial and, most of all, genuine friendship. Thank you, Ted, for your generosity.

Professor Joe Scarpaci, Department of Urban Affairs and Planning, Virginia Polytechnic Institute and State University, and Dr. Harriet Bauer, Principal, St. Mary's Catholic School, Blacksburg, Virginia, read various draft sections of the manuscript and provided very helpful suggestions. In spite of the many demands on their time, both Professor Scapaci and Dr. Bauer always found time to review the materials with me, with their characteristic sugar-coated criticisms.

Susan Malone, Malone Editorial Services, Colleyville, Texas, did a great job editing the manuscript and, in the process, giving vitality to some of the issues. Her comments and suggestions were extremely professional and very helpful too. Her unforgiving red pen notations are something any serious writer would like to see. Thank you, Sue. You've just added another satisfied customer to your list.

Su Clauson-Wicker of Su Clauson-Wicker Public Relations and Communications, Blacksburg, Virginia, painstaking proofed the final draft, questioning certain word uses and identifying grammatical and punctuation errors that I could easily have missed. Su's help, by itself, was invaluable. What I appreciated even more was her accommodating attitude and willingness to help even at very short notice.

Mary Holliman and **Bruce Wallace**, Pocahontas Press, Blacksburg Virginia, have been wonderful friends and a real blessing to this work: editing, typre-setting, and providing invaluable professional advice.

Professor **Michael Bliss**, Department of English, Virginia Polytechnic Institute and State University, reviewed the manuscript and provided many editorial and substantive comments and suggestions. His insights and willingness to help are deeply appreciated.

Nathan Skreslet, a Virginia Tech student with many demonstrable talents, designed and produced the cover of this project. And he did so *pro-bono*, in spite of the many time-consuming changes occasioned by my indecision, and in the middle of his end-of-semester examination. I describe Nathan as a young man with a heart many times bigger than one would expect for someone his age.

Lou Bergeron, President, Friends International, Portland Maine, USA, has been a great friend and supporter of this project.

I particularly want to acknowledge the support and encouragement of the following individuals and couples for making my stay in the Blacksburg - Christiansburg area of Virginia a "home away from home." They are: **Lucille Calhoun**, **Larry** and **Betty Foy**, **David** and

Susan Gibbs, Henry and Susan Henderson, Wayne and Dee Lagan, Mr. and Mrs. Lookabill, Carolyn Moore, Freddie Oliver, Dr. Arthur Roberson, Tom and Betsy Roberts, Linda Robinson, and Chip and Donna Worley.

Loy and Mary Burch have been a most wonderful host family, providing every conceivable need to make my family comfortable in Blacksburg. Their kindness and generosity was simply overwhelming. Thank you so kindly, Loy and Mary.

Five very special people have consistently encouraged and supported my creativity promotion activities over the years. They are:

General Ibrahim Babangida, former Head of State, Federal Republic of Nigeria, has been one of my greatest motivators. His innovative public policies, his highly visible support for new ideas and, in particular, his encouragement for Nigerians to "think outside the box" gave me the all-important "political platform" to stand on. Thank you, General, for your presidential injunction: "Our people have to be creative." Translating this statement into practical action is a major reason for this project.

General Cletus Emein (Rtd.), Nigerian Army, former Military Governor, Niger State, was the first state governor to make creative thinking the official way of doing business in the state's civil service and local government administration. The role that he asked me to play in implementing that visionary policy initiative added impetus and strengthened my resolve for this project.

My uncle, Engineer Jackson Anana, former director (highways), Federal Ministry of Works and Housing, Lagos, Nigeria, has been my mentor all my life. His total identification with the poor and the less fortunate members of society, his vision of a more just and more equitable human future, and his faith in human ingenuity to bring about that future have undoubtedly influenced my thinking and personal orientation.

Mr. Nelson Essien Ekanem, Obong Uforo Ibibio ("Pillar of Progress in Ibibioland"), former managing director, Anchor Insurance, Uyo, Nigeria, was a remarkable success in his own right. What made Nelson even more remarkable was his personal commitment to helping the people around him to succeed. The well-deserved traditional title, "Pillar of Progress," speaks volumes of a young man whose life demonstrated that nobody can count himself a success unless and until everyone around him has succeeded.

Mrs. Moji Ruffai, former director (training), Federal Ministry of Works and Housing, Lagos, Nigeria, has been my friend and intellectual sparring partner for twenty-two years. Moji and I are as different as any two people can be. We find reason to disagree with each other on practically every thing, except one: The colossal waste of human talents, and the need for urgent salvage action. The idea of demystifying creativity – making it a more popularly accessible and less elitist subject – came out of one of our sparring encounters nine years ago.

My elder brothers, **Solomon Etuk, William Etuk,** and **Essien Etuk** prematurely but graciously withdrew from school to make money available for the last-born to stay on. Their love, concern, and support for the "baby of the family" has continued to grow over the years. Thank you, brothers, for all the pampering. I can never have enough of it.

My greatest debt goes to my wife and children:

My eldest daughter, **Enobong Etuk,** endured years of my absence while I was working on this project. Even in that very difficult condition, her love for Daddy never diminished. Her letters, telling Daddy to press on with the task, did exactly what she intended them to do – encourage me! Thank you, Enobong, for your understanding and fortitude. I love you!

Destiny, Uwem, and **Nelson Etuk** learned to put up with a dad who was as good as absent. Their assistance turning the computer on and off, saving and closing document files when Dad was occupied with something else, looking up words in the Dictionary for Dad, and asking "Daddy, when are you going to be done with this project?" was a great source of support.

My wife, **Kate Ndudi,** has been a wonderful companion throughout this project – encouraging, advising, word-processing, editing, managing the files, and keeping the house. If there is just one person who has brought this project to this stage, it is, without a doubt, Kate. Certainly, only she could endure some of the conditions and experiences that the work entailed. There were times when every road seemed closed and it looked more honorable, at least more convenient, to give up than to persist. But Kate would not brook recreance. Rather, she kept reminding me that what was at stake (i.e., blighted human potential) was more important than our temporary inconvenience. Thanks, Kate. I salute your courage. As you are very well aware, the journey is just beginning!

E. E.

My use of the pronouns *he, him, his,* and *himself* for the more universal *he or she, him or her, his or her,* and *himself or herself,* respectively, is in no way intended to offend; I do so purely for the sake of simplicity and concision.

Foreword

Sixteen years ago, Dr. Efiong Etuk of Nigeria discovered my 1962 publication (with Dr. H.F. Harding), *A Source Book for Creative Thinking*. It was the first book he had seen about creativity and fortunately the most comprehensive and authoritative one available at that time. He was excited about what he read and determined to devote his professional life to the study and development of creativity in Africa. He was determined to influence the continent of Africa to accept and promote creative thinking programs and to see their positive effects as these programs were acted upon. The challenge is powerful in developing Africa.

I first met Dr. Etuk at the Creative Education Foundation's 41st Annual Creative Problem Solving Institute in 1995. Before I became acquainted with him personally, I heard him speak eloquently at leadership sessions of the Institute. He impressed us all with his knowledge of the creativity field and with what he had already done in Nigeria – also with his courage and commitment to helping Africa understand and use creativity to move forward.

At that time, after reading several important pieces of his writing that he shared with me, I told him that I felt he could be as important to the continent of Africa as Alex Osborn has been in the United States and throughout the world. I feel that Dr. Etuk has the vision, the fire, the determination that Dr. Osborn had in his many decades of commitment to nurturing and spreading creativity. I urged Dr. Etuk to carry the image of Dr. Osborn as his symbol – to become the Alex Osborn of the African continent. *Great Insights on Human Creativity* signifies the seriousness with which he took that solemn charge in the interest of both his continent and the rest of humanity.

Ever since reading *A Source Book for Creative Thinking*, Dr. Etuk began noting and collecting important brief quotations on creativity and innovation in everything he read over the years. During the past half-dozen years, he has worked tirelessly to complete a useful organization and synthesis of thousands of brief quotations. This first of five volumes will begin a yearly publication of the other four volumes of *Great Insights on Human Creativity*.

Great Insights on Human Creativity is a unique collection of mostly one- and two-line statements, highlighting important facts about human creativity and suggesting ways to nurture, to deploy, and to preserve this all-important human resource. In this and subsequent volumes, Dr. Etuk brings together some of the most authoritative and credible statements on human creativity, with particular emphasis on its species-wide distribution, its necessity for wholesome development and mental well-being, its relevance in every area of human activity, and our collective responsibility for its development and promotion.

In this and each succeeding volume, Dr. Etuk provides essays and general overviews of each special creativity theme covered by that volume. Written with a remarkable sense of responsibility and commitment, the introductory essays try to bring creativity to bear on key contemporary problems and the human condition, frequently calling public attention to some of the issues that are sometimes regarded as "settled."

Universal in its appeal, *Great Insights on Human Creativity* speaks directly and persuasively to individuals who are struggling both to actualize their potential and to help others realize their own. The total collection will provide a seminal work in the field for scholars, students, writers, practitioners – in government, business, education, and other professions.

I am deeply appreciative of the service provided by Dr. Etuk to all of us in the field. I am also proud and delighted to have stimulated his initial interest in the subject of creativity and innovation.

Sidney J. Parnes, Ph.D.
Professor Emeritus and Founding Director
Center for Studies in Creativity
State University of New York College at Buffalo

Lifetime Trustee, Creative Education Foundation

I
The Essence of Human Creativity

Let each become all that he was created capable of being.

— Aristotle

A Shift in Values

A fundamental shift in values is transforming the way we live, work, educate, lead, perceive, and relate to one another and to our world. People are no longer satisfied just to exist; they want to exist more fully and to realize more of their latent potentialities.* Food, clothing, and shelter no longer suffice: over and above these essentials, people want meaning, identity, and personal fulfillment. More than ever before, individuals are recognizing that they are specially gifted and talented; and they want to be able to actualize their potential – to develop and express their talents in things that they perceive as important and beneficial to themselves as well as to their societies and the natural environment. Increasingly, also, they are rejecting conditions and experiences they perceive as artificially limiting their capacities and/or diminishing the scope of their existence as human beings. As practical illustrations of this worldwide trend:

- Women are asserting not only equality with their male counterparts, but also identity, respect, mutuality, and opportunity to actualize their natural abilities and to make a difference in their families, organizations, national societies, and the world.

- Workers are increasingly rejecting the "nose-to-the-grindstone" concept of work and are seeking not only to participate in the management of their organizations, but also to develop and express their unique capabilities in the work they are doing and, therefore, to increase their productivity and also experience meaning and personal fulfillment on the job.

- Career professionals are increasingly realizing that the stress and burnout that frequently attend "fast-track, high-tech lives"** are too high a price to pay for

---

* A yearning in Henry David Thoreau's time is becoming a practical reality in our own.
** The phrase is Douglas LaBier's (1986: 147).

material success, and they are searching for more balanced, more meaningful, and more fulfilling life-styles.

• Students in institutions of higher education are increasingly demanding a voice in major school policy decisions, including subject-matter contents and the way they are taught and assessed. Furthermore, they want to be able to relate what they learn to the things that really matter to them, as well as to their socioeconomic circumstances and daily life experiences.

• Minority populations around the world are increasingly rejecting marginal positions and are asserting their right to develop themselves and to participate fully in their nations' political, economic, and cultural activities.

• Former colonials are asserting the integrity of their indigenous cultures as well as the right to develop in their own ways and to contribute their insights to the urgent task of global civilization building.

(See, for example, Freire, 1972; Moustakas, 1973: 13; Bloomfield *et al.*, 1975: 1-9; The Club of Rome, 1979: 13, 15; Toffler, 1980: 81-82, 372-394; Watts and Gerber, 1982: 162; LaBier, 1986: 133-161; Harman and Hormann, 1990: 61-95; Laszlo, 1994: 179-180, 190-193; Spady and Bell, Jr., 1997: 87).

Two observations, one by a human potential advocate and the other by a class of students, poignantly (even passionately) illustrate the near-universal clamor for identity, for meaning, for participation, and for personal fulfillment.

Jack Forem, commenting on the ceaseless and universal human search for happiness and fulfillment, says:

> ... despite all that we have, all our abundance, our freedom of choice, action and expression, we feel restless, dissatisfied, bored, tired. We don't feel really alive. We are not so happy as we could be, and we are always on the lookout for something more (Forem, 1974: 5)

A class of high school students, reacting to an evaluation system, calls attention to increasing pressures to "conform" and the attendant threats to personal identity, meaning, and fulfillment. They say:

> We have all kinds of pressures.
> People are always telling us what to do.
> We have to take courses that have no meaning to us.

Adults tell us to decide, and then they don't like the decision.
We're not all the same – there are different points of view
    among us.
We want to move without too many restrictions.
We want to become more aware of things by ourselves.
Even though things are complicated, we're still enthusiastic.
Adults want us to conform, and so we lose our identity.
We have to conform to the group, so our friends will like us.
We have to have good ideas to be somebody
(See Weinstein and Fantini, 1970: 154).

Some humanistic psychologists, postmodernists, and social philosophers interpret the growing demand for identity, meaning, and personal fulfillment as an indication that people are not physical entities alone, but physical, emotional, and spiritual beings *combined.* Economists, too, are saying that there is more to human existence than the satisfaction of material needs, or the "utility functions" of possession, consumption, power, and the pleasures that those things give. Studies of the emotional lives of numerous working people also suggest that "success" is more than a position on the corporate hierarchy. The personal accounts of otherwise very successful individuals who "feel empty inside" give evidence that human well-being does not consist in material comfort alone, but also in the extent to which one is able to realize one's potential and to contribute to the common good (see, for example, Gardner, 1964; Terkel, 1974; LaBier, 1986; Sinetar, 1987; Frankl, 1992; Csikszentmihalyi, 1996).

A signal indication of the growing significance of meaning and personal fulfillment is the renewed interest in human creativity, recognizing, in particular, its inherence in human nature; its primacy among the forces that drive human behavior; its implications in our physical, mental, and emotional well-being; its actualization as the healthiest possible state of being and the ultimate goal of human existence; its blockage as the source of many psychological and social problems; and, finally, *the right of every human being to be creative* – to develop and express one's unique set of abilities in something that one intuitively feels one must do in order for one's life to be "complete." These are the reasons for this section and, indeed, for the entire project.

The Eclipse and Rise of Interest in Human Creativity

There was a time when wealth, power, and pleasure were widely regarded as the most powerful human motivations, and acquiring them the ultimate purpose of human existence. That assumption permeated many areas of thought and gave rise to several important economic, social, and political principles, arrangements, and practices.

To illustrate: Money came to be regarded as the sole motivation to work, and financial profit the primary reason for undertaking an enterprise. Education was regarded as a process of producing good citizens and a disciplined and skilled labor force for a highly competitive global market. Many governments saw their primary responsibility as creating jobs for their people, maintaining law and order, providing the infrastructure for people to go about their legitimate businesses, and defending their citizens against possible external aggression. National societies were regarded as "economies" and largely organized for the production and distribution of goods and services as well as for the resolution of attendant conflicts. The science and technology that brought about so many products and services were expected to solve any problems that might arise from the exponential growth and expansion which the world had virtually taken for granted. Material standards of living became equated with development, and both individual worth and national prestige were measured almost exclusively by the quantum of goods and services produced, owned, and consumed. Many people came to believe that the really important things in their lives were to mature, secure a good education, acquire marketable skills, get a job, amass wealth and fame, marry, produce and educate their children, and finally retire (ideally, in material comfort). Parental responsibility in many cultures was regarded as giving children the best that parents could afford and also molding and guiding one's offspring to be materially successful and socially well-adjusted.

For the most part, many aspects of human life, including social relations, came to be looked upon in "business" terms, driven by economic principles and valued for the material rewards that they entailed. Wealth and its acquisition increasingly became the dominant human concern, with corresponding influence on the thoughts and actions of most people.

The aggregate success of the resulting civilization is well known: record production and consumption of goods and services, instantaneous communication across the globe, space exploration, mass literacy; eradication of certain deadly diseases, longer life spans, and a

4

long list of technological products. Many people see the spectacular economic and social transformations of the past two hundred years as a vindication of the largely economic principles upon which modern civilization has been built. Some social commentators have already characterized the present era as "the most brilliant civilization in human history" and "the highest standard of living the world has ever known."

That "verdict," however, is not universally shared. Ecologists and human potential advocates in particular have a different opinion.

While acknowledging rising levels of material well-being (at least, in some parts of the world), ecologists call attention to the attendant (sometimes irreparable) damage to the natural environment. They even fear imminent breakdown of the ecosystem and possible extinction of life on earth as the results of such human-induced effects such as population explosion, overconsumption, overuse of land, toxic wastes, acid rain, air pollution, groundwater contamination, species loss, and so on. Ecologists, of course, recognize the need for "the good things of life," but doubt whether some of those things are worth the harm they are causing to the natural environment.

Human potential advocates broadly categorize existence into basic livelihood and personal fulfillment, and they perceive the relation between the two as "means-and-end." Describing basic livelihood as the means, and personal fulfillment as the end, human potential advocates believe that in the pursuit of material well-being, most people and cultures have given too much attention to basic livelihood (the "means") and relatively little concern for personal fulfillment and the actualization of human potential (the "end"). (See, for example, Montagu, 1962: 58-60, Schumacher, 1975: 55-58.) They attribute the preeminence of material well-being over human fulfillment to the assumptions and social practices listed above (page 4). Following are some of the perceived linkages:

1. The belief that financial profit is the only reason for business has led to the predominance of activities that offer monetary rewards.

2. The perception of money and the things that money can buy as the primary motivation to work has given rise to jobs that merely pay good salaries, with little regard for meaning, purpose, or personal fulfillment.

3. The view of education primarily as an instrument for preparing young people for the labor market has tended to under-serve or totally ignore talents that are not perceived as having marketable value and, inadvertently, to discourage the people who possess those talents.

4. The gradual shift of the goal of human existence from becoming one's potential to acquisition and consumption has made many people define themselves and measure their worth almost exclusively by their academic credentials, bank accounts, real estate, and other material assets.

5. Many parents' eagerness to bring up materially successful children has steered many young people into economic activities that offer high salaries but without the intrinsic satisfaction of doing something one is passionate about and deeply enjoys.

(See, for example, Fromm, 1955; Rogers, 1961; Montagu, 1962; Gardner, 1964; Moustakas, 1967; Maslow, 1968; Schumacher, 1975; LaBier, 1986; Sinetar, 1987).

In all of these familiar situations, the real, but often unnoticed and unintended "casualty" has been human potential and its fulfillment. Because of their near-total concern with material well-being, many people probably have lived and died without ever finding themselves, without ever recognizing their special abilities and being able to express them in things and ways that they perceive as important and worthy. To illustrate: The assumption that economic considerations are the primary motivations in human life has been described as "one-sided view of human nature" and is believed to have stripped human existence of meaning and purpose (Schumacher, 1975: 95; Griffin, 1988a: 149). Defining human well-being exclusively in terms of money and the things that money can buy, measuring people's worth by the goods and services that they own and/or consume, and equating standard of living with development is believed to have alienated human beings from their spirit (Solzhenitsyn, 1978: 49). Perceiving everything as a marketable product and constructing social relationships upon commercial premises are believed to have brutalized and dehumanized human nature (Montagu, 1962: 56, 58; Toffler, 1980: 271, 272). Jobs that offer no meaningful challenge to a worker's imagination or that provide no opportunity for the worker to achieve something significant are regarded as meaningless and, in the long run, unproductive (see the section entitled "Creative Work"). Having to work on something that one is not passionate about or with which one does not feel deeply involved is described as "stultifying" and "soul-destroying" (see, for example, Fromm, 1955: 111-137; Schumacher, 1975: 55). Steering one's children into the so-called prestigious and high-paying occupations that may not necessarily suit their natural abilities and predispositions is believed to have denied many young people the opportunity to realize their unique potentialities. Turning education into an instrument for producing skilled and disciplined workers for the economy and inducing learners to acquire skills in areas that are not natural to them is believed to have artificially constrained their capabilities as well as their personal growth and development (see the section entitled "Creative Education").

The net effect of these patterns of existence is the phenomenon that humanistic psychologists commonly refer to as "unfulfilled human potential." The condition has been linked to many psychological and social problems. Abraham Maslow (1968), for example, believes that persons who are unable to realize their potential tend to become angry and even dangerous. Their unused capacities, according to the humanistic psychologist, become "disease centers," giving rise to a variety of problems such as anxiety, depression, meaninglessness, feelings of incompleteness, hatred, violence, and criminality (see, also, Fromm, 1955; Rogers, 1961; Moustakas, 1967; Ryan, 1972; Buscaglia, 1978; Eitzen and Zinn, 1997). Studies of the emotional lives of professional people largely corroborate Maslow's conclusions. Their findings identify three broad groups of professionals: (a) the "successful-yet-troubled" individuals who have everything that they could possibly desire but still "feel empty inside"; (b) angry, violent, bored, or depressed individuals whose problems, reportedly, arise from lack of something that they are passionate about — something to which they could commit themselves, and in the promotion of which they could constructively engage their talents and find meaning in their lives; and (c) deeply satisfied individuals who attribute their happiness to being able to find something that gives expression to their unique abilities and meaning to their lives (see, for example, Gardner, 1964: 120, 125-128; LaBier, 1986; Sinetar, 1987).

Since the works of Abraham Maslow and other humanistic psychologists (approximately fifty years ago), interest in possible connections between actualization of human potential and behavior has grown phenomenally. Human potential advocates ascribe this interest to two related situations: (a) a rapid increase in the number and complexity of social and psychological problems and, as a result, the rapidly deteriorating human condition (e.g., widespread poverty, alienation, boredom, depression, hatred, violence, destructiveness, criminality, substance abuse, feelings of personal insecurity, meaninglessness, and worthlessness) even at a time when the world is experiencing unprecedented levels of material well-being; and (b) the increasing difficulty of conventional theories of social and psychological problems (e.g., "innate-inferiority," "deviant value system," "troubled childhood," or "neurosis," etc.) to explain many of the problems. In place of the so-called "person-blame" theories of social and psychological problems, human potential advocates and some social scientists are suggesting reexamination of the social, economic, political, and intellectual conditions in which people live and work and, in particular, the extent to which those conditions facilitate or hinder what is perceived as the "essential core" of people and the "deepest needs" of their hearts. The thoughts and writings of Ashley Montagu, Erich Fromm, Carl R. Rogers, Abraham Maslow, John W. Gardner, and William Ryan reflect this view and are believed to have given rise to the so-called "systems approach" to social and psychological problems (see, for example, Eitzen and Zinn, 1997).

The systems approach to social and psychological problems, unlike its person-focused counterpart, attributes some of the problems that so many societies are facing to the inability of some of their members to realize their potentials, to participate in productive activities that engage their talents and interests and, therefore, to find meaning in their lives and feel good about themselves. Advocates of this view of social problems believe that the only way that people are going to be genuinely responsible as citizens, productive as employees, and happy as individuals is if they are enabled to recognize their unique abilities and to develop and express them in things that they perceive as important and beneficial both to themselves and to their societies. Advocates of the systems approach to social and psychological problems further suggest that the only way that societies, groups, and organizations are going to survive and thrive in the rapidly changing and increasingly uncertain environments in which they find themselves is to increase their capacity to innovate by recognizing and nurturing the creativity of all of their members (see the section entitled "Wanted: Society-Wide Creativity" – Volume V, forthcoming).

8

The creative action of all people is also seen as the best hope for humanity to avert impending disaster, which declining social and environmental conditions seem to portend. Statements by Carl R. Rogers, John W. Gardner, and George R. Eckstein, respectively, illustrate both the apprehension and the sense of urgency regarding the situation:

> Unless individuals, groups, and nations can imagine, construct, and creatively [devise] new ways of relating to these complex changes [in the world], the lights will go out. Unless man can make new and original adaptations to his environment as rapidly as his science can change the environment, our [civilization] will perish ... [and] international annihilation will be the price we pay for a lack of creativity (Rogers, 1962: 64).

> Unless we cope with the ways in which modern society oppresses the individual, we shall lose the creative spark that renews both societies and men. Unless we foster versatile, innovative and self-renewing men and women, all the ingenious social arrangements in the world will not help us (Gardner, 1964: xiv – xv).

> If, as is generally conceded, the world is in a rather sorry mess, crying for solutions to problems that are staggering in complexity and magnitude, the encouragement of creative thinking would seem to be the most necessary and immediate goal of all concerned people (Eckstein, 1972: 1).

> (See also Fromm, 1955: 310; North-Whitehead, 1964: 103; Heilbroner, 1975: 144; The Club of Rome, 1979: iii, 10, 12, 72; Woodcock and Francis, 1979: 65; Theobald, 1981: 25, 84, 150-151; Laszlo, 1993: 117, 194).

Analysis of the renewed and growing interest in human creativity identifies three vital concerns: personal fulfillment; social well-being; and the survival of the human species. Increasingly, it is becoming clear that in order to achieve a livable and fulfilling global society, people must be given the encouragement and support to develop and to express their unique abilities in important and socially beneficial activities – in other words, to be creative! The remainder of this introductory review focuses on what it means to be creative, why creativity is so central to human life, and the many ways in which it manifests itself.

9

The Essence of Creativity

A leading creativity scholar recently remarked that it is possible to have three or more people talk about creativity and find out that all of them are talking about different things. This is the general impression that one gets from the rapidly growing literature on human creativity. Apparent differences of opinion can be observed in practically every aspect of the construct: essence, distribution, process(es), expression, and significance. However, closer examination of many of the things that have been written and said about human creativity indicates that some of those "differences" are not mutually exclusive, but complementary representations of various dimensions of the same human essence.

One of the most significant shifts in modern thinking has been the growing consensus that every human being is inherently creative. Rejecting the traditional view of creativity as the special endowment of a select few, more and more scholars, writers, and social commentators are saying things such as: "we are all born with creativity"; "the power to create exists within each of us"; "each of us has a gift"; "to be human means to be creative" (see, for example, Mearns, 1958: 263-272; Syrus, 1991: 2; Varèse, 1993: 142; Csikszentmihalyi, 1996: 318; Barrett, 1998: 3). According to this "universal-human-attribute" view of creativity, if a person is not producing as much novelty as others, it is not because of a lack of innate ability or talent; it is very likely because the conditions of his existence* may have constrained his ability to live up to his potential.

Table I.1 (pages 11-13) presents eighty-eight increasingly popular notions of creativity, signifying, as indicated earlier, its inherence in human nature, its universal distribution, its implications in every human activity, and and its primacy among the forces driving human behavior.

---

* "Condition of existence," as the term is used in this context, includes, among other things, parental upbringing, educational system, cultural expectations, group membership, availability of role models, economic circumstances, and material resources.

Table I.1. Various Representations of Human Creativity

1. "a natural ability that we are all endowed with"
2. "man's most important characteristic"
3. "inner nature"
4. "inner essence"
5. "the central core of the person"
6. "genetically coded mystery of life"
7. "the most valuable human quality"
8. "that self which one truly is"
9. "psychic imperative"
10. "existential necessity"
11. "the ultimate answer to being human"
12. "the strongest force in human life"
13. "the motive energy that impels all our actions"
14. "the essential core [of a person]"
15. "the defining characteristics of humanness, or personhood"
16. "the hidden sources of our personality"
17. "the healthiest and highest expression of human nature"
18. "the compelling necessity which the individual feels to search for and become himself"
19. "the most common and the most powerful motivation"
20. "the greatest of all natural resources"
21. "what people would like to become if they could"
22. "the most crucial of our needs"
23. "the deepest human experience"
24. "the best human qualities"
25. "the best of what it is to be human"
26. "the highest of all [human] values"
27. "what is most important for [our] lives"
28. "our healthiest impulse"
29. "our inmost selves"
30. "your meant-to-be"
31. "your calling ... [your] own inner voice"
32. "your undiscovered energy:
33. "[the] vast untapped energy within you"
34. "your most precious resource"
35. "your own signature on life"
36. "peak experience"
37. "feeling of transcendence"
38. "the central source of meaning in our lives"

Table I.1., continued

39. "the center and what is highest in humanity"
40. "the highest expression of human nature"
41. "the inner compulsion to be all that one ought to be"
42. "the buried longings of our lives that are always urging
    to be satisfied"
43. "the unique and the universal in the individual and in mankind"
44. "the first, foremost, and last essence of the human species"
45. "the urge for self-transcendence"
46. "inner urge to grow and to develop [according to one's endowment]"
47. "the life-force within every individual [that is constantly pressing
    to be developed and expressed]"
48. "the heart, the soul, and the innermost core of our being"
49. "the most significant dimension of man that distinguishes him
    from all other beings"
50. "that which sets humans apart from other creatures"
51. "wellspring of [human] growth and change"
52. "areas of [our] maximum potential"
53. "the vast potential that our humanity gives us as a birthright"
54. "what is most important for [our] lives"
55. "the mysterious power behind some of our most ordinary mental
    activities"
56. "that natural instinct that propels us toward creation, choice,
    liberation and change"
57. "the goal the individual most wishes to achieve, the end which he
    knowingly and unknowingly pursues"
58. "the wellspring of our very essence"
59. "the aim and purpose of human life"
60. "life's ultimate purpose"
61. "the deep center"
62. "the ground of any well-lived life"
63. "who you are at a deep level and what your life, at best,
    should really be about"
64. "the root of the tree of life, the ultimate cause of all the innumerable
    effects which constitute the relative field of life.
65. "[personal] perspective on the world"
66. "your unique point of view"
67. "the center of [our] life [and] origin of [our] thinking and acting"
68. "the forces that drive you"
69. "inner"[personal] perspective on the world"

Table I.1., continued

70. "the wellspring of all our actions"
71. "your true center, the place from which you act as yourself"
72. "the basis of all success and happiness in life"
73. "the universal Self in us"
74. "the basic personhood that we all have"
75. "what it means to be a person"
76. "[your] reason to live"
77. "[your] role in life"
78. "that which only you can do"
79. "what is supremely important to you"
80. "the one thing I must do before I die"
81. "something meaningful to accomplish each day [that you] can't wait to get started on it...[the] one thing that is worth waking up for...tasks you look forward to"
82. "[the] tremendous dynamo of energy and intelligence within man [that] is constantly empowering and directing human activity"
83. "a pressure toward a fuller and fuller being, more and more perfect actualization of [one's] humaness in exactly the same naturalistic...sense that an acorn may be said to be pressing toward an oak tree"
84. "what seems different in yourself ... the rare thing you possess"
85. "living realities ... which are still at work in our hearts, and which fashion our person"
86. "the one thing that gives each of us his worth"
87. "the foundations of one's sense of personal worth"
88. "the basis of everything we do"

(See, for example, Fromm, 1955: 188; Tournier, 1957: 131, 132; Grabo, 1962: vi; Moustakas, 1967: 92, 133; Rogers, 1961: 108, 111; Kierkegaard,, 1961: 110; Montagu, 1962: 156; Parnes and Harding, 1962: vii; Maslow, 1959: 128, 161, 193; O'Connor, 1971; Peterson, 1971: 202; Buhler and Allen, 1972: 44; Freire, 1972: 76, 77; 14; Davidson, 1974: 325, 373; Foren, 1974: 79, 96, 104, 106, 111, 161; Bloomfield et al., 1975: 8, 160; Koestler, 1975: 363-364; Murray, 1975: 90; Schuller, 1975: 141, 142; Arieti, 1976: 5, 13, 31; May, 1976: 55; Buscaglia, 1978: 17, 21; Theobald, 1981: 144; Harman and Rheingold, 1984: xxii, 2, 7; Viscott, 1984: 13, 152, 234; Gide, 1987: 34; Fuller, 1987: 131; Harmon and Hormann, 1990: 85; Pearson, 1991: 165; Parnes, 1992:16; 1997: 55; Pinchot and Pinchot, 1993: 246, 247; Mayor, 1994: 200; Damon, 1995: 15, 19; Swindoll, 1995: 499; Thiss, 1995: 169; Csikszentmihalyi, 1996: 1, 182, 349; Maclaurin, 1998: xi; Bleedorn,1998: 3).

Notions of Creativity

Different people perceive and describe creativity differently: some, in terms of the mental attributes associated with extraordinary achievement; others, in terms of the feelings that spectacular achievements generate; still others, in terms of the procedures for achieving novel ideas and products. As a result, no unified theory of creativity exists, and there is no generally accepted definition of the construct. In spite of their apparent differences, however, many notions of creativity overlap in meaning and are complementary. The following widely-accepted representations of the construct illustrate the point:

Creativity as "authenticity"

"Uniqueness" and "individual differences" are two popular notions in creativity literature. Both concepts signify differential "endowment," or the particular combination of abilities that are believed to define every individual and also to distinguish him from every other human being.

One of the earliest recorded references to the notion of uniqueness is believed to be Aristotle's notion of *entelechy* (see Davidson, 1974: 197-200). The Greek philosopher believed that every organism is imbued with an essence (potentiality) that he referred to as a "natural principle" (i.e., *entelechy*). According to Aristotle, an organism's *entelechy* determines what the organism can become, drives the organism toward achieving or becoming its potential, and distinguishes the particular organism from all others. The principle is believed to be true of all living things, including humans, plants, and animals.

Since Aristotle, many thinkers have called attention to the tremendous similarities and variations in human nature. Carl Rogers (1961), for example, suggests that human beings are created differently and are endowed with unique potentialities which one must be able to actualize to feel good about oneself. The humanistic psychologist calls attention not only to the differential endowments of individuals, but also to the inner (psychic) necessity to live in accordance with one's nature. Abraham Maslow's (1968) concept of "authentic selfhood" also recognizes differential genetic constitutions of people which, according to him, explain observed differences in the ways that different people perceive and prefer to relate to themselves, to other human beings, and to nature. Like Aristotle, Maslow and Rogers also emphasize the psychic necessity of actualizing one's potentialities, a condition which they perceive as the healthiest and highest expression of human nature. Howard Gardner (1993) uses the term "intelligences" to describe the unique combinations of abilities that characterize individuals and also differentiate them from one another. To enhance the prospects of creativity, the educational psychologist advocates a system of education that recognizes and facilitates the individual learner's unique configuration of abilities.

Unique personal endowment and the psychic necessity to achieve, or to become, one's potential are perhaps why some scholars define creativity as *authenticity*. Authenticity, of course, connotes "genuineness" — the ability to perceive, think, feel, act, and relate in ways that express one's potential as well as one's predispositions. Paulo Freire's (1972: 32, 76, 77) famous "speak-their-word" and "name-their-world" metaphors aptly describe that condition of existence. Other scholars and writers define authenticity as a "personal outlook on life," or the ability to be oneself, to recognize and appreciate one's natural abilities, to sense the world in one's unique way, to express one's unique perspectives on issues, to find and try to fulfill what one perceives to be one's special purpose in life (see the section entitled "Uniqueness, Eccentricity, and the Creative Selfhood" – Volume III, forthcoming).

Creativity as "deviance"

To be creative, by definition, is to be "different" — at times, very different. Scholars attribute part of this difference to genetic makeup and part to personal history and one's sociocultural environment.

"Deviance" takes many forms. Its widely reported variants in creativity literature include: personal world view; inclination to tasks that seem to fit one's abilities, interests, and temperaments; constructive dissatisfaction with certain aspects of life, coupled with a desire to bring about improvement; deviation from established traditions; doubting the so-called obvious; questioning the orthodox; challenging the tried-and-true; rejecting the structured and the ordered; raising new questions; finding new solutions to old problems; breaking free of concepts and dogmas to be able to see the world in fresh new ways; and foregoing the certainty and the comfort of established traditions and settled existence (see the section entitled "Uniqueness, Eccentricity, and the Creative Selfhood" Volume III, forthcoming).

Creativity as "transcendence"

Most creatures are said to survive by passively adapting to their natural circumstances, relying only on the hereditarily fixed responses of their species (Fromm, 1955: 29, 30, 31, 131, 314). Human beings differ in this respect. They are distinguished from other creatures by the urge to exceed themselves, to rise above perceived limitations of their era, culture, gender, age, economic or social circumstances – to be more than they are currently defined.

Other powerful forces in human nature are fascination with things not normally found in everyday experience, a penchant for goals that no one has achieved, the quest for the extraordinary, and the urge to transcend existing boundaries of knowledge. Generally referred to as "trail-blazing" or "pioneering spirit," this is the urge to break perceived limits of physical and/or biological laws; to reach beyond the scope of existing knowledge; to create new possibilities; to develop new ways of seeing life and nature; or to discover new forms, new symbols, new metaphors, and new patterns on which to build a new "order." The seeming impracticality of such goals, coupled with the intensity of commitment, is why this notion of creativity is sometimes euphemistically equated with "thinking the unthinkable," "doing the undoable," "solving the unsolvable," and "making the impossible possible" (see, for example, May, 1976; Boorstin, 1985; Csikszentmihalyi, 1996).

Creativity as "self-fulfillment"

Although every human being is talented, not everybody seems to realize this fact. By the same token, not everyone seems to recognize his special abilities. Also, although differences in individual abilities are widely acknowledged, many life experiences are frequently provided as if people had identical abilities or similar interests. The result is that some talents are nourished, while others tend to be neglected, underserved and, at times, actively blocked.

Humanistic psychologists suggest that an essential characteristic of every human being is the urge to grow and develop according to one's nature – to actualize one's unique potential, to recognize and express one's unique talents, to liberate and give full play to all of the impulses that inherently lie within each of us (see, for example, MacKinnon, 1962: 19; Eckstein, 1972; Suzuki, 1974: 415; Harman and Rheingold, 1984). According to this principle, whether recognized or not, human potentialities never stop wanting to be expressed, pressing to be fulfilled.

Sigmund Freud's psychoanalytic theory compares these potentialities to a river which, if dammed up at one place, tends to find outlets through any available channels, or even bursts through its banks at the weakest spot (see Steele, 1987: 55).

Abraham Maslow's (1968) phrase "capacities clamor to be used" and Paulo Freire's (1972) "existential necessity" imply that whatever an individual's natural abilities or potentialities, their recognition, development, and utilization in meaningful and worthwhile activities are necessary conditions for mental health and personal fulfillment. ("Meaningful and worthwhile activities," in this sense, refers to the things that one genuinely believes to be important, that make one feel good about oneself, and that one perceives as providing benefits to fellow human beings and the natural environment).

Creativity as "transformational thinking" or "reconstruction of reality"

Hardly any human experience comes with its value fixed or its meaning preestablished. Most situations are fluid and therefore amenable to different interpretations. When confronted with a phenomenon, a problem, or an event, one typically has three options: ignore it, take it literally as presented, or try to make something new out of the situation. The third option is what creativity scholars refer to as "transformational thinking" or "reconstruction of reality."

Creativity literature represents transformational thinking as the ability to turn seemingly familiar items and mundane situations into spectacular ones. Underlying this type of thinking is the ability to perceive hitherto unnoticed properties in a familiar thing or event; find hidden similarities between things that are traditionally perceived as different; perceive unnoticed differences among things that hitherto were thought to be similar; relate familiar ideas in new and more productive ways; combine seemingly disparate elements into a useful synthesis; perceive hitherto unnoticed relationships between things that were thought to be discrete and independent of one another; find new and more fruitful applications for an existing theory; invent new symbols for interpreting and dealing with an existing situation or condition; perceive paradoxes in situations that were believed to be settled; find things that appear to contradict common sense; challenge the so-called "universally accepted interpretation of nature"; "transform apparent randomness into organized structure"; or identify an important but hitherto unrecognized problem, challenge, or opportunity (see, for example, May, 1975: 17, 148, 150;

Arieti, 1976: 405; Theobald, 1981: 159; Morris, 1983; Root-Bernstein, 1987; Roskos-Ewoldsen *et al.*, 1993: 317; Popper and Eccles, 1993: 553; Cuatrecasas, 1995: 201, 202).

Creativity as "bissociation," or the "magic synthesis"

Not all creative breakthroughs are consciously planned. Some of them occur fortuitously, as unplanned and unexpected events. Countless instances have been reported in which a random event or totally unrelated idea provided the missing piece to an outstanding puzzle, or in which ideas from two or more seemingly unrelated areas of knowledge came together to provide a solution to a problem in a third area. Silvano Arieti (1976) refers to this phenomenon as the "magic synthesis." Mihaly Csikszentmihalyi (1996: 256) describes it as the coming together of "domains that appear to have nothing in common."

Arthur Koestler's book *The Act of Creation* (1975) provides extensive discussion of this notion of creativity. This widely-referenced resource describes creativity variously as: "bissociation"; the coming together of two previously separate frames of reference; the fusion of seemingly incompatible, or previously unrelated matrices of thought; the "unearthing of a hidden analogy" which solves a previously insoluble problem; and the "fruitful fusion of different elements" (Koestler, 1975: 27, 94, 120, 182, 195, 220, 229, 230, 320).

Creativity as "expanded horizon of existence"

Ralph Waldo Emerson once observed that "man is the dwarf of himself." One interpretation of Emerson's statement is that many people are not living up to their natural capacities or are using only a fraction of the immense potential with which they are endowed. Before Emerson, Jean-Jacques Rousseau had described the human condition as "born free but everywhere in chains." Rousseau was denouncing the political, social, and economic conditions that he perceived as diminishing the scope of life of his contemporaries. Two and a half centuries after Rousseau, the human condition is not believed to be significantly different, especially with respect to capacities and their actualization. At the end of the twentieth century, creativity literature was still replete with phrases such as "limited existence," "meaningless life," "stoppage places," "deprivation pockets," "inability to live out [one's] purpose," and the "necessity" of having to "conform to the plans designed for [one]" (see, for example, Moustakas, 1967; Pritzkau, 1970, Freire, 1972).

Observers of the human condition believe that, in spite of significantly higher standards of living (at least, in some parts of the world), large segments of the human population are still not able to realize their full potential as human beings. Humanistic psychologists, in particular, call attention to what they perceive as gaps between human capacity and its utilization, between talents and their expression. They attribute the problem to personal and sociocultural factors that, presumably, constrict people's experience and the range of things that they can do (see the section entitled "Barriers to Creativity" – Volume II, forthcoming).

As restricting as some of the conditions appear, however, indications are that human potential cannot be totally suppressed. Like the river in Freud's analogy, human creativity ceaselessly seeks to develop and to express itself. People naturally, even intuitively, try to reach their potential, to increase awareness of themselves, to break free of conditions that tend to confine their abilities, to expand their understanding of the world and become more effective in it – to be creative! (see, for example, Rogers, 1961: 35, 38; Maslow, 1968: 152; Pritzkau, 1970: 1-62; Thoreau, 1987: 61, 63, 65; von Schiller, 1987: 50; Csikszentmihalyi, 1996: 317). (The exceptions are those instances in which one is not aware of one's apparent "confinement," feels too comfortable in the existing arrangement to perceive any deprivations, or is too busy implementing the system and too committed to its maintenance to question the system's goodness.)

Creativity as "personal breakthrough"

Some creative acts originate from direct, conscious experience. Others, reportedly, come from outside the regions of conscious awareness, – regions that psychoanalysts describe as the "subconscious" or the "unconscious" mind. Some of the names used to refer to this area of the human mind are the "hidden mind"; "the deep center"; "innate divinity"; "divine oracle within"; "the self's divine potential"; "untapped psychic potential"; "the largely unexplored and vastly underdeveloped aspects of human potentialities"; "the collective unconscious"; "accumulated wisdom of the ages"; "inner source"; "universal energy"; "vast storehouses of rich golden treasure"; and "the wellspring of our very essence" (see, for example, Barron, 1969; Peterson, 1971; Arieti, 1976; Gowan, 1978; Harman and Rheingold, 1984). Existentialist and psychoanalytic thinkers (such as Willis Harman and Howard Rheingold) describe the subconscious mind as part of everyone's inheritance and, therefore, as potentially available to every human being.

Some of the most momentous creative achievements in human history are believed to have originated from these regions of the human mind. Because of their seemingly mysterious origins, knowledge and ideas that purportedly emanate from these regions are frequently looked upon with awe and reverence. Their mystique is reflected by some of the terms used to describe them: "revelation"; "vision"; "knowing from within"; "breakthrough of deeper intuition"; "immediate insight"; "understanding that is not based on reason or observation"; "a moment of knowledge recognizable as something beyond the usual reach of the cognitive mind"; "the still, small voice of the unconscious [that] emerges from beneath the outer layers of consciousness"; "divine unconscious expressing itself from within" (see, for example, May, 1976: 57, 74-75, 102, 104; Harman, 1984: xxiii; Harman and Rheingold, 1984: 2, 7, 97, Steele, 1987: 43).

Creativity scholars of the psychoanalytic tradition believe that, though "collective," the unconscious regions of the mind are not universally accessible. They suggest that, in most human beings, subconscious materials lie "buried" under a series of inhibitions, including mistrust of one's intuition and the seemingly irrational forms of understanding that are not based on reason, logic, or empirically verifiable observation.

However, as buried and hidden as the subconscious mind is believed to be, psychoanalysts claim that it can be accessed and some of the materials that it holds retrieved. They define creativity mainly as the ability to get in touch with the unconscious regions of one's mind and to be able to use their resources to solve practical problems and handle everyday life experiences. However, to be able to reach the subconscious mind and tap into the resources that it holds, psychoanalysts maintain that one has to break through the barriers that tend to disconnect one from one's "inner source." (The exploding literature on "personal growth" provides numerous suggestions for breaking through one's inhibitions and reconnecting with one's inner essence.)

Creativity as "encounter"

Human beings are regarded as a pattern-recognizing and meaning-making species. Unlike other species, the human individual does not take the world as a given, but tries to make sense of events – to *interpret* them. Interpretation, of course, presupposes a preexisting idea or belief system that specifies what things are and how they work. When confronted with an observation, phenomenon, information, or situation, an individual is believed to try to make sense of it by "fitting" it into his existing frame of reference.

Many life experiences are satisfactorily interpreted by these extant models. Occasionally, however, one encounters a problem that cannot be understood in the light of an existing construct; or a situation arises that contradicts one's existing view of things. Such an anomaly creates dissonance, anxiety, tension — in short, "disequilibrium." To restore equilibrium, one could choose to ignore the disturbing event; or one could try to force-fit the phenomenon into the existing frame of reference and assume that it isn't anything new; or one could decide to "encounter" the paradox frontally. Where encounter is chosen, one might need to revise one's preexisting model to accommodate the new idea. Alternatively, one might have to reject the earlier presupposition and replace it with another that more adequately represents the set of phenomena in question (see, for example, Pritzkau, 1970: 21, 55; May, 1976: 39-56, 87-109; Bussis et al, 1987: 9-21; Root-Bernstein, 1989: 351; Gardner, 1993: 116-117; Fosnot 1996: ix, 30; Schifter, 1996: 78).

Parenthetically, dissonance and the resultant "encounter" are not restricted to the discrepant and the paradoxical. Even the traditional and the commonplace sometimes agitate the mind. Those who choose to "re-perceive"* the old or to "reconstruct the world"** report the thrill of being able to see the familiar in new and more fruitful ways, to raise questions that appear to have been answered, to call attention to a previously ignored but significant element, to formulate relationships that were hitherto not recognized, or to find a new "metaphor" for making sense of the apparent confusion of life (see, for example, Root-Bernstein, 1989; Barrett, 1998). Humanistic psychologists describe encounter variously as "passion for form"; "a desire powerful enough to turn on your whole being"; "something to believe in and to be devoted to"; being caught up and totally absorbed in a purpose, value, or challenge that gives life meaning (see, for example, Rogers, 1961: 216, 217; Maslow, 1970: 82; May, 1976: 43, 96, 154; Barret, 1998: 73).

There are two basic aspects to encounter. The first is to be able to find a task, a need, or a problem that one considers too important or too compelling to wait. The second is to be prepared to confront the obstacles associated with this self-imposed responsibility.

---

* The term is Willis Harman and Howard Rheingold's (1984: 185).
** The phrase is Henry David Thoreau's (1987: 60).

21

Creativity as "problem solving"

Ours has come to be known as a problem-ridden world. In academe as in the media, in executive suites and on street corners, from local neighborhoods to international organizations, the central concern frequently is "problems" and how to solve them. Problems, of course, come in different forms: personal, institutional, social, business, political, environmental, and so on. Some are considered minor, others life-threatening. Some are treated as local issues, while others receive global attention.

The problem with many problems is their apparent persistence. Despite good intentions and effort, most of them neither go away nor yield to solution. Rather, they tend to increase both in number and in complexity, thereby casting doubt on the efficacy of available solutions and prompting the search for new, even unconventional, ones. The remarkable success of many unconventional approaches, otherwise known as creative solutions, has created the impression that creativity is about problem solving. The problem-solving notion of creativity is particularly evident in business and industry, in which scores of systematic creative problem-solving techniques have been developed, tested, and used in the design, proposal, development, and marketing of new products and services, as well as in the management of human and material resources.

The much-advertised success of creative problem-solving techniques in business and industry is probably the reason for the growing interest in creativity in several so-called nontraditional areas, such as sports, education, public administration, personal growth, social relations, and community building. In those areas, as in business and industry, individuals, groups, and organizations are reportedly solving very difficult problems by adapting, combining, magnifying, rearranging, reversing, transforming, or otherwise manipulating ideas and things in new and unusual ways.

Creativity as "personal integration"

Some people regard modern civilization as the best thing that has happened to humanity; others describe the present era as a "humanitarian and environmental disaster." For purposes of this brief review, we can refer to the former group as "modernists" and the latter as "postmodernists."

"Modernists," as has been indicated earlier, characterize modern times as "the most brilliant civilization in human history," calling attention to the high and rising standards of living that have been achieved, the wide range of goods and services for human consumption, relatively long life spans, jet travel, space exploration, global communication, and so many other good things of life. Postmodernists acknowledge the unprecedented levels of material well-being in some parts of the world. However, they deplore the degrading and still deteriorating economic and social conditions in which the vast majority of human beings live – the "forgotten four-fifths" around the world for whom poverty, starvation, malnutrition, illiteracy, and diseases have become a way of life.

One outgrowth of modern civilization that is not so generally recognized is the reportedly large and growing number of "troubled-yet-successful"* individuals whose economic and social circumstances are making it difficult for them to tap their latent creative abilities and to live more fully. Humanistic psychologists, sociologists, and social critics attribute this phenomenon to a number of factors, including alienation, dissatisfaction with work life, boredom, meaninglessness, or personal sense of futility. Certain social practices are also believed to be involved, among them: (a) defining human life almost exclusively in material terms, thus denying its emotional and spiritual dimensions; (b) categorizing (i.e., stereotyping) people by their gender, age, skin color, or economic circumstances, and defining them solely by the group into which they happen to fall; (c) separating the human species from the rest of nature, thus denying the systemic wholeness and essential unity of all life; and (d) the prevalence of jobs that offer little or no meaning or personal fulfillment, but only money (see, for example, Fromm, 1955:163, 258; Moustakas, 1967: 135; Suzuki, 1974: 415; Schumacher, 1975: 55, 250; May, 1975: 61; Heilbroner, 1975; Toffler, 1980: 76-105, 251-273; Harman and Rheingold, 1984; LaBier, 1987; Harman and Hormann, 1990; Naisbitt and Aburdene, 1990: 273, 277; Griffin, 1988; 1988a; Eitzen and Zinn, 1997: 318-322).

Therapists, counselors, and other helping professionals view the emotional problems arising from these conditions as a major reason why many people are resorting to spiritual and/or psychotherapeutic procedures, presumably to "regain [their] wholeness" and restore meaning and balance in their lives.

A comprehensive list of psychotherapeutic procedures would be too long to provide here, even if it were available. Some of the more frequently-mentioned programs include: centering; creative visualization, encounter groups, hypnosis, various forms of meditation, prayer, sensitivity training, structural integration, various forms of yoga, and many more. Advocates and practitioners ascribe several benefits to these procedures including, for example, the ability to (re)connect with one's

---

* The phrase is Douglas LaBier's (1986)

inner wisdom, which some thinkers regard as the source of creative break-throughs. Advocates further claim that these programs and procedures can, and do, help one to become more aware of oneself and one's abilities, feelings, interests, and needs; break down artificial mind-body-spirit separation and integrate the various dimensions of oneself; bring balance into one's inner and outer lives and achieve greater harmony with oneself, with fellow human beings, and with the rest of nature; discover more of the world around oneself, become more intimately aware of the "whole" of which one is a part, and feel more at home in the universe; and, generally, recognize and be able to tap one's creative potentialities that might have been denied, repressed, dormant, or unused (see, for example, Peterson 1971; Henderson, 1975; Laurie and Tucker, 1978; Gawain, 1982).

Conclusion

Modern creativity scholars have called attention to its inherence in human nature; its primacy among the forces that drive human behavior; its implication in every human action; the necessity of its recognition, development, and constructive expression for personal fulfillment and meaningful existence; and its unfulfillment as the root cause of much of today's widespread dissatisfaction with life. Beyond these general observations, however, considerable differences exist regarding the exact nature of human creativity (its essence) and the manner(s) of its expression.

The limited understanding of the essence of human creativity has given rise to several seemingly competing suppositions that are sometimes referred to as "theories of creativity." Many of these presumptions remind one of the "Six Blind Men and the Elephant" story, in which a group of blind men each probed a different part of an elephant and concluded, based on his "findings," that the shape of the whole animal corresponded to the part that he probed. As different as they appear, the various notions of creativity reviewed in this introductory synopsis can hardly be called "competing theories." With so much concordance in their main ideas, it is more appropriate to regard them as complementary rather than as conflicting propositions. It might even be more appropriate to view them as different dimensions of the same human essence.

Selected Insights
on
The Essence of Human Creativity

What we can't express runs our lives.

— Anonymous.

[Genius is] someone who sees things *very very* clearly but sees them with the eyes of a child.

— Anonymous.

Creative thinking is the relating of things or ideas which were previously unrelated.

— Anonymous.

Few of the things we want most are attainable by means that appear possible. It is the function of planning [and of creativity] to make the impossible possible.

— Russell L. Ackoff (1981: 121).

Creativity is largely a matter of identifying self-imposed constraints, removing them, and exploring the consequences of doing so.

— Russell L. Ackoff (1981: 193).

Whatever creativity is, it is in part a solution to a problem.

— Brian Aldiss (1993: 193).

It takes little talent to see clearly what lies under one's nose, a good deal of it to know in which direction to point that organ.

— W. H. Auden (1993: 890).

The knowledge of man is as the waters, some descending from above, and some springing from beneath; the one informed by the light of nature, the other inspired by divine revelation.

— Francis Bacon (1977: 24).

Creativity springs from having a different attitude toward the world. It accepts nothing as a given and everything as subject to improvement.

— Derm Barrett (1998: 14).

To find a form that accommodates the mess, that is the task of the artist now.

— Samuel Beckett (1993: 130).

[I]t seems to me, any individual seeking to reclaim his creativity must first break the patterns of the familiar.

— Warren Bennis (1976: 80).

Seek and ye shall find — whether it is there or not.

— David Berlo (1979: 209).

[Creative] problems have no one solution that is absolutely correct. [Instead,] they offer an infinite number of solutions, good and bad, new and traditional, feasible and seemingly impracticable. They even present solutions that may be impossible to implement at the moment.

— Angelo M. Biondi (1972: 19).

Contrary to the long-held belief that people must be ever restricted to conditioned personalities and confined to suffering, mounting evidence suggests that fulfillment is everybody's birthright.

— Harold H. Bloomfield (1975: 191).

By tapping his full measure of creative intelligence, an individual may begin to reflect humanity's highest ideas in his life. ... Such individual development offers the key to solving modern man's social problems.

— Harold H. Bloomfield (1975: 193).

Creativity is not only concerned with *generating new ideas* but with *escaping from old ones.*

— Edward de Bono (1971: 2).

Writing is nothing more than a guided dream.

— Jorge Luis Borges (1993: 37).

One of the idiosyncratic needs inherent in the human organism is the need to create, to bring order out of chaos.

— Berenice Bleedorn (1998: 49).

[Creative] problems have no one solution that is absolutely correct. [Instead,] they offer an infinite number of solutions, good and bad, new and traditional, feasible and seemingly impracticable. They even present solutions that may be impossible to implement at the moment.

— Angelo M. Biondi (1972: 19).

Contrary to the long-held belief that people must be ever restricted to conditioned personalities and confined to suffering, mounting evidence suggests that fulfillment is everybody's birthright.

— Harold H. Bloomfield (1975: 191).

By tapping his full measure of creative intelligence, an individual may begin to reflect humanity's highest ideas in his life. ... Such individual development offers the key to solving modern man's social problems.

— Harold H. Bloomfield (1975: 193).

Creativity is not only concerned with *generating new ideas* but with *escaping from old ones.*

— Edward de Bono (1971: 2).

Writing is nothing more than a guided dream.

— Jorge Luis Borges (1993: 37).

One of the idiosyncratic needs inherent in the human organism is the need to create, to bring order out of chaos.

— Berenice Bleedorn (1998: 49).

If there are obstacles, the shortest line between two points may be the crooked line.

— Bertolt Brecht (1993: 242).

Creativity is using your imagination to see something different from what it [sic] appears to everyone else.

— Steve Brockmeyer (1993: 113).

In the act of creation, a man brings together two facets of reality and, by discovering a likeness between them, suddenly makes them one.

— Jacob Bronowski (1965: 51).

That is the essence of science: ask an impertinent question, and you are on the way to a pertinent answer.

— Jacob Bronowski (1993: 807).

To innovate is not to reform.

— Edmund Burke (1977: 103).

It does not matter how new an idea *is*: what matters is how new it *becomes*.

— Elias Canetti (1993: 437).

In everything that can be called art there is a quality of redemption.

— Raymond Chandler (1993: 23).

No one was ever great without some portion of divine inspiration.

— Cicero (1992: 222).

If I cannot do great things, I can do small things in a great way.

— James F. Clark (1991: 54).

When you have eliminated the impossible, whatever remains, *however improbable*, must be the truth.

— Arthur Conan Doyle (1992: 425).

[A] great deal of new technology is not new knowledge; it is new perception. It is putting together things that no one had thought of putting together before, things that, by themselves had been around a long time.

— Peter F. Drucker (1970: 44).

The man who regards his life as meaningless is not merely unhappy but hardly fit for life.

— Albert Einstein (1969: 50).

[Creativity is the ability] to see the miraculous in the common.

— Ralph Waldo Emerson (1991: 201).

Invention breeds invention.

— Ralph Waldo Emerson (1992: 225).

Making mental connections is our most crucial learning tool, the essence of human intelligence: to forge links; to go beyond the given; to see patterns, relationship, context.
— Marilyn Ferguson (1997: 108).

Our task is to *discover* the primordial, absolutely unconditioned first principle of all knowledge ... It is intended to express that *Act* which does not and cannot appear among the empirical states of our consciousness, but rather lies at the basis of all consciousness and alone makes it possible.
— J. G. Fichte (1992: 133).

Too keen an eye for pattern will find it anywhere.
— T. L. Fine (1992: 136).

Creativeness often consists of merely turning up what is already there. Did you know that right and left shoes were thought up only a little more than century ago?
— Bernice Fitz-Gibbon (1991: 47).

Creative thinking may mean simply the realization that there's no particular virtue in doing things the way they always have been done.
— Rudolf Flesch (1991: 47).

Man has to solve a problem, he can never rest in the given situation of a passive adaptation to nature.
— Erich Fromm (1955: 34).

We tend to think of innovators as those who contribute to a new way of doing things. But many far-reaching changes have been touched off by those who contribute to a new way of thinking about things.
— John W. Gardner (1964: 36).

Creativity requires the freedom to consider "unthinkable" alternatives, to doubt the worth of cherished practices.
— John W. Gardner (1968: 83).

There are no right ways of doing things, only better ways. [The best way to do things remains to be discovered].
— James E. Gates (1962: 313).

To discover a truth oneself, without external suggestions or assistance, is to create – even if the truth is an old one.
— Antonio Gramsci (1985: 10).

[S]o many inventions involve simply putting the same old elements together in some new ways.
— J. P. Guilford (1962: 157).

Much creative effort is in the form of the transformation of something known into something else not previously known.
— J. P. Guilford (1962: 162).

It is obvious that invention or discovery, be it in mathematics or anywhere else, takes place by combining ideas.

— J. Hadamard (1975: 120).

Life has more questions than answers.

— George Halsey (1994: May 19).

All of history supports the observation that the desire to create is a fundamental urge in humankind.

— Willis Harman and John Hormann (1990: 26).

[W]hen one comes to truly know oneself, the pull of the material body and ego personality become greatly decreased and one finds that the deepest motivation is to participate fully ... in the evolutionary process and the fulfillment of humankind. ... [O]ne becomes aware that what appeared to be driving motivations were mainly illusory ego needs and that the desires of the true Self [psychological and spiritual growth and transformation] are one's real needs...

— Willis Harman and Howard Rheingold (1984: 135).

At one level creativity may be synonymous with novelty; the re-arrangement of traditional components into a new or unique pattern.

— John Hayes and Patricia Hough (1976: 90).

Creativity enables people to think the unthinkable, do the undoable.

— Roger Hayes and Reginald Watts (1986: 78).

[W]hether it occurs in painting a picture; writing a poem or symphony; inventing a new jet-propulsion system, marketing technique, or wonder drug; or managing a creative organization, the creative process is a manifestation of a fundamental ability -- that of relating previously unrelated things ... the ability to look at things with a fresh eye.
— Herbert G. Hicks and C. Ray Gullet (1976: 203).

A moment's insight is sometimes worth a life's experience.
— Sir Oliver Wendell Holmes (1992: 427).

Little minds are interested in the extraordinary; great minds in the commonplace.
— Elbert Hubbard (1967: 1308).

Those who refuse to go beyond fact rarely get as far as fact; and anyone who has studied the history of science knows that almost every step therein has been made by ... the invention of a hypothesis which, though verifiable, often had little foundation to start with ...
— T. H. Huxley (1975: 233).

Creativity is about being new and being different.
— Yuji Ijiri (1993: 394).

New things are made familiar,
and familiar things are made new.
— Samuel Johnson (1997: 47).

The two most engaging powers of an author are to make new things familiar, and familiar things new.
— Samuel Johnson (1990: 55).

In all chaos there is a cosmos, in all disorder a secret order.
— Carl Jung (1993: 131).

The supreme paradox of all thought is the attempt to discover something that thought cannot think.
— Søren Kierkegaard (1992: 233).

It's surprising how much of memory is built around things unnoticed at the time.
— Barbara Kingsolver (1995: 201).

Metaphor and imagery come into existence by a process, familiar from scientific discovery, of seeing an analogy where nobody saw one before. …the discovery of hidden similarities.
— Arthur Koestler (1975: 27, 343).

The creative act is not an act of creation in the sense of the Old Testament. It does not create something out of nothing; it uncovers, selects, re-shuffles, combines, synthesizes already existing facts, ideas, faculties, skills. The more familiar the parts, the more striking the new whole.
— Arthur Koestler (1975: 120).

True creativity often starts where language ends.
— Arthur Koestler (1975: 194).

No model exists for certain problems.
— Robert Lawrence Kuhn (1993: 394).

There are fundamentally two kinds of innovation: the "breakthrough" [and] ... the "improvement".
— Ralph Landau (1982: 54).

Much of the literature is devoted to the "heroes" of invention, whether inventors or entrepreneurs; very little is written about the improvements.
— Ralph Landau (1982: 56).

[C]ourage is the ability to act when you are afraid.
— Michael LeBoeuf (1979: 148).

The irony is that the creative areas in philosophy today do not lie in the region of academic work.
— Michèle Le Boeuff (1992: 246).

That's the way things come clear. All of a sudden. And then you realize how obvious they've been all along.
— Madeleine L'Engle (1997: 62).

It is not the finding of a thing, but the making [of] something out of it after it is found.
                                        — James Russell Lowell (1991: 47).

All people yearn toward self-actualization or tend toward it.
                                        --Abraham Maslow (1968: 128).

We are called upon to do something new, to confront a no man's land, to push into a forest where there are no well-worn paths and from which no one has returned to guide us.
                                        — Rollo May (1976: 2).

Creative courage ... is the discovery of new forms, new symbols, new patterns on which society can be built.
                                        — Rollo May (1976: 14-15).

[T]he struggle with limits is actually the source of creative productions.
                                        — Rollo May (1976: 137).

There are no new truths, but only truths that have not been recognized by those who have perceived them without noticing.
                                        — Mary McCarthy (1992: 436).

Rather than existing as slaves of instinct or even of prior experience, as humans we can, through choice, become more and do more than we can now imagine.
                                        — J. W. McLean and William Weitzel (1991: 56).

There are some enterprises in which a careful disorderliness is the true method.

— Herman Melvile (1993: 243).

Art enables us to find ourselves and lose ourselves at the same time.

— Thomas Merton (1996: 191).

The mind is its own place, and in itself
Can make a heaven of Hell, a hell of Heaven.

— John Milton (1993: 251).

The creative cannot be scaled down to the level of facts or observable data. It rides on the horizons and fills the heavens. It is incomparable and can never be subsumed under categories of definition, communication, and logic.

— Clark Moustakas (1967: 32).

To be creative means to experience life in one's own way, to perceive from one's own person, to draw upon one's own resources, capacities, roots.

— Clark Moustakas (1967: 27).

The clearest way into the universe is through a forest wilderness.

— John Muir (1993: 269).

What is originality? To *see* something that has no name as yet and hence cannot be mentioned although it stares us all in the face. The way men usually are, it takes a name to make something visible for them.

— Friedrich Nietzsche (1992: 322).

Art raises its head when religions relax their hold.

— Friedrich Nietzsche (1992: 324).

I mistrust all systematizers and I avoid them. The will to a system is a lack of integrity.

— Friedrich Nietzsche (1992: 324).

To see what is in front of one's nose requires a constant struggle.

— George Orwell (1995: 177).

The grandeur of human actions is measured by the inspiration from which they spring.

— Louis Pasteur (1975: 262).

Creativity is the ground of any well-lived life.

— Carol S. Pearson (1991: 165).

Our creations are not separate from us. We create as the expression of who we are, and as a way to discover who we are and what we think and know.

— Carol S. Pearson (1991: 174).

[T]he kind of creativity that most of us in business deal with ... is most often *not* fundamental innovation; it is most often relatively minor rearrangements of things that have already existed.

— Peter G. Peterson (1965: 182).

Great literature is simply language charged with meaning to the utmost possible degree.

— Ezra Pound (1992: 527).

It is important to emphasize that creativity ... does not mean the discovery of new and unknown facts. All the information is known, but new concepts are created by the mixing of known and previously unrelated facts.

— J. G. Rawlinson (1978: 5).

Invention is little more than new combinations of those images which have been previously gathered and deposited in the memory. Nothing can be made of nothing; he who has laid up no material can produce no combinations.

— Sir Joshua Reynolds (1975: 8).

Novel projects can [hardly] be executed through routine methods.

— Admiral Rickover (1962: 37).

Take something common and make it uncommon.

— John D. Rockefeller (1991: 95).

The very essence of the creative is its novelty, and hence we have no [objective] standard by which to judge it.

> — Carl R. Rogers (1962: 66).

But we cannot expect an accurate description of the creative act, for by its very nature it is indescribable.

> — Carl R. Rogers (1962: 68-69).

Less is more.

> — Ludwig Mies van der Rohe (1993: 26).

There is material enough in a single flower for the ornament of a score of cathedrals.

> — John Ruskin (1993: 276).

The answer to any question 'pre-exists.' We need to ask the right questions to reveal the answer.

> — Jonas Salk (1996: 130).

The smart person solves problems, the genius avoids them.

> — E. F. Schumacher (1992: 222).

The ability to relate and to connect, sometimes in odd and yet in striking fashion, lies at the very heart of any creative use of the mind.

> — George J. Seidel (1978: 12).

Nothing will come of nothing.
> — William Shakespeare (1993: 485).

Great art is never produced for its own sake. It is too difficult to be worth the effort.
> — George Bernard Shaw (1993: 60).

The becoming of man is the history of the exhaustion of his possibilities.
> — Susan Sontag (1993: 715)

.

Creativity has to do with the development, proposal, and implementation of *new* and *better* solutions ...
> — Gary A. Steiner (1965: 4).

[Creativity is] the ability to develop and implement new and better solutions.
> — Gary A. Steiner (1969: 353).

The poet is the priest of the invisible.
> — Wallace Stevens (1993: 35).

To have ideas is to gather flowers. To think is to weave them into garlands.
> — Anne-Sophie Swetchine (1997: 107).

Alleged "impossibilities" are opportunities for our capacities
to be stretched.

> — Charles Swindoll (1995: 466).

The essence of creativity lies in sensitivity to defects, the
recognition of a disturbing element.

> — E. Paul Torrance (1962: 42).

When we remember that we are all mad, the mysteries disap-
pear and life stands explained.

> — Mark Twain (1993: 230).

The surprise element of so many creative ideas arises because
they *do not result from the exercise of logical thought processes*
and conventional wisdom.

> — Brian C. Twiss (1980: 80).

Any activity becomes creative when the doer cares about
doing it right.

> — John Updike (1998: 49).

Excellence is to do a common thing in an uncommon way.

> — Booker T. Washington (1994: Jan. 20).

Of course no novelty is wholly novel.

> — Alfred North Whitehead (1961: 16).

[T]he greatest invention of the nineteenth century was the invention of the method of invention.
— Alfred North Whitehead (1961: 22).

Familiar things happen, and mankind does not bother about them. It requires a very unusual mind to undertake the analysis of the obvious.
— Alfred North Whitehead (1993: 374).

No great artist ever sees things as they really are. If he did he would cease to be an artist.
— Oscar Wilde (1992: 458).

II
The "Creative Individual"

No insignificant person was ever born.

— George W. Bush

The extraordinarily creative individual may simply be extraordinarily good at whatever skill is required to do a great job in a given domain. ... [T]hese extraordinary skills will not be relevant to every problem the individual works on, which means there will be cases in which the "genius" may produce merely ordinary work.

— Robert W. Weisberg

Creative and "Uncreative"

Conventional wisdom holds that some people are creative and others are not. This view is reflected in such familiar epithets as creative person, creative teacher, creative student, creative scientist, creative artist, creative engineer, creative manager, creative writer, and so on. Academic support for the creative-uncreative dichotomy comes from a long research tradition that has been trying to identify those attributes that characterize "creative individuals" and, presumably, distinguish them from the rest of the human population. A major human development study, for example, found two groups of children: (a) "creative unintelligent children," who could solve problems in unusual ways; and (b) "intelligent but uncreative children," who could solve difficult problems using conventional ways. Additional support for the creative-uncreative dichotomy comes from a section of literature on leadership which perceives leaders as "creative pioneers" who chart the course of change and bring the "uncreative rank and file" into line. There is, finally, the general tendency to associate creativity with a few domains of human activity and, *ipso facto,* their practitioners, i.e., arts and artists, architecture and architects, music and composers, fashion and fashion designers, painting and painters, poetry and poets, science and scientists, and so on.

Of course, characterizing one individual as "creative" implies that others in the same situation are not. By the same token, regarding certain gests that other domains and their practitioners are not creative – a belief that, in many parts of the world, seems to have translated into both public policy and social relations. Practical illustrations include: (i) perceiving certain individuals as having extraordinary ability, regarding them as different from the rest of the population, and according them special recognition and privileges; (ii) sorting young people into different academic streams (e.g., "secondary grammar," "secondary commercial," "secondary technical") according to their perceived intellectual abilities, and providing them with different curricular experiences; and (iii) making extra corporate efforts to attract, motivate, and retain the so-called "creatives."

The widespread notion of creativity as the rare and mysterious ability of a select few individuals has been particularly significant for its impact on people's self-perception as well as their creative functioning. Reports speak of self-fulfilling prophecy: People who perceive themselves as creative tend to believe in themselves and their abilities and, frequently, go on to achieve great things. By the same token, people who believe that they are not creative tend to doubt their abilities and usually fail to deploy them (see the section entitled "Self-Concept and Creativity"– Volume III, forthcoming.)

Characteristics of the "Creative Individual"

Because of the awe that creative ideas and products nearly always evoke, and the economic and cultural capital that are frequently made of those products, considerable research effort has been made to identify specific qualities (personality attributes) that characterize creative individuals. The following is a brief summary of some of the personality attributes that researchers have found to correlate with creative expression and that the general reading public has come to associate with creativity and "creative individuals."

Gary A. Steiner's widely-referenced *The Creative Organization* (1965) brings together a set of attributes that are believed to describe the creative individual. These are originality, conceptual fluency, ability to produce a large number of ideas quickly, ability to separate source from content in evaluating information, ability to suspend judgment and avoid early commitment, independence of judgment, playfulness, relativistic view of life, and bizarre fantasy

46

life. Steiner's review also describes the creative individual as less conforming and less authoritarian.

E. J. Shapiro's (1966) profile of the creative scientist includes twenty-seven personality attributes. The "creative scientist," according to the researcher, is outspoken, quick-thinking, self-centered, persuasive, impulsive, demanding, dedicated to research, intellectually curious, uninhibited, aggressive, adventurous, confident of his own ability, aesthetically inclined, intuitive, introverted and introspective, independent in judgment, flexible, emotionally unstable and sensitive, socially detached, radical, and dominant. Other characteristics of the "creative scientist," as the research indicates, are high sense of humor; initiative, broad theoretical interests, and achievement orientation.

J. H. McPherson's (1967) research on creative engineers suggests that these persons are above average in certain kinds of intelligence, dedicated to solving problems, nonconforming in ideas, receptive to ideas for testing, and extremely rigorous and scientific at times. Moreover, they tend to pursue their goals aggressively but quietly, seek and cherish autonomy and privacy, and are constructively dissatisfied with themselves and with things around them.

The "personality behind innovation" and the characteristics necessary for creativity, according to P. R. Whitfield (1975: 32-34), include: sensitivity, broad knowledge, general interests, imagination, flexibility, high need for achievement, risk-taking, commitment, self-confidence, forward-looking attitude, acceptance of individual responsibility, little urge for control over others, little interest in the power game, internal direction, propensity to explore and to experiment, openness to new information and flexibility in organizing it, nonconformity, optimism, and ability to use all senses.

Abraham Maslow's "clinically observed characteristics" of creative ["healthy"] people include: superior perception of reality; increased acceptance of self and of others, increased spontaneity, increase in problem centering, increased detachment and desire for privacy, increased autonomy and resistance to enculturation, greater freshness of appreciation and richness of emotional reaction, higher frequency of peak experiences, increased identification with the human species, improved interpersonal relations, more democratic character structure, and more. (Maslow, 1968: 25-26).

Barry Staw's (1995:162) review of creativity theories identifies the following characteristics as "shared by many of those who are creative": risk taking – willingness to take chances with unproven solutions rather than stick with the orthodox; nonconformity – a tendency to do something out

47

of the ordinary and the conventional; persistence – the tendency to keep at a problem in spite of frustrations or rebuff; flexibility – the ability to change perspectives on a problem when facing failure; dedication – total absorption in work, even to the exclusion of family and personal life.

Mihaly Ciskszentmihalyi's (1996: 51-76) "creative personality" embodies seemingly contradictory tendencies: physical energy and seeming idleness; smartness and naiveté; playfulness and discipline; fantasy and a rooted sense of reality; extroversion and introversion; humility and pride; masculinity and femininity; tradition and rebellion; iconoclasm and conservatism; passion and objectivity; pain and bliss.

We can make two general observations from these characterizations of "creative individuals." First, little agreement exists on the exact constellation of attributes that defines creative individuals. Second, the personality attributes associated with creative individuals are so many and so varied that the derived (composite) profile essentially describes human beings in general.

That, then, raises the question: Is creativity a special endowment of a select few or a widely-distributed human essence?

Creativity Distribution

One of the most controversial issues in creativity literature concerns its distribution. Opinions differ on whether or not creativity is a special endowment or a widely distributed human attribute. Four historically competing views of creativity deserve mention (see, for example, Weisberg, 1986). These are: (a) "genius"; (b) "genetic inheritance"; (c) "domain-restricted"; and (d) "universal human attribute."

The "genius" view of creativity perceives creative talent as an extraordinary, rare, and even mysterious ability that only a few highly-gifted individuals possess. In this view of creativity, geniuses possess the power to do what other human beings cannot do. They are the channels through whom divine ideas are communicated to humanity. They arrive ever so rarely, and their monumental contributions make them "benefactors" of humanity.

The "genetic inheritance" theory of creativity takes the observed frequency of creative products within certain families, clans, tribes, or racial groups as proof that creativity is genetically inherited or, so to speak, runs in the family, clan, tribe, or race. In this view, the children of

48

creative parents are more likely to be creative than the children of noncreative parents. By extension, people from clans, tribes, or racial groups that have distinguished themselves by their creative achievements are more likely to achieve creativity than are people from other clans, tribes, or racial groups.

The "domain-restricted" view of creativity ascribes this ability to selected human activities and their practitioners. In this view of creativity, architecture and architects can be creative; arts and artists can be creative; and so also can engineering and engineers, literature and writers, music and composers, poetry and poets, science and scientists. Certain other human activities presumably do not admit of the creative approach; as such, their practitioners cannot be creative.

The "universal-human-attribute" view of creativity points to the spectacular, sometimes unexpected, achievements of people from social groups and occupational categories that are normally not associated with creativity as evidence that creative ability is more widely distributed than was previously thought. Much of the thinking and writing about human creativity, particularly in the last quarter of the twentieth century, indicates a gradual shift from the previously exclusive notion of creativity to a more universal one. Contrary to the long-held belief that creativity is the special ability of a gifted few, more and more people are saying, for example, that we are all born creative, each with his own special abilities, talents, or gifts.

Reactions to Various Views of Creativity

The "genius" view of creativity takes the spectacular achievements of the great men and women in history as evidence of a special breed. In this view, only those individuals, and no one else, could achieve what they have done. The obverse, even if unspoken, view is that other human beings are not as gifted and therefore are not capable of achieving "great things."

Human-potential advocates acknowledge that there could be only one Confucius, one Socrates, one Shakespeare, one Mozart, one Einstein, one Gandhi, one Mandela, one Wole Shonyinka. They further acknowledge that probably only those individuals could have achieved the great things for which they are justifiably celebrated. It is suggested, however, that, by reason of his unique, one-of-a-kind genetic constitution, every human being has the potential (i.e., the innate capacity) to achieve something spectacular, unprecedented, and unequaled. Statements by Martin Buber (1958), Maurice Friedman (1967), and Willis Harman and Howard Rheingold (1984) summarize these arguments. According to Martin Buber:

> Every person born into this world represents something new, something that never existed before, something original and unique. It is the duty of every person ... to know ... that there has never been anyone like him in the world, for if there had been someone like him there would have been no need for him to be in the world. Every single man is a new thing in the world and is called upon to fulfill his particularity in this world (Buber, 1958: 139-140).

Maurice Friedman, also arguing the giftedness of every human being and the uniqueness of everyone's purpose, reminds us that:

> Each man is created for the fulfillment of a unique purpose. His foremost task, therefore, is the actualization of his unique, unprecedented and never-recurring potentialities, and not the repetition of something that another, and be it even the greatest, has already achieved (Friedman, 1967: 134).

Willis Harman and Howard Rheingold focus on the genius in every human being. They, however, believe that this aspect of the human individual often tends to be crowded out by other concerns and has to be deliberately tuned into. In their words:

> Perhaps what we call genius has something to do with a learned state of consciousness, a way of attending to the stream of mental experience. Perhaps many more of us could hear inner melodies, find guidance and inspiration, achieve breakthrough insight – if we could only pay more attention to the fleeting images [sic] and the quiet intuitions presented to us by the creative mind (Harman and Rheingold, 1984: 7-8).

The view of creativity as "genetic inheritance" regards differential creative achievements between families and between social groups as evidence that creative ability is inherited and restricted to certain families, clans, tribes, racial or ethnic groups.

Human potential advocates acknowledge the immense contribution that some families and social groups have made to the human heritage. They also observe enormous variations in creative expression between siblings and between members of any particular social group. Based on these observations, human potential advocates suggest that something other than genetic inheritance might be involved in human creativity. In this connection, they argue that if creativity were genetically inherited, as the inheritance theory seems to suggest, children of the same parents and members of the same social group would, more or less, be uniformly creative. Human potential advocates suggest that while creative ability is part of one's genetic constitution, the surprising but frequent occurrence of creativity in unlikely places indicates that its distribution is not restricted to particular families or social groups. Rev. Jesse Jackson's (1988) reference to his personal achievements and his rise to political and social fame illustrates the point. In his words:

> Great things happen in small places. Jesus was born in Bethlehem. Jesse Jackson was born in Greenfield (Jackson, 1988).

John Vaizey's criticism of the "tracking" system of education (i.e., the practice of grouping students according to perceived ability) also calls into question the view of creativity as a group-restricted attribute. Here is Vaizey's statement:

> The contemporary view posits that the correlation between intelligence and high socioeconomic class is probably not due to genetic selection but rather to social conditioning ... If this is so (and it seems reasonable to suppose that it probably is), [sic] then the division of the curriculum according to the 'innate' capacity of the children to acquire knowledge is no longer an acceptable basis for classification (Vaizey, 1967: 45).

The "domain-restricted" view of creativity holds that only a few areas of human activity and their practitioners can be creative. By implication, other activities are ordinary, and so also are their practitioners.

Human potential advocates acknowledge that architecture, arts, engineering, literature, music composition, painting, poetry, science, and sculpture, for example, actively encourage novelty and are traditionally approached as such – hence the high incidence of novelty and "creative individuals" in those professions. However, these advocates believe that every other human activity can be approached creatively, even the presumably mundane and routine. According to them, the important consideration is not so much the complexity of the task as the personal "encounter," the struggle, the absorption, the passion, or the anguish involved in trying to change established patterns and/or to bring about a new order (see, for example, May, 1975: 39-56, 87-109).

Two influential statements, one by Carl Rogers and the other by Abraham Maslow, indicate the relevance and applicability of creativity across domains. According to these eminent humanistic psychologists, even so-called routine things can be done in great and creative ways.

Here's how Carl Rogers puts it:

> Creativity is not, in my judgment, restricted to some particular content ... there is no fundamental difference in the creative process as it is evidenced in painting a picture, composing a symphony, devising new instruments of killing, developing a scientific theory, discovering new procedures in human relationships, or creating new formings of one's own personality ... The action of the child inventing a new game with his playmates; Einstein formulating a theory of relativity; the housewife devising a new sauce for the meat; a young author writing his first novel; all of these are, in terms of our definition, creative, and there is no attempt to set them in some order of more or less creative (Rogers, 1962: 65).

Like Carl Rogers, Abraham Maslow also believes that no activity is too routine or too mundane to be approached creatively. In his words:

> I had unconsciously confined creativeness to certain conventional areas ... of human endeavor, unconsciously assuming that *any* painter, *any* poet, *any* composer was leading a creative life. Theorists, artists, scientists, inventors, writers could be creative. Nobody else could be. Unconsciously I had assumed that creativeness was the prerogative solely of certain professionals ... I [have] come to apply the word "creative" to many products other than the standard and conventionally accepted poems, theories, novels, experiments or paintings. ... a first-rate soup is more creative than a second-rate painting ... a perfect [athletic] tackle could be as esthetic a product as a sonnet and could be approached in the same creative spirit. ... A good cabinet-maker or gardener or dressmaker *could* be more truly creative [than a competent cellist]. ... almost any role or job could be ... creative ... (Maslow, 1968: 135, 136, 137).

Parenthetically, Derm Barrett has reminded us of the unproductiveness and, indeed, the dangers of continuing to ascribe creativity to a few areas of human activity. In his words:

> The belief that creativity is limited to artists is dangerous and costly. It stops many people who work outside of the arts from using their creative abilities, since they believe they don't have any ... (Barrett, 1998: 15).

While "universal distribution of creative abilities" is not a universally accepted theory, it is more publicly affirmed than are competing theories. Now, more than ever before, scholars are acknowledging creativity as the distinguishing human attribute, and they are suggesting that the attribute is species-wide. As noted in section I, "The Essence of Human Creativity," more and more people are realizing that they are more creative and more capable than they are normally made to feel. Accordingly, they are asserting their right, in Paulo Freire's famous words, "to speak their word," "to name their world," and to participate in changing it (Freire, 1972: 76). The activities of social activists, ecologists, women's liberation movements, human potential movements, and other "new world order" movements illustrate the trend.

Intellectual support for some of these movements comes from a variety of sources. For purposes of this review, statements by George R. Eckstein (1962: 320), Leo B. Moore (1962: 304), and Derm Barrett (1998: 3) are particularly pertinent. Independently, the three sages call attention to the creativity in every human being, and they urge every society to recognize that fact and to provide the conditions that call forth the vast reservoir of inherent creative ability in their people.

A Different Notion of "The Creative Individual"

Reference has already been made to the principle of individual endowment – the unique set of abilities that characterizes every individual and the inner necessity to actualize one's potential. It remains to be explained why endowment is so important and what its implications are for human development.

The principle of endowment, as was noted in Section I, holds that every human being "comes" with a unique combination of abilities, an urge to actualize one's potential, and a force that ceaselessly impels the individual toward becoming his potential. The Greek philosopher Plato described this principle as "spirit"; Aristotle, as noted earlier, called it "natural principle" (or *entelechy*). The central idea of endowment ("spirit," *"entelechy,"* "natural principle"), as it relates to human beings, is that there is a force within every individual that determines what the individual can become, that distinguishes the individual from all other human beings, and that drives or guides the individual toward becoming its potential. Differences in the ways people think, feel, act, perceive, and prefer to relate to themselves and to their world are partially attributed to this principle (see, for example, Boss, 1963: 43; Buber, 1958; Maslow, 1968: 152, 191).

While every human being is innately endowed, not everybody has been able to realize his potential or to fulfill his unique purpose. That depends on one's total condition of existence, including parental upbringing, education, cultural stimuli, economic and social circumstances, professional standards, the political climate and, very importantly, self-definition (see the sections entitled "The Innovative Society" and "Barriers to Creativity" -- Volume II, forthcoming).

The principle of individual endowment and its derivatives, to the extent that they are valid, call into question the continued division of human beings into "creative" and "uncreative" and, in particular, the assumption that some individuals are "not talented." Categorizing a person as "not creative" or "uncreative" simply because he has not been able to produce novelty in a particular area amounts to equating creative expression with creative potential. Given the enormous variety of human talents, as Howard Gardner (1988; 1993) and many others have identified them, it is conceivable that some people's type of creativity may not currently be recognized or particularly valued. As such, the "creative individual" may simply be someone whose unique abilities happen to be recognized and valued at a particular time or in a particular culture or domain (see, for example, Arieti, 1976: 293-311; Tart, 1976; Weisberg, 1986). The lives of people whose works were recognized as creative many years after their death illustrate the point.

Conclusion

Human civilization has been built largely on the efforts of creative individuals – the men and women who broke the limits and made the seemingly impossible possible. Its future direction and, indeed, the destiny of the human species depend even more critically on that resource.

Creative individuals, as it appears, are the product of four main influences: *inner resources* (talents, intelligence, endowment, or the power to create); *courage* (willingness to endure the complexity, the tension, and the emotional stress that nonconformity frequently entails); *cultural stimuli* (favorable economic, social, political, and intellectual climate); and *a receptive public* (social recognition, support, and encouragement of new ideas). To the extent that the principle of individual endowment is valid, the first of these factors, inner resources, can be taken for granted. However, endowment alone is not always sufficient for creativity to occur. The other three factors – personal courage, cultural stimuli, and a receptive public – are also necessary.

Therefore, where some individuals or groups of people do not seem to be producing as much novelty as other individuals and groups, it is not due to "inferior genetic endowment," as was once believed; these individuals' apparent "lack of creativity" may be due to sociocultural and/or psychological factors, including: (a) the limited number of domains in which human creativity is currently recognized in many cultures, as against the extraordinary range of human talents; (b) inadequate encouragement and, sometimes, downright disapproval of ideas and things that seem to contradict official thinking or an existing belief system, or that are perceived as a threat to the way things have always been done; (c) deprived and constraining economic, social, political, and/or intellectual environments that, in some cultures, tend to stifle the creativity of certain categories of people and certain members of an organization; and (d) complacency, self-doubt, and other self-limiting assumptions and life-styles (see the section entitled "Barriers to Human Creativity" – Volume II, forthcoming).

The immense contributions that the great men and women in history have made to civilization may have given rise to ongoing efforts to identify their present-day successors and nurture their talents. As part of that effort, several attempts have been made to identify the traits of creative people, measure creative potential, and evaluate creative growth across the life span. The problem with some of these "creativity assessment" procedures, however, is the (often) unspoken assumptions that: (a) creativity is a unidimensional and undifferentiated ability that an individual either has or does not have, either has so much or so little of; and (b) everyone's type of creativity can be measured by currently available techniques and expressed in currently available terms. If, as the principle of individual endowment suggests, creativity is peculiar to the individual, one wonders whether one person's creativity can validly be assessed by a few "tests of creativity" designed by another (see, for example, Shapero, 1985: 196; Badawy, 1988: 54; Gardner, 1993: 13-34). Furthermore, one wonders whether part of the effort that has gone into identifying "creative individuals" might not have been more productively used to identify and remove the constraints that tend to prevent the vast majority of human beings from ever realizing their natural abilities.

Again, to the extent that the principle of individual endowment is valid, it is doubtful whether any useful purpose can be served by continuing to categorize and treat some human beings as "creative" and others as "not creative" or "uncreative." The last thing that any human being should be told or made to believe is that he is not creative. Such degradation could become a self-fulfilling prophecy. Daily experience and behavioral science research findings suggest that people who believe, or are made to believe, that they are creative tend to exert themselves more and, in fortunate circumstances, go on to achieve great things. By the same label-confirming behavioral tendencies, individuals who are presumed not creative, and are made to believe that they have no talents, often fail to sufficiently stretch their abilities and, frequently, settle for less than they are capable of (see the sections entitled "Self-Concept and Creativity" and "The Great Waste" – Volumes III & V, respectively, forthcoming).

Self-fulfilling prophecy aside, how can we justify the perception of some people as creative and others as not creative in a world that, as Charles Tart (1976: 106) observes, selectively recognizes and develops a small number of human abilities, actively inhibits some others, and is ignorant of many more?

As global problems continue to increase both in magnitude and complexity, and as the human condition continues to deteriorate, it is doubtful whether humanity can afford to continue to leave the solution to these problems to a small group of individuals, however gifted or talented. Further progress, evidently, will require the full and active participation of a greatly enlarged pool of creative individuals, one that includes every human being.

Perhaps the time has come to shift the focus of the creativity debate from the mystique of great men and women who possess supernatural and inaccessible talents to creating the conditions in which everybody's type of creativity is recognized, nourished, and channeled to the urgent tasks of moral reconstruction and civilization building. As an essential part of that project, we will need to come up with more durable national, regional, and planetary goals that individuals see as giving meaning to their lives and, therefore, as being worthy of their commitment and the investment of their unique creative abilities.

Selected Insights
on
The "Creative Individual"

The power to create exists within each of us.

— Anonymous

There lie buried in our subconscious selves
Vast store houses of rich golden treasure,
A God Himself dwells within;
If we can but touch this hidden divinity of life,
And bring it forth into triumphant expression,
We may rise to a glorious and more abundant existence.

— Anonymous

The creative person is able to transform the sea of irrelevancy
in which he finds himself into a vision of order and beauty, or
he sees how a tiny fragment of seeming cosmic futility collides
and coincides with a piece of obviousness. He is provided
with the capacity to transform randomness and disparity into
organized structure.

— Silvano Arieti (1976: 405).

Realize that you can be very talented in one area and just
normal in others.

— George Barany (1985: 117).

[N]othing is more natural to human beings than to be inventive and creative ...

— Derm Barrett (1998: xiii).

Don't associate the ability to create new solutions only with persons of great genius. Creative and inventive abilities are present in all people, to varying degrees. ... All normal human beings by sheer virtue of being human, have the inborn skill to be creative and inventive.

— Derm Barrett (1998: 3).

Creative and inventive abilities are present in all people. ... [A]nyone who wants to be more creative can be. ... Our ability to discover, create, and invent has been built into our brain through millions of years of evolution.

— Derm Barrett (1998: 3).

Some people with high levels of intelligence but weak will are not at all creative, while others of ordinary intelligence but passion and will can sometimes be exceedingly so.

— Derm Barrett (1998: 14).

The belief that creativity is limited to artists is dangerous and costly. It stops many people who work outside of the arts from using their creative abilities, since they believe they don't have any ...

— Derm Barrett (1998: 15).

Creative persons are, or have learned to be, mental free-spirits.
Their curiosity is quite uninhibited.

— Angelo M. Biondi (1972: 20).

[C]ould Mozart's genius have been due to his exceptionally
skillful use of a computational resource we all share: the
human mind?

— Margaret A. Boden (1992: 240).

[T]he more innovative individuals are not as deferent, obedi-
ent, flattering, conventional, predictable, easy to control, or
flexible to external demands and changes as their less innovative counterparts. Generally, they tend to view authority as
conventional rather than absolute.

— Kenneth E. Boulding (1982: 45-52).

To be human means to be creative.

— Mihaly Csikszentmihalyi (1996: 318).

[C]entral among the traits that define a creative person are
two somewhat opposed tendencies: a great deal of curiosity
and openness on the one hand, and almost obsessive
perseverance.

— Mihaly Csikszentmihalyi (1996: 326).

Creativity is God-given; born into each of us. It is not an
oddity, but a naturalness long neglected.

— George R. Eckstein (1962: 320).

Intelligence can be a trap. It can lead a young person to expect that success will come easily. It almost never does. ... In the real world outside of school, drive, persistence, hard work, task commitment, and a little bit of luck count as much or more than intellect.

— Ruth Duskin Feldman (1985: 118).

[O]n the whole, we Quiz Kids are not as outstanding as in our youth. Some have done well, some not so well; we performed no better than others less gifted.

— Ruth Duskin Feldman (1985: 118).

Genius is the ability to put into effect what is in your mind.

— F. Scott Fitzgerald (1991: 76).

Mankind is not divided into two categories, those who are creative and those who are not. There are degrees of the attribute.

— John W. Gardner (1964: 40).

The creative individual has the capacity to free himself from the web of social pressures in which the rest of us are caught.

— John W. Gardner (1964: 44).

We don't live up to the potential for excellence that is the birthright of every person.
— John W. Gardner (1996: 309).

Everybody ought to feel that whatever his or her calling, they can be excellent.
— John W. Gardner (1996: 309).

Perhaps what we call genius has something to do with a learned state of consciousness, a way of attending to the stream of mental experience. Perhaps many more of us could hear inner melodies, find guidance and inspiration, achieve breakthrough insight — if we could only pay more attention to the fleeting, images, and the quiet intuitions presented to us by the creative mind.
— Willis Harman and Howard Rheingold (1984: 7-8).

The capacity for achieving fundamental insights isn't only for geniuses, but is at least partially a learned skill. ... Profound inspiration isn't strictly reserved for artists, but can be a meaningful dimension of anybody's life.
— Willis Harman and Howard Rheingold (1984: 15).

Each of us has the capacity to become much more than we think we can be, if we choose to stop believing otherwise.
— Willis Harman and Howard Rheingold (1984: 16).

Some persons are more creative than others, but everyone has some creative ability.

— Herbert G. Hicks and C. Ray Gullet (1976: 214).

Great things happen in small places. Jesus was born in Bethlehem. Jesse Jackson was born in Greenfield.

— Jesse Jackson (1993: 597).

Genius ... means little more than the faculty of perceiving in an unhabitual way.

— William James (attributed).

Inventors are very much a type whether they work inside or outside an institution. ... The inventor is absorbed with his own ideas and disposed to magnify their importance and potentialities. He tends to be impatient with those who do not share in his consuming imagination and leaping optimism... his crucial characteristic is that he is isolated; because he is engrossed with ideas that he believes to be new and therefore mark him out from other men... The world is against him, for it is normally against change, and he is against the world, for he is challenging the error or the inadequacy of existing ideas. It is precisely because of these eccentric qualities that society had always found it so difficult to fit the inventor into its scheme of things... He is capable of self-deception yet he can be right when most others are wrong.

— J. Jewkes, D. Sawer, and R. Stillerman (1961: 176).

A man of genius makes no mistakes. His errors are volitional
and are the portals of discovery.

— James Joyce (1992: 164).

Though innovators are diverse people in diverse circumstances, they share an integrative mode of operating which
produces innovation: seeing problems not within limited
categories but in terms larger than received wisdom; they
make new connections, both intellectual and organizational;
and they work across boundaries, reaching beyond the limits
of their own jobs-as-given.

— Rosabeth Moss Kanter (1983: 212).

It would be appealing to say that corporate entrepreneurs are
idealists captivated by the idea itself and eager to show its
value; but they are human like the rest of us and driven by the
same mixes of "pure" and "impure" human emotions and
needs.

— Rosabeth Moss Kanter (1983: 211).

The majority of our children are being led to believe that they
are doomed to failure in a world which has room only for
those at the top.

— Eda J. LeShan (1997: 18).

Everyone is a genius at least once a year.

— G. C. Lichtenberg (1995: 11).

Talent is that which is in a man's power; genius is that in whose power a man is.
— James Russel Lowell (1992: 165).

Thus it comes about that doubt, tentativeness, uncertainty, with the consequent necessity for abeyance of decision, which is for most a torture, can be for [creative people] a pleasantly stimulating challenge, a high spot in life...
— Abraham H. Maslow (1968: 206).

Even though we are "gifted" we still are human. We can make mistakes. No matter how smart we are supposed to be, inside we are just like everyone else.
— Matt ("Gifted" Student) (1985: 21).

Forever unsatisfied with the mundane, the apathetic, the conventional, [creative individuals] always push on to newer worlds. Thus they are the creators of the "uncreated conscience of the race."
— Rollo May (1976: 28).

Each of us has a gift.
— Hughes Mearns (1958: 263).

Genius does what it must, and Talent does what it can.
— Owen Meredith (1992: 165).

All of us have an innate creative ability. Unfortunately, we suppress it, preferring to use the proven safer techniques.
— Alex F. Osborn (1963: xi).

Highly creative people are uniformly intelligent, but not all intelligent people are creative.
— Anne Roe (1965: 80-81).

[F]amous scientists aren't any more intelligent than those who aren't famous. ... [S]uccessful ones aren't right any more often than their colleagues, either. ... [T]he architects of science are simply more curious, more iconoclastic, more persistent, readier to make detours, and more willing to tackle bigger and more fundamental problems.
— Robert Scott Root-Bernstein (1989: 407).

Highly creative individuals in all fields have been found to be overwhelmingly intuitive.
— Helen Rowan (1969: 353).

There is no great genius without some touch of madness.
— Senecca (Attributed)

[T]here is some degree of nonconformity in us all, perhaps conquered or suppressed in the interest of our general well-being, but able to be touched or rekindled or inspired ...
— Ben Shahn (1971: 101).

[W]e do not have to postulate any special kind of "genius" to explain the creative act.

— Herbert A. Simon (1986: 19).

At the extreme, [highly creative people] sometimes feel lonely and apart, with a sense of mission that isolates them, in their own minds, from average men with average concerns.

— Gary A. Steiner (1965: 8).

Everyone excels in something.

— Publilius Syrus (1991: 2).

The truly creative personality is ready to abandon concepts and sees in life many rich and new possibilities.

— E. Paul Torrance (1962: 37).

The contemporary view posits that the correlation between intelligence and high socio-economic class is probably not due to genetic selection but rather to social conditioning ... If this is so (and it seems reasonable to suppose that it probably is), [sic] then the division of the curriculum according to the 'innate' capacity of the children to acquire knowledge is no longer an acceptable basis for classification.

— John Vaizey (1967: 45).

Everybody is born with genius, but most people only keep it a few minutes.
— Edgard Varèse (1993: 142).

It is the triumph of genius to make the common appear novel.
— Johann Wolfgang von Goethe (1991: 76).

Creativity is not a "you have it or you don't" proposition. It is a continuum and a fundamental attribute of all humanity. No organization can tap all the creativity that resides deep within the individual ... The important point is that the organization must not operate in a manner that poses insurmountable obstacles to all but the most creativity gifted or most aggressive individuals.
— Ross Webber (1979: 492).

[N]ovel products develop through the use of ordinary thought processes when a particular individual is placed in a particular situation.
— Robert W. Weisberg (1993: 25).

[A] genius is a person in whose psyche a significant synthesis of cultural elements has occurred.
— L. A. White (1976: 302).

A sensitive being, [is] a *creative* soul.
— William Wordsworth (1977: 579).

III
Creative Aging

Most of us go to our graves with our music still inside
— Oliver Wendel Holmes, Jr.

Born Unique

Jean Jacques Rousseau once portrayed the human condition as "born free, but everywhere in chains." Rousseau's seemingly pessimistic remark was in reaction to what he saw as the curtailment of individual freedom due, first, to the increasing regulation of life by the state and, second, to inexorable social pressures to which people had to conform* (see, for example, Havens, 1962: 235-261; Crocker, 1968).

While Rousseau's comments pertained specifically to the human condition that he observed in France in the middle of the eighteenth century, historical evidence indicates that the situation in many parts of the world was not much different then. Frequently mentioned examples include so-called traditional societies in which conformity was near-total and deviation not tolerated, political regimes that virtually excluded women and minorities in the decision-making process, despotic rulers who brooked no dissent, judicial systems in which only the rich and powerful could afford justice, economic systems in which only the fittest could survive, and imperial systems within which colonized peoples had very little say in how they were governed.

Since Rousseau's time, however, considerable progress has been made, particularly in the domain of political freedom: Women and minorities around the world have won the right to vote and a place in the decision-making process; civil rights have been enacted into law in many coun-

---

* Besides the curtailment of individual freedom, Rousseau also criticized what he saw as: (a) lack of moral progress despite the tremendous increase in knowledge and material comfort; (b) artificial inequality of race, class, education, and economic circumstances; and (c) a system that "favored a noble over a commoner, the strong over the weak" (Havens, 1962: 243).

tries; slavery has been abolished; formerly colonized peoples have attained political independence; the UN-sponsored Fundamental Human Rights doctrine is protecting individual freedom in many parts of the world; and there are even calls for a new world order, based on the principles of equity and justice for all.

Human potential advocates acknowledge the gains in political freedom, but describe the human condition as still less than satisfactory. Two and a-half centuries after Rousseau's comments, human life in many parts of the world still shows signs of serious deprivation. If we could extend Rousseau's "chains" metaphor to reported human conditions in many parts of the world, many people's experiences can be described as born unique and incomparable, but categorized and compared as statistics and abstractions; born whole (mind, body, and spirit), but largely regarded as rational economic man *(Homo economicus);* born original, but socialized into standardized roles; or born creative, but expected to produce patterned responses in most situations. A number of institutional arrangements that were originally designed to expand human capacity sometimes tend to constrain it.

Awareness of one's capacities, interests, and goals, and the ability to transcend the constraints that tend to prevent one from realizing one's potential and reaching one's goals are what is meant in this anthology as *creative aging.*

Endowment and Socialization

The concept of creative aging derives from the principle of individual endowment and, in particular, the goal-directedness of human life. According to this principle (already reviewed in sections I and II), every human individual, like all other living things, has within him innate potentialities (capacities) that determine what the individual can become and that also tend to impel him to increasingly realize and express his capacities – of course, *within the limits of his sociocultural environment.* The same principle is also believed to predispose the individual toward certain goals and away from others.

The literature describes becoming one's potential alternatively as "living according to one's own nature", "following one's own interests," and "living out one's purpose." This multiplicity of endowments, however, means that an individual's interests have to be expressed in the context of other individuals, other institutions, and, of course, the natural environment. That notion raises the possibility of conflict between individual and community interests, between personal existence and orderly social life, between free will and control. The process by which societies try to forestall or minimize potential conflicts and to ensure that individual interests do not unreasonably interfere with the interests of other individuals is known as *socialization.*

Sociologists define socialization as the process by which the individual acquires the culture of his or her society. While specific forms of socialization vary from culture to culture, the goals of socialization are largely the same: (a) to relate the individual and his interests with other individual and their interests, and (b) to teach individuals what society feels they should know and be able to do, and how they should behave in specific situations.

The benefits of socialization to individuals and society are many and wide-ranging. Sociologists speak of orderly living, social stability, and continuity, by virtue of which certain traditions are passed from one generation to the next. Social psychologists point to personality development, social interaction, and interpersonal and intergroup exchanges that are essential for community life. Social anthropologists identify "cultural mindsets" or the relatively stable patterns of thought, feelings, and actions that typify the people of a given society. The existence of food, clothing, shelter, values, customs, conventions, voluntary associations, religious institutions, and political organizations explain why socialization is so vital for the survival of the individual and continuity of the society (see, for example, Robertson, 1987: 138).

Human potential advocates recognize the many benefits of socialization and its absolute necessity for orderly living. However, they perceive the acculturation process as a mixed blessing, pointing to certain social arrangements that, in some cultures, tend to suppress originality and creativity. To illustrate:

- the pressure to think, feel, or adhere to approved group symbols sometimes makes it difficult for people to be genuine and to act in accordance with their true feelings.

- perceiving the individual as a role (male, female, son, daughter, parent, politician, scientist, farmer, teacher, student, worker, supervisor, etc.) tends to ignore several of his "other" attributes that are normally not associated with the role that is assigned to him and, therefore, minimizes him as an integrated human being.

- relating to the individual as an abstraction (black, white, yellow, African, American, Asian, European, intelligent, strong, weak, and so on), like perceiving him as a role, tends to ignore "other" attributes of the individual that are normally not associated with the category to which he is being assigned and, therefore, limits the range of his potential contributions to society.

- the difficulty of gaining acceptance for ideas that seem to challenge accepted beliefs or official thinking tends to discourage divergent thinking, which is the hallmark of creativity.

Ironically, then, the same (socialization) process that holds society together sometimes makes it difficult for people to realize their potential and, thus, to maximally benefit society.

Patterns of Adjustment

Behavioral sciences observe varying degrees of socialization and different patterns of internalization. Forms of "socialization" range from the totalitarian societies (with high degrees of conformity and low tolerance for deviance) to the so-called permissive societies (where most forms of behavior are accepted). Most societies fall between these two extremes, with varying degrees of regimentation and permissiveness. Patterns of internalization also vary greatly. One extreme consists of people who, as Harman and Hormann (1990: 125) observe, unquestioningly accept the suggestions of their society or culture without examining their reasons, implications, or long-term consequences. The other extreme consists of individuals who reject the way of life of their society and their compatriots. The vast majority of human beings probably fall between the two extremes, with varying degrees of conformity and "rebellion."

Creative Aging

Ironically, "conformity" and "rebellion," represent the type of existence that is referred to here as *creative aging*. As distinct from routine existence or merely growing old and maturing physiologically, creative aging can be described as a dynamic lifelong process of continuously discovering, developing, and engaging one's unique abilities in ways that one perceives as important and beneficial to oneself, to fellow human beings, and to the natural environment. Related experiences go by different names: "self-actualization"; "coming into existence," "becoming a person," "the struggle to become an individual"; "the art of being fully human"; "the life you were born to live," "finding your life purpose"; "the work you are here to do"; "[learning] to follow our own threads through the tapestry of life with authenticity and resolve" (see, for example, Rogers, 1961; 1967; Maslow, 1968; Buscaglia, 1978; Kabat-Zinn, 1994: 209; Millman, 1994; Redfield and Adrienne, 1995: 198).

Analysis of some of the things that have been written about this pattern of existence identifies several recurring predispositions. Following are five of those conditions:

Authenticity

By reason of his endowment or the unique combination of abilities that define him, the human individual is predisposed in certain ways and to certain things. He has a unique and very personal way of perceiving and relating to himself, to fellow human beings, and to nature. Moreover, he has things that he deeply yearns to do or feels that he must do to be genuinely satisfied, things that he tends to cling to in spite of circumstances, things that seem to come naturally to him and that feel right when he does them (see the section entitled "Creative Work"; see also Maslow, 1968: 152; Gardner, 1993: 17-26; Pearson, 1991: 171-172; Csikszentmihalyi, 1996: 371-372).

Endowment, as explained earlier, is only one part of being human. The other part is the inner urge or the psychic necessity to actualize one's potential. Humanistic psychologists suggest that in order to feel fulfilled, one must be able to discover and to follow one's inclinations and interests, to live according to one's nature, to sense and relate to oneself and the outside world as one perceives them. Paulo Freire (1972) euphemistically describes this experience as the ability to say one's word, to name one's world, and to participate in changing it. Jon Kabat-Zinn (1994: 209, referenced above) metaphorically defines it as following one's own threads through "the tapestry of life." The obvious implication here is genuineness – being able to recognize and accept the integrity of one's perceptions, feelings, goals, and interests, and to live and act accordingly (of course, in the context and for the benefit of other human beings and the rest of nature).

Meaning and personal fulfillment
Two of the most crucial human needs are meaning and fulfillment. Most human actions, recognized or not, are directed primarily at satisfying these needs.

Meaning consists, first, in discovering an ideal, a task, or a goal that really matters to one. The second part of meaning is perceiving that ideal, task, or goal as part of one's life purpose – something without which one's life would be empty or incomplete (Mitin, 1972: 527). Fulfillment is the ability to achieve what one perceives as one's life purpose or to be part of a collaborative enterprise that brings about realization of one's deepest desires. Meaning and personal fulfillment, therefore, consist in finding and doing something that one perceives as the reason for one's existence. This is the relationship between creative aging and the genuinely successful life.

"Expanded landscape of being"
Henry David Thoreau's (1987: 40-66) notion of "expanded landscape of being," Abraham Maslow's (1968) theory of the "hierarchy of human motivations," and Philo Pritzkau's (1970: 50) concept of "greater existence" suggest that human fulfillment is not a goal to be reached, but a process that never ends; a journey, as the cliché goes, rather than a destination; an ever-widening spiral of becoming, rather than a consummation of one's nature.

Contrary to conventional wisdom, human fulfillment does not consist in contentment, but in constructive dissatisfaction with things as they are, coupled with an effort to bring about improvement. Support for that conclusion is the universal human tendency to try to exceed the current situation; to reach beyond the scope of existing knowledge; to imagine and construct new possibilities; to find new things to do, new challenges to take on, higher standards to attain, or new avenues within which to use one's abilities.

Creativity scholars perceive human existence as a continuing process of transcending the present condition (however "satisfactory" it may seem) and, in the process, overcoming the barriers that tend to limit one's possibilities and the scope of one's existence. Highly productive and genuinely successful people attribute their success to such experiences (see, for example, Sinetar, 1987; Csikszentmihalyi, 1996).

Breakthrough Experience

Perceiving the human condition as "born free, but everywhere in chains" does not mean that the so-called "chains" can't be broken. Anecdotal evidence and numerous success stories of self-actualizing individuals suggest that most social and psychological chains *can* be broken.

Existentialist literature represents human existence as a continuing struggle with limiting conditions, and it contains several suggestions for breaking through and escaping some of the conditions that tend to constrain one's abilities and to diminish one's existence. Some of the suggestions are embodied in a series of self-confrontation questions: Who am I? Why am I here? What am I doing? Why am I doing the things that I am doing? What do I want to do with my life? To what extent do the "conditions" in which I find myself nourish my abilities and promote the things that I really want to do? What opportunities are there for me to break free of the factors that tend to limit my growth and development? How can I turn the present condition to my advantage? (see, for example, Pritzkau, 1970: 9).

Passion and verve

The universal human tendency to want to transcend ourselves suggests that human beings are constituted for excitement rather than torpor, for passion rather than languor. Contrary to the once-popular nose-to-the-grindstone perception of the work-life in particular, a growing body of research and anecdotal evidence suggests that human existence need not be dull, uninteresting, or stultifying, but, rather, challenging, fascinating, and deeply satisfying (see the section entitled "Creative Work"). People who claim to have found their "work" describe their experience as something that you relish so much that you don't want to give it up as you grow older; something that you care so much about that you don't seem to have enough time to do it; something that you want to do more than anything else in the world; a desire that can never be satisfied; something that you like so much that, if necessary, you would pay to do it; or an activity that is its own reward.

Ways of living that reflect these general conditions go by different descriptions in both academic literature and popular parlance. Henry David Thoreau, for example, refers to it as the ability to restore one's unity that had been disrupted by abstractions, to complete the humanity within oneself, and to pass over from limited conditions of existence into an infinite one (see Steele, 1987: 40-66). Abraham Maslow talks of an ongoing actualization of one's potentials, capacities, and talents; fuller knowledge and acceptance of one's intrinsic nature; and an unceasing trend toward unity, integration, or synergy within oneself (Maslow, 1962: 25). Philo Pritzkau (1970, already referenced) refers to breaking through perceived deprivation pockets and the barriers to greater existence.

"Growing old without feeling old," "staying alive throughout life," "finding your passion and following it," and "getting better on the inside even though the outer body is disintegrating" are popular but witty epigrams for the same pattern of existence.

The recurrence of terms like "ongoing," "unceasing," and "trend" suggests that creative aging is not an episodic growth or development, but a continuing, lifelong process of self-affirmation and self-renewal that begins very early in life and continues through school, employment, and retirement. To emphasize: Creative aging does not begin at fifty-five or sixty-five (whatever a country's official retirement age happens to be), and does not end until "the end."

Finally, if people's creative expressions appear to be declining as they grow older or, perhaps more accurately, if they are not producing as many novel ideas and products as they did when they were younger, it probably is not because their creative potential has declined. The belief exists that, as the price of mistakes gets higher, as the risk of failure increases, as the penalty for deviance gets stiffer and the rewards for conformity become ever more enticing and indispensable, and as the sanctity of established traditions becomes unquestionable, people tend to regard any "deviant" ideas that they might have as childish, frivolous, irresponsible, and even dangerous. Given such a cautious approach to life, the likely tendency is to be wary of the new and untried or, in popular parlance, to choose to be on the safe side.

Implications for the Aging and the Aged

Gerontologists have been warning that as a result of advances in public health and improved sanitation and nutrition, more and more people will live beyond the age when they are capable of performing useful work or even of maintaining themselves. Gerontologists further estimate that, in the foreseeable future, as much as one third of a person's lifetime may be spent in retirement, traditionally perceived as a period of inactivity during which an individual's productive capacity is presumed to have depreciated to a level that cannot be supported on economic grounds. Finally, because of the high value that many cultures place on youth and the productive capacity of young people, gerontologists believe that the elderly population in those societies is not likely to be especially valued and could even be discriminated against in the distribution of resources.

Obsession with youth and the tendency to devalue elderly people have been common cultural practices at least since ancient Greece. Through the ages in many human societies, people who lived beyond a certain culturally-defined age of economic productivity have tended to be denigrated. Although not universal, public opinion and even expert comments in those societies have tended to associate old age with senility, physical deterioration, memory loss, mental decline, helplessness, and loss of contact with reality. Plato, for example, described old age as "a dreary solitude." Euripedes, another ancient Greek thinker, characterized the elderly as "voice and shadow." Seneca, of ancient Rome, perceived old age as "an incurable disease." His hypothesis was that "old age and happiness seldom go together." William Shakespeare, in *Much Ado About Nothing* (III.v), suggests that "when the age is in, the wit is out." A great nineteenth-century thinker simply postulated that "nature abhors the old." Up to the last quarter of the twentieth century, a few gerontologists were still perceiving old age as a disability and something to be dreaded. In obvious reference to their presumed declining economic productivity, elderly people have been portrayed variously as "the spent and maimed," "the twentieth century social problem," a "surplus population," "social leeches" who live off the productivity of the young, and a "useless and unnecessary" group "whose wisdom represents another age that is irrelevant now."

It is not clear how widely these negative stereotypes about age and aging are shared. However, to the extent that elderly citizens are devalued as "useless and helpless relics of the past," the stigma can become a self-fulfilling prophecy. Such epithets as "senility," "memory loss," and "physical decline," for example, tend not only to lower society's expectations of elderly persons but also to diminish the way members of that segment of the population perceive themselves. Studies in self-concept indicate that negative labeling and stigmatization, to the extent that they are actually believed and internalized by the stigmatized, tend to devalue these people's self-image and to generate behaviors that eventually confirm those stereotypes. Social psychologists suggest that persons, including the elderly, who perceive their environment as rejecting them, as underestimating their contributions and personal worth, tend to minimize their participation, withdraw into solitary activities, or totally disengage. With diminished utilization, of course, most human abilities atrophy and, eventually, decline.

The problem of aging and the anxiety that it frequently generates are not peculiar to the aged alone, but cut across several age strata, possibly beginning as early as adolescence. Gerontologists report considerable apprehension among people approaching old age, and attribute the phenomenon to several factors, including: (a) impending retirement and fear of the declining sense of self-worth that regular work provides; (b) anticipated loss of income and the financial independence that regular income provides; and (c) diminishing social network and possible isolation.

The literature on self-actualization, and anecdotal evidence from people who, self-reportedly, "love" their work, suggest that some of the apprehensions about old age need not arise and can be minimized, if people are encouraged and able to recognize their unique abilities and talents engage in activities that cultivate their most enduring attributes, and practically express their talents in their current jobs. Bernard Haldane's personal testimony illustrates the point. The octogenarian declares:

> "At 84, I feel I have lived a good life, given much, and have more to give" (Haldane, 1996: ix).

78

Conclusion

There is no denying the absolute necessity of every human society to socialize its members and organize their activities in ways that ensure that society's continued existence and proper functioning. However, when building orderly and prosperous societies entails minimizing human potential and diminishing the scope of people's existence, there is the risk that the world could end up with a "brilliant civilization" comprised of alienated, stressed, unfulfilled, and deeply unhappy people, a situation reminiscent of the one described in Oliver Goldsmith's "The Deserted Village," "where wealth accumulates and men decay."

There is no question that people have a right to economic and material well-being. However, when people come to define themselves and measure their worth almost exclusively by their bank accounts and the size of their private estates, the world could end up with rich but unfulfilled and inwardly disenchanted human beings. Also, where production and consumption of the "good things of life" become the goal of human existence, people could easily lose sight of what is in their long-term interest and that of the natural environment upon which all life depends.

The fear is sometimes expressed that if human beings are allowed to follow their inclinations, things could fall apart and society could disintegrate, possibly resulting in anarchy or chaos. That probably would be the case, without a shared vision of something worth preserving and worth committing to, without a larger and integrating purpose toward which individual actions can be directed, without a system of values that individuals perceive as giving meaning to their lives and as benefiting themselves, their societies, and the natural environment (see, for example Gardner, 1964: xv, 123, 127, 128; Schumacher, 1974: 95, 101, 297; Laszlo, 1994: 123-124). Numerous episodes of patriotic fervor, collective self-sacrifice, and acts of heroism (whether resulting from perceived threats or crises, or in response to a challenge) suggest that people willingly commit their energies and talents to a cause and even take personal responsibility for its realization, if they perceive it as promoting their personal growth and development, as expressing qualities that they like about themselves, and as expressing values they regard as important and worthy.

The social and political trends of the past few decades (e.g., New Age, workers' rights, women's liberation, participatory corporation, deep-ecology, spirituality, etc.) suggest that people are no longer content with routine existence, but want to live meaningful and fulfilling lives; are no longer excited about "any work that brings in the money," but look for projects that continuously expand their capacities and deeply engage their talents and interests; are no longer enamored with high social status as such, but are looking for opportunities to significantly benefit their society and/or the natural environment; and are no longer satisfied with material "progress," *per se,* but are eager to build a more humane, more fulfilling, and more durable civilization.

To the extent that people's economic productivity as well as their physical, mental, and spiritual well-being depend on the actualization (development and expression) of their natural abilities, neither the problems of dependency, helplessness, and depression among the elderly, nor the "burden of old age pensions on workers," are likely to be solved in the long-term by extended family obligations, or by patronizing programs for the elderly, or by generous retirement benefits, or by lowering the age at which people are entitled to draw their retirement benefits. What is more likely to help people (the aged as well as the aging) live creative, productive, meaningful, and fulfilling lives is the opportunity to develop and to engage one's talents in things that one is passionate about and that one also sees as beneficial to one's society and the rest of nature. That, precisely, is the essence of "creative aging." Strategies for promoting this pattern of existence are discussed throughout this anthology.

Selected Insights
on
Creative Aging

The man who views the world at 50 the same as he did at 20 has wasted 30 years of his life.

— Muhammad Ali (1997: 73).

We grow neither better nor worse as we get old, but more like ourselves.

— Mary Lamberton Becker (1992: 242).

[I]t's clear that some people … continue to learn and grow throughout their lifetimes.

— Warren Bennis (1989: 100).

[A] person aspiring to wisdom knows that the bottom line of a well-lived life is not so much success but the certainty we reach, in the most private fibers of our being, that our existence is linked in a meaningful way with the rest of the universe.

— Mihaly Csikszentmihalyi {1996: 233).

When we live creatively, boredom is banished and every moment holds the promise of a fresh discovery.

— Mihaly Csikszentmihalyi (1996: 344).

[People can] keep being creative even when the body fails and when societal opportunities become restricted.

— Mihaly Csikszentmihalyi (1996: 220).

Creative individuals don't have to be dragged out of bed; they are eager to start the day. This is not because they are cheerful, enthusiastic types. Nor do they necessarily have something exciting to do. But they believe that there is something meaningful to accomplish each day, and they can't wait to get started on it.

Most of us don't feel our actions are that meaningful. Yet everyone can discover at least one thing every day that is worth waking up for.

— Mihaly Csikszentmihalyi (1996: 349).

[T]o be nobody but yourself in a world which is doing its best, night and day, to make you everybody else, means to fight the hardest battle which any human being can fight; and never stop fighting.

— ee. cummings (1995: 532).

The important thing is this: To be able at any moment to sacrifice what we are for what we could become.

— Charles Dubois (1976: vii).

It is never too late to be what we might have been.

— George Eliot (1993: 422).

The man who is true to his "Genius" need not feel subject to the weary kingdom of time.
— Ralph Waldo Emerson (1988: 219).

Most people die before they are fully born.
— Erich Fromm (1971: 60).

Creative living means to be born before one dies.
— Erich Fromm (1971: 60).

[W]e know that men and women need not fall into a stupor of mind and spirit by the time they are middle-aged. They need not relinquish as early as they do the resilience of youth and the capacity to learn and grow. Self-renewal is possible.
— John Gardner (1964: xiii).

Human beings have always employed an enormous variety of clever devices for running away from themselves, and the modern world is particularly rich in such stratagems. We can keep ourselves so busy, fill our lives with so many diversions, stuff our heads with so much knowledge, involve ourselves with so many people and cover so much ground that we never have time to probe the fearful and wonderful world within.
— John Gardner (1964: 15)

By middle life most of us are accomplished fugitives from ourselves.

— John Gardner (1964: 15).

[T]rue happiness involves the full use of one's powers and talents.

— John Gardner (1964: 121).

The conception of individual fulfillment and lifelong learning finds no adequate reflection in our social institutions.

— John W. Gardner (1968: 107).

Older people differ not at all from their younger contemporaries in the requirement that life should have some meaning.

— John W. Gardner (1968: 154.

One of the most useful things a society could do to help people adapt to retirement would be to give all its members in their early and middle years the kinds of experience that will build the capacity for self-renewal.

— John W. Gardner (1968: 154).

If we want to improve the quality of life for older people, we should do everything possible to increase the number of persons with the capacity for self-renewal.

— John W. Gardner (1968: 155.

Our greatest mistake is to neglect the cultivation of those virtues a person has, and to try to exact from each person virtues he does not possess.

— Hadrian (1996:1).

At 84, I feel I have lived a good life, given much, and have more to give.

— Bernard Haldane (1996: ix).

Lives based on having are much less free than lives based either on doing or on being.

— William James (1964: 63).

The minute a man ceases to grow, no matter what his years, that minute he begins to be old.

— William James (attributed).

When you're through learning, you're through.

— Vernon Law (1997: 69).

[Although older people are apt to lose other faculties such as memory], creative imagination is ageless.

— George Lawton (1963: 18).

Unless you try to do something beyond what you have mastered, you will never grow.

— C. R. Lawton (attributed).

You are as young as your faith; as old as your doubt; as young as your confidence; as old as your fear; as young as your hope; as old as your despair.
> — General Douglas MacArthur (1975: 137).

[The creatively ageing] person rather than coming to rest becomes more active.
> — Abraham Maslow (1962: 28).

Imagination grows by exercise, and contrary to common belief, is more powerful in the mature than in the young.
> — W. Sommerset Maugham (1963: 19).

Creativity is not merely the innocent spontaneity of our youth and childhood; it must also be married to the passion of the adult human being, which is a passion to live beyond one's death.
> — Rollo May (1976: 27).

Self-knowledge is not a static undertaking.
> — J. W. McLean and William Weitzel (1991: 75).

Unrest of spirit is a mark of Life.
> — Karl Menninger (1996: 19).

Our first duty to society is to be somebody, that is to say, to be ourselves.

— Clark Moustakas (1967: 1).

Every individual embodies and contains a uniqueness, a reality, that makes him unlike any other person or thing. To maintain this uniqueness in the face of threats and pressures ... is the ultimate challenge and responsibility of every man.

— Clark Moustakas (1967: 1).

How can the individual develop latent resources and hidden talents when he is urged to conform, to compete, to achieve, to evaluate, to establish fixed goals?

— Clark Moustakas (1967: 17).

When a person's involvement in a situation is based on appearances, expectations, or the standards of others; when he acts in a conventional manner, or according to prescribed roles and functions, when he is concerned with status and approval; his growth as a creative self is impaired.

— Clark Moustakas (1967: 35).

New opportunities and different stages in life call on us to use different gifts and to make different contributions.

— Elizabeth O'Connor (1971: 44).

New opportunities and different stages in life call on us to use different gifts and to make different contributions.
— Elizabeth O'Connor (1971: 44).

We know what our part is [in solving the great world problems of our time and creating a more just, humane, and beautiful world] by what feels not just familiar, but deeply true and right when we do it. We know it by what we love and what makes us feel fulfilled. We know it by what we cling to when everything around us and sometimes in us is falling apart.
— Carol S. Pearson (1991: 171-172).

It is only when we begin to uncover who we are – beneath insecurity and grandiosity, beneath ingrained habit and social conditioning, beyond our outer appearance and our persona – that we can have some confidence that our actions are helping to expand rather than shrink our individual, collective, and world Soul.
— Carol S. Pearson (1991: 174).

All men have the capability of creating their own form, not simply using that of others.
— Philo T. Pritzkau (1970: 11).

Today's children are too often raised in a passive way with little or no opportunity to find their identity and recognize their talents before they are thrust out into a society that is increasingly more specialized and technical.
— James Redfield and Carol Adrienne (1995: 224).

It's important to remember that each child brings in his or her own issues to work through in this lifetime. They are not born to be simply molded by parental influence.
— James Redfield and Carol Adrienne (1995: 225).

Perhaps the greatest failure of the ... socialization process is its inability to equip people adequately to face old age ...
— Ian Robertson (1987: 136).

One of the final challenges for human beings is to get old with as much verve and gumption as possible. Old parents who keep on being interested in life give a subtle kind of sustenance to their children: they are givers of hope and affirmers of life.
— Alice Judson Ryerson and Wendy Coppedge Sanford (1978: 129).

A man is not old until he has lost his vision. A man is young as long as he sees possibilities around him.
— Robert H. Schuller (1975: 136).

The tragedy of life is what dies inside a man while he lives.
— Albert Schweitzer (attributed).

Nothing is less worthy of honor than an old man who has no other evidence of having lived long except his age.
— Seneca (1969: 11).

There are people who, like houses, are beautiful in dilapidation.
— Logan Pearsall Smith (1969: 11).

The art of life is not controlling what happens to us, but *using* what happens to us.
— Gloria Steinem (1992: 22).

I'm fortunate to have a future of active work I love and look forward to …
— Gloria Steinem (1992: 246-247).

The adult with a capacity for true maturity is one who has grown out of childhood without losing childhood's best traits. He has retained the basic emotional strengths of infancy, the stubborn autonomy of totterhood, the capacity for wonder and pleasure and playfulness of the preschool years, the capacity for affiliation and the intellectual curiosity of the school years, the idealism and passion of adolescence. He has incorporated these into a new pattern of development dominated by adult stability, wisdom, knowledge, sensitivity to other people, responsibility, strength, and purposiveness.
— Joseph Stone and Joseph Church (1982: 41).

There are too few people who have anything important to do with their time.
— Robert Theobald (1962: 121).

Most of us have diminished the scope of being by pursuing life styles that retard attention to the world and interest in our experience.
— Henry David Thoreau (1987: 47).

Your ultimate goal in life is to become your best self. Your immediate goal is get on the path that will lead you there.
— David Viscott (1987: 72).

One can go on learning until the day one is cut off.
— Fay Weldon (1997: 69).

IV
Creative Education

Is not the true purpose of education to help you to find out [your particular talents, goals, and interests], so that as you grow up you can begin to give your whole mind, heart and body to that which you really love to do?

— Jiddu Krishnamurti.

Education, to justify itself, should enable a man to use the full potential of his body, mind, and spirit.

— Maharishi Mahesh Yogi

Views of Education

*"What is our aim in educating our children?"** Answers to that question vary enormously and are some of the most contentious issues of our time. Fundamental differences exist in practically every aspect of education: philosophy, curriculum, pedagogy, goal, assessment, school structure and administration, and others. Examination of some of the things that have been written and said about education indicates a near-universal agreement on the importance of formal, school-based education, but substantial disagreement over what should be taught and learned, how teaching and learning should be conducted, how schools should be organized, and the type of people that educational institutions should "produce." The contending parties and obvious stakeholders include parents, teachers, school administrators, policy makers, national think tanks, business, the media, and, of course, learners (i.e., students).

Following are seven contending notions of education, with potentially significant implications for curriculum, pedagogy, goals, and outcomes:

- Education as an instrument for *developing a "disciplined and skilled labor force"* for the economy – preparing young people for the labor market; producing,

---

* The question has been raised by Charlotte Bühler and Melanie Allen (1972: 92).

93

distributing, and upgrading knowledge for a rapidly changing and highly competitive global market.

• Education as civics – *preparing learners for "adult roles and the responsibilities of citizenship"*; inculcating common political, cultural, and moral values in young people and, through them, transmitting and preserving the national heritage and established cultural, political, and economic institutions.

• Education as *"the great equalizer"* – creating avenues for disadvantaged populations to "move upward" socially, economically, and politically; redressing social inequalities, including gender, tribal, ethnic, and other social imbalances; integrating hitherto marginalized groups into the mainstream of society.

• Education as an instrument for *social empowerment and "participatory democracy"* – involving students, parents, teachers, and local residents in the management and administration of schools and in the determination of curricula, pedagogy, and evaluation.

• Education as *"passport" to the good things of life* – "equipping" learners with the knowledge and skills that they need to achieve and sustain decent standards of living; preparing young people for careers in high-paying jobs.

• Education as scholastics, for the *preservation of the human heritage* – transmitting formal, theoretical knowledge and introducing learners to the wisdom of the ages; developing a cadre of literate and well-informed "intellectuals" who can think critically and make informed choices in matters pertaining to society, politics, culture, and the economy.

• Education as a continuing, life-long process of *self-discovery, self-renewal, and the unfolding of human potential* – enabling the learner to discover, to develop, and to engage his talents as fully as possible in, for example, pursuing ever-higher levels of productivity as employee and increased responsibility as citizen; constructing new knowledge and adding to the human heritage; improving relations between people and with nature; and cooperating with fellow human beings to build a more fulfilling human civilization.

(For more detailed discussion of the concept of education and the role of schools, see, for example, Gardner, 1968; Pritzkau, 1970; Freire, 1972; Aronowitz and Giroux, 1985; Gardner, 1993; Eitzen and Zinn, 1997: 391-421).

Two Educational Traditions

The purpose of education and the role of schools have been looked at in many different ways. For purposes of this anthology, we shall focus on two of the most widely-discussed approaches to teaching and learning: *traditional education* and *creative education*.* The reason for focusing on these two educational traditions is their likely impact on (a) the types of individuals, workers, and citizens that schools produce; (b) the quality of learning achieved; (c) the attitude to school and satisfaction with academic life; and (d) the willingness to continue to learn beyond formal school experience.

Traditional education, as the term is used in this synopsis, is an approach to teaching and learning that is primarily concerned with transmitting knowledge, skills, and values, as well as with producing skilled workers and an informed citizenry.

Creative education, as the term is used here, is an approach to learning and human development that is primarily concerned with helping each learner recognize his unique talents and, then, providing him with relevant experiences, facilities, and resources (including academic skills) to strengthen and, eventually, engage his natural abilities in things that he perceives as important and beneficial to himself, his employer, and his society.

The difference between traditional education and creative education consists mainly in what the two models of learning see as the purpose of education, as well as in the significance that the two traditions attach to the learner's innate potential. First, while traditional education tends to focus on the quantum of knowledge and skills taught and learned in schools, creative education tends to focus on helping learners discover their special abilities and interests. Second, while traditional education frequently presents knowledge and skills as ends in themselves, creative education regards knowledge and all academic skills as tools for enhancing the learner's competence in areas of his unique abilities and/or special interests. Third, while traditional education, in many cases, prescribes what the learner is to *be*

---

* There probably are no purely traditional and no purely creative education systems anywhere in the world. Most reported teaching practices and learning experiences appear to incorporate elements of both systems, albeit in varying degrees. Also, "traditional education" and "creative education" as the terms are used in this review do not in any way imply superiority or inferiority. It all depends on what a country selects as its goal in educating its citizens.

95

and to do as a result of his formal education, creative education is concerned with helping each learner realize his natural potential. Relatedly, while traditional education is concerned with training, grooming, and developing certain types of people and certain types of competencies, creative education is concerned with enlarging the pool of talents available.

Education and Social Problems

Notwithstanding substantial differences regarding educational philosophy, curriculum, pedagogy, and goals, many people, national governments, international development agencies, and, ironically, teachers, agree that the standards and quality of education are declining and that schools are failing in their crucial responsibility. Three of the most widely reported indicators of this problem are (a) falling test scores in critical subjects, functional illiteracy, technical and managerial skills deficits, and declining productivity at work; (b) falling standards of morality and ethics, dwindling participation in public service and governance, disrespect of cherished values, abandonment of traditional ways of life, and environmental irresponsibility; and (c) boredom, alienation, feelings of personal worthlessness, dissatisfaction with life, attrition (dropping out of school), and disillusionment with academic life. Authoritative world and national education reports acknowledge the amazing successes that have been achieved in several fields of learning, but criticize what they see as excessive ("single-minded") preoccupation with technical and material progress and the increasing difficulty of handling the attendant social, psychological, and environmental problems.* Phrases such as "the human gap"; "world *problematique*"; "rising tide of mediocrity"; "rapid deterioration of the human condition"; "real emergency ... upon us"; "impending disaster"; and "ultimate catastrophe" indicate the apprehension and sense of urgency with which several national and global education reports view the situation.

As human and environmental conditions in many parts of the world continue to decline, education, more than any other single tool, is increasingly being looked upon as the key to recovery and, indeed,

---

* Some of the problems are non-recognition or under-utilization of the natural abilities of learners, too much emphasis on material well-being and relatively too little on the actualization of human potential, marginalization of the vast majority of human beings, and a dangerously polluted and impoverished natural environment.

the surest way out of what has come to be known as the "human predicament." This quip reflects that faith: "To fix people and their societies, we must first of all fix general education."

Ironically, while most stakeholders are dissatisfied with the outcomes of formal education, the reasons for their dissatisfaction vary considerably. Advocates of traditional education, for example, hold that the quantum of knowledge and skills that are being taught in schools is not enough. Proponents of creative education, on their part, are dismayed by what they see as excessive preoccupation with the transmission of knowledge and skills, and the tendency to under-serve learners' growth and development. While both models of learning agree on the need for reform, significant disagreement exists regarding what aspects of education to reform, how to manage the reform, and what to adopt as goals.

To illustrate: Traditional educators takes observed deficits in critical skills (e.g., reading, writing, science, and mathematics) as evidence that young people are not learning enough. They cite, for example, instances of primary (elementary) school pupils who can hardly read or write; secondary (high) school graduates who lack basic mathematical skills; university undergraduates (college freshmen) who need remedial courses in writing and mathematics to be able to cope with college work; college graduates who "know far less than their predecessors"; and teachers who, themselves, lack adequate literary and mathematical skills. Those and related observations are viewed with concern not only in education circles but also by the general public. Ian Robertson summarizes the worry:

> Critics have accused the schools of failing in their most basic educational tasks ... [attacking them] for encouraging mediocrity rather than excellence; for wasting time on trivial electives that interfere with the learning of basic subject matter; for failing to create a sufficiently disciplined learning environment; and for abandoning academic standards in a misguided attempt to bring about fairness and equality (Robertson, 1987: 389).

The belief that inadequate amount of knowledge and skills taught in schools is the "cause" of declining standard of education has led to the design and development of more rigorous curricula and better instructional practices in many countries. Most of these innovations have one aim: To transmit the most material, in the shortest possible time, as efficiently as possible, and to get learners to "work harder and learn more." Here's how a policy recommendation in one country expresses this goal:

> Providing materials that were centrally developed and successfully field tested would: 1) reduce greatly the time needed to prepare and organize materials; 2) require little inservice time; 3) be economical for schools ... to implement; 4) standardize the definition, sequencing, and quality of instruction necessary for mastery of each objective; 5) reduce greatly the time needed for developing lesson plans; and 6) be easy for substitutes to use.

Advocates of creative education also observe a decline in the motivation to learn, but attribute the problem to a different factor. They suggest that if learners do not seem to be working harder and learning more, it is not because they are lazy; it is probably because formal education, as presently designed and presented in many places, is not doing enough to actualize (i.e., recognize, develop, and give expression to) the learner's unique abilities and, thus, to promote his sense of self-worth. They point to the large number of learners who say that they "hate school" or describe their academic experience as "boring"; others who see schooling as an inconvenience that they would rather avoid, and who anxiously look forward to the end of the school year or to the end of their academic program; and still others who drop out of school or cheat in one way or another to make the required grades. Finally, advocates of creative education point to the large number of otherwise knowledgeable and well-informed individuals who, self-reportedly, have not been able to find meaning, purpose, or fulfillment in their lives and who, also self-reportedly, are not happy with themselves or with their work. In this connection, advocates of creative education call attention to the growing incidence of depression and feelings of incompleteness and worthlessness among otherwise educated people who, under "the pain and strain of nonfulfillment," resort to spirituality and other therapeutic regimes purportedly to "bring meaning and balance into [their] lives."

The belief that formal education is not doing enough to enhance learners, or that schools are failing in their responsibility to maximize human potential can be found not only in humanistic psychology circles but elsewhere.* Stanley Eitzen and Maxine Bacca Zinn's (1997) observation summarizes some of the criticisms:

---

* The remarks in this section provide a partial list of the many "disciplines" from which dissatisfaction with the traditional, knowledge-transmission concept of education has been expressed.

Radical critics of the educational system argue that the schools fail all children, whether they are from the ghettos or suburbs. Schools, as they are presently structured, damage, thwart, and stifle children. Inquisitive children become acquisitive children with little desire to learn. Schools shape children to fit into a society where citizens follow orders and do assigned tasks without questioning (Eitzen and Zinn, 1997: 421).

Those who perceive the central problem of education as inadequate enhancement of the learner or the degradation of his unique potential argue that mere accumulation of facts and information, however extensive, does not necessarily improve the learner as a human being, or make him a more effective, more productive, or inwardly-fulfilled person. Further, they suggest that the only knowledge that can enhance an individual is the knowledge that the learner himself has helped to construct, that he can personally relate to in his concrete situation, and that he also perceives as fostering the development of his capacities and as promoting the things that he perceives as important and worthwhile. Based on those assumptions, advocates of creative education suggest that what is widely regarded as falling standards of education won't be remedied by more rigorous curricula or by better instructional practices designed to get people to "work harder and learn more," but by basing education on the learner's natural abilities and inclinations, and by enabling him to nourish and express his potentialities in things that he regards as important and beneficial to himself and his world.

Indications are that most formal education systems are changing (or will soon be changing) from merely transmitting and assimilating knowledge to using existing bodies of knowledge as tools for bringing out the best that is within learners, enabling them to develop and express their talents in ways that benefit their employers and society and that make them feel good about themselves. The remarks that have been selected for this section are intended to facilitate that transition. Together with this introductory synopsis, they highlight critical aspects of traditional education that need to be rethought in order to enhance the learner's potential and make his learning experience meaningful, exciting, fun, and lasting. By way of elaboration, a tentative profile of creative education is provided, highlighting some of its key elements and indicating its critical importance in developing inwardly fulfilled and happy individuals, passionate and committed workers, good and responsible citizens.

Traditional Education and Human Creativity

For a long time, many cultures and schools regarded the acquisition, transmission, application, and verification of knowledge as the primary (if not the sole) purpose of education. One went to school to acquire "knowledge" and was classified as a good or bad student on the basis of the amount of knowledge that he was able to imbibe and to regurgitate on demand or during an examination. Clichés such as "hunger for knowledge," "in search of the golden fleece," and "better drink deep [at the fountain of knowledge], or not at all" indicate the near-total focus on the acquisition of knowledge.

Just as most individuals went to school to acquire knowledge, most schools regarded the production and transmission of knowledge as their sole *raison d'être*. For the most part, the "good schools" acquired that status by generating and disseminating the most knowledge.

Human potential advocates suggest that, in the apparent preoccupation with the transmission and acquisition of knowledge, many educational programs tended to ignore learners' unique abilities, goals, and interests. Knowledge, they observe, came to be regarded as an end in itself, rather than as a *tool* for enhancing the individual learner, respecting the integrity of his special talents and interests, and promoting his growth and development in accordance with his aptitudes and natural inclinations, thereby making education and learning a meaningful personal experience. This trend has been blamed for some of the reported dissatisfaction with academic life and disillusionment with school, including, as previously indicated, fear of certain subjects, tardiness, dropping out, cheating, and certain undesirable behaviors.

Preoccupation with the transmission and acquisition of knowledge is only one of the many aspects of traditional education with which considerable dissatisfaction has been expressed. Critics identify several related assumptions and classroom practices that they blame for taking meaning and creativity out of education (see, for example, Cremin, 1964; Gardner, 1964; 1968; Krishnamurti, 1964; Vaizey, 1967; Pritzkau, 1970; Buhler and Allen, 1972; Freire, 1972;

Moustakas, 1973; Club of Rome, 1979; Aronowitz and Giroux, 1985; Bloom, 1987; Bussis et al., 1987; Lay-Dopyera and Dopyera, 1987; Steinem,1992; Gardner, 1993; Dykstra, Jr., 1996; Fosnot, 1996; Greene, 1996; Schifter, 1996; Eitzen and Zinn, 1997: 392-421). The following are a subset of those assumptions and classroom practices:

Assumed uniformity of worldview

The belief that there are "objectively true" meanings of things and events that everybody shares (or should share) and, therefore, the tendency to present a body of knowledge as self-evident; the often unspoken assumption that what things mean to the teacher is what they mean to learners; the belief that learners perceive a given situation, construe a given problem, or interpret a given event in the same way that the teacher perceives, construes, or interprets it.

Uniform curricula and methods

The perception of learners as having the same abilities and interests, and as responding in the same way to a given educational experience and, therefore, uniform, centrally (i.e., nationally or internationally) planned curricula and delivery methods; the priority of national interests and goals and, therefore, preoccupation with preparing learners to play important socially-defined roles; a view of people as learning in the same way; and, therefore, the predominance of certain methods of instruction – lectures, for example.

Standardization

National, regional, and, in some cases, international standards of achievement by which learners are measured and compared in order to be certified; mass education in which teachers offer the same materials, usually in the same sequence, through the same medium, using the same assessment criteria; "lock-step learning" in which everyone learns the same things, produces the same answers, and adopts the same reasoning process; programmed instruction in which a given body of knowledge is codified, packaged, and presented in easy-to-deliver, easy-to-memorize, easy-to-regurgitate, and easy-to-assess formats.

Limited curricula experiences

The assumption that currently recognized academic disciplines and professions represent (or exhaust) the range of human abilities and possibilities; a selective focus on socially-defined "important" human abilities and, *ipso facto*, neglect of those abilities that are either not yet recognized or have not been accorded sufficient importance to warrant systematic development.

101

Compartmentalization of knowledge

Division of knowledge into specialized (academic) disciplines and their presentation as separate bodies of knowledge; perception of both societal and global problems as autonomous and unconnected and, therefore, the separation of the academic disciplines that deal with these problems.

Intellect-bias

"Right answer-centered";* the tendency to confuse facts with knowledge and memorization with learning; the priority of literacy and numeracy and, therefore, a preference for the ability to think in words, equations, and formulas; the belief that intellectual development consists of the ability to think, speak, and write "logically"; disdain (in some cultures) for nonlinear thinking and other "non-rational" ways of knowing; the relative unimportance (in some cultures) of athletic skills, musical skills, intra-personal skills, social skills, feelings, various forms of mental imagery, and the ability to think in pictures.

Passivity

Preoccupation with what is already known (as against what remains to be discovered); a view of education as the acquisition of factual knowledge about the world – an accumulation of ideas, solutions, results, outlooks, methods, and rules for handling known problems and familiar situations; a view of teachers as custodians of knowledge, dispensing what they think learners should know; a view of learners as inert and in constant need of the teacher's guidance (empty containers to be filled, *tabula rasa* to be written on, pieces of clay to be molded and shaped); emphasis on teaching, instruction, and other methods of "transmitting" existing bodies of knowledge; the tendency to reward unquestioning acceptance, memorization, and accurate regurgitation of existing ideas and, possibly, prejudices.

"Narration Sickness" **

Perception of the teacher as the talker and learners as the listeners who take notes, memorize what the teacher says, and repeat what they heard (when required to do so); a view of teaching as consisting largely of telling learners what they need to know; a view of learning as a process of listening to and memorizing what the teacher says; defining academic success or failure, brightness or dullness, as the ability or inability to accurately regurgitate what was said, read, or heard.

---

* The phrase is John Holt's (1976: 120)
** The phrase is Paulo Freire's.

External Symbols of Success

Focus on accreditation, certification, distinction, honors, and other signs of academic excellence; ever more rigorous standards in literacy, mathematics, science, or whatever happens to be a country's preoccupation at the time; a concern primarily with producing "world-class skills" in nationally important areas; institutional success measured by enrollment statistics, test scores, retention and graduation rate, and positions held in society by alumni; individual success measured by scholastic ability; a tendency to make those who are not able to "make the grade" feel ashamed of themselves or believe that something is wrong with them.

Alienation

Centrally planned curricula that, in many cases, overlook local conditions and ignore the learner's interests, needs, and priorities; (in some Third World countries) materials, illustrations, cases, and examples that are drawn from other places and that hardly reflect the practical realities of the learner's situation; scant regard for the learner's capacity for self-direction – with parents, educators, government, the clergy, and the business community deciding what young people should know and be able to do; curriculum design geared toward jobs, rather than toward the unfolding and actualization of the learner's unique potential; relatively few opportunities for authentic self-expression – for learners to pose their own problems and work out their own solutions to those problems, and to participate in the types of inquiry that make sense to them.

Creative Education

Jiddu Krishnamurti's rhetorical question (presented above, as introduction to this section) aptly summarizes the purpose of creative education, as the term is used in this anthology:

> Is not the true purpose of education to help you to find out, so that as you grow up you can begin to give your whole mind, heart and body to that which you really love to do? (Krishnamurti, 1964: 52).

In this view of education, the goal is not to shape or mold the learner into what the school wants him to be, but to facilitate the success potential that he already embodies. Rather than make some learners feel that they are talented and others that they are not, creative education implicitly acknowledges each learner's particular set of talents and attempts to enable the learner to discover and to develop his particular set of abilities, so he can engage them as fully as possible in things that give meaning and purpose to his life.

Unlike its traditional precursor, creative education is not about giving learners knowledge for the sake of knowledge, or because that's what society, government, industry, and business want people to know and be able to do. Creative education is about enabling all learners to discover their unique abilities or talents (i.e., what they are best "equipped" to do and in what ways they can best serve society, industry, business, government, and nature), and then providing them with the types of knowledge, skills, and experiences that enhance their particular abilities and, thus, imbue their learning with meaning and purpose.

Following is a brief outline of some key features of creative education. This outline is based on the literature from which the remarks in this section were selected:

Tentative worldview
Represents the "universe" as a *terra incognito,* still largely unknown – something to be explored and discovered – rather than as a set of facts to be memorized and regurgitated; rejects claims of absolute truth and irrefutable certitudes; regards existing bodies of knowledge as tentative and as a useful starting point toward fuller understanding of our universe, as a foundation to build upon, as a challenge to meet and exceed.

Relevance
Embeds its curriculum in the practical concerns of learners and the community or society in which they live, rather than on any standardized notion of what they should know; draws upon the realities of the learner's existence, using the materials and experiences that are available in his economic, social, political and physical environments; organizes teaching, training, coaching, mentoring, research, and other learning experiences around real-life issues and concrete situations in which these ideas and principles can be observed.

Emphasis on meaning and personal fulfillment
Finds out the learner's special talents, goals, needs, aspirations, and interests and organizes materials and learning experiences to promote these personal orientations; tries to find out the things that really matter to the learner – things that he perceives as important to him and/or to his world; respects the validity

and the integrity of the learner's own interpretation, understanding, perception, and personal opinion about things, i.e., how things appear and what they mean to the learner; encourages and supports the learner to explore his own world, to follow his own inclinations, to develop and practically express his natural abilities.

Flexible curriculum

Respects the integrity of the learners' diverse needs, interests, and personal goals and therefore gives them real choices, rather than confining them to a few traditional areas; provides learners with a wide range of experiences in traditional and non-traditional areas; readily modifies programs and their delivery in accordance with the needs of the times.

Psychological safety

Provides and maintains an environment in which being "wrong" is acceptable and safe; encourages diversity of views, approaches, and conclusions, rather than restricting learners to established conventions; encourages and supports experimentation, trial-and-error, mistakes, and "failure"; allows learners to try out different things and to "fail" as many times as it takes for them to discover their natural inclinations, or to find out what they consider truly interesting, meaningful, and personally rewarding; helps learners to appreciate their uniqueness and to accept the validity of their own perceptions.

Problem-sensitivity

Encourages the learner to explore, to discover, or to find things out for himself; rewards problem finding and problem recognition as much as problem solving; encourages and supports learners to find new challenges to meet, new needs to satisfy, and better ways to deal with old problems or to satisfy existing needs; tries to develop learners into producers of knowledge, rather than just consumers; cherishes new questions, fresh perspectives on "settled" matters, and unusual responses to issues; encourages learners to think freely and to develop their own perspectives, rather than close learners' minds by giving them definitive conclusions and cut-and-dried answers.

Challenge

Doubts the obvious, questions the seemingly self-evident, and challenges the so-called tried-and-true; focuses more on challenges than on solutions, more on questions than on answers; challenges and supports the learner to conceptualize new problems, to frame new issues, and to synthesize new directions; encourages the learner to see opportunities where before he saw problems, to appreciate and be able to deal imaginatively with change, complexity, and uncertainty.

Empowerment

Emphasizes what the learner can do himself − metaphorically, as John Gardner puts it, encourages the learner to grow his own plants rather than wait to receive "cut flowers"; helps the learner to discover, to develop, and to be able to use his unique abilities; sensitizes the learner to concepts, notions, traditions, and conditions that tend to limit his possibilities; gives the learner responsibility for his own growth and development, encouraging him to decide on his own projects, set his own goals, and define his own standards of achievement.

Constructivist approach to knowledge and meaning

Believes that knowledge and meaning are not "immanent" in things, but are individually and socially "constructed," reflecting the experiences, the interests and concerns, the needs and purposes, and the hopes and aspirations of the person, group, society, or generation that happens to be interested in the particular phenomenon; believes, further, that meaning is not transferable/transmittable from one person (teacher) to the other (learner), but are *personal* to the individual learner, reflecting his needs, goals, and interests.

Collaborative community of learners

Rejects the view of education as a "competitive sport" in which learners try to outsmart one another to see who succeeds and who fails, who comes first and who comes last, who receives the honors and who goes home psychologically bruised and humiliated; views teacher and learners as a community of people who come together to construct their own reality − a "cooperative" whose members help one another to succeed; learning projects are designed collaboratively in such a way that learners' interests and the teacher's agenda are reconciled; organizes the classroom (or learning situation) as a forum in which both teacher and learners present, discuss, and share their personal interpretations and perspectives, during which each develops a better understanding of the matter of their common interest; in Genishi, McCarrier, and Nussbaum's words, perceives learning as a:

dialogue [involving teachers and learners as participants] in which teachers and [learners] inform, err, question, correct, self-correct, think aloud, repeat, make sense – in other words, develop together (Genishi et al., 1988: 190).

Learner-centeredness
Recognizes the uniqueness of each learner – his special abilities, perceptions, interests, goals, and modes of understanding; pays attention to the questions, the problems, issues, concerns, stories, songs, jokes, writings, drawings, paintings, fantasies, daydreams, and even favorite toys that learners bring to the learning situation; regards learners' spontaneous activities as revealing their goals and passions as well as their perceptions, understandings, fears, hopes, and desires (the assumption being that what people perceive as important is what they tend to talk about and to do); believes that people learn best when they are motivated, and that the most durable form of motivation to learn frequently stems from "projects" that the learner himself has helped to design – things that resonate with his own interests and in which he sees purpose and meaning.

Individualized pedagogy
Recognizes the plurality of "languages" in which people think and the multiplicity of ways (aesthetic, artistic, conceptual, kinesthetic, metaphorical, musical, spatial, symbolic, visual, etc.) in which they try to apprehend their world; listens to, and makes use of, the learner's interpretation and understanding of events and things; respects the validity and integrity of every learning style, and acknowledges the right of everybody to learn in ways that best suit them; believes that no pedagogical tool can be right for every learner and, therefore, provides a variety of learning experiences and tools that take individual preferences into account; as far as possible, encourages and allows the learner to follow his own inclinations.

Integrative curriculum
The curriculum recognizes the essential unity of all things and, in particular, the interconnectedness of global problems and, therefore, tries to organize learning around issues rather than around academic specialties; perceives knowledge as indivisible and, as far as possible, encourages exchange of ideas, methods, tools, materials, and personnel among disciplines.

Personal enhancement

Focuses on human possibilities and the actualization of the success potential that every learner represents, rather than intimidating people with the threat of failure; activities and experiences that are designed to: (a) enhance that the learner's unique potential, personal effectiveness, and success; and (b) promote his personal sense of worth, rather than ridicule assumed inadequacies.

Inner development

Enables the learner to see the "big picture" and to appreciate the critical importance of his unique role in the larger scheme of things; believes that (as one school of Eastern thought suggests), in order to achieve social order, equity, peace, and harmony, people must be "improved inwardly," and not just punished for showing negative tendencies; periodically provides opportunities for the maturing learner to address himself to some of the basic questions of human existence: Who am I? Why am I here? Where am I going? What are my responsibilities to my fellow human beings and the rest of creation? How can my life benefit them?

Assessment

Rejects exclusive concern with transmitting knowledge and skills and evaluating learners on their ability to memorize and regurgitate information; assessment, where relevant, is used in the context of personal-best to encourage more learning and greater personal effort, rather than as a pretext for weeding out the unsuccessful, or for prematurely terminating people's growth and development.

(See, for example, Vaizey, 1967; Gardner, 1968; Katz et al., 1968; Pritzkau, 1970; Buhler and Allen, 1972; Freire, 1972; The Club of Rome, 1979; Theobald, 1981; Aronowitz and Giroux, 1985; Bloom, 1987; Bussis et al., 1987; Lay-Dopyera and Dopyera, 1987; Steinem, 1992; Gardner, 1993; Dykstra, Jr., 1996; Fosnot, 1996; Grenz, 1996; Schifter, 1996).

Rationale for Creative Education

The previous section has highlighted selected features of creative education, and the type of rethinking necessary for its implementation. This section presents six reasons why this approach to human development is so critically important both for enhancing learners as self-actualizing individuals and also for developing productive employees, responsible citizens, and inwardly-fulfilled human beings:

(a) The centrality of creativity in human life

The human species, it has been suggested, is distinguished by its creative potential, an essence that drives most of our actions and also tends toward its fulfillment (see the section entitled "The Essence of Human Creativity"). The principle is as applicable in education as it is in other domains of human life. Whether the aim is equipping learners with marketable skills, preparing them for adult roles, introducing them to the classics, or making them economically and socially more equal, the implications are that: (a) only those educational experiences that the learner perceives as enhancing his personal growth and development are likely to generate and sustain his interest and personal involvement in and out of school; and (b) only people whose educational experiences enable them to recognize and actualize their innate potential, to develop and use their particular capacities and, therefore, to feel inwardly fulfilled *can* be maximally productive, responsible, and culturally highminded.

(b) The enormous variety of human abilities, interests, and goals

Creativity, while a uniquely human attribute, is not a uniform or unidimensional ability. Enormous variations exist in talents or gifts, as the ability is commonly referred to in popular parlance. In his seminal work, appropriately entitled *Multiple Intelligences,* Howard Gardner (1993: 5-12) identifies several of those abilities including, for example: (i) *linguistic* intelligence – the ability to use words effectively to communicate one's thoughts, to share one's feelings, and to affect social outcome; (ii) *logical-mathematical* intelligence – the ability to reason in the Cartesian sense and solve problems that require step-by-step procedures; (iii) *spatial* intelligence – the ability to conceptualize the world in three or higher order dimensions; (iv) *musical* intelligence – the ability to compose and/or to produce melodies; (v) *bodily-kinesthetic* intelligence – the ability to solve problems by the movement of parts of one's body; (vi) *interpersonal* intelligence – the ability to understand other people and to relate effectively with them; and (vii) *intrapersonal* intelligence – the ability to understand one's abilities, interests, and goals and to build an effective life based on that understanding.

John W. Gardner, Charles Tart, Howard Gardner, and many others further suggest that only a small set of human capacities are currently being recognized and promoted by formal education, as presently constituted and implemented. According to these writers, several human abilities probably still lie outside the domains of traditional curricula.

To the extent that the idea of "multiple intelligences" is valid, this idea calls for a different philosophy and a different pedagogy from traditional uniform curricula, unidimensional assessment,* and the "pass-fail syndrome," among others. For example, instead of providing all learners with the same curriculum, more varied learning experiences need to be provided to promote the multiplicity of abilities, interests, and goals that learners represent. Second, instead of assessing all learners on exactly the same set of abilities (some of which an individual may not possess or might not particularly care about), a more productive method is to try to identify each learner's "area of maximum potential" ** and to facilitate his development in accordance with his natural abilities. Third, given the infinite range of human talents as well as the psychic necessity to fulfill one's potential, careers need to be custom-built around learners' particular abilities and interests, rather than grooming learners to fit established occupational molds or steering them to particular vocations because of money or glamour. As Howard Gardner (1993) suggests:

> the purpose of school should be to develop intelligences and to help people reach vocational and avocational goals that are appropriate to their particular spectrum of intelligences (Gardner, 1993: 9).

Fourth, instead of appearing or acting as arbiters of human success and failure, educational institutions need to acknowledge the creativity and, therefore, the success potential that every learner embodies. Accordingly, more schools need to shift their focus from testing and measuring learners and (by implication) "sentencing" some people to a life of inferiority and low self-esteem (because they lack a particular set of skills) to "midwifing" the success that is every learner's birthright. Additionally, many more academic institutions need to realize that paying attention to, and positively cultivating learners' unique abilities, is not a "deviation from essential educational priorities," as it is sometimes perceived, but is, in fact, a necessity if schools are to produce genuinely motivated learners, highly productive employees, and good and responsible citizens. Finally, the near-universal tradition of rank-ordering human abilities and designating some of them

---

* The phrase is Howard Gardner's (1993: 11).
** The phrase is Robert Theobald's (1981: 50)

as more important than others may be useful from the standpoint of a society's current priorities and, therefore, for purposes of allocating scarce economic resources. Beyond that, there doesn't appear to be much biological support or moral defense for such a distinction. Carol Pearson's statement indicates the relevance of every ability and, by implication, the disservice to society of promoting some skills and devaluing others. According to her:

> Each of us has a piece of the puzzle of solving the great world problems of our time and creating a more just, humane, and beautiful world. ... If everyone who loved to create beauty did so, we would live in a beautiful world. If everyone who loved cleanliness and order, cleaned up, we would live in a clean and orderly world. If everyone who yearned to heal the sick did so, we would live in a healthier world. If everyone who cared about world hunger shared his creative ideas and acted to alleviate the problem, people would all be fed (Pearson, 1991: 171-172).

(c) The huge variety of thinking tools and learning styles that learners employ

Just as people are different in abilities, they also differ in the ways they learn and the tools that they employ in their learning processes. Significant differences exist not only in the way that learners apprehend their world (see, smell, taste, hear, feel, perceive, interpret, act, etc.) but also in the ways that they think about things and the "languages" that they use in their thinking. Alternatively referred to as "individual learning styles," these languages include artistic, aesthetic, conceptual, kinesthetic, linguistic, logical, mathematical, metaphorical, musical, poetic, spatial, symbolic, visual, and many more (see, for example, Gardner, 1993: 9).

Educational psychologists generally agree that no one instructional method is right for all learners. They also suggest that learners are likely to be more interested and more involved in materials and experiences that appeal to, or make use of, their peculiar thinking tools.

To the extent that the theory of individual learning styles is valid, certain educational assumptions and practices need to be reconsidered. For example, the perception of learners as an undifferentiated mass of listeners who learn by being told needs to take account of the personal nature of knowledge and the role of learners in constructing their

111

own knowledge. Methods of instruction also need to be considerably varied to accommodate the multiplicity of tools that learners employ in their thinking. More teachers, trainers, and mentors need to recognize and respect the validity and integrity of every learning style and, also, the right of learners to employ their preferred thinking styles and to learn in ways that best suit them.

(d) Other "logics," other systems of knowledge

The history of human civilization is essentially the story of one endless struggle to understand the universe and relate ever more effectively to its elements. In that struggle, several traditions have provided the tools: astrology, legend, mythology, mysticism, philosophy, religion, ritual, and many other transcendental experiences. In spite of their successes, as claimed by their adherents, these systems of knowing have traditionally been criticized as subjective and unverifiable, conditions that initially spurred the search for the (presumably) more objective scientific method and the Cartesian logic upon which it has been erected.

With its emphasis on objectivity, neutrality, and verifiability, modern logic (epitomized by the scientific method) gradually came to be regarded in many parts of the world as the consummation of human knowledge. In this view, the only reliable information about the world was that obtained through logical-mathematical thinking. The spectacular achievements in agriculture, astronomy, engineering, medicine, and technology justified that claim. So successful has been the scientific method that many of its conclusions virtually went unchallenged for a long time and in many parts of the world. With the advance in science and technology, of course, other ways of knowing tended to decline in significance, losing both credibility and adherents.

One of the most significant intellectual turning points of the Twentieth Century may well be the realization that, in the realm of human knowledge, there are no absolute truths and that much of what is regarded as "objectively true" is actually a social construction, incomplete and, almost without exception, falsifiable. Well-known illustrations include: (i) quantum mechanics, which experts say is challenging some of the once-unassailable principles of Newtonian physics; (ii) the growing spirituality in orthodox (hitherto purely physical, purely scientific) medicine; and (iii) so many other shifts in social thinking that, together, are redefining the purpose of human existence and the

112

practice of life (see the section entitled "Paradigm Shift and Human Creativity").

Collectively known as postmodernism is the belief that scientific principles, as useful and successful as they have been, do not have all of the answers to the human quest; that many of the ideas that are being touted as self-evident and objectively true are not necessarily so; and that certain areas of human existence are not yet accessible to the tools of modern logic and the scientific method.

The influence of "postmodernist thinking" evidently is spreading, even in places where it is not yet officially acknowledged. To illustrate: The idea of the one correct logic, one correct method, and one intellectual tradition is increasingly being challenged. More and more people are realizing that not everything worth knowing can be apprehended by any one of the existing logics or methods of inquiry. Systems of knowledge once regarded as "primitive," "native," "mystic," "supernatural," and "unscientific" are increasingly being recognized and their capabilities explored. More and more areas of business, government, medicine, and science are finding ways to integrate hitherto separate traditions of knowledge and to complement one logic with others, for a fuller understanding of the universe and for greater effectiveness in dealing with its elements. A growing number of educational institutions are recognizing the limitations of existing logics and, therefore, the tentativeness of bodies of knowledge founded upon those traditions.

(e) Intrinsic motivational nature of learning

A radically different approach to teaching and learning is gradually transforming the way that young people are being educated in some parts of the world. Based on the intrinsic motivational view of learning, the new thinking is that:

- What goes on in the mind of the learner is extremely important in understanding his learning behavior, his attitude to school and, eventually, his educational achievement.

- People learn best when they are motivated to do so.
- The most powerful form of motivation is something in which the learner sees meaning, purpose, and relevance.

Meaning, in this context, refers to two things: (a) learning experiences and materials that are based on the learner's view of the world and that therefore make sense to him; and (b) projects that the learner himself has helped to design and that also resonate with his own interests. *Purpose* refers to: (a) goals that the learner perceives as important to him and/or to his world; and (b) knowledge, skills, and experiences that enable the learner to realize more of his potential and to be able to relate more effectively with his world. Gloria Steinem's (1992:155) phrase "educating through individual interest" aptly defines "purpose" in education. *Relevance* refers to educational experiences and materials that derive from the learner's concrete situation or that relate to his personal circumstances and daily life experiences.

The central idea of the intrinsic motivational view of learning is that we cannot ignore the learner's thoughts, feelings, interests, and goals if we are to understand why he responds the way that he does to his educational experience. Nor can we overlook the practical economic, social, cultural, and political circumstances in which the learner experiences his life. Paulo Freire (1972: 39), for example, suggests that no truly liberating system of education can be removed from the learner's daily life experiences, from the actual circumstances in which he lives. Stanley Eitzen and Maxine Zinn's rhetorical questions dramatically state the point:

> What is the relevance of conjugating a verb when you are hungry? What is the relevance of being able to trace the path of how a bill becomes a law when your family and neighbors are powerless? (Eitzen and Zinn, 1997: 410).

To the extent that the intrinsic motivational theory of learning is valid, educational curricula and instructional practices need to be driven more by the needs and interests of the learner (i.e., what the learner perceives as best for himself and his society), than by any hard-and-fast notion of what he should know and be able to do.

The suggestion is that only in learning things that he perceives as strengthening and giving expression to his natural abilities, as deriving from and relating to his personal circumstances, and as increasing his understanding of the world and enhancing his personal effectiveness and sense of self-worth will a learner likely "work harder and learn more," and even make learning a lifelong experience and an integral part of his daily life.

(f) The personal nature of knowledge, meaning, and human understanding

In an article poignantly entitled "... because wisdom can't be told," Charles Gragg (1940) argues that, contrary to received wisdom, meaning and insight cannot be transmitted, nor can they be received passively. To really understand or be able to make sense of an (educational) experience, the learner has to be actively involved. "Involvement," as the term is used in Gragg's and similar writings, is the process of *interpreting* and relating a new piece of information, a new experience, or a new material to one's belief system and/or personal circumstance. In Gragg's words:

> It can be said flatly that the mere act of listening to wise statements and sound advice does little for anyone ... no amount of information, whether of theory or fact, in itself improves insight and judgment or increases ability to act wisely under conditions of responsibility ... We cannot effectively use the insight and knowledge of others; it must be our own knowledge and insight that we use ... So far as responsible activity in the business world is concerned, it is clear that a fund of ready-made answers can be of little avail. Each situation is a new situation, requiring imaginative understanding as a prelude to sound judgment and action (Gragg, 1940: 1, 10-11).

In one of the most powerful commentaries on teaching and learning, Kahlil Gibran argues that the proper aim of education is *not* to transmit to the learner what the teacher already knows, but to help the learner in his search for meaning, in his effort to construct his own knowledge and to develop his own understanding. According to Gibran:

> No man can reveal to you aught but that which already lies half asleep in the dawning of your knowledge.
> The teacher who walks in the shadow of the temple, among his followers, gives not of his wisdom but rather of his faith and lovingness.
> If he is indeed wise he does not bid you enter the house of his wisdom, but rather leads you to the threshold of your own mind.
> The astronomer may speak to you of his understanding of space, but he cannot give you his understanding.
> The musician may sing to you the rhythm which is in all space, but he cannot give you the ear which arrests the rhythm nor the voice which echoes it.

And he who is versed in the science of numbers can tell of the regions of weight and measure, but he cannot conduct you thither ..." (Gibran, 1973: 56-57).

The personal nature of understanding, meaning, and insight is central to what has come to be known as "constructivist" education. According to this theory, people "construct," rather than passively absorb, knowledge; and they will learn what they *want* to learn – what, to them, is important and meaningful. Constructivist educators further suggest that understanding and insight are not achieved by top-down, teacher-to-student transmission of knowledge, but through dialogue.

This belief holds that people come to a learning situation with personal ideas in mind, and they try to interpret the material in the light of those ideas. According to this view, when encountering a new learning experience or when presented with new material, the learner tries to make sense of it by "fitting" it into his personal frame of reference, or relating it to his preexisting ideas. Some materials and experiences fall within the learner's existing mental model. Others, conceivably, contradict his preconceptions. Resolving such contradictions and the tension to which they frequently give rise is regarded as the essence of learning. Constructivist educators believe that integrating new material into an existing frame of reference and increasing one's understanding are most effectively achieved through dialogue (involving teacher and learners) in which a learner, for example, shares his own perspectives with fellow learners and the teacher, while also using other people's interpretations to expand his own understanding and to achieve greater meaning (see, for example, Fosnot, 1996).

To the extent that the idea of personal insight and personal construction of meaning is valid, certain critical aspects of education need to be rethought. Knowledge, for example, needs to be perceived as a catalyst and a resource for greater personal meaning, rather than as a finished product to be consumed. Learners need to be viewed as capable, self-directed people with personal goals and needs and personal models of the world, rather than as "empty containers" to be filled with whatever information the teacher thinks that they should know. Learning itself needs to be viewed as a continuing process of making and expanding personal meaning, interpreting and being able to relate more effectively and more responsibly with one's world, rather than as the art of memorizing and regurgitating prescribed information. Teachers and students, trainers and trainees, mentors and mentees need to see themselves as a "community of learners" – cooperating, collaborating, and helping one another to increase their own understanding – rather than as contestants trying to outsmart one another for accolades or for a few designated honors.

Conclusion

There is a near-universal recognition of school-based education as a tool for teaching knowledge and skills and preparing learners for the labor force, fostering civic responsibility, equalizing economic and social opportunities, allowing parents and local residents to participate in decisions affecting the lives and welfare of their children, and preserving the human heritage. A problem arises, however, when these vitally important societal functions are perceived as separate and complete in themselves and, even worse, when their promotion tends to ignore the learner's unique potential, goals, interests, or makes it difficult for him to recognize, develop, or express his unique talents.

Of course, we need a skilled workforce to do necessary jobs and a well-informed citizenry to maintain civic institutions. Of course, we need to expand economic and social opportunities and to give everybody a sense of belonging and a piece of the action. Of course, we need a knowledgeable population to carry the culture and to transmit the human heritage. But, even more importantly, we need creative, self-actualizing, and inwardly-fulfilled human beings who can achieve and maintain ever-higher productivity for employers, develop and maintain evermore humane and civilized institutions, carry and continuously enrich the culture, and participate effectively and constructively in the human enterprise.

Indications are that, at least for the foreseeable future, we will continue to teach reading and writing, mathematics and science, civics and ethics, etc. But, stressful and boring as the acquisition of these skills is sometimes (mis)represented as being, learning them could be more meaningful, more rewarding, more interesting, even compelling, if they were taught in the context of the things that really matter to the learner, and if they could be perceived by him as: (a) fostering the development and

117

expression of the capacities and attributes that he really likes about himself; (b) promoting what he perceives as important and useful to himself and the larger society; (c) relating to his daily life experiences or to the concrete realities of his economic, social, and/or political situation; and (d) allowing him to genuinely participate in the construction of knowledge pertaining to the material that he is learning.

It could be asked: How do we find out the things that really matter to the learner? The simple answer to that question is that every child and, indeed, every person "provides" clues to his personal goals, motives, inclinations, and interests by the things that he likes to do or talk about and by the way that he chooses to act in specific situations (see, for example, Dinkmeyer and Mckay, 1973: 23; Moustakas, 1973: 1-19).

The fear exists that if education encourages learners to follow their own interests, societal goals might be compromised. There is a two-part response to that apprehension. First, as is becoming increasingly clear, personal and societal goals are mutually constitutive and synergistic. Aligning them, however, requires a larger system of values that people perceive as giving meaning to their lives and to which they therefore are willing to commit their energy and resources (see, for example, Tillich, 1952: 47; Gardner, 1964: 128; Schumacher, 1975: 101).

The second part of the response to the "individual-versus-societal-goals" controversy is simply that any human experience (including education) that fails to enhance people as human beings can hardly be regarded as socially expedient. The standardized curriculum has a lot to recommend it: time, convenience, economy, uniform worldview, interchangeable skills, and more. But, as some educational psychologists have observed, drawbacks exist, including alienation, tardiness, attrition, estrangement from school, and "turned-off" learners. Some humanistic psychologists wonder whether certain presumably anti-school attitudes and behaviors might not be attempts by academically "unsuccessful" individuals to "get even" with an institution that they perceive as sentencing them to a life of mediocrity and stripping them of their sense of self-worth, especially when "something" deep inside seems to tell them that they have useful contributions to make to society – even if it is not reading, writing, mathematics, science, or technology.

Stories of people who have achieved great things without formal school-based education and of those who went on to literally change the world after being told that they were academically unsuccessful suggest that not all human abilities are currently being recognized or adequately served by existing curricula, instructional practices, or assessment procedures, impressive as they are. To the extent that such an assumption is valid, what is widely regarded as "declining standards of learning" might actually be a subtle rejection of an experience that some learners perceive as devaluing their talents and alienating them from their goals and interests. Changing such a perception or getting learners who hold it to "work harder and learn more" is not likely to be achieved by more rigorous reading, writing, mathematics, or science programs *alone;* nor by such laudable innovations as adult literacy programs, distance learning, itinerant schools (for nomadic herdsmen), more teachers, small class sizes, or more books and equipment. What will likely make learning exciting, meaningful, self-regenerating, and life-long are problems which learners themselves help to formulate and solutions which they help to develop.

A commonly expressed belief is that extrinsic motivation (such as grades or test scores, certificates, and diplomas) is necessary to inspire learning. In the words of a renowned educator:

> Many students need the spur of extrinsic rewards to get them going, or to keep them going in the face of learning challenges that they find too daunting, too frustrating, or too unfamiliar to tackle on their own initiative. Many students, for example, never discover the intrinsic joys of reading until given an extrinsic push that enables the student to overcome the anxiety of cracking a formidable-looking book.

That sounds quite plausible, especially given the importance that most students attach to diplomas and certificates and the amount of effort that they put into their preparation for the required examinations. However, the eagerness with which many students dispose of, sell back, or permanently close those "formidable-looking" books, and the relief that they frequently express after completing some of the courses that they took "in partial fulfillment of the requirements" for a particular diploma or certificate, indicate the temporary nature and limited usefulness of extrinsic motivations to learning. They rarely, if ever, sustain genuine and lasting interest.

Finally, if we can assume that every learner, by reason of his unique natural endowment, is equipped to succeed, then the goal of education needs to shift from transmitting knowledge to facilitating individual success – from testing and measuring how much information a learner has acquired to providing him with experiences and resources (including knowledge) that awaken and maximize his natural abilities. Accordingly, existing bodies of knowledge need to be regarded as tools for catalyzing the learner's potential, rather than as "truths" to be imbibed or pursued for their own sakes. Also, instead of assessing all learners on the same set of abilities and dividing them into "the successful" and "the unsuccessful," schools need to explicitly recognize the creativity and, therefore, the success potential, that is latent in every learner. (In this connection, they need to rethink their responsibility – from transmitting knowledge for the sake of knowledge to facilitating learners' success.) By the same token, learners themselves need to shift their focus from passing examinations and acquiring certificates to realizing more of their innate potentialities and contributing them to the common good.

In sum, if we want to build a more humane and fulfilling society – one in which people can find meaning in their lives and feel good about themselves – education needs to do *more than* transmit accumulated knowledge or preserve the culture, *more than* prepare learners for the labor force or teach them the responsibilities of citizenship, *more than* expand economic opportunities or allow local residents to participate in the management of schools. Very critically, it needs to recognize and respect the integrity of learners' unique abilities and, then, provide appropriate experiences and resources to enable them to develop and engage their talents as fully as possible in their various roles as human beings and as national and planetary citizens: construct new knowledge and add to the human heritage; pursue ever-higher levels of productivity and responsibility as employees; improve relations among people and with nature; and cooperate with fellow human beings to build a more fulfilling human civilization.

Selected Insights
on
Creative Education

Learning is not a spectator sport.

— Anonymous

He who creates a desire to learn in a child, does more than he who forces it to learn much.

— Anonymous

Teachers kill creativity by inducing students to give them the answers that students think teachers expect. Answers that are expected cannot be creative.

— Russel L. Ackoff (1991: 73).

There is ... qualified support for the prediction that relatively informal classroom environments will facilitate creativity more effectively than traditional restrictive classroom environments.

— Teresa M. Amabile (1983: 163).

The larger the number of creators in one generation, the larger will be the number of creators in the next.

— Teresa M. Amabile (1983: 185).

[I]t may increase the creativity of all children if they can be taught to resist peer pressure toward conformity.
— Teresa M. Amabile (1983: 197).

[C]reativity may best be maintained and enhanced by class-room teachers who encourage independence and self-direction in their children.
— Teresa M. Amabile (1983: 198).

[A]t a time when nearly everyone is anxious about his/her place in a rapidly shifting job market, [educational] relevance has come to mean little else than job preparation.
— Stanley Aronowitz and Henry A. Giroux (1985: 1).

If educational systems really want to prepare students to function effectively and productively in a democratic [sic] society and/or workplace, they will have to add to their curricula the specific teaching of thinking procedures.
— Berenice Bleedorn (1998: 11).

Our present educational problems cannot seriously be attributed to bad administrators, weakness of will, lack of discipline, lack of money, insufficient attention to the three R's, or any of the other common explanations that indicate that things will be set aright if ... professors would just pull [their] socks. All these things are the result of a deeper lack of belief in the university's vocation.
— Allan Bloom (1987: 312).

The challenge for educators ... is to reclaim the image of the competent child. ... [P]romoting a single image of children is a ... potentially dangerous task.

— Sue Bredekamp (1993: 14).

What is our aim in educating our children?

— Charlotte Buhler and Melanie Allen (1972: 92).

An economically or culturally deprived child may have special talents – developed or latent. Attention must be directed to the development of these talents, these gifts, if the ideal of ... the full development of the individuals and through them the advancement of society ... is to be met. National self-interest, indeed, survival ... depends upon it.

— William Cassels (1971: 278).

Teachers who had the greatest facilitating influences on their [students'] creative development ... were [those who] treated students as individuals; encouraged students to be indepen- dent; served as model; spent considerable amount of time with students outside of class; indicated that excellence was expected and could be achieved; [were] enthusiastic; accepted students as equals; directly rewarded student's creative behavior or work; [were] interesting, dynamic lecturer[s]; and [were] excellent on one-to-one basis.

— J. A. Chambers (1983: 164).

Teachers who had the greatest... inhibiting influences on their [students'] creative development ... were [those who] discouraged students' (ideas, creativity, etc.); [were] insecure (hyper-critical, sarcastic); lacked enthusiasm; emphasized rote learning; [were] dogmatic and rigid; did not keep up with the field; [were] generally incompetent; had narrow interests; and [were] not available outside the classroom.

— J. A. Chambers (1983: 164).

The chief object of education is not to learn things but to unlearn things.

— G. K. Chesterton (1997: 20).

The empires of the future are the empires of the mind.

— Sir Winston Churchill (1993: 249).

It is astonishing how the practice of cooperation so essential to contemporary life is neglected in formal educational systems where competition is the fundamental rule.

— The Club of Rome (1979: 37).

[T]he schools' goal of preparing for life is turning to separation from life.

— The Club of Rome (1979: 65).

At a time when creative ideas are needed quickly, many administrators, teachers, and the unions are resisting change.

— The Club of Rome (1979: 69).

[I]f the next generation is to face the future with zest and self-confidence, we must educate them to be original as well as competent.

— Mihaly Csikszentmihalyi (1996: 12).

[T]he bottom line for schools is job preparedness.

— Conservative Ideology (1985: 187).

The preoccupation in most schools with subject-matter content has led to a situation in which sociomoral and affective development are negatively influenced. Ironically, this one-sided preoccupation has created a situation in which intellectual development and understanding of subject-matter content do not thrive, either.

— Rheta DeVries and Betty Zan (1996: 103).

The educational center of gravity was in the teacher, the textbooks, anywhere and everywhere you please except in the immediate instincts and activities of the child.

— John Dewey (1964: 118).

When you have invented an idea for yourself, it is much more a part of you than when you memorize a description of it from someone else.

— Dewey Dykstra, Jr. (1996: 202).

If there is a key to reinventing our educational system, it lies in what our teachers believe about the nature of knowing. Without a reexamination and change in beliefs about the nature of knowing, there will be no substantial change in the enterprise of education; we will stay in a vicious circle.
— Dewey Dykstra, Jr. (1996: 202).

Formerly, it was education for degrees; now it is education for living.
— Sri Eknath Easwaran (attributed).

[T]he educational system is a product of society and hence shapes its products to meet the requirements of society. The present system is predicated on the needs of an industrial society in which citizens must follow orders, do assigned tasks in the appropriate order and time span, and not challenge the status quo. But these behaviors will not be appropriate for life in the near future or perhaps even the present.
— D. Stanley Eitzen and Maxine Bacca Zinn (1997: 419).

The curriculum ... is not very germane to the poor child. What is the relevance of conjugating a verb when you are hungry? What is the relevance of being able to trace the path of how a bill becomes a law when your family and neighbors are powerless? ... Schools ... have a way of ignoring real-life problems and controversial issues. Schools are irrelevant if they disregard topics such as race relations, poverty, and the distribution of community power.
— D. Stanley Eitzen and Maxine Bacca Zinn (1997: 410).

Schools perform a number of functions that maintain the prevailing social, political, and economic order: (a) socializing the young, (b) shaping personality traits to conform with the demands of the culture, (c) preparing for adult roles, and (d) providing employers with a disciplined and skilled labor force.
— D. Stanley Eitzen and Maxine Bacca Zinn (1997: 421).

The secret of Education lies in respecting the pupil. It is not for you to choose what he shall know, what he shall do. It is chosen and foreordained, and he only holds the key to his own secret. By your tampering and thwarting and too much governing he may be hindered from his end and kept out of his own. Respect the child.
— Ralph Waldo Emerson (1997: 71).

[Wisdom is] not what comes from reading great books. When it comes to understanding life, experiential learning is the only worthwhile kind; everything else is hearsay.
— Joan Erickson (1992: 349).

[The educational system is like] twelve years in a Roman circus wherein the winners get gold stars, affection, envy; they get A's and E's, honors, awards, and college scholarships. The losers get humiliation and degradation. The fear of losing the game is a great fear. It's the fear of swats, of the principal's office, and above all the fear of failing.
— Jerry Farber (1972: 98).

The accumulation and manipulation of knowledge is not truly education.

— Jack Forem (1974: 92).

True education should certainly help an individual discover and create meaningful values, meaningful goals and a direction in life.

— Jack Forem (1974: 94).

Why has inner development, the basis of all success and happiness in life, the most fundamental aspect of our education, been neglected?

— Jack Forem (1974: 96).

Certainly the need for a way to unfold the full potential of man is the greatest need of the age, and it is the legitimate province and fundamental function of education.

— Jack Forem (1974:98).

[I]t is very important for us that the child feel the teacher to be not a judge but a resource to whom he can go when he needs to borrow a gesture, a word.

— Tiziana Filippini (1990).

The students are not called upon to know, but to memorize the contents narrated by the teacher. ... Hence in the name of the "preservation of culture and knowledge" we have a system which achieves neither true knowledge nor true culture.

— Paulo Freire (1972: 68).

Education either functions as an instrument which is used to facilitate the integration of the younger generation into the logic of the present system and bring about conformity to it, or, it becomes the "practice of freedom" — the means by which men and women deal critically and creatively with reality and discover how to participate in the transformation of their world.

— Paulo Freire (1988: 28).

In the banking concept of education, knowledge is a gift bestowed by those who consider themselves knowledgeable upon those whom they consider to know nothing.

— Paulo Freire (1972: 58).

Whereas banking education anesthetizes and inhibits creative power, problem-posing education involves a constant unveiling of reality.

— Paulo Freire (1972: 68).

(a) the teacher teaches and the students are taught;
(b) the teacher knows everything and the students know nothing;
(c) the teacher thinks and the students are thought about;
(d) the teacher talks and the students listen – meekly;
(e) the teacher disciplines and the students are disciplined;
(f) the teacher chooses and enforces his choice, and the students comply;
(g) the teacher acts and the students have the illusion of acting through the action of the teacher;
(h) the teacher chooses the program content, and the students (who were not consulted) adapt to it;
(i) the teacher confuses the authority of knowledge with his own professional authority, which he sets in opposition to the freedom of the students;
(j) the teacher is the subject of the learning process, while the pupils are mere objects.

— Paulo Freire (1972: 59).

The task of impressing on people the guiding ideals and norms of our civilization is, first of all, that of education. But how woefully inadequate is our educational system for this task. Its aim is primarily to give the individual the knowledge he needs in order to function in an industrialized civilization, and to form his character into the mold which is needed ... Our high schools and [universities] continue with the task of providing their students with the knowledge they must have to fulfill their practical tasks in life, and with the character traits wanted on the personality market. Very little, indeed, do they succeed in imbuing them with the faculty of critical thought, or with character traits which correspond to the professed ideals of our civilization.

— Erich Fromm (1955: 299).

If work is to become an activity based on [the individual's] knowledge and on the understanding of what he is doing, then indeed there must be a drastic change in our method of education.

— Erich Fromm (1955: 300).

Schooling, be it transmission of knowledge or formation of character, is only one part, and perhaps not the most important part of education; using "education" here in its literal and most fundamental sense of "e-ducere" = "to bring out," that which is within man. Even if man has knowledge, even if he performs his work well, if he is decent, honest, and has no worries with regard to his material needs – he is not and cannot be satisfied.

— Erich Fromm (1955: 301).

You cannot teach a man anything.
You can only help him discover it within himself.
— Galileo (1977: 1).

Educators have a particular responsibility to see that education
is not social conditioning. This means the elimination of all
distinction between useful and unuseful fields of learning...
— John Kenneth Galbraith (1974:227).

[I]t has now been established quite convincingly that individuals have quite different minds from one another. Education ought to be so sculpted that it remains responsive to these
differences. Instead of ignoring them, and pretending that all
individuals have (or ought to have) the same kinds of minds,
we should instead try to ensure that everyone receive an
education that maximizes his or her own intellectual potential.
— Howard Gardner (1993: 71).

Now that we know something about teaching styles, learning
styles, and individual intelligences, it is simply inexcusable to
insist that all students learn the same thing in the same way.
— Howard Gardner (1993: 73).

Nearly all educators ... acknowledge the failure of the en-
trenched factory model of education, in which students are all
served the same curriculum in the same assembly-line fashion
and teachers are cogs in a massive bureaucratic apparatus.
— Howard Gardner (1993: 82).

[E]ducators need to make it clear that merely taking a temperature over and over again does not heal a patient and that a person who can only spit back facts cannot be expected to solve an unfamiliar problem or to create something new.

— Howard Gardner (1993: 84).

Striking differences among individuals ... call into question whether individuals ought all to be taking the same curriculum and whether, to the extent that there is a uniform curriculum, it needs to be presented in the same fashion to all individuals.

— Howard Gardner (1993: 170).

If anything, education has proceeded according to the ... assumption [that] there is one way of teaching, one way of learning, and individuals can be arrayed in terms of their skills in this mandated form.

— Howard Gardner (1993: 228).

[M]ost schools are content to accept performances that are rote, ritualized, or conventionalized; that is, performances that in some way merely repeat or give back what the teacher has modeled.

— Howard Gardner (1993: 229).

[T]he great majority of people are capable of using their competences in a skillful way; [sic] we need to explore how such use can be encouraged...

— Howard Gardner (1993: 248).

Much education today is monumentally ineffective. All too often we are giving young people cut flowers when we should be teaching them to grow their own plants.
— John W. Gardner (1997: 47).

If we indoctrinate the young person in an elaborate set of fixed beliefs, we are ensuring his early obsolescence. The alternative is to develop skills, attitudes, habits of mind and the kinds of knowledge and understanding that will be the instruments of change and growth on the part of the young person. Then we will have fashioned *a system that provides for its own continuous renewal.*
— John Gardner (1964: 25).

All education worthy of the name enhances the individual.
— John W. Gardner (1968: 73).

The schools and colleges must equip the student for a never-ending process of learning; they must gird his mind and spirit for the constant reshaping and re-examination of himself. They cannot content themselves with the time-honored process of stuffing students like sausages or even the possibly more acceptable process of training them like seals.
— John W. Gardner (1968: 99.

Perhaps the greatest challenge in education ... is to discover what it is that keeps alive in some people the natural spark of curiosity, eagerness, hunger for life and experience, and how we may rekindle that spark when it flickers out.

— John W. Gardner (1968: 105).

The important thing is that [every individual] have the kinds of experience and education that will bring out the best that is in him ... that every individual fulfill his own potentialities and live a meaningful and satisfying life in the context of those potentialities. College will do that for some kinds of people with some kinds of abilities. Other kinds of experience will do it for people with different abilities.

— John W. Gardner (1968: 110).

One of the most appalling and unhappy errors of much popular education has been to assume that youngsters incapable of the highest standards of intellectual excellence are incapable of any standards whatsoever and can properly be subjected to shoddy, slovenly and trashy educational fare.

— John W. Gardner (1968: 111).

No society can properly define for any individual the purpose and meaning of his life. The good society will create conditions in which the individual can find his own purpose and meaning in life.

— John W. Gardner (1968: 152).

A student of business with tact,
Absorbed all the answers he lacked.
But acquiring a job,
He said with a sob,
"How does one fit answer to fact?"
— (Anonymous limerick).

No man can reveal to you aught but that which already lies half asleep in the dawning of your knowledge.

The teacher who walks in the shadow of the temple, among his followers, gives not of his wisdom but rather of his faith and lovingness.

If he is indeed wise he does not bid you enter the house of his wisdom, but rather leads you to the threshold of your own mind.

The astronomer may speak to you of his understanding of space, but he cannot give you his understanding.

The musician may sing to you the rhythm which is in all space, but he cannot give you the ear which arrests the rhythm nor the voice which echoes it.

And he who is versed in the science of numbers can tell of the regions of weight and measure, but he cannot conduct you thither

For the vision of one man lends not its wings to another man ...

— Kahlil Gibran (1973: 56-57).

Your children are not your children.
They are the sons and daughters of life's longing for itself.
They come through you, not from you.
And though they are with you, they belong not to you.
You may give them your love but not your thoughts,
For they have their own thoughts.
You may house their bodies but not their souls,
For their souls dwell in the house of tomorrow, which you cannot visit, not even in your dreams.
You may strive to be like them, but strive not to make them like you.
For life goes not backward nor tarries with yesterday.
You are the bows from which your children as living arrows are sent forth.
The archer sees the mark upon the path of the infinite, and he bends you with his might that the arrows may go swift and far.
Let your bending in the archer's hand be for gladness;
For even as he loves the arrow that flies, so he loves the bow that is stable.

— Khalil Gibran (1973: 17-18).

Since every effort in our educational life seems to be directed toward making ... the child a being foreign to itself, it must of necessity produce individuals foreign to one another, and in everlasting antagonism with each other.
— Emma Goldman (1992: 156).

It can be said flatly that the mere act of listening to wise statements and sound advice does little for anyone ... no amount of information, whether of theory or fact, in itself improves insight and judgment or increases ability to act wisely under conditions of responsibility ... We cannot effectively use the insight and knowledge of others; it must be our own knowledge and insight that we use ... So far as responsible activity in the business world is concerned, it is clear that a fund of ready-made answers can be of little avail. Each situation is a new situation, requiring imaginative understanding as a prelude to sound judgment and action.
— Charles I. Gragg (1954: 10-11).

No one knows as yet how we can educate for creativity.
— J. P. Guilford (1962: 164).

An answer without a question is devoid of life. It may enter the mind; it will not penetrate the soul. It may become part of one's knowledge; it will not come forth as a creative force.
— Abraham Heschel (1986: 92).

[A]lmost all children fail. ... [T]hey fail to develop more than a tiny part of the tremendous capacity for learning, under-standing, and creating with which they were born and of which they made full use during the first two or three years of their lives.
— John Holt (1976: 15).

Schools are a kind of temple of worship for "right answers," and the way to get ahead is to lay plenty of them on the alter.
— John Holt (1976: 120).

Books ... rarely if ever talk about what children can make of themselves, about the powers that from the day or moment of birth are present in every child.

— John Holt (1992: 65).

[Traditional] academic education is the act of memorizing things read in books, and things told by college professors who got their education mostly by memorizing things read in books and told by college professors.

— Elbert Hubbard (1997: 101).

The idea of an education which will develop all man's natural gifts is certainly a true one. ... Under the present system of education, man does not fully attain the object of his being.

— Immanuel Kant (1974: 93).

The frightening thing is [students'] unquestioning acceptance of whatever is taught to them by anyone in front of the room.

— Bel Kaufman (1997: 110).

A child miseducated is a child lost.

— John F. Kennedy (1997: 7).

[O]ur schools have in the past chosen from the whole of life certain intellectualistic tools ... have arranged these under the heads of reading, arithmetic, geography, and so on, and have taught these separately as if they would, when once acquired, recombine into the worthy life. ... Not only do these things not make up the whole of life; but we have so fixed attention upon the separate teaching of these as at times to starve the weightier matters of life and character.

— William Heard Kilpatrick (1964: 217-218).

The important thing in education is to insure that the
purposes and plans are those of the learners, and not the
teachers.
> — William Heard Kilpatrick (1964: 218).

True education is to learn *how* to think, not *what* to think.
> — Jiddu Krishnamurti (1997: 9).

[I]s not the true purpose of education to *help* you to find out,
so that as you grow up you can begin to give your whole
mind, heart and body to that which you really love to do?
> — Jiddu Krishnamurti (1964: 52).

If schools are to become cradles of social creativity, basic
textbooks need to be rethought and rewritten. ... Most school
texts do not call for debate and critical thinking, only for
acceptance.
> — Ervin Laszlo (1994: 116).

There is an urgent need for educational programs that lead to
discovery and do not stop at instruction; that encourage
insights, not merely the accumulation of information,
and that foster personal involvement rather than passive
emulation.
> — Ervin Laszlo (1994: 116).

The common view is that the child's own interests and inclinations are not as important in constructing [educational] programs as the adult conceptions of what the child can become, given appropriately structured and managed experiences.
— Margaret Lay-Dopyera and John Dopyera (1987: 182).

He who can be educated can be re-educated.
— Luis Alberto Machado (1980: 15).

School is not at all like billiards. When you play billiards you push the ball with a certain force and it hits the table and bounces off; there's a definite way the ball will go, depending on force and direction. Children are not all like this, predictable. But sometimes schools function as if they were; these are schools with no joy.
— Lorris Malaguzzi (1994: 53).

Educators focus on implanting the greatest possible amount of information in the greatest number of children, with a minimum of time, expense and effort. ... Children in the usual classroom learn very quickly that creativity is punished, while repeating a memorized response is rewarded, and concentrate on what the teacher wants them to say, rather than understanding the problem. Since classroom learning focuses on behavior rather than thought, the child learns exactly how to behave while keeping his thoughts his own.
— Abraham Maslow (1992: 216-217).

The student's values are inevitably shifted to external signs. He is validated by scores; he experiences himself of worth only in terms of a series of marks on a technical scale. The shift of validation to the outside shrinks his consciousness and undermines his experience of himself. And again it is not that the criteria are external (we all must live, at whatever stage, by many external criteria) but rather criteria are not *chosen by the person himself* but brought to bear upon him by others, in this case parents and school authorities.

— Rollo May (1972: 98).

All the data on what makes a person more human
are not yet in.

— Marshall McLuhan (1970: 1).

We are familiar enough with the general picture of traditional school learning with its fixed curriculum, its single textbook, its lessons mapped out for all to learn and recite upon at the same hour, its material limited to specially selected information about the outside world past and present — and mostly past ...

— Hughes Mearns (1958: 242).

We must recognize that today ... we have far too much instruction and all too little education. We are far too busy filling up the young with what we think they ought to know, to have much time left over for helping them to become what they ought to be.

— Ashley Montagu (1974: 93).

We need to reform our ideas concerning the meaning and purposes of education. ... We need to understand that the very concept of education requires to be revised in the light of our growing understanding of the nature of human nature, and that what we are doing in the schools must be completely revamped so that they become schools for the teaching not of the three R's as such, but for the teaching of the theory and practice of human relations, and the three R's as skills or techniques in the service of more effective human relations.

— Ashley Montagu (1962: 157).

What is all the instruction in the world worth if it is not accompanied and integrated by an understanding of man's responsibility to man?

— Ashley Montagu (1962: 303).

A scientific approach to education must begin with the basic assumption that values must in the long run be tested by their capacity to contribute to the happiness and creativeness of human beings living together.

— Ashley Montagu (1962: 303).

Much of the disillusionment with education today, and specifically with schools, is the result of academic climates that are impersonal and unrelated to student interests, experiences, and needs. The basic philosophy and methods of traditional education lead to alienation of the child from himself, alienation from peers and from teachers, and alienation from society.

> — Clark E. Moustakas (1973: 1).

In no way should expediency, efficiency, organization, and achievement push the self of the learner away, for the self of the learner is his one unique contribution to humanity, his one tie to meaning and to life.

> — Clark E. Moustakas (1973: 19).

Education — the great mumbo jumbo and fraud of the ages — purports to equip us to live and is prescribed as a universal remedy for everything from juvenile delinquency to premature senility. For the most part it serves to enlarge stupidity, inflate conceit, enhance credulity, and put those subjected to it at the mercy of brainwashers ...

> — Malcolm Muggeridge (1995: 23).

If we aim to re-invent the corporation, we must give some thought to re-inventing education too.

> — John Naisbitt and Patricia Aburdene (1985: 139).

[W]hat good does it do us to achieve excellence in an education system that no longer fits our society?
— John Naisbitt and Patricia Aburdene (1985: 140).

Today's education system – the one some reformers want to elevate to a level of excellence – was never meant to serve the needs of today's information society; it was custom-made to fit the industrial society – a time when it made sense to treat everyone the same.

Uniformity, control, centralization in the factory and in management were the ideals of industrial society. And the schools were modeled in the image and likeness of these industrial values – right for their time, but horrendously wrong today.

Individuality, creativity, the ability to think for one's self – the values we treasure now – were hardly considered assets on the assembly line or even in the executive suite.

Were we to, in effect, freeze our children in the educational paradigm of the industrial society, we would condemn them to being as ill-equipped to function in the information society as their grand parents would be.
— John Naisbitt and Patricia Aburdene (1985: 140).

We have essentially the same education system as we had in the industrial society and we are trying to use it to equip us for the information age.
— John Naisbitt and Patricia Aburdene (1985: 140).

Young people brimming with creative potential are run through a system that recognizes and deals only with the linear, logical, rational side of human and social reality.
— John Naisbitt and Patricia Aburdene (1985: 140).

Creativity often fades after children enter school, where they are rewarded for doing what adults want them to do.
Diane Papalia and Sally Wendkos Olds (1992: 271).

A pleasant, success-oriented program enhances the child's self-esteem. ... [Educational] content relevant to the life of the learner fosters self-motivated involvement. ... Encouraging different solutions to the same problem recognizes that each child has his own learning style.
Cereta Perry (1973: 84).

Interest is expanded when the child is free to select his favorite number and to create a story about that number. A child takes great pride in his own creation. Self-direction and self-affirmation are important ingredients in real learning.
Cereta Perry (1973: 85).

When children are free, they are happy. When children are happy, they learn more.

Cereta Perry (1973: 166).

The principal goal of education is to create men and women who are capable of doing new things, not simply of repeating what other generations have done. ... men and women who are creative, inventive discoverers. The second goal of education is to form minds which can be critical, can verify and not accept everything they are offered.

Jean Piaget (1998: 17).

[L]et early education be a sort of amusement; you will then be better able to find out the natural bent. For no one will love that which gives him pain, and in which after much toil, he makes little progress.

Plato (1974: 176).

Our pedagogy consists in pouring answers into children without their having asked questions, and the questions they do ask are not listened to.

Karl Popper (1997: 142).

Real education must ultimately be limited to one who INSISTS on knowing, the rest is mere sheep-herding.

Ezra Pound (1992: 527).

There can be no answer that is not [the learner's] personally responsible decision.

Philo T. Pritzkau (1970: 5).

Most would [say] that education should be associated with the development of a meaningful life. Most would also agree that education should be central to the evolvement of a more human person.

Philo T. Pritzkau (1970: 15).

[O]ne of the criteria of great teaching is *not to teach* in the usual sense.

— Philo T. Pritzkau (1970: 18).

The point to consider is the adamant reluctance of the school to acknowledge that it is fraught with conditions which seem meaningless to youth.

— Philo T. Pritzkau (1970: 23-24).

The teacher must seek to liberate the mind. ... Great teaching will result only if everything which is brought into the conditions for learning is secondary to the mind, and thus to the individual [learner].

— Philo T. Pritzkau (1970: 16).

What must a child think when the behavior of teachers and other adults precludes all or almost all of the experiences he encounters in the daily eighteen or so hours spent outside of the classroom? What must he think when most of the encounters which are relevant to him are never brought into focus as he pursues his school tasks?

— Philo T. Pritzkau (1970: 22-23).

Curiosity is reduced, inquiry is narrowed, the direction is settled, the individual is devalued.

— Philo T. Pritzkau (1970: 58).

We have all kinds of pressures.
People are always telling us what to do.
We have to take courses that have no meaning to us.
Adults tell us to decide, and then they don't like the decision.
We're not all the same —
　　　there are different points of view among us.
We want to move without too many restrictions.
We want to become more aware of things by ourselves.
Even though things are complicated, we're still enthusiastic.
Adults want us to conform, and so we lose our identity.
We have to conform to the group, so our friends will like us.
We have to have good ideas to be somebody.

— (Reactions of a class of high school students to the evaluative system; see Weisntein and Fantini, 1970: 154).

149

The schools and colleges teach very little (other than basic literacy and numeracy) that is directly relevant to the world of work.

— Ian Robertson (1987: 392).

Good knowledge of unsolved problems of science, and how we know that they're problems, would probably be better education for students than all the "facts" we could cram into their heads.

— Robert Scott Root-Bernstein (1989: 191).

We spend so much time trying to teach students how to answer pre-solved problems in the pre-approved manner that we fail to teach them how to pose new problems for themselves.

— Robert Scott Root-Bernstein (1989: 353).

[W]e are generally educated and socialized with an overwhelming emphasis on situations and learning experiences for which there is only one correct answer.

— Martin B. Ross (1981: 129).

The problems of education are merely reflections of the deepest problems of our age. They cannot be solved by organisation, administration, or the expenditure of money, even though the importance of all these is not denied. We are suffering from a metaphysical disease, and the cure must therefore be metaphysical. Education which fails to clarify our central convictions is mere training or indulgence. For it is our central convictions that are in disorder, and, as long as the present anti-metaphysical temper persists, the disorder will grow worse. Education, far from ranking as man's greatest resource, will then be an agent of destruction, in accordance with the principle *corruptio optimi pessima*.

— E. F. Schumacher (1975: 101).

All men who have turned out worth anything have had the chief hand in their own education.

— Sir Walter Scott (1997: 61).

There is no such thing as a *neutral* educational process. Education either functions as an instrument which is used to facilitate the integration of the younger generation into the logic of the present system and bring about conformity to it, *or* it becomes "the practice of freedom," the means by which men and women deal critically and creatively with reality and discover how to participate in the transformation of their world.

— Richard Shaull (1972: 15)

[E]very child has something worthy to contribute and should be encouraged to express it.

— Geraldine Brain Siks (1958: ix).

Learning must be sought; it will not come of itself.

— Simeon (1991: 109).

No one knows how many would-be engineers and inventors have been steered away from their own potentials in high school career counseling sessions.

— Marsha Sinetar (1987: 64).

Children don't belong to us. ... They are little strangers who arrive in our lives and give us the pleasure and duty of caring for them — but we don't own them. We help them become who they are.

— Gloria Steinem (1992: 65).

[W]e do know that children who are encouraged to follow their own interests actually learn more, internalize and retain that learning better, become more creative, and have healthier and more durable self-esteem than those who are motivated by reward, punishment, or competition with other children.

— Gloria Steinem (1992: 154).

The first problem for all of us ... is not to learn,
but to unlearn.
— Gloria Steinem (1997: 21).

Perhaps the most flagrant examples of the undervaluing of
creativity are found in the schools.
— Robert J. Sternberg and Todd I. Lubart (1995: 20).

Most schools discourage error.
— Edmund Sullivan (1985: 187).

We need to understand that all of us can be better off if we
share our divergent perspectives and thus develop a more
complete view of reality.
— Robert Theobald (1981: 99).

We must teach students how to develop their own philosophy
so that they will not always require support from an authority
but will be willing to work out their *own* conclusions.
— Robert Theobald (1962: 101).

In education, ... teachers stand in front of their classes and tell people what they should know. Consequently, students come to believe that somebody always understands, and controls, all situations. This training for passivity causes us to blame others for the failures of our culture ... More to the point, it prevents each of us from believing that we, ourselves, can be effectively involved in change processes.

— Robert Theobald (1981: 24).

[W]e must find ways to reverse the damage done by our educational system to young people and adults who have passed through them.

— Robert Theobald (1981: 44).

It is a minimal obligation of society today to provide people with the capacity to learn for themselves.

— Robert Theobald (1981: 45).

We need to break out of the model whereby people consider certain subjects more valuable and more respectable than others.

— Robert Theobald (1981: 46).

People need to be helped to discover their areas of maximum potential through guidance rather than iron control.

— Robert Theobald (1981: 50).

[T]he educational process of the industrial era has sapped people's sense of their own worth.

— Robert Theobald (1981: 144).

Schools are organized like factories in order to socialize people to work in factories.

— Alvin Toffler (1985: 139).

I believe... it is important that children be permitted and encouraged to manipulate, to play around with, objects and ideas.

— E. Paul Torrance (1962: 35).

Education has produced a vast population able to read but unable to distinguish what is worth reading.

— G. M. Trevelyan (1990: 44).

Education consists mainly in what we have unlearned.

— Mark Twain (1997: 20).

[R]elevance is the test of an appropriate curriculum ...

— John Vaizey (1967: 42).

[T]he schools teach what their teachers know...

— John Vaizey (1967: 42).

There can be little doubt that the concern with numbers of
pupils to be educated, teachers to be trained, schools to be
built, has enabled people to avoid the pressing question of
who is to be taught what and why.

— John Vaizey (1967: 49).

The question as to what should be taught to whom is not
an empty philosophical question; it is now the question
which faces all of us — parents and teachers — most urgently.

— John Vaizey (1967: 50).

Traditional educational experiences gave young persons the
painful sense that they had to deny their feelings, lock away
their questions, and stay quiet for fear of looking stupid.

— John Vasconcellos (1974).

The goal of self esteem, and the demands of many humans,
make it clear that the very questions about humanness and
human nature and human potential are the most important
questions for schools and education today.

— John Vasconcellos (1974).

[S]chools should be places where human beings are encouraged to be open and express themselves – rather than places where they are conditioned to feel bad about themselves, to take orders and fit in, to pursue studies without questioning, and to perpetuate the old system and its stereotypes.

— John Vasconcellos (1974).

Education ought to be a process that affirms the right of a child not to be ashamed of him/her self, not to be afraid to declare his/her own needs and wants. It ought rather to enable him/her to recognize his/her body and mind and emotions as legitimate and valuable and equal components of being/becoming fully human. Education ought to affirm and respect the whole child.

— John Vasconcellos (1974).

Much of our educational system is an elaborate game of "guess what the teacher is thinking."

— Roger von Oech (1983: 10).

The Nature of this Flower is to Bloom.

— Alice Walker (1992: 65).

Learning is nothing if not a process of discovery and unfolding.

— Diana Chapman Walsh (1997: 297).

Education, to justify itself, should enable a man to use the full potential of his body, mind, and spirit.

— Maharishi Mahesh Yogi (1974: 93).

157

The child
is made of one hundred.
The child has
a hundred languages
a hundred hands
a hundred thoughts
a hundred ways of thinking
of playing, of speaking.
A hundred always a hundred
ways of listening
of marveling of loving
a hundred joys
for singing and understanding
a hundred worlds
to discover
a hundred worlds
to invent
a hundred worlds
to dream.
The child has
a hundred languages
(and a hundred hundred hundred more)
but they steal ninety-nine.
The school and the culture
separate the head from the body.
They tell the child:
to think without hands
to do without head
to listen and not to speak
to understand without joy
to love and to marvel
only at Easter and Christmas.
They tell the child:
to discover the world already there
and of the hundred
they steal ninety-nine.
They tell the child:
that work and play
reality and fantasy
science and imagination
sky and earth
reason and dream
are things
that do not belong together.

And thus they tell the child
that the hundred is not there.
The child says:
No way. The hundred is there!
--Loris Malaguzzi (1996:3).

V
Creative Work

Do you show up to work more for the paycheck or more for the passion, because you love what you are doing?

— Ricky Rainbolt

Growing Dissatisfaction with Work and Disloyalty to the Organization

Could it be true that "an organization's worst enemy is its own employees?"

It sounds incongruous, but that is the conclusion that some management consultants seem to be reaching. Shari Caudron reviews the evidence in an article poignantly entitled "Fighting the Enemy Within" (*Industry Week*, September 4, 1995). Caudron's review observes increasing incidents of frustration, resentment, alienation, and fear among workers. The review also talks of a "massive breakdown" in the level of corporate loyalty and the emergence of a "frightening new breed of get-even employees" who are doing what they can to sabotage the companies for which they work, and who feel justified in doing so. Seven common forms of corporate sabotage are identified: theft, sabotage of products, overspending, diversion of business, time-wasting, indifference, and withdrawal. Probable reasons for these maladies are given as: (a) vengeance, the desire to get even with an organization that workers feel is not sufficiently sensitive to their needs; (b) alienation, perceived distance between workers and management and between personal needs and corporate goals; and (c) resentment of unimaginative routines, i.e., tasks that workers perceive as stunting their creativity and ingenuity and minimizing them as human beings (see, also, Greenberg, 1993; 1993a; Greenberg and Scott, 1995).

It should be observed that corporate vengeance is not the only reported symptom of discontent with work. Psychological and more

159

personal problems show up as well. Among these problems are "un-happiness," "low morale," "stress," "boredom," "depression," "burn-out," "career shock," and the "who-cares?" attitude. Practical indica-tors include lateness, truancy, phony sick leave, lengthy vacations, absenteeism, labor turnover, frequent trips to the bathroom or to the water fountain, and other time-wasting practices. The large number and trans-occupational spread of "busy yet bored," "involved yet in-different,"* successful-yet-troubled" ** individuals give evidence of the pervasiveness of these corporate pathologies.

Less obvious but also widely reported indicators of the growing disenchantment with work include: (i) increasing recourse to psycho-therapy and other stress-reducing practices that, presumably, assist disenchanted workers in dealing with their experience and, in par-ticular, in bridging the separation that they feel between work and their physical, emotional, and spiritual needs; (ii) increasing con-sumption of tranquilizers by workers to "keep [them] from going nuts"; (iii) the growing popularity of self-employment, even in places where wages are increasing and working conditions are continuously im-proving; (iv) the importance that workers attach to vacation and lei-sure activities, and the lengths to which they go to find interests out-side of their jobs; (v) the large number of workers who, reportedly, feel "entrapped in a life that is meaningless;" and (vi) common employee jokes that portray work as a nuisance, for example: "Thank-God-It's-Friday!" "Sunday evening blues!" "Keeping Saint Monday!" "Don't work too hard!" and "I'd rather be sailing!" This is not to ignore the all-too-familiar industrial actions: strikes, walkouts, sit-ins, etc.

The prevalence of these and other seemingly anti-work attitudes has led to the suggestion that, intrinsically, many people do not like the work that they are doing.

Alvin Gouldner observes that "many people hate their work, or find themselves socially crippled and demeaned by this aspect of their lives" (Gouldner, 1987: 260). Glenn E. Watts and Lou Gerber (1982: 162) also observe what they describe as a "growing conviction among both white-collar and blue collar employees that the 'nose to the grind-stone' way of life is too high a price to pay for material success." Re-ports of how people feel about their work more often speak of disen-

---

* The expression is Charles Swindoll's (1995: 548).
** The phrase is Douuglas LaBier's (1986).

chantment than of satisfaction and personal fulfillment. Why there is so much disaffection with work is the subject of extensive research. The next few paragraphs synthesize some of the findings.

Why There is so Much Disaffection with Work

Erich Fromm, in his seminal work *The Sane Society* (1955: 258), asks: "Is there any empirical evidence that most people today are not satisfied with their work?"

Going by the literature upon which this synthesis is based, the answer to Fromm's question is a resounding "Yes." The follow-up question, however, arises: Is it work, *per se*, that people hate, or the structure and organization of certain types of work? Available evidence points to the latter answer which suggests that human beings naturally like work and want to work. However, they (often unconsciously) hate experiences (work- and nonwork-related) that are devoid of meaning and personal fulfillment, or that tend to violate what is most important in their lives – their creativity, identity, integrity, and dignity as human beings.

Underscoring the "spiritual" essence of work, several management scholars and human potential advocates describe work variously as life's ultimate purpose, a deeply satisfying and fulfilling part of one's everyday life, a calling, a mission, an activity that gives one the greatest joy and pleasure, the ultimate source of meaning and fulfillment in one's life, "the ultimate seduction" (see, for example, Drucker (1955: 161; Fromm, 1955: 253; Smith (1986: 113; Sinetar, 1987; Covey, 1992: 178-182). John W. Gardner (1961: 148) and John Applegath (1982: 27) suggest that people would rather work hard for something that they believe in – something that is compatible with their basic needs and fundamental values – than enjoy ease or leisure.

Unfortunately for many people around the world, the joy of work remains elusive. Rather than experiencing meaning, purpose, and personal fulfillment, a disturbingly large proportion of workers are reporting dissatisfaction, meaninglessness, and a personal sense of futility (see, for example, Fromm, 1955: 258; Heron, 1955: 197; Applegath, 1982: 20; Smith, 1986: 113; LaBier, 1986; Sinetar, 1987; Harman and Hormann, 1990, 119; Tumin, 1992: 106). E. F. Schumacher (1975: 250) pointedly observes that most people have no interest in the work that they are doing because it provides neither challenge nor satisfaction, but only a paycheck. Schumacher (1975: 55) attributes this phenomenon principally to patterns and organization of work that (perhaps inadvertently) strip certain economic activities of meaning, purpose, and personal fulfillment. An influential newspaper editorial, deploring the standardization, routinization, repetitiveness, and unimaginativeness of certain types of work organization, once satirically compared the experience of doing them to being in hell. Part of the editorial read:

> Dante, when composing his visions of hell, might well have included the mindless, repetitive boredom of working on a factory assembly line. It destroys initiative and rots brains, yet millions of ... workers are committed to it for most of their lives.

Studs Terkel (1974: xi), reviewing the personal accounts of hundreds of workers, portrays some traditional workplaces as a nightmare, characterized by violence to the spirit as well as to the body, by ulcers as well as accidents, by shouting matches as well as fistfights, and by nervous breakdowns.

Modern literature on job satisfaction suggests that, contrary to conventional wisdom, so-called workplace disenchantment does not occur because people inherently hate work, but because the principles and underlying assumptions by which many workplaces are organized, and the resulting patterns and operational relationships, are out of sync with human nature and the real reasons why people work (see the remarks in this section; see also the section entitled "Creative Management" — Volume II, forthcoming).

Following are some work-related assumptions, practices, and operational relationships that are frequently associated with reported hatred for work and dissatisfaction with work-life:

The view of work as alien to human nature
The "nose-to-the-grindstone" concept of work (i.e., the assumption that work is something hard and disagreeable) has given rise to the belief that its performance has to be bought, sold, coerced, or externally motivated, as the case may be. The related assumption that money and material rewards are the main reasons why people work has tended to put wages, benefits, bonuses, promotion, and tenure above intrinsic satisfaction and personal fulfillment.

Complex division of labor
Operational procedures in which the worker is not responsible for any meaningful whole, or is not aware of his relative contribution to the final product, are believed to create a sense of alienation.

The priority of tools and machinery (technology)
Methods of work and systems of production in which tools and machines are considered more important than the people who design, operate, and maintain them have been described variously as "salaried servitude," "mindless labor," "soul destroying," and "dehumanizing."

Partial involvement of the person
The practice of selectively recognizing only those abilities of the worker that his employer perceives as having utility and, *ipso facto,* the tendency to ignore, suppress, or even sanction aspects of the worker that are not considered instrumental to the objective for which he is employed are said to deny the essential wholeness of the person. Characterized as "repressive utilitarianism,"* this practice is perceived as capable of alienating the individual from some aspects of himself and, therefore, of generating a sense of "uselessness," of an "unemployed self," or of an "unlived" or "wasted life."

Categorization and the separation of workers from one another
Status differentials and formalized patterns of interaction that categorize and relate workers by their ranks or professions are perceived as turning them into role performers, replacing personal identity with official job titles and encouraging game-playing rather than authentic and spontaneous self-expression. These practices are also perceived as capable of creating psychological barriers between workers, eliminating friendships, peer relationships, mutual support, and emotional involvement in the work place, and giving rise to loneliness and depression.

The practice of separating thinking from doing, decision making from implementation
Management practices that effectively divide workers into "thinkers" and "doers" and that give managerial and leadership responsibilities exclusively to high-ranking corporate officers are perceived as demeaning, or as telling mature and otherwise responsible adults, husbands, fathers, wives, mothers, and community leaders. that their judgment cannot be trusted.

---

* The phrase is Alvin Gouldner's (1989: 263).

Belittling and demeaning staff control mechanisms
Rules, regulations, and operational procedures that create the impression that
employees are not capable of responsible self-direction and could not be trusted
to do the "right things" frequently, but inadvertently, produce precisely the
same unhappy outcome.

Standardization of operational procedures
The belief that only one correct way exists for achieving a given objective is
believed to stifle workers' creativity and to limit the exercise of their imagination – a condition that can provoke untoward reactions. Unchallenging
routines and repetitive work (i.e., having to do the same thing over and
again and in the same way) are believed to breed boredom.

The distinction between work and leisure
Perceiving work as qualitatively different from pleasure and designing the
former to exclude the latter are seen as potential sources of stress and boredom
in the workplace.

Corporate and institutional goals that the worker had no part in setting
Tasks that the worker was not involved in designing, and the control of
which lies elsewhere, are believed to create an inadequate sense of contributing,
of belonging, of recognition, of respect, and of responsibility.

Perceived discrepancy between corporate and employees' goals
Disregard of the worker's interests, goals, and personal inclinations is
perceived as capable of giving rise to alienation and the "couldn't-care-
less" attitude and, possibly, of minimizing commitment.

(See, for example, Heron, 1948; Fromm, 1955: 253-280; Theobald, 1961:
121; Terkel, 1974; Schumacher, 1975; Arieti, 1976: 406; May, 1976: 96;
Stokes, 1981; LaBier, 1986; Sinetar, 1987; Cooley, 1989; Gouldner, 1989;
Harman and Hormann, 1990; Covey, 1992; Gournay, 1995; Csikszentmihalyi,
1996: 371; Eitzen and Zinn, 1997: 318-327.)

Paradigm Shifts

Although by no means universal, the problem of worker disaffection is widespread and serious enough to warrant the global attention
that it is currently receiving. Its solution is one of the fastest growing
areas of management consulting and a major reason for the large and

growing number of management reform experiments, including automation of tedious and repetitive routines, improvements in physical working conditions, higher wages and benefits, individualized compensation packages, flexible hours, training, job enrichment, job enlargement, job rotation, reengineering, empowerment, delayering, "360° appraisal ratings," quality circles, continuous improvement, total quality, self-management teams, worker-ownership, and other participatory programs. The success of many of the experiments is too obvious to be argued. Rising levels of workforce competence and the resulting increase in productivity and morale (even if temporary) frequently justify the investment. The growing popularity of some of these tools indicates their perceived relevance.

Even with so many successes, the phenomenon of "worker discontent" still persists. While improved conditions and benefits and other performance-improvement programs have definitely brought about increased productivity and even morale, those successes rarely endure for the long-term. Experience indicates that, to produce the desired results, the programs have to be sustained and continuously strengthened (see, for example, Schaef and Fassel, 1989).

The isolated and temporary successes of many management reform and performance improvement programs raise two fundamental but related questions:

(a) Why do people work?

(b) To what extent do conventional patterns of work take cognizance of the real reasons (financial and nonfinancial) why people work?

For a while, the conventional wisdom was that people worked to earn a living. Based on that assumption, "reward" in workplaces came to be defined almost exclusively in terms of salary, pay, bonuses, and benefits. Workers tended to look for high-paying jobs, while employers relied on generous pay packages and opportunities for advancement to attract and hold qualified people. Emerging evidence suggests, however, that money and material rewards alone do not necessarily produce job satisfaction. One of the biggest surprises of contemporary management research is the finding that money is *not* the most important reason why people work (see, for example, Heron, 1948; Schumacher, 1975; LaBier, 1986; Sinetar, 1987; Schaef and Fassel, 1989; Harman and Hormann, 1990; Csilszentmihaly, 1996).

Personal accounts of individuals who claim to have "found their work" (i.e., something they are passionate about and feel they must do in order to be fulfilled) suggest that money is only *one* of the many powerful motivations for work. Others are:

- *association* – the desire to join with fellow human beings in a common enterprise.

- *cause* – the desire to promote a particular value, to advance a deeply held position, or to contribute to what one perceives as a worthy and important undertaking.

- *service* – the desire to do something that one perceives as bringing benefits to one's community, state, nation, fellow human beings, and/or the natural environment.

- *purpose* – the search for meaning and the desire to do something that one perceives as one's reason for existence.

- *personal fulfillment* – the desire to actualize one's potentialities, to develop and give expression to those attributes (abilities) that one values most about oneself.

These and related reasons for work are the focus of this section and, indeed, are the essence of *creative work*. The remainder of this introductory synopsis explains the concept. The remarks that follow indicate its importance for personal and social well-being as well as for corporate success.

Creative Work

Creative work, as the term is used here, is something that one intuitively feels one must do in order for one's life to be "complete" – an activity in the performance of which one finds oneself, in which one discovers one's special abilities and interests and maximally contributes to one's society and the planet. It could be a hobby, a charity, or a paid job. It could be done in a factory or in an office, on a farm or at a construction site. It could be a family enterprise or part of a communal project, self-employment or a cooperative. It could be mental or physical, tangible or intangible, temporal or spiritual.

The following is a partial synthesis of some of the ways that people describe creative work. The synthesis is developed from published comments of individuals who claim to have experienced the greatest joy and satisfaction from what they do and from the reports of the scholars who study those individuals (see, for example, Heron, 1948; Fromm, 1955; Krishnamurti, 1964; Maslow 1968; Pritzkau, 1970; Wilson, 1972; Terkel, 1974; Schumacher, 1975; Theobald, 1981; Watts and Gerber, 1982; Amabile, 1983; LaBier, 1986; Sinetar, 1987; Gouldner, 1989; Schaef and Fassel, 1989; Harman and Hormann, 1990; Pinchot and Pinchot, 1992; Steinem, 1992; Csikszentmihalyi, 1996; Haldane, 1996; Wolf, 1997; Barret, 1998; Jaccaci and Gault, 1999; Jaccaci, 2000).

Appeal: Something one passionately loves to do, and to which one gives one's whole mind, heart, and body; something about which one feels "psychologically saturated" while doing it; so absorbing that minor irritations don't matter; well-suited to one's abilities, talents, and temperament; passionate; "burning love"; "single-minded devotion"; something one feels "naturally drawn to"; one's "personal priority" to which one is willing to subordinate everything else; an activity to which one commits oneself in spite of the drudgery, the costs, the frustrations, the pressures, anxieties, deadlines, conflicts, and other difficulties; something one cares so much about that one would pay to do it.

Personal sense of identity: Enables one to gain deeper insight into one's feelings, beliefs, values, and orientations; provides a sense of one's place and worth in the corporation, the community, and/or the planetary scheme of things; builds confidence in one's strengths and potentials; helps one to discover who one is and to accept oneself for what one is; makes one feel proud of oneself and of what one is doing; makes one proud to tell friends and relatives where one works and what one does.

Authenticity: Enables one to express one's true self and uniqueness; provides a channel for communicating one's feelings, ideas, fears, and anxieties; enables one to do things in ways that resonate with one's rhythm and style; serves as a vehicle for expressing one's inner longings, values, desires, and priorities; utilizes one's talents and abilities more completely and constructively than any other activity.

Ecstasy: Euphoric; delightful; something one does joyfully and finds genuine happiness and satisfaction in doing; feels right; gives one the greatest pleasure and joy; feels more satisfying than any other thing one could do; time doing it is experienced as the best time one could have; refreshing; fun; exciting; combines playfulness with the dedication necessary to achieve results; seems to come naturally; intensely involving; "totally absorbing"; done with "calm sureness" as if it were one's second nature; done without any sense of striving, straining, struggling, or laboring; a "feeling of grace"; smooth; easy; effortless; "fully functioning"; "everything clicks"; "everything is in the groove"; "everything is in overdrive"; feels like the perfect thing to do and the perfect place to be.

Intrinsic satisfaction: Deeply satisfying; something that is worth doing for its own sake; makes sense and is rewarding in and of itself; the only reason for doing it is the inner satisfaction one derives and the enjoyment that comes from confronting the attendant challenges and frustrations; something one does not out of fear, nor to avoid pain or deprivation, nor as a price for some other reward; something one would happily do even without being paid for doing it.

Personal growth and development: Enriching; promotes the fullest possible development of one's unique potentialities; strengthens and gives practical expression to attributes that one really values about oneself; reveals and channels one's hidden talents and abilities to the ends that one desires; enables one to understand one's strengths and weaknesses, and to realize more of one's potential.

Personal integration: Holistic; something that simultaneously engages one's mind, body, spirit, and the senses; enables one to engage and express one's hitherto "unemployed self" – to identify and (re)integrate those personal resources (talents, strengths, and abilities) that other responsibilities have tended to minimize or to ignore altogether; enables one to "tune into one's own world"; combines economic productivity with personal satisfaction, financial rewards with emotional health, material success with personal fulfillment.

Meaning: Central to one's life; provides a framework within which every other thing that one does acquires meaning; something without which one's life would not be complete; gives one reason for living; expresses one's passions as well as one's potential; the most deeply satisfying and fulfilling part of one's everyday life; appeals to one's deepest longings; enables one to find and fulfill one's goals; produces and provides products and services that one perceives as important, worthy, socially beneficial, and environmentally responsible.

Fulfillment: Personally rewarding; creates a feeling of "life's ultimate purpose"; a calling, vocation, mission, or "service to life"; something one most enjoys doing and that also resonates with one's personal interests and abilities; an activity that most expresses the attributes that one deeply values about oneself; promotes personal sense of worth and pride; provides a greater sense of achievement than any other thing one could do; deeply engages one's abilities and interests; creates a feeling of doing something worthy and being useful to oneself, one's employer, one's community, and the world.

Connectedness: Promotes a sense of being related with fellow humans, of contributing to a worthwhile cause, and of participating in the human experience; provides recognition and respect; enhances awareness of the "big picture" and, in particular, one's duties and obligations to the corporation, the community, and the planet.

Life-renewing: Life-regenerating, life-enriching, and life-enhancing; continues to engage one's interests and efforts long after the formal employment situation. Studs Terkell aptly describes the experience as opportunity "for daily meaning as well as daily bread, for recognition as well as cash, for astonishment rather than torpor." (Terkell, 1974: xi).

The foregoing descriptions of creative work underscore three basic needs: (a) the centrality of work in human life and, in particular, the critical importance of meaningful and fulfilling work for personal and corporate success; (b) greater humanization of work, whereby the fulfillment of human potential is accorded at least as much significance as corporate profit, and within which meaningful existence is given at least as much consideration as income and the material things of life; and (c) periodical audit of one's interests to find out what is important in one's life, and the extent to which one's present job provides or promotes one's emotional and spiritual needs.

With respect to the first need, even if jobs cannot be invented for every conceivable human ability, it is possible to increase opportunities for employees to nurture and to express their creativity in their current jobs. Even if we cannot create enough institutionalized jobs for everybody who wants to work, there are unlimited avenues (at least, more than we are currently exploring) for people to engage in things that meaningfully and usefully engage their talents (see, in particular, Pearson, 1991: 171-172). With respect to the second need, even if managers and supervisors must decide what has to be done, they can minimize the degree of alienation or disaffection by letting employees figure out how to do their work. Even if drudgery and stress cannot be eliminated totally from the workplace, these problems can be mitigated by making jobs more fun, more meaningful to the worker, and more suited to his disposition. With respect to the last need, human potential advocates recommend taking up an occupation with which one is emotionally connected, rather than persisting in "a Monday through Friday sort of dying" * because that's "where the money is," or because the job is glamorous, or even because doing it is the wish of significant others (parents, spouse, siblings, friends, teachers, counselors, or mentors).

The frequent reference to paid employment both in this introductory overview and in the remarks that follow is not to ignore the significance of self-employment, hobbies, "outside interests," and other forms of human activity, but merely to recognize the predominance of institutionalized economic, commercial, and administrative activities as the biggest consumers of human energy. To repeat: *Creative work* is not confined to the "Nine to Five" or the "Monday through Friday" job. Practically any human activity can be creative if it gives expression to the performer's unique abilities and makes him feel like it's "the perfect thing to do" and if, at the same time, it provides benefits to one's employer, the community, and the natural environment. Furthermore, an activity is not "creative" just because it results in something new and unusual, important as these criteria are. An activity is *creative* only if it practically engages and expresses the worker's unique abilities or perspectives in socially and ecologically beneficial ways.

Summary and Conclusion

It has been suggested that many people are in jobs that they do not intrinsically enjoy. This conclusion is based on widely reported incidents of worker disenchantment, job dissatisfaction, low morale, tension, stress, boredom, depression, burnout, alienation, anger, industrial disputes, disloyalty to organizations, and sabotage. Additional support for this view comes from a frequently expressed desire to "get away from it all," the anticipation with which many people look to vacations, and the excitement with which they talk about the "fun things" that they do on holidays and weekends.

While apparently increasing in recent times, worker disaffection is not a new phenomenon. Historical evidence of the malaise goes as far back as the beginning of organized labor. Traditional remedies include incentive pay, bonuses, improved conditions, flexible hours, structural reorganization, motivational seminars, internal security, and coercion, among others. The limited and often temporary success of so many widely advocated "productivity improvement programs" suggests that some of these well-thought-out management tools are not tackling the real problem. Although no one knows what that problem is, there are several helpful clues to go by, such as the personal accounts of former corporate employees who have opted for self-employment. Claims by many of these former employees-turned-self-employed that their post-corporate lives are "much richer," "more meaningful," and "more balanced," and also that they are now able to "gain control" of their time and their lives, challenge employers of labor and designers of institutionalized jobs to find out what makes self-employment so "seductive" and to see how they could factor some of those elements into regular corporate activities.

Contrary to long-held belief, apparent "hatred for work" does not occur because work is incompatible with human nature, an inconvenience that people would rather avoid. The stories of individuals who claim to have found and followed their passions suggest that observed dissatisfaction with work, and the attendant personal, corporate, and social problems, occur probably because the structure and organization of certain jobs tend to violate what is most important in people's lives, to suppress rather than reveal workers' talents, to frustrate rather than promote the exercise of workers' imagination, to stunt rather than foster their growth as persons of intrinsic worth. There are also suggestions that many workers do not fully understand or personally identify with the core values of the "business" that they are in and, for that reason, they do not feel that the work they are doing is helping them to be the type of persons they deeply desire to be – to realize their potential and become more fulfilled human beings.

The assumption here is that every worker/employee has something he is passionate about or a unique way of doing things which, if found, would require little or no external motivation to achieve and maintain consistently high productivity. It is also suggested that only to the extent that an individual engages in things he deeply believes in and perceives as important, things he sees as promoting his unique capabilities and expressing his goals and values, can he maximally benefit his employer, organization, or institution. The extent to which an institution's activities challenge and engage the whole person, to which an organization's objectives incorporate the seemingly personal interests of its workers, could make the difference between apathy and enthusiasm, between lip-service loyalty and genuine commitment, between short-term profit and lasting corporate success.

Selected Insights
on
Creative Work

Man fulfils himself in work; properly challenged, he will
strive for higher goals than ease or leisure.

— (Anonymous).

I'm looking for something more than money out of my
work. I expect deep fulfillment and a little fun too.

— (Anonymous Corporation Executive;
see Marsha Sinetar, 1987: 8).

It's too late. I have spent too many years doing exactly what
was expected of me: being a good son, a good husband, a
good father. In my company, I'm known as a "good soldier."
When I ask myself what I am about, I'd have to say I don't
know anymore. I have tried for so long to fit in, I've held
back for so long, I don't know what or who I am.

— (Anonymous Corporation Executive;
see Marsha Sinetar, 1987: 19).

Creativity can be further fostered by a clearly intrinsic
motivational orientation toward work.

— Teresa M. Amabile (1983: 202).

Why are so many people dissatisfied with traditional jobs?
— John Applegath (1982: 22).

We are predisposed to think that employment cannot be enjoyable. Work is work – that is why you get paid for it. Doing what you want to do – leisure, entertainment – comes after work. We have grown to feel that doing what you want, whether frivolous or deeply spiritual, is personal and doesn't belong in the category of work, Right? Wrong.
— Lucy Anderson (1977: 153).

[T]he traditional "military" model by which most work is organized survives only as long as individuals choose to put up with it.
— John Applegath (1982: 3).

For too many people, our work systems are incompatible with their basic needs and fundamental values.
— John Applegath (1982: 27).

Indeed, it is a fact that work organizations which make it a point to maximize employees' autonomy, flexibility, and personal growth often enjoy lower turnover and higher employee morale and productivity.
— John Applegath (1982: 25).

The crucial need to confront the problem of stress and lack of fulfillment in our society has become painfully evident in the breakdown of people's relations to social institutions. Work, which had once provided an opportunity for achievement, has largely degenerated into a purely economic necessity.
— Harold H. Bloomfield *et al.,* (1975: 4).

Encourage talents, not roles.
— Dorothy Corkille Briggs (1975: 164).

When work is soulless, life stifles and dies.
— Albert Camus (1996: 123).

[P]eople are not just resources or assets, not just economic, social, and psychological beings. They are also spiritual beings; they want *meaning,* a sense of doing something that matters. People do not want to work for a course with little meaning.
— Stephen R. Covey (1992: 178-179).

[Some organizations] are only dealing with the economic
need of people ... That's why everybody is looking elsewhere
to meet their other needs and make more meaningful contributions.

— Stephen R. Covey (1992: 182).

Find a way to express what moves you.

— Mihaly Csikszentmihalyi (1996: 364).

Few of us know in advance what domains we may have an
affinity for. ... [I]t takes us decades of trial and error to find
out what we are best cut out for. ... something that then
[turns] out to be just right.

— Mihaly Csikszentmihalyi (1996: 370-371).

[A] pay check is not enough to base one's self-respect on.

— Peter F. Drucker (1955: 161).

Modern man does not know what to do with himself, how to
spend his lifetime meaningfully, and he is driven to work in
order to avoid an unbearable boredom.

— Erich Fromm (1955: 160).

Is there any empirical evidence that most people today are not satisfied with their work?
— Erich Fromm (1955: 258).

Dissatisfaction, apathy, boredom, lack of joy and happiness, a sense of futility and a vague feeling that life is meaningless, are the unavoidable results of [alienated work].
— Erich Fromm (1955: 258).

If nobody were forced any more to accept work in order not to starve, work would have to be sufficiently interesting and attractive to induce one to accept it.
— Erich Fromm (1955: 293).

The alienated and profoundly unsatisfactory character of work results in two conditions: one, the ideal of complete laziness; the other a deep-seated though often unconscious hostility toward work and anything and everybody connected with it.
— Erich Fromm (1955: 163).

Even if man had no monetary, or other reward, he would be eager to spend his energy in some meaningful way because he could not stand the boredom which inactivity produces.
— Erich Fromm (1955: 253).

The best kept secret ... today is that people would rather work hard for something they believe in than enjoy a pampered idleness.

— John W. Gardner (1961: 148).

The self-renewing man knows that if he has no great conviction about what he is doing he had better find something that he can have great conviction about. Obviously all of us cannot spend all of our time pursuing our deepest convictions. But everyone, either in his career or as a part-time activity, should be doing *something* about which he cares deeply. And if he is to escape the prison of the self, it must be something not essentially egocentric in nature.

— John Gardner (1964: 19).

The man who wants to get back to the sources of his own vitality cuts through the false fronts of life and tries to understand the things that he really believes in and can put his heart into.

— John Gardner (1964: 20).

What seems different in yourself; that's the rare thing you possess. The one thing that gives each of us his worth, and that's just what we try to suppress. And we claim to love life.

— Andre Gide (1987: 34).

Instead of men of being used as insensate units to produce increasing quantities of components, they should be trained and given the opportunity to improve the quality of their work.

— Edward Goldsmith, *et* al. (1974: 43).

Many people hate their work, or find themselves socially crippled and demeaned by this aspect of their lives.

— Alvin Gouldner (1989: 260).

[J]ust as there are unemployed men, there is also the unemployed self.

— Alvin Gouldner (1989: 261).

The wasted life is the big secret that everyone suspects but that all are embarrassed to discuss and may, therefore, remain thankfully uncertain about.

— Alvin Gouldner (1989: 263).

[M]ost workers believe in the validity of the very arrangements that waste their lives.

— Alvin Gouldner (1989: 263).

Just about everyone has job frustrations. Traditional ways of dealing with them have failed to increase job satisfaction.
— Bernard Haldane (1996: 17).

Most people do not need to quit their employers in order to enjoy job satisfaction.
— Bernard Haldane (1996: 17).

Humans thrive not on mindless pleasure, but on challenge.
— Willis Harman and John Hormann (1990: 29).

Survey data as well as less formal observation makes it clear that the traditional motivators for job performance — job security, high pay, and good benefits — no longer work. Employees want such intangibles as being treated with respect, having work that is personally satisfying, having ample opportunity to learn new skills and to grow personally, having a reasonable amount of autonomy, being recognized for good work.
— Willis Harman and John Hormann (1990: 67).

Humans ultimately seek meaning, not comfort; creative work, not inactivity.
— Willis Harman and John Hormann (1990: 119).

[C]reative work ... [is] the closest anyone has ever come to defining the meaning of life.
— Willis Harman and John Hormann (1990: 119).

Much business practice is still oriented around outdated theories of motivation which assume that people are motivated by money, power, status, or a hierarchy of needs.
— Willis Harman and John Hormann (1990: 144).

The human being who has resigned himself to a life devoid of thinking, ambition, pride, and personal achievement, has resigned himself to the death of attributes which are distinctive elements of human life.
— A. R. Heron (1955: 197).

We must never abandon the material benefits we have gained from technology and mass production and specialization of tasks. But we shall never achieve the ideals of [improving human potentialities] if we create a class of workers denied the satisfactions of significant work.
— A. R. Heron (1955: 197).

Without some cause in which to lose themselves, some creed in which to find themselves, or some loved object of value for which to sacrifice themselves, men live lives without point and purpose.
— Cyril E. M. Joad (1962: 78).

What do I care about so much that I would pay to do it?
— Jon Kabat-Zinn (1994: 207).

That is the challenge innovative organizations face: to combine the necessity for routine jobs with the possibility for employee participation beyond those jobs.
— Rosabeth Moss Kanter (1983: 181).

The problem for innovation and change is not the *existence* of [routine, repetitive] tasks but the *confinement* of some people within them. [This is the case] when people are never given the chance to think beyond the limits of their job, to see it in a larger context, to contribute what they know from doing it to the search for even better ways ... when job definitions become prison walls and when the people in the more constrained jobs become viewed as a different and lesser breed.
— Rosabeth Moss Kanter (1983: 180-181).

[Y]ou can't buy people's commitment ... with ringing bells, thank you notes, or plaques. ... [O]verall organizational effectiveness and efficiency depend on employees' personal dedication and sense of responsibility.
— James M. Kouzes and Barry Z. Posner (1987: 249).

When you feel very strongly about something, do you consider it difficult to put it into action? ... It is only when you don't vitally feel the truth of something that you say it is difficult to put it into action. You don't love it. That which you love you do with ardour, there is joy in it, and then what society ... may say does not matter.

— Jiddu Krishnamurti (1964: 155).

It is hard to take pride in a bridge you've never gonna cross, in a door you've never gonna open. You're mass-producing things and you never see the end result of it.

— Mike Lefevre (1974: xxxi).

We can conclude that money is not necessarily an incentive for the industrial workers, nor are short hours, safety, seniority, security and bargaining power an incentive for work. The only potent incentive is recognition of our abilities by our contemporaries and ourselves.

— J. F. Lincoln (1955: 212).

Nowhere has the meaning of creativity been more disastrously lost than in the idea that it is something you do only on week ends!

— Rollo May (1976: 38).

[T]here are millions of human beings who work at jobs which they detest and despise but who are shackled to them because they don't want to starve. This is madness and it drives millions of human beings mad.

— Ashley Montagu (1962: 56-57).

We have spent billions in training programs trying to change people to fit jobs and virtually nothing to change jobs to fit people.

— Jeffrey Parker (1977: 176).

A quiet revolution is taking place ... in the business corporation ... Individuals are awakening to the possibility of personal growth and finding opportunities to attain it.

— Perry Pascarella (1990: 151-152).

We work better when we're doing what we like to do/are good at. Everyone benefits when individual goals can be aligned with organizational goals.

— Petrocorp Department Philosophy (1983: 116).

[M]ost [entrepreneurs] leave corporations not primarily because they find their pay and benefits insufficient but because they feel frustrated in their attempt to innovate.

— Gifford Pinchot III (1985: xvii).

Do you show up to work more for the paycheck or more for the passion, because you love what you are doing?

— Ricky Rainbolt (2000: 33).

The work you are to do might not be summed up with a particular title on an office door.
— James Redfield and Carol Adrienne (1995: 198).

[The assembly line] is clearly a dehumanizing setting in which to work. Human beings, equipped with a wide array of skills and abilities, are asked to perform a limited number of highly simplified tasks over and over. Instead of expressing their human abilities on the job, people are forced to deny their humanity and act in a robot-like manner. People do not express themselves in their work, but rather deny themselves.
— George Ritzer (1993: 26).

[Y]ou must find a goal that drives you despite the dangers.
— Robert Scott Root-Bernstein (1989: 410).

Do what makes your heart leap.
— Jonas Salk (attributed).

The test of a vocation is the love of the drudgery it involves.
— Logan Pearsall Smith (1986: 113).

If it doesn't absorb you, if it isn't any fun, don't do it.
— Logan Pearsall Smith (1986: 113).

It is your work in life that is the ultimate seduction.
— Logan Pearsall Smith (1986: 113).

To organise work in such a manner that it becomes meaning-less, boring, stultifying, or nerve-racking for the worker would be little short of criminal; it would indicate a greater concern with goods than with people, an evil lack of compassion and a soul-destroying degree of attachment to the most primitive side of this worldly existence.
— E. F. Schumacher (1975: 55).

How could we explain the almost universal refusal on the part of the rulers of the rich societies – whether organised along private enterprise or collectivist enterprise lines – to work towards *the humanisation of work.*
— E. F. Schumacher (1975: 37).

Many [people] have no desire to be in [the productive stream] because their work does not interest them, providing them with neither challenge nor satisfaction, and has no other merit in their eyes than that it leads to a pay-packet at the end of the week.
— E. F. Schumacher (1975: 250).

Few men enjoy what they do to earn a living, and those who do are fortunate no matter how little they make.
— Philip Van Doren Stern (1970: 16).

[T]he creative individual works and is sustained in his efforts by intrinsic interest in the problem, by what he perceives to be its significance. Now, what he perceives to be its significance may have nothing to do with its significance to the firm ... what [he] perceive[s] to be the significance of the problem will not necessarily be its corporate significance.
— Gary A. Steiner (1965: 104).

Sullen employees who hate their jobs are less productive, more unreliable, and often prone to engage in creative sabotage just to enliven their days.
— Bruce Stokes (1981: 24).

The majority work to make a living; some work to acquire wealth or fame, while a few work because there is something within them which demands expression.
— Edmond Boreaux Szekely (1987: 157).

Do not hire a man who does your work for money, but him who does it for love of it.
— Henry David Thoreau (1955: 190).

Society's concern is far more with the extent to which ... jobs are performed effectively than with the problem of whether the performers are deriving esthetic gratifications out of their activities.
— Melvin Tumin (1992: 106).

If you can find the work that nourishes you, it will make you whole. You are your best when you're giving the most. You give the most to a cause you believe in.

— David Viscott (1984: 234).

Your work should be a celebration of the best you can be, and you should always be getting better.

— David Viscott (1984: 234).

[A]s useful as incentive pay is in raising output, it does not in itself solve the problem of obtaining workers' cooperation. In some circumstances it may intensify that problem.

— M. S. Viteles (1955: 255).

There is nothing I would enjoy more than a job that was so meaningful to me that I brought it home.

— Nora Watson (1974: 523).

Most people are looking for a calling, not a job; but, unfortunately, are saddled with jobs that are too small for their spirit.

— Nora Watson (attributed).

People are motivated by three things in terms of doing work. One is money, another is a desire to be helpful, and the third is a need to be creative.

— Michele Williams (1982: 73).

A person who is bored or alienated form most of what she spends her life doing is one whose life can be said to lack meaning. ... [S]he may in fact be performing functions of worth, ... but because she is not engaged by her work, ... she has no categorical desires that give her a reason to live.

— Susan Wolf (1997: 211).

VI
Creative Leadership

... the function of leadership is to produce more leaders, not more followers.
— Ralph Nader

... what leaders do, as paradoxical as it may seem, is make followers into leaders.
— James M. Kouzes and Barry Z. Posner

Basic Human Motivation and Leadership

What (if anything) do the following real-life incidents have in common?

- A four-year-old girl tells her six-year-old brother: "I don't have to do everything you tell me to do."

- A class of political science students tells its teacher, who is about to distribute examination question papers, "Sir, in accordance with the principle of democracy that we've been talking about, can we vote on whether or not this examination should proceed?"

- A subordinate tells his bossy boss: "Do you think I am a stone or some kind of insensate object?"

- Leaders of a group of minority tribes ask their counterparts from the ruling majority tribes: "When is it ever going to be our turn to rule this country?"

- An underprivileged population tells the ruling class: "Give us freedom or give us death."

- Protesters in a small, civil war-torn nation tell a regional "Big Brother" upon which their country has depended for such things as food, technical assistance, and peacekeeping: "Get your troops out of our land and leave us alone."

189

The motivations expressed or implied in all of those seemingly isolated incidents will become clearer as we review the concept of creative leadership and reflect on the selected remarks in this section.

Definition of Leadership

What, exactly, is leadership?

That question has engaged some of the world's greatest thinkers for centuries; it is still not decisively answered. Opinions vary considerably: One extreme position regards leadership as a rare and extraordinary ability that only a few individuals possess. The other extreme views the ability as a widely distributed human essence, the expression of which, however, is contingent upon personal qualities, situational forces, and the characteristics of other members of a group or organization. The one position perceives leadership as the right to set goals and, if necessary, coerce compliance. The other regards leadership as inspiring principles and visions that make others want to follow the person who exudes those values and to pursue the goals that he envisions.

As part of the debate, two scholars independently have proposed definitions of leadership with which many people seem to agree. One scholar defines leadership as "setting goals and policies to achieve those goals, [and] inspiring followers to work toward those goals." The other scholar regards leadership as "the art of getting others to want to do something you are convinced should be done." Common to both definitions of leadership are (i) something that the leader is convinced should be done, and (ii) the ability to influence other people to want to do it. This introductory synopsis examines the two widely accepted components of leadership and, in particular, the extent to which the leader's convictions dovetail with what people deeply desire to do.

Distribution of Leadership Abilities

Unequal distribution of abilities is a widely accepted basis of social differentiation and social organization. Nowhere is the principle more evident than in the domain of leadership. Historical evidence indicates a near-universal tendency to divide people into two groups: the "wise" and the "ignorant," "leaders" and "followers." The wise and leaders are be-

190

lieved to be distinguished by their superior intelligence, knowledge, wisdom, and reasoning that, presumably, predispose them to direct others toward what they (the wise and the leaders) see as desirable ends. This thinking dates back at least to ancient Greek civilization. Socrates, for example, described the wise and leaders as "Philosopher Kings." His successor, Plato, posited that "the wise shall lead and rule, and the ignorant shall follow." The only hope for resolving the human predicament, Plato suggested, was for true lovers of wisdom to assume political office, or for those who rule to become lovers of wisdom. Another venerated Greek philosopher, Aristotle, argued that "from the hour of their birth, some are marked out for subjection, others for rule" (see, for example, Heilbroner, 1986: 39; McLean and Weitzel, 1991: 33-34). Modern versions of the principle of unequal distribution of leadership abilities are not difficult to find. A line in a popular novel compares the human experience to a journey on which the strong shall lead the weak and the more endowed shall guide the less gifted. It reads: "We are all pilgrims on the same journey – but some pilgrims have better road maps." A modern philosopher agrees, suggesting that a few "naturally selected," "socially pure" men must rule over the rest of mankind. He goes on to say that the "noble and powerful" "may act toward persons of a lower rank just as they please" (see Castell, 1946: 340).

Many contemporary descriptions of leadership also reflect assumptions of extraordinary ability. Examples are "born leader," "natural ruler," "great man/woman," "the cream of society," "high and mighty," and "the best and brightest." Assumptions of extraordinary ability can also be observed in the allocation of responsibilities as well as in the distribution of power and privileges. By reason of their presumed superior knowledge, longer vision, and better sense of direction, leaders in many cultures tend to be looked upon to set directions; assign tasks; make key decisions; energize other members of the society, group, or organization; enforce compliance; evaluate performance; reward loyalty; and punish recalcitrance. "Followers,"* by reason of their presumed inferior endowment, are sometimes regarded as ignorant and, therefore, to be led; powerless and, therefore, to be "empowered"; lacking vision and, therefore, to be guided; unable to manage themselves and, therefore, to be "governed." There have even been sugges-

---

* Hereafter referred to as "people," "constituents," or "others."

tions that subordinates cannot be trusted to do the right things and, therefore, have to be controlled; that they do not always know what is best for them and, therefore, need their leaders to decide for them. *

Not everybody, however, subscribes to superior inheritance as the sole explanation for leadership. Cases of individuals whose circumstances are not ordinarily associated with leadership but whose personal vision and inspiration have propelled their organizations, communities, or societies to uncommon success have given rise to the suggestion that leaders are not only born, but are sometimes made. William Shakespeare's "some are born great; some achieve greatness, and some have greatness thrust upon them" is frequently cited in support of the "leaders-as-born" and "leaders-as-made" theses.

A synthesis of the two theoretical extremes is the "leadership-as-part-born, part-made" thesis. This view of leadership holds that inherited leadership attributes still require training, coaching, and/or mentoring to develop and actualize. The view further suggests that just as people can learn other skills, they can also learn the knowledge, attitudes, behaviors, and skills that they need to become effective leaders (see, for example, Kouzes and Posner, 1987: 297).

A fourth notion of leadership is its presumed species-wide distribution: "a universal human attribute" (see, for example, Spady and Bell, Jr., 1997: 41). This notion of leadership suggests that every functioning human being has an inherent ability to lead in some particular area related to his natural abilities. Proponents of this view of leadership argue that actual development and actualization of the ability depend on personal factors as well as external circumstances, including: (a) the individual's behavioral disposition; (b) the characteristics of other members of the group or organization; and (c) situational factors. Behavioral factors include such things as the leader's value system; his rapport with other members of the group or organization; the way the leader handles meetings; his communication style; his willingness to delegate; and the amount of respect, friendship, trust, and concern that he shows to other members of the group or organization. Factors pertaining to other people include, for example, their need for autonomy, desire to share in the decision-making process, identification with the group, interest in the task at hand, and

---

* These early ("scientific") management assumptions can still be observed in many contemporary groups, organizations, and cultures.

possession of the knowledge and experience needed to perform the task. Situational factors include such things as the nature of the task involved, the group's performance track record, and the availability of relevant information and other performance resources (see, for example, Tannenbuam and Schmidt, 1958; Fiedler, 1971, Spady and Bell, Jr., 1997: 41-48).

Emergence, Personality Attributes, Styles, and Functions of Leadership

Distribution of the ability to lead is not the only contentious issue in leadership. Considerable differences exist regarding how leaders emerge, what their characteristics are, how they lead, and what they do.

Emergence

The multiplicity of routes through which people achieve leadership gives a partial clue to its presumed distribution. Depending on the culture, group, or organization, one or more of the following considerations have been accepted as the bases of leadership: (a) *innate superiority* – individuals who are believed to be endowed with extraordinary abilities (e.g., "intelligence") are elected, appointed, or accepted as leaders; (b) *inheritance* ("aristocracy") – leadership runs along genealogical lines and passes from a deceased or deposed incumbent to his descendants; (c) *expert knowledge* – the most highly educated person in the focal area of concern assumes leadership or is appointed to lead the group (akin to the "philosopher king"); (d) *seniority* – the most experienced person in the group assumes leadership; (e) *increasing group/organizational complexity* – someone with organizational ability steps forth or is appointed to   coordinate the large number of disparate activities and the efforts of other members of the group; (f) *social status* – the highest-ranking or the most widely recognized person in the group is looked upon as leader; (g) *rate of participation in group activities* – the member with the most significant contribution to the group's activities is elected or accepted as leader; (h) *conformity to group norms* – the most loyal or the most committed member of a group is elected or accepted as leader; (i) *crisis* – a group or organization is beset with an unusual problem and someone who ordinarily might not have "qualified" to lead the group comes up with a viable solution to the problem and thereafter emerges as its leader; (j) *charisma* – the most charming or the most likable member of a group is accepted as leader (see, for example, Davidson 1974: 178, 184-186; Johnson, 1989: 194-195; McLean and Weitzel, 1991: 1-34).

Personality Attributes

The mystique surrounding leaders, the marvelous things that many of them have achieved, and the tremendous difference that some of them have made in their respective fields, have inspired numerous research projects designed to identify attributes that effective leaders presumably share and that also set them apart from other members of their groups or organizations. One result of these studies is a very long list of human attributes* – physical, emotional, behavioral, social, philosophical, and intellectual. To mention but a few, leaders have been found to be generally taller, more attractive, more self-confident, more empathic, more intelligent, more liberal in outlook, more sociable, more talkative, more determined, more enthusiastic, more mature, more open-minded, more collaborative, more highly educated, and more inspiring than the other members of their groups or organizations. Studies have also observed a correlation between leadership effectiveness and such attributes as foresight, creativity, integrity, decisiveness, aggressiveness, verbal skills, strong learning orientation, and a strong sense of direction (see, for example, Stogdill, 1948; Mann, 1959; Tannenbaum and Schmidt, 1958; Fiedler, 1971; Thompson, 1992: 214, 218-219).

While certain personality traits have been found to correlate with leadership in specific situations, no particular trait or cluster of traits has yet been found that consistently defines effective leaders across situations. In the absence of universal, cross-situational "leadership traits," scholars suggest that the qualities that make successful leaders are not uniform, but are contingent on the circumstances in which a group finds itself, including, as indicated earlier: (i) the leader's values, attitudes, behavior, and relationships with other members of the group; (ii) mem-

---

* One study is said to have found approximately 17, 000 one-word descriptions of individual leadership qualities in the literature.

bership profile, patterns of interaction, group norms, and operational procedures; and (iii) the nature and structure of the tasks at hand.

Styles

Just as leaders differ in the way that they emerge and in the characteristics that presumably make them effective, significant differences have been observed in the way they lead and exercise their powers. Social scientists identify three basic styles of leadership: (a) *authoritarian leadership:* the leader gives orders, enforces compliance, and controls major group processes; (b) *democratic leadership:* the leader gives suggestions, invites ideas and recommendations from other members of the group, and respects decisions reached by the group; and (c) *laissez faire leadership:* the leader allows members of the group the freedom to determine what they want to accomplish and allows them to plan how to do it. Stephen R. Covey (1991: 101-108) identifies three types of leadership power: (a) *coercive power:* people do what they are asked to do out of fear of adverse consequences if they should fail to comply; (b) *utility power:* people do what they are asked to do solely for the rewards they expect to receive for their compliance; and (c) *principle-centered power:* people do what the leader asks them to do, not out of fear of punishment or expectation of reward, but because they trust the leader and also believe in the goal that he espouses.

The amazing success of the different ways in which leaders do their work in different circumstances has given rise to the general conclusion that no one leadership style is effective in all situations.

Functions

Leaders, by definition, lead. Leading, however, means different things to different people. The following is a short list of some of the tasks that are commonly associated with leadership:

• organize group activities; allocate resources; disseminate information; monitor and control the group's performance; coach group members; maintain solidarity in the group; manage conflict among group members; represent and negotiate on behalf of the group in its external relations; cope with external threats and deal with internal forces of disintegration; discipline erring group members; and "keep the gates" by deciding who joins or leaves the group and what comes into, or goes out of, the group.

- develop a vision of some desirable goal or ideal, map out a strategy for translating this vision into action, promote and "sell" the vision, and motivate other people to contribute to the realization of the vision.

- inspire a shared vision that other members of the group or organization perceive as important and worthy of their individual and collective allegiances; find the way, show the way, and model the way; uphold the group's ideals and live out its values and purposes.

The Leadership Crisis

By all accounts, the world has had many great leaders. The names come from practically every culture and every field of human endeavor: agriculture, industry, education, politics, religion, philosophy, science, technology, human development, environmental protection, and more. Most of the advances in civilization and the spectacular progress that the human species has made have been inspired, at least in part, by the visions and the dedication of these great men and women.

Unfortunately, however, at a time when the human condition is rapidly deteriorating* and the world seems to need more and more effective leaders, both their numbers and their capacity to lead seem to be declining.

Warren Bennis, a foremost leadership scholar and writer, poignantly asks: "Why can't leaders lead?" "Why are people unwilling to follow?" Answering his rhetorical questions, Bennis identifies the following as some of the reasons for the phenomenon of declining leadership: bureaucratic thinking and a commitment to the way that things have always been done; the preeminence of individual rights over the common good; self-interest and unwillingness to make sacrifices today for a greater tomorrow; self-imposed isolation, "cocooning," and unwillingness to reach out, to make connections, or to cooperate with one's neighbors.

Examination of some of the things that have been written and said about leadership identifies the following as additional reasons why leaders are finding it increasingly difficult to lead and why people seem reluctant to follow:

---

* Increasing poverty, illiteracy, social segregation, hatred, crime, avarice, greed, moral decadence, and, of course, environmental degradation that threaten all life on planet earth.

- The "alpha dog syndrome," or the practice by which one or a few members of a society become the messiah to whom all others are expected to defer: By denying other members the opportunity to reveal and express their own potential (including *leadership*), "one-man-show" styles of leadership frequently breed disaffection and even resentment.

- The "great person" notion of leadership: the practice of giving all of the credit for a group's success to the leader denies other forces at play and, in particular, tends to minimize the contributions of countless individuals whose efforts and, in some cases, personal sacrifices, have brought about that success. This is regarded as another potential source of disaffection.

- The absence of a unifying idea toward which people can focus their individual actions: part of the "declining loyalty" and even "sabotage" that institutional, corporate, and even national leaders frequently complain about could be due to the absence of a higher (moral) purpose that people perceive as reflecting what they value most and deeply believe in and which, therefore, is worthy of their personal commitment.

- "Credibility gap": perceived variance between what leaders are expected to do and what they actually do, or between what leaders say they are doing and what they are perceived by constituents to be doing.

- Insufficient opportunity for personal growth and development: the tendency by some leaders to want to think for the people, to create a vision and then invite others to work to achieve that vision, or to decide what has to be done and also plan how to do it tends, perhaps inadvertently, to restrain the exercise of people's imagination and creativity and, therefore, to create disenchantment.

The growing demand for identity, meaning, purpose, and personal fulfillment and the concomitant rejection of experiences (leadership- and nonleadership-related) that people perceive as devaluing them or as making inadequate use of their capacities (including leadership) suggest that the current wave of "disenchantment with leadership" is not likely to be reversed by more threat or coercion, nor by generous bonuses and other material inducements, but by goals that people see as enhancing their worth as individuals and worthy of their commitment, and by relationships and operational procedures that recognize, nourish, and engage their own leadership abilities. That, basically, is the essence of *creative leadership*.

Creative Leadership

"Creative leadership" refers to the values, principles, behaviors, and relationships of the person at the head of an institution, group, or organization that inspire other members of the group or organization to willingly exert themselves toward the realization of its goals, while, at the same time, nurturing their creativity as well as their own individual capacities to lead in areas in which they have special abilities. The literature describes related styles of leadership variously as "inspiring leadership," "energizing leadership," "catalyzing leadership," "enlightened leadership," "transforming leadership," "servant leadership," "post-heroic leadership," "principle-centered leadership," and "mutualistic leadership." Distinguishing features of creative leadership, as reported in the literature, include: considering people as physical, emotional, and spiritual human beings; inspiring people to think in new ways and to "rise above the level of mediocrity"; "[raising] one another to higher levels of motivation and morality"; and handling problems and challenges in ways that call forth the creativity of other members of a group or organization as well as build their capacity both to handle similar situations and also to lead (see, for example, Burns, 1978: 20; Bass, 1985: 219; Sinetar, 1987: 89; Handy, 1989: 166-167; Covey, 1992; Kouzes and Posner, 1995: 321; Swindoll, 1996; Greenleaf, 1997; Spady and Bell, Jr., 1997; 1999). Suggestions for achieving this style of leadership include:

(i) *Self-knowledge and inner "housekeeping"*
The age-old injunction "know thyself" is of particular relevance in leadership. This wise but deceptively simple counsel enjoins the leader to be aware of his internal (psychological) conditions – his belief system, his perception of himself, as well as the assumptions he holds about people and the world. The suggestion is that what goes on in the mind of the leader almost inevitably translates into his attitudes, actions, and relationships with the people for whom he is responsible.

Variously referred to as "leading from within," "understanding yourself at a deeper level," and "authentic outward expression of the inner character of an individual," the belief is that who the leader is on the inside (his fears, anxieties, concerns, interests, motivations, values, and principles), could perhaps inadvertently be projected onto the people for whom he is responsible or with whom he has to deal, with serious implications for these people's lives and work (see, for example, Covey, 1992; Thompson, 1992: 221; Palmer, 1997: 296-297; Rosen, 1997: 304). Two statements, one by Ashley Montagu and the other by Warren Bennis, underscore this point. According to Montagu:

> [M]an creates his world according to the kingdom that is within him (Montagu, 1962: 157).

Warren Bennis regards self-knowledge as the primary responsibility of a leader. In his words:

> For the task of the leader is to lead, and to lead others he must first of all know himself (Bennis, 1976: 176).

The importance of self-knowledge for aspiring and incumbent leaders is a recurring theme in two very influential books: *Leadership – Magic, Myth, or Method?* by J. W. McLean and William Weitzel and *The Leadership Challenge: How to Get Extraordinary Things Done in Organizations* by James M. Kouzes and Barry Z. Posner. McLean and Weitzel (1991: 66) remind aspiring and incumbent leaders that awareness of their own character and knowing how best to use, improve, or compensate for their natural abilities are "clearly the leading criteria for being a successful leader." Kouzes and Posner suggest that "you cannot lead others until you have led yourself through a struggle with opposing values" (Kouzes and Posner, 1987: 301). Apparently inspired by Parker Palmer's essay on the subject (self-knowledge), Diana Walsh suggests that all leaders have a special responsibility to confront what goes on inside themselves, lest they unintentionally project their fears, personal insecurities, and self-delusions onto their constituents, their organizations, or the larger society. To explain that position, Walsh argues that:

> Leaders who are insecure about their own identity and self-worth create institutional settings that deprive other people of their identities. They tend to perceive the universe as essentially hostile and life as competitive battleground (Walsh, 1997: 296).

"Lest the act of leadership create more harm than good" is how Palmer (1997: 296) alerts his readers to the harm that can be done when a person performs his leadership role without being aware of his inner conditions and without examining how those conditions impact his own life as well as the life and well-being of other people. In this view, only those leaders who have developed a strong sense of self, who understand and can express their true feelings and values, can facilitate genuine and authentic self-expression by others, which is essential for collective success.

(ii) *Respect for the integrity of others and a commitment to the actualization of their innate potentialities*

The experience of many successful leaders suggests that leadership involves more than getting things done through people; more than the ability to plan, organize, direct, and control; more than the power to reward or to punish; more than the right to hire or fire. Antithetical as it seems to the more generally accepted command-and-control principles of human resources management, there are growing indications that so-called "touchy-feely" things are critically important for successful leadership. Referred to as the "principle of the heart," the belief exists that while people's skills can be sold and bought, their loyalty and commitment can only be inspired. Stephen Covey pointedly observes that: "you can buy a man's hands and back, but not his heart and mind" (Covey, 1992: 179). Also emphasizing the critical importance of the emotional sides of people, James M. Kouzes and Barry Z. Posner suggest that "the true force that attracts others is the force of the heart" (Kouzes and Posner, 1987: 125).

The "force of the heart," as described in modern leadership literature, implies, among other things: (i) treating people as whole persons and, therefore, catering to their material, emotional, social, and spiritual needs; (ii) being sensitive to people's interests, feelings, needs, and aspirations; (iii) recognizing the unique set of abilities that each person represents and his right to maximize his potential; and (iv) providing opportunities for people to do something that really matters to them and that also engages their talents.

The absolute necessity of recognizing and engaging people's talents has been indicated by three eminent thinkers. Carl Rogers (1961: 350-351) calls attention to the universal human tendency to want to actualize oneself, to become one's potential, to develop and be able to express one's capacities. John Gardner (1963: 121) suggests that "true happiness" consists in the full use of one's talents. According to Abraham Maslow (1968: 196-197), psychological health is impossible unless one's natural abilities are recognized, respected, and appreciated by oneself and others. To the extent that these views are valid, it can be suggested that the only way that people are going to be "loyal and productive members of a group or organization," the only way that they are going to be "compassionate," "cooperative," "trusting," "humane," and "responsible" is if they can be enabled to realize their unique abilities, even in the context of a formal organization.

(iii) *Sensitivity to, and respect for, diversity and the ability to unify seemingly disparate interests*

The fact that members of a group or an organization are individuals with unique mindsets, interests, and values is a potential source of *differences* and even divisions. Manifestations of this phenomenon vary from group to group and from organization to organization. Its adversarial forms go by different descriptions: "competition," "conflict," "rivalry," "turf protection," "empire-building," "infighting," and "back-stabbing." Probably every human group and organization has had to deal with one or more of these problems at one time or another and in one form or another.

In a sense, this is to be expected. Bringing together people with different talents, different styles of thinking, and different personal histories to achieve a common goal is bound to create tension which, in turn, can strain working relationships, with considerable loss to the organization. The ability to manage these divisions and avoid the "negative synergy" * that they frequently portend is regarded as one of the most critical tests of leadership. Several conflict-minimizing options and a variety of tools are available to the leader for this purpose. A very short list includes "conflict resolution," "denial," "suppression," "exclusion," "isolation," "tolerance," "assimilation," "mutual adjustment," "accommodation," and "understanding" (see, for example, Thomas, Jr., 1997: 333-334).

As experience has indicated, the problem with some conflict-minimizing procedures is their inability to bring to the surface some of the underlying differences that gave rise to the observed disharmony and, therefore, the tendency of those procedures to "paper over" deep divisions. The characteristically short life of solutions that fail to address people's (private) interests, concerns, and perceptions, or that try to make everybody conform to one position, be it majority or "official," suggests why a growing number of organizations are turning away from "conflict resolution" to "diversity management."

Diversity management, as some organizations are trying to implement it, involves two things: (a) recognition (even celebration) of inevitable differences among members of the organization; and (b) transforming observed differences into a positive force for corporate renewal and vitality.

Rather than adopt the more convenient "quick-fix" conflict resolution approach, rather than manipulate people to (superficially) accept the "official

---

* Colloquially, this is the tendency for people to do their own thing or, as Stephen Covey (1992: 179) describes it, to spend their creative energy on "their own goals and dreams."

position," rather than pretend that differences don't exist or, as the saying goes, sweep them under the carpet, rather than suppress dissent by intimidating or getting rid of people who hold divergent opinions, more and more leaders are recognizing the vitality that is inherent in diversity and the challenge of finding a purpose, a vision, or an ideal that reconciles or even unifies seemingly conflicting interests and inspires collective allegiance. Terms such as "larger purpose," "worthy objects," "higher imperative," "higher order values," "larger system of ideas and values," and "the central project of society" reflect the increasing recognition of inevitable differences among people and, therefore, the need for higher and *unifying* principles. Kouzes and Posner (1987: 225) aptly characterize this (leadership) challenge as recognizing and being sensitive to people's interests and desires and framing issues to align with those interests. Terry Mollner (1992: 105-106) perceives the challenge as redefining self-interests so that they all have "the common good" as their highest priority. The growing realization is that even in the most diverse groups and organizations, some unifying vision or purpose can be found that people perceive as beneficial not only to their groups and organizations, but also to themselves and the larger society.

Successful diversity management, however, depends on four related conditions: (a) respect for the uniqueness of every individual and the attendant differences in perception, interests, and orientation; (b) perception of various interests and desires as equally valid, equally necessary, and equally deserving of consideration; (c) valuing and validating every member and maximizing his unique capabilities for improved group or corporate performance; and (d) a unifying vision that resonates with people's self-interests and that therefore induces their voluntary commitment.

(iv) *Commitment to the enhancement of "subordinates" and constituents*
First and foremost, creative leadership is about enhancing other members of a group or organization – recognizing and strengthening their unique capabilities, expanding areas of their responsibility, and giving them opportunities to acquire new knowledge and skills. Following are five critical aspects of this responsibility:

(a) Challenging tasks and responsibilities
"To draw out the best in people" is an increasingly recognized leadership responsibility. Key elements of this responsibility include confidence in people's ability to get extraordinary things done, a commitment to excellence and the highest standards of performance, and the availability of challenging or even seemingly "impossible" goals that stretch people's imagination.

(b) Continuous improvement

Creative leaders realize that the current situation of their group or organization, however successful, can always be better. The experience of the proverbial dinosaur that failed to learn new ways and eventually had to face definite extinction serves as a constant reminder that complacency in today's turbulent environment almost inevitably will engender decline and eventual demise. As part of challenging their constituents to ever higher standards of performance, creative leaders also encourage them to question accepted ways of doing things as well as the assumptions upon which existing practices and methods are based (see, for example, Senge, 1992: 87). Recognizing that more than one right answer can be found for every problem, they deliberately frame issues in ways that encourage other members of the group to think in different ways and/or to try new and different approaches.

Another critical aspect of a leader's continuous improvement responsibility pertains to the capacities of the people that he leads. Carol Sanford (1992: 204) aptly summarizes this leadership responsibility. Arguing that every individual is unique and continuously developing, with a potential for making a value-adding contribution to his group or organization, Sanford suggests that the leader's responsibility is to collaborate with the individual to continuously upgrade and match the individual's unique abilities to the needs of his group or organization.

(c) Empowerment

The inherence of creativity in human nature does not necessarily guarantee that people will always be able to achieve extraordinary things for their groups or organizations. How they perform and what they acheieve largely depend on the prevailing conditions of their lives and work. Some of those conditions have been found to facilitate creativity, while others tend to inhibit it. Maximizing the former conditions and minimizing the latter and, thereby, unleashing human creativity, is how this anthology defines empowerment.*

Several useful recommendations for empowering people and maximizing their creativity and productivity can be found in the literature. They include, among others: (a) building trust between the leader and the people and, therefore, breaking down hierarchical thinking and related barriers; (b) allowing people to propose and try to implement new initiatives; (c) meaningfully involving people at all stages of a task and making them genuinely feel capable and important, valued and valuable, cherished and appreciated for their contributions; (d) giving people tasks that make them feel gifted and talented; (e)

---

* Empowerment carries several different meanings in management literature. "Participative management"; "participative decision making," "delegation," and "moving decision making down to the lowest level" are some of the more popular ones.

placing people, rather than the leader, in charge of solving critical business; (f) involving people in the decision-making process regarding what has to be done and in planning how to do it; (g) sharing information with people and enabling them to act as though they were the "owners of the business"; (h) enabling everyone in the organization to understand the business, to feel responsible for its success, and to know how they can contribute to that success; and (i) allowing people to try, to fail, and to learn from their mistakes (see, for example, Kouzes and Posner, 1995: 185-187, 201, 204-205; Hammer and Champy, 1993: 168; Thiss, 1995; Blanchard, Carlos, and Randolph, 1996; Harris and Moran, 2000: 109).

(d) Capacity building

Transforming people into effective and successful leaders in their own right, or building the type of relationships that encourage people to come forth and exercise their unique gifts of leadership, are perceived by many modern writers as the quintessential responsibilities and the ultimate tests of creative leadership. Strategies for achieving these ends are given considerable attention both in business and behavioral science literature. Suggested leadership development activities include:

- training and equipping people with relevant skills and attitudes that they presumably need in order to be able to influence others and direct their actions toward group or organizational goals.

- enlarging people's sphere of influence, giving them ever-larger responsibilities, and putting them in charge of things that really matter in the group or organization.

- encouraging and supporting people in their efforts to discover their unique abilities and to exercise their "latent gifts of leadership"* in areas where they seem to have the greatest potential.

Advocates of training as a strategy for developing leaders perceive leadership as a set of skills, attitudes, and knowledge that, according to them, can be taught and learned. In this view, just as people can be socialized to perform practically any other societal role, they can also be trained to influence people and get extraordinary things done in their groups or organizations. James Kouzes and Barry Posner's statement summarizes this view:

> By viewing leadership as a non-learnable [inherited] set of character traits, a self-fulfilling prophecy has been created that dooms societies to having only a few good leaders. If you assume that leadership is

---

* The phrase is M. Scott Peck's (1987: 72).

learnable, you will be surprised to discover how many good leaders there really are (Kouzes and Posner, 1987: 297).

Delegating higher responsibility as a strategy for leadership development is based on the assumption that people learn to lead by actually leading. A related assumption is that high expectations tend to produce high levels of performance, i.e., people tend to perform to the level that authority figures and significant others expect of them. Conversely, low expectations tend to produce low-level performance (see, for example, Kouzes and Posner, 1987: 295). The evidence indicates that people who are given leadership responsibilities tend to behave like leaders and, other things being equal, eventually become effective and successful in that role.

Suggestions of group-wide (or organization-wide) spread of leadership are based on the assumption that leadership is not a singular, cross-situational ability, but a multi-varied and largely situation-specific one. As already discussed, no single trait, or particular set of traits, has yet been found that, alone, defines all successful leaders. The emerging consensus is that different situations demand different leadership characteristics and, where nothing interferes, every member of a group or organization, by reason of his unique endowment and talents, can lead in something.

(v) *Team (nay, Community) building*
Many institutions and organizations tend to equate leadership with team-building – the ability to bring different individuals together and get them to work on problems or issues of common interest, drawing upon and blending their individual expertise. The "team-building" metaphor, evidently derived from sports, is increasingly popular in business and public service organizations. According to reports, some of these teams are successfully performing functions that hitherto were viewed exclusively as managerial responsibilities – hiring, discipline, resource allocation, quality assurance, performance evaluation, and more (see, for example, Blanchard, Carlos, and Randolph, 1996: 101-106; Hammer and Champy 1993: 52).

As successful as teams are reported to be in many organizations, there are suggestions that they can be more successful, more deeply satisfying to their members, and more compelling of members' commitment and allegiance if they (teams) could be transformed into "communities" – replacing ego-centeredness and win-lose thinking with relatedness and a win-win mindset; recognizing, appreciating, enhancing, and complementing members' unique capabilities; coming into communion with members/ feelings (hopes and fears, joy and grief, pleasure and pain); providing comfort and company for one another; committing themselves to collective as well as to one another's success; and, generally, trusting each member to promote the common good (see, for

205

example, Toffler, 1980: 347-352; Theobald, 1981: 74-76; Peck, 1987: 59-85, 171; Griffin, 1988a; Spretnak, 1988; Mollner, 1992; Jaccaci and Gault, 1999: 127-153). Scott Peck's comments typify this notion of community and its rewards. Describing community as "collective spirit" (intense, powerful, moving, healing, and deeply satisfying relationships in which members commit to one another and share one another's experiences) Peck writes:

> Remember that community is a state of being together in which people, instead of hiding behind their defenses, learn to lower them, in which instead of attempting to obliterate their differences, people learn not only to accept them but rejoice in them. It is not a place for "rugged" individualism. As a place for "soft" individualism, … it actually encourages pluralism. Through community … pluralism ceases to be a problem. Community is a true alchemical process that transforms the dross of our differences into golden opportunity (Peck, 1987: 171).

"Community building," as described, is a clear departure not only from the zero-sum perception of group and organizational processes, but also from the individual-excellence concept of teamwork – the mechanistic "you-do-your-job, I'll-do-mine"* mindset which assumes that if everybody does his job well, all of the pieces will fit and produce the desired result.

While no formulas have yet been found for "welding" together people with divergent interests and values, leaders who have been trying to promote community spirit in their groups and organizations attribute whatever success they have had to such things as recognition of the common humanity of people; transcending individual differences; collaborating, (rather than competing); generalized support (rather than segmental relationships); integration (rather than excessive specialization); collective success (rather than individual excellence); collegialism (rather than superiority, subordination, and control); shared, collectively-evolved vision; and, finally, an inclusive, "win-win" environment within which people practically complement one another.

---

* The phrase is Appleseed Associates' of Glen Ellyn, Illinois, USA.

Rationale for Creative Leadership

The idea of creative leadership as outlined in this synopsis and suggested by many of the selected remarks in this section derives from one fundamental assumption: the inherence of creativity and leadership potentials in human nature, coupled with the psychic necessity to actualize one's potential. This is the belief that every functioning human being has within him an innate capacity to excel (and even to lead) in some domain.

Extending the journey and pilgrims analogy, this assumption acknowledges our pilgrimage on the same journey, but also recognizes that the accuracy of our individual "maps" depends on the terrain that is being traveled. Accuracy of our individual "maps" probably also depends on the historical epoch during which the journey is undertaken and what we see as the "destination" or the goal. The assortment of talents that are said to have characterized highly successful leaders, both historical and contemporary, supports this position. The rise to fame of "no-chance" individuals – persons whose perceived attributes are not normally associated with heroism – also attests to the universal distribution of leadership potential. Cases of individuals who accomplished extraordinary things in one domain but could not repeat their success in other situations provide additional argument for the universal but domain-specific nature of "leadership."

To the extent that assumptions of universal distribution of leadership potential is valid, facilitating the leadership potential of constituents (or other members of a group) becomes a cardinal responsibility of incumbent leaders. Robert Spady and Cecil Bell, Jr. elaborate:

> The adoption of new administrative philosophy and processes by those who govern and are the administrators of public and private organizations and institutions can provide organizational members and constituents the opportunity to participate viably and contribute their "leadership" to the planning processes affecting them. Such participation holds the key to the release of a fabulous amount of human creativity and energy, for "leadership," [sic] like creativity, is a quality that infuses all people from the highest to the lowest in an organization, and from the lower to the younger in a society – it is not a quality reserved only for the titular heads of organizations and society (Spady and Bell, Jr., 1997: 126-127).

Facilitating the leadership potential of one's constituents, as paradoxical as it seems, is a responsibility with an all-win outcome – first, to the leader; second, to constituents; and third, to an organization. Here are a few pragmatic considerations:

Events of the past few decades suggest that it is in the (enlightened) self-interest of every modern leader to make as many more leaders as he can by: (a) recognizing the unique capabilities of his constituents or subordinates; (b) giving them challenges that nourish and strengthen their individual competencies; and (c) spreading responsibility and engaging the pool of talents available. The experience of highly successful leaders indicates that getting more people to work on a task, problem, or issue almost always produces better results. Better group or organizational results, of course, nearly always translate into one's effectiveness, success, or even greatness as a leader.

Shared responsibility, reduced work-load for the leader, and better results are just three of the many pragmatic reasons for producing more leaders, rather than more followers. Other reasons have to do with the growing demand for identity and personal fulfillment. Reference here is to (a) the large and growing number of people who no longer accept being treated as a statistic, but want to be recognized as individuals with "something to say" who can contribute to their groups and organizations; (b) increasing disenchantment with autocratic organizations that people perceive as not making adequate use of their talents and, therefore, as diminishing them as human beings; and (c) increasingly strident protests of marginalization and, in particular, the growing agitation by women, minorities, and employees for recognition and inclusion in the decision-making process.

The second consideration in "making followers into leaders" has to do with the emotional (psychological) well-being of the people concerned. There is a growing realization that members of a group or organization are not just physical entities ("flesh and blood"), but emotional and spiritual beings as well, and that all aspects of their lives need to be given expression for the individual to be maximally productive and to feel fulfilled. The growing popularity of "new age" and "human potential" movements, with their emphasis on "integration," "spirituality," and "harmonious balance" illustrate the significance of this need. Additional support for the potency of emotional and spiritual needs are (a) the growing popularity of intangible, nonmaterial rewards in formal organizations; (b) the reported success of corporations that claim to be managing their employees as whole persons, providing their material as well as their emotional and spiritual needs; and (c) reported feelings of emptiness by some ostensibly successful individuals and their self-confessed search for something that their material success has not been able to provide them.

The third and final consideration in "making followers into leaders" is the survival and/or success of an organization. Contrary to the messianic notion of leadership of earlier times, it is becoming increasingly clear that leaders and other members of a group or organization are inextricably linked by the goals they are pursuing. Alternatively referred to as "interwoven destiny," this is the realization that in most modern leadership situations (group, institution, organization, community, national society, or international relations), neither the leader nor the other members can hope to succeed unless all of the parties in the relationship succeed. More than ever before, it is becoming increasingly obvious that the common interest – be it productivity, profit, community spirit, social order, or whatever – is best served through the cooperation and mutual support of all concerned.

Leaders, everywhere, desire and cherish loyal group members, productive and committed employees, good and responsible citizens. In the past, these "behaviors" could be taken for granted. It is not so any more. For reasons that are reviewed in several places in this work, the amount of loyalty, productivity, commitment, and responsibility that today's leaders can expect increasingly depends on the extent to which people perceive the (leadership) situation and/or relationship as fostering their talents and enhancing them as people of worth. As indicated earlier, people increasingly want to participate in the decisions affecting their lives and their future, and they tend to commit themselves more to actions that they themselves have helped to plan than to programs that are handed down to them. K. F. Jackson (1975) summarizes this emerging trend:

> Most people like to feel that they are well in command of their circumstances and are able to make their own decisions. They do not like to feel that they have to submit to other people's will. They are much more likely to be prepared to commit themselves to a course of action which they themselves have planned or decided upon, than one planned or decided upon by others. That is why it is so valuable

to arrange for all concerned to participate as much as possible in decision-making and problem-solving (Jackson, 1975: 214).

Evidence of a growing sense of personal worth and the desire to assert oneself can be found almost everywhere, from family relations to international diplomacy. Practical illustrations, even if isolated, are the incidents with which we began this introductory synopsis: the four-year-old girl who tells her six-year-old brother that she does not have to do everything he tells her to do; the class of political science students that reminds its teacher that he had forgotten to consult them beforehand about an upcoming examination; the subordinate who wants his boss to treat him with respect; leaders of a group of minority tribes who remind their counterparts from the ruling majority tribes that they too have a right to rule their country; an under-privileged population that seemingly prefers death to perpetual servitude; and protesters in an impoverished, war-torn nation who resent their "Big-Brother's" apparent encroachment and arrogance.

Conclusion

It is an irony of modern times that at the same time that many groups, organizations, communities, and even national societies are pining for strong and effective leadership, many incumbent leaders are complaining of declining loyalty on the part of the public.

Analysis of some leadership situations, however, suggests that what is sometimes perceived of as a "lack of strong and effective leadership" might be due in part to the tendency to rely on a few "gifted and talented" individuals (e.g., chief executive officers, the political leadership, traditional rulers, or the rich and famous) to plan for the rest of the population, to find a solution to every conceivable problem and, metaphorically, to be everything for everybody. Even as local and global problems are increasing both in number and complexity, even as incumbent leaders' wit is being stretched to its apparent limits, many people still continue to look to designated leaders for answers.

One obvious result of excessive dependence on a few individuals for leadership is the much-talked-about "decision overload," with its attendant delays, and the increasing difficulty of getting things done. Known variously as "devolution" in political literature, "empowerment" in management literature, "grassroots participation" in development literature, and "strengthening others and turning them into leaders themselves" in creativity literature, a way out of the decision-overload problem might be to redistribute the decision-making responsibility, so that more people at more levels can contribute their information, their perspectives, and their unique capabilities to the enterprise.

If, as is generally believed, people are primarily driven by the need to actualize their potential, then what many incumbent leaders sometimes perceive as "declining loyalty" may actually be a subtle rejection of an arrangement and a relationship that people perceive as inhibiting their talents and stunting their growth as human beings. If, indeed, that is the case, then those parents who are experiencing increasing "defiance" by their children, those teachers who are encountering increasing "student confrontation," those corporate executives who are finding it difficult to achieve set targets because of "declining employee commitment," and those political leaders who are facing "declining loyalty" might wish to do some personal stocktaking – to assess the extent to which their leadership practices are providing for people's material, emotional, and spiritual needs and also maximizing their creativity. Any one of the following questions could serve as guide:

- To what extent do the visions that I communicate and the values that I exude accommodate the self-interests of the people for whom I am responsible and therefore inspire their willing allegiance?

- To what extent do the goals that I am promoting enable people to find and to do the things that really matter to them and that therefore give meaning to their lives?

- To what extent do my policies, actions, and interactions with people enhance their sense of worth or help them to strengthen and be able to express the qualities that they really value and like about themselves?

- To what extent does the exercise of my leadership abilities help others to recognize and actualize more of their own?

- Generally, to what extent do my actions and behavior as leader improve the ability of my constituents and those for whom I am responsible to do the work for which they are specially equipped, to find purpose and fulfillment in their lives and, therefore, to be happy with themselves and grateful for my being their leader?

Finally, to the extent that the current wave of self-assertion, self-determination, and seeming rebellion represents a rejection of institutionalized arrangements that people perceive as diminishing them or inhibiting their natural abilities, it is unlikely that genuine commitment to a group or organization will be achieved by coercion, behavior modification (reward or punishment), manipulation, or diplomacy. What is more likely to induce people's loyalty as followers, productivity as employees, responsibility as citizens, and humaneness toward one another are values, principles, behaviors, and actions that enhance them as human beings and that also foster their own natural ability to lead.

Selected Insights
on
Creative Leadership

The best indication of the quality of leadership is not what happens when you are in "control," but what happens when you are gone.

— (Anonymous).

One of the tests of leadership is the ability to recognize a problem before it is an emergency.

— (Anonymous).

Each of us has within us the capacity to lead.

— David Aronovici (1995: 317).

It is both an irony and a paradox that precisely at the time when trust and credibility in leaders are lowest, when people are angry as well as cynical, when we in leadership positions feel inhibited from exercising what power we have ... this is precisely the time when the nation most needs people who can lead and who can transcend that vacuum.

— Warren Bennis (1976: 134).

What I think most people in institutions really want ... is affection, acceptance, a belief in their growth, and esteem.

— Warren Bennis (1976: 99).

The process of becoming a leader is much the same as becoming an integrated human being.
— Warren Bennis (1992: 210).

[A]n *essential* factor in leadership is the capacity to influence and *organize meaning* for the members of the organization.
— Warren Bennis and Burt Nanus (1987: 484).

If people in authority are to succeed, they must know themselves and listen to themselves, integrating their ideals and actions ...
— Warren Bennis (1989: 156).

The hero reveals the possibilities of human nature; the celebrity reveals the possibilities of the media.
— Daniel J. Boorstin (1995: 193).

The ability to participate in a challenge and to make it a shared challenge is an incredible task for a leader.
— Patricia M. Carrigan (1987: 29).

The great and decisive test of genius is [sic] that it calls forth *power* in the souls of others. It not merely gives knowledge, but breathes energy.
— William Ellery Channing (1987: 4).

There is a great man who makes every man feel small. But the real great man is the man who makes every man feel great.
— Gilbert Keith Chesterton (1992: 178).

He who requires much from himself and little from others will be secure.
— Confucius (1991: 161).

To get the best out of a man go to what is best in him.
— Daniel Considine (1991: 63).

True greatness is often unrecognized. That is sure.
— Russell H. Conwell (1915: 44).

If people sense that we are "talking down" to them or that our motive is to manipulate them into making a change, they will resist our efforts.
— Stephen R. Covey (1992: 222).

A great man is always willing to be little.
— Ralph Waldo Emerson (1993: 150).

Our chief want in life is somebody who shall make us do what we can.
— Ralph Waldo Emerson (1991: 63).

Why is it that in spite of the good intentions of leaders and citizens of every country for hundreds of years the world continues to be burdened with suffering?

— Jack Forem (1974: 221)

Our age demands more decisive, dynamic action, coming from a higher level of consciousness, a deeper insight, a clearer mind and a purer heart. We must have more intelligent, creative leadership and action that is all life-supporting, if we are to have a really *new* world, not just a replay of the same old songs.

— Jack Forem (1974: 227).

Men who lack humility (or have lost it) cannot come to the people, cannot be their partners in naming the world. Someone who cannot acknowledge himself to be as mortal as everyone else still has a long way to go before he can reach the point of encounter. At the point of encounter there are neither utter ignoramuses nor perfect sages; there are only men who are attempting, together, to learn more than they now know.

— Paulo Freire (1972: 79).

[D]ialogue cannot exist without humility. The naming of the world, through which men constantly re-create the world, cannot be an act of arrogance. ... How can I dialogue if I consider myself a member of the in-group of "pure" men, the owners of truth and knowledge, for whom all non-members are "these people" or the "great unwashed"? How can I dialogue if I start from the premise that naming the world is the task of an elite and that the presence of the people in history is a sign of deterioration, thus to be avoided? How can I dialogue if I am closed to – and even offended by – the contribution of others? How can I dialogue if I am afraid of being displaced ...?

— Paulo Freire (1972: 78-79).

Leaders who do not act dialogically, but insist on imposing their decisions, do not organize the people – they manipulate them. They do not liberate, nor are they [themselves] liberated: they oppress.

— Paulo Freire (1972: 179).

When one element in a pluralistic system becomes very powerful in relation to the others, the pluralism of the system itself is in danger.

— John W. Gardner (1964: 88).

Very few of our most prominent people take a really large view of the leadership assignment. Most of them are simply tending the machinery of that part of society to which they belong ... They may tend it very well indeed, but they are not pursuing a vision of what the total society needs. They have not developed a strategy as to how it can be achieved, and they are not moving to accomplish it.

— John W. Gardner (1968: 126-127).

[W]e must invent ways in which local leaders in and out of government can work together to formulate community policies and purposes.

— John W. Gardner (1999: 45).

I don't believe in just ordering people to do things. You have to sort of grab an oar and row with them.

— Harold S. Geneen (1991: 105).

The ability to recognize a problem before it becomes an emergency.

— Arnold H. Glasow (1991: 105).

Leadership is more than just having individuals reaching goals, it's having them reach their fullest potential.
— Otis N. Glover (attributed).

It would ... be sensible to promote the social conditions in which public opinion and full public participation in decision-making become as far as possible the means whereby communities are ordered.
— Edward Goldsmith et al. (19974: 38)

Leadership in community is more than a person. ... When the time, situaiton, or need is right, anyone can take up the staff of leadership.
— Kazimierz Goozdz (1993: 216).

A good leader takes a little more than his share of the blame, a little less than his share of the credit.
— Samuel I. Gravely (1994: May 6).

[T]he great leader is seen as servant first, and that simple fact is the key to his greatness.
— Robert K. Greenleaf (1997: 429).

The post-heroic leader lives vicariously, getting kicks out of other people's successes – as old-fashioned teachers have always done.
— Charles Handy (1989: 166).

No really great man ever thought himself so.
— William Hazlitt (1991: 81).

How do we pull the best out of ourselves and others – and help put the best into practice?
— Shad Helmstetter (1982: 187).

Leadership which taps the creativity of those who are at the center of the project ... will always do better than leadership that uses its authority.
— Harold Howe, II (1996: 229).

Respect a man, he will do the more.
— James Howell (1991: 64).

Leadership in today's world requires far more than a large stock of gunboats and a hard fist at the conference table.
— Hubert H. Humphrey (1993: 511).

Most people like to feel that they are well in command of their circumstances and are able to make their own decisions. They do not like to feel that they have to submit to other people's will. They are much more likely to be prepared to commit themselves to a course of action which they themselves have planned or decided upon, than one planned or decided upon by others. That is why it is so valuable to arrange for all concerned to participate as much as possible in decision-making and problem-solving.
— K. F. Jackson (1975: 214).

Changing things is central to leadership, and changing them before anyone else is creativeness.

— Antony Jay (1980: 66).

Instead of continuing to think that they can run the organization from the top, effective leaders will be those who know how to take advantage of the [creative] capacity of those below.

— Rosabeth Moss Kanter (1983: 363).

[W]hen the leader is the sole creator of the organization vision, the members' own ability to envision the future atrophies, and they grow ever more dependent on that leader.

— Charles F. Kiefer (1992: 179).

In a metanoic organization, each person's vision for the organization can be as vital as any other's, because it is in the differences of these visions as well as their similarities that the underlying purpose of the organization is clarified. Since each person's contribution is vital to that clarity, each person participates in the leadership of the organization, whether or not they occupy formal leadership roles.

— Charles F. Kiefer (1992: 180).

How can we really change the thinking of the world unless we change our own thinking first?

— Elizabeth Duncan Koontz (1975: 85).

Leadership is the process of moving people in some direction mostly through noncoercive means.

— John P. Kotter 1990: 218-219).

The true force that attracts others is the force of the heart.
— J. M. Kouzes and B. Z. Posner (1987: 125).

To take the determinist's view that only some of us have [leadership qualities] and others do not is to settle for less than we can become.
— James M. Kouzes and Barry Z. Posner (1987: 297).

There is no one way to lead, nor is there one and only one leadership personality.
— James M. Kouzes and Barry Z. Posner (1987: 294).

You cannot lead others until you have first led yourself through a struggle with opposing values.
— James M. Kouzes and Barry Z. Posner (1987: 301).

Empowering others is essentially the process of turning followers into leaders themselves.
— James M. Kouzes and Barry Z. Posner (1987: 179).

[W]e become the most powerful when we give our own power away.
— James M. Kouzes and Barry Z. Posner (1995: 185).

To strengthen others, leaders place their constituents, not themselves, at the center of solving critical problems and contributing to key goals.
— James M. Kouzes and Barry Z. Posner (1995: 197).

[T]he truest measure of what leaders deeply believe is how they spend their time. Constituents look to see this measure and use it to judge whether a leader measures up to espoused standards.
— James M. Kouzes and Barry Z. Posner (1995: 222).

Unleashing people power is the key to organizational creativity, whether for a company or for a country. Enlightened leadership should do whatever it can to enhance people as individuals.
— Robert Lawrence Kuhn (1993: 393).

The bad leader is he who the people despise. The good leader is he who the people praise. The great leader is he who the people say, "We did it ourselves."
— Lao-tzu (attributed).

The leader knows that constant interventions will block the group's process.
— Lao-tsu (1991: 106).

Instead of trying to overcome resistance to what people are not ready to do, find out what they are ready to do.
— (Anonymous; See Charles Robert Lightfoot, 1991: 1200).

Globally thinking persons give up looking to leaders and larger-than-life heroes to take matters into hand; they recognize their own role in the evolutionary transition.

— Ervin Laszlo (1994: 123).

There is nothing more difficult to take in hand, more perilous to conduct, or more uncertain in its success, than to take the lead in the introduction of a new order of things.

— Niccolo Machiavelli (1976: 228).

[I]f you wish to have influence on other people, you must be a person who had a really stimulating and furthering influence on other people.

— Karl Marx (1955: 121).

The most important quality in a leader is that of being acknowledged as such.

— André Maurois (1993: 511).

[L]eadership should be regarded as a relationship among various persons in a given setting, rather than as a particular set of characteristics of the isolated individual.

— J. W. McLean and William Weitzel (1991: 54).

Leadership begins with greater self-knowledge.

— J. W. McLean and William Weitzel (1991: 65).

In the guerrilla wars we all encounter in the battle of life, there are times when everyone must lead. Leadership, then, is the product of a relationship that provides sufficient support for one (and more!) in the relationship to attempt to affect how the group will accomplish its desired goals.
— J. W. McLean and William Weitzel (1991: 184).

[An important] step in attempting to utilize the potential you have for leadership is to expect to take and then relinquish leadership depending upon the situation and the needs of those in the relationship.
— J. W. McLean and William Weitzel 1991: 184).

The real leader has no need to lead — he is content to point the way.
— Henry Miller (1993: 512).

Let those of us who are to teach and lead the others learn how to be good ourselves, so that we can properly teach the others.
— Ashley Montagu (1962: 158).

The new leader is a facilitator, not an order giver.
— John Naisbitt (1982: 188).

The dominant principle of organization has shifted, from management in order to control an enterprise to leadership in order to bring out the best in people and to respond quickly to change.
— John Naisbitt and Patricia Aburdene (1990: 218).

A [creative] leader is an individual who builds followership by ... creating an environment where the unique potential of the individual can be actualized.
— John Naisbitt and Patricia Aburdene (1990: 308).

[I]t is the leader's job to invent – or stimulate others to invent – a range of alternative visions from which the most desirable can be chosen.
— Burt Nanus (1992: 80).

We have a lot of managers — short-term, control-oriented, report-oriented ... Leaders think longer term, grasp the relationship of larger realities, think in terms of renewal, have political skills, cause change, affirm values, achieve unity.
— Russell E. Palmer (1990: 219).

[A] community is a group of all leaders.
— M. Scott Peck (1987: 72).

The role of current leadership will be to develop leadership in all their people.
— Gifford and Elizabeth Pinchot (1993: 216).

The challenge in intelligent organization is to establish strong and effective community so that everyone contributes leadership.
— Gifford and Elizabeth Pinchot (1993: 217).

Our job as leaders and members of any organization or community is to create an environment that brings out the best, not the worst, of what it is to be human.
— Gifford and Elizabeth Pinchot (1993: 246).

Submission destroys initiative, creativity, self-esteem, and judgment and increases dependency and apathy.
— Gifford and Elizabeth Pinchot (1993: 245).

People ask the difference between a leader and a boss ... The leader leads, and the boss drives.
— Theodore Roosevelt (1993: 512).

Learning to lead starts with getting to know yourself. You must first dig deep and get your own house in order before you can lead others.
— Robert H. Rosen (1997: 304).

[We should] look at each individual as unique, continuously developing and having the possibility of making an increasing value-adding contribution. Our challenge is to collaborate with people as a leader to discover, develop, and match that uniqueness to the contributions that are needed by the business.

— Carol Sanford (1992: 204).

In a learning organization, leaders are designers, stewards, and teachers. They are responsible for *building organizations* where people continually expand their capabilities to understand complexity, clarify vision, and improve shared mental models — that is, they are responsible for learning.

— Peter M. Senge (1990: 340).

You need to engage in quality deeds, not just quality words.

— Daniel T. Seymour (1993: 57).

A unifying, guiding, and distinctive vision is the foundation on which a "house of quality" is built.

— Daniel T. Seymour (1993: 60).

If we want people to collaborate in our ... societies ... and to participate vitally in their institutions, then we must recognize that the quality of "leadership" is not something reserved exclusively for the titular heads of organizations. It is, in reality, a universal human quality that infuses all people from the highest to the lowest "rank" in every organization.
— Richard J. Spady and Cecil H. Bell, Jr. (1999: 45-46).

[A]pathy among people may be less a function of people's attitude and more a function of leadership style.
— Richard J. Spady and Cecil H. Bell, Jr. (1999: 125).

If people believe that a telephone they have is not working properly – and that no one could hear at the other end – no one will take the time and energy to talk into it. The same is true if people believe that their leaders (church, school, political, community) do not want to hear and listen – in fact, are not even interested...
— Richard J. Spady and Cecil H. Bell, Jr. (1999: 124).

Dictators and authoritarian leaders cannot prevail. Time itself will see them fall due to the liberating energies of [current] trends toward freedom.
— Richard J. Spady and Cecil H. Bell, Jr. (1999: 168).

Many believe that authoritarianism provides the strongest "leadership," but that is not the case.
— Richard J. Spady and Cecil H. Bell, Jr. (1999: 167).

A leader cannot raise a people's self-esteem by placing himself above them.

— Gloria Steinem (1992: 53).

[A] lack of core self-esteem can produce totalitarian leaders for whom no amount of power is enough, grandiose money-makers or spenders of inherited money for whom no amount of display is enough, and authoritarian parents for whom no obedience is complete.

— Gloria Steinem (1992: 67).

You can accomplish by kindness what you cannot do by force.

— Publilius Syrus (1991: 64).

[W]e have to help everybody find a community in which they can be personally effective.

— Robert Theobald (1981: 75).

Our present forms of leadership are ... profoundly inappropriate.

— Robert Theobald (1981: 140).

We ... could not expect any individual or small group of individuals to manage our society for us. Instead, ... the majority of the population must feel able to make decisions for themselves ...

— Robert Theobald (1981: 140).

Our society makes a profound distinction between people who have the capacity to make decisions for others and those who have not. ... One of our most urgent tasks is to convince people that the chaos is real and that *nobody* is in effective charge of our world.

— Robert Theobald (1981: 83-84).

Leadership mobilizes the spirit of people. Its essence is spiritual.

— Tom Thiss (1995: 125).

Managers mobilize material resources. In doing so, they materialize the organization. They monitor the quantitative side of business. Leaders, as opposed to mere managers, mobilize spirit. As such, they spiritualize an organization. Their realm is the qualitative side of business. ... If you do not attend to the qualities of the human spirit, the qualities of your products and services will suffer.

— Tom Thiss (1995: 131).

[Y]ou cannot "teach" or "bestow" leadership qualities on someone, any more than you can give them freedom. What you can do is create situations in which people recognize and express their own abilities and in which they are free to act. In short, you can elicit these qualities only by creating a world in which they are relevant.

— John W. Thompson (1992: 219-220).

[A]t its foundation, true leadership is the authentic outward expression of the inner character of an individual. ... It is not what visionary leaders do that makes them extraordinary; it is who they are as human beings.
— John W. Thompson (1992: 221).

Correction does much, but encouragement does more.
— Johann Wolfgang von Goethe (1991: 64).

Leaders who are insecure about their own identity and self-worth create institutional settings that deprive other people of their identities. They tend to perceive the universe as essentially hostile and life as competitive battleground. They believe and act as though ultimate responsibility for everything rests with them.
— Diana Chapman Walsh (1997: 296).

VII
Creativity, Personality, Community, and Human Progress

Learning to live together is not simply a moral imperative; it is our only chance of survival.

— Federico Mayor

"Inward Improvement"

The story * is told of a certain clergyman who, one morning, ran amok in his town's main market. Like a bull in a china shop, he overturned the fruit and vegetable stalls, shouting hoarsely as he rampaged. A large crowd gathered, dismayed by the clergyman's unseemly behavior. In accordance with the town's justice system, the rioter was apprehended and promptly summoned to the Emir's court to explain his actions. Before stating his case, the clergyman requested that all of the town's doctors of law, chief courtiers, senior administrators, commanders of the army, and important businessmen be summoned to hear him. He was obliged. To everybody's surprise, the clergyman offered no apologies. Rather, he used the incident to teach an important lesson: the presence of potentially destructive tendencies in people. According to the clergyman, every day, every hour, in every man and woman, there are thoughts and inadequacies which, if given expression, would result in actions as damaging to the individual and the community as his rampage in the marketplace. The Emir, apparently acknowledging the validity of this assertion, asked him for a solution to the problem. "The solution," said the clergyman, "is to realize that people must be *improved inwardly*, not just prevented by custom from showing their coarseness and destructiveness, and applauded if they do not" (emphasis added). The court was so pleased with the clergyman's teaching that it called a three-day public holiday to celebrate the new wisdom.

---

* Paraphrased from Idries Shah (1971: 132-133).

233

The point of this story is that human beings are endowed with enormous potentialities (i.e., creativity, talents) that can be put to good and constructive ends, or to bad and destructive ones. As Dan Millman observes:

> We create in constructive ways,
> or we create in destructive ways;
> either way, creative energy finds expression.
> (Millman, 1993: 330)

Whether or not people use their creative abilities to build or to destroy, to repair or to damage themselves and/or their societies, probably depends on a combination of factors, including: (a) the extent to which that ability is recognized, valued, and nurtured; (b) the moral values by which people live, or to which they commit their energies; and (c) the types of opportunities and avenues that are available for people to express their talents.

Recognizing, valuing, and developing one's natural potentialities is what is meant in the allegory by "inward improvement." At this stage of human development and with so many life-threatening, man-made problems facing the world, the question is no longer: Can people improve inwardly? Rather, the issue is: How can we persuade, encourage, and support people to improve inwardly – to recognize that it is in their own best interest to think, feel, and act in ways that benefit not only themselves but also their society and the rest of nature? That is the focus of this introductory overview and the theme of the remarks selected for this section.

Linkages

The points of departure for this introductory overview include Viktor Frankl's "man's search for meaning"; Erich Fromm's "well-being"; Carl Rogers' "fully functioning individual"; Abraham Maslow's "self-actualization"; John Gardner's "personal fulfillment within a framework of [shared] moral purpose"; Ervin Laszlo's "interexistence"; Ernesto Cortes' "interwoven destiny"; the United Nation's Commission on Environment and Development's "our common future"; Alvin Toffler's "practopian future"; Robert Theobald's "new society"; Sidney Parnes' "high-level wellness"; Howard Gardner's "multiple intelligences"; and August Jaccaci and Susan Gault's "planetary community of all life." These and related notions suggest probable linkages among human creativity, personality, community, and social progress. To summarize:

- Human *creativity*, perceived as the ability to discover, develop, and express one's unique talents in things that one perceives as important and as providing benefits to oneself and one's society, is believed to be the foundation of a healthy, self-actualizing personality.

- Healthy, self-actualizing *personality*, perceived as a way of thinking, feeling, and acting that expresses one's natural abilities and that also recognizes the necessity and the right of other people to fulfill their own potential, is regarded as the critical "building block" for genuine and viable community.

- Genuine *community*, perceived as the relatedness and interdependence of all life and a framework for human beings to develop and express their unique abilities and to complement one another in mutually beneficial actions, is regarded as the basis of human progress.

- *Human progress* is defined as an increasingly more fulfilling, more satisfying, more humane, and more collaborative pattern of existence in which all members of society are able to realize their potential and to contribute to mutually and environmentally beneficial ends.

Human Creativity

Sections I, II, and III suggested that contrary to conventional wisdom, creativity is a universal, species-wide human attribute, rather than a mysterious ability of a select few supernaturally endowed individuals. Also, contrary to the conventional wisdom, it was suggested that the realization of one's creative potential – its discovery, nurture, and expression in socially and environmentally important and worthy ways (rather than power, possession, or material success) – is the basis of a healthy, productive, and responsible personality.

Support for these two assertions derives from several influential notions, including: Aristotle's *entelechy* – "natural principle," "inner necessity," and "the center and what is highest in man" (see, for ex-

235

ample, Davidson, 1974: 197-201; Bloom 1987: 176); Ralph Waldo Emerson's "the God within," "innate divinity," "untapped psychic potential," "the ground of [our] being," "inner essence," "the center of meaning," "the self's divine potential" (see Steele, 1987: 2, 37, 134); Kierkegaard's the right to be that self which one truly is (see Rogers, 1961: 110, 166); Abraham Maslow's the "heart," the "soul," and the "essential core of the person," the "innermost core" of our being (1968: 190, 191, 196, 197); Elizabeth O'Connor's "buried longings of our lives that are always urging to be satisfied" (1971: 14); Paulo Freire's the right to "speak [one's] word," to "name the world" as one sees it (1972: 32, 76, 77); Willis Harman and John Hormann's "the vast potential that our humanity gives us as a birthright" (1990: 85); Morris Stein's "the God-given right to achieve success in this world and the God-wherewithal to do so" (1992: 86); Howard Gardner's "multiple intelligences" (1993); Guiford Pinchot and Elizabeth Pinchot's "the best of what it is to be human" (1993: 246, 247); Taylor and Crain's "energy [that is always seeking] unblocked channels in which to flow" (1994: November 5); Charles Swindoll's "inner compulsion to be all that one ought to be" (1995: 499); Mihaly Csikszentmihalyi's "the central source of meaning in our lives" (1996: 1); Sidney Parnes' "the magic of your mind (1997); and Jaccaci and Gault's "evolutionary best [that is] in all of us" (1999: xvii).

All of these descriptions of human creativity point to six facts: (a) its *naturalness* – intrinsic nature of the human species and embedded in the human psyche; (b) its *universality* – widely distributed throughout the human population; (c) its *uniqueness* – personal abilities, talents, and gifts, expressive of one's peculiar way of perceiving, thinking, and acting; (d) its *compulsion* – irresistible "life-force" within every individual that is constantly "urging" to grow and to become, to develop and to express; (e) its *ubiquity* – expressible in every domain of human activity; and (f) its *centrality* – influencing every aspect of our life, and essential for personal growth and development and for one's psychological well-being.

The parts of these ideas that are of particular relevance to this section of the anthology are (a) the view of creativity as a multiplicity of abilities that characterize the human species; (b) the natural urge of every ability to be developed and expressed; and (c) the necessity of realizing one's creative potential for one's emotional and spiritual well-being.

The next subsection discusses probable relationships between creativity and human personality indicating, in particular, probable ways in which recognition, development, and use of one's talents affect one's thoughts, feelings, and actions – in short, one's personality.

Personality

Psychologists and sociologists define human personality as the unique and enduring pattern of thinking, feeling, and action that characterizes an individual in his relationship and interaction with other human beings. The thinking element of personality includes beliefs, perceptions, memory, and other mental processes by which the individual acquires, manipulates, stores, recalls, and uses knowledge. Feelings are the emotions, such as love, hate, anger, fear, anxiety, pride, attitudes, and more. Action consists of the overt behavior of the individual.

Psychologists further tell us that some personality attributes are inherited – that they are an integral part of a person's genetic makeup. Other behavioral characteristics, they also suggest, are the product of the sociocultural environment in which the individual lives.

Inheritance, alternatively referred to as "nature," "heredity," "trait," "proclivity," "intelligences," or "innate potentialities," is the set of inborn abilities that characterize an individual and, presumably, predispose him to certain things and certain ways of doing things. The same abilities probably account for the individual's unique way of seeing the world (perspective), his peculiar interpretation of events and phenomena, as well as his interests, goals, tendencies, and preferences.

Environment, alternatively referred to as "nurture," "learning," "socialization," or "acculturation," is the economic, social, cultural, political, intellectual, and technological conditions in which the individual lives. Psychologists and sociologists ascribe three roles to environment in personality formation. First, it determines which abilities (out of the total range of an individual's talents) are socially beneficial, and then it selects and develops those potentialities. Second, in selectively recognizing and developing certain abilities, environment inadvertently decides which of an individual's talents are not valuable, and thus

237

discourages or actively blocks their development. Third, most social environments are believed to be ignorant of certain human potentialities and, therefore, tend to neglect them (see, for example, Gardner, 1961: 65-90, 101; Tart 1974: 105, 106, 170; Gardner, 1993: 183, 236).

The relative importance of inheritance and environment in human personality formation has intrigued sociologists and psychologists for generations. At various times, human personality has been perceived as the product of one or the other factor. Inheritance theorists emphasize the role of genetic traits and attribute human behavior to the hereditary predisposition to think, feel, or act in a certain way. The environment viewpoint locates the source of behavior in cultural factors outside of the individual, such as previous experience, anticipated reward, or fear of punishment. In this view, regardless of genetic inheritance, any individual could be "molded" into the type of person that society wants him to become.

The fallacy of both theoretical positions and the futility of the so-called "nature versus nurture" controversy have since been recognized. Current thinking holds that human personality is neither biologically pre-programmed, as inheritance theorists postulate, nor a pattern of learned responses to rewards and punishment, as some environment viewpoints maintain. Most theorists today perceive personality as a product of the dynamic interaction between biology and culture, between one's genetic endowment and one's socioeconomic, sociocultural, and sociopolitical circumstances – between genetic inheritance and the social environment.

Humanistic psychologists suggest that human potentials, by their very nature, ceaselessly press to be developed and expressed in their carriers' daily activities. In reality, however, not all potentials are ever realized. Many are never recognized at all. Others are neglected as unimportant. Still others are deemed dangerous and are actively repressed. In the final analysis, only the presumably valuable or socially beneficial few abilities get developed or partially developed. The vast majority simply die, become dormant, or atrophy from nonrecognition and persistent neglect (see, for example, Maslow, 1968; Gardner, 1988; 1993).

Persons who are able to realize a significant portion of their potential are described as "wholesome," "fully functioning," and "healthy" personalities. Theoretically, they are more likely to contribute positively to their society and their employers and more likely to enjoy high degrees of mental and physical health than those who are not able to actualize their own talents. Humanistic psychologists suggest that undiscovered, blocked, or neglected human potentials don't always atrophy without resistance, but frequently create pent-up energy that, at times, "erupts," giving rise to a number of psychological and social problems. According to Abraham Maslow (1968, already referenced), persons who are unable to develop and express their talents constructively or who feel their creativity blocked, repressed, or frustrated, tend to become angry and perhaps dangerous. Their unused capacities, the humanistic psychologist maintains, frequently become "disease centers," giving rise to such problems as anxiety, depression, hatred, criminality, violence, substance abuse, a sense of meaninglessness or uselessness, feelings of incompleteness, self-rejection, and other psychological and antisocial behaviors (see, also, Fromm, 1955; Rogers, 1961; Moustakas, 1967; Pearson, 1991; Millman 1993).

This is to say that the personalities (i.e., beliefs, assumptions, attitudes, emotions, values, and behaviors) that individuals bring to their relationships with fellow human beings and to their interaction with the natural environment are, by and large, the product of selectively recognized, selectively developed, and selectively utilized creative potentialities. The next subsection examines the implications of this selective process for community building.

Community

In *Beyond Despair: A Policy Guide to the Communications Era,* Robert Theobald (1981: 146) suggests that the human species today is suffering from "amondie," a condition which he defines as lack of a world in which men and women can live and function effectively, creatively, humanely, and in accordance with their natural abilities. Theobald's observation corroborates those of many others, including Abraham Maslow's, John Gardner's, Erich Fromm's, and Emilé Durkheim's. Abraham Maslow, for example, suggests that the "ultimate disease of our time is valuelessness, rootlessness, emptiness, and the lack of something to believe in and to be devoted to" (Maslow, 1970: 82). Writing in the same vein, John W. Gardner characterizes some of the major psychological problems of modern times as "feelings of alienation, anonymity, loss of identity, an oppressive sense of the impersonality of the society, loss of any sense of participation or of any social context in which participation would have meaning" (Gardner 1968: 146-147). Erich Fromm, reviewing and synthesizing the thoughts of some earlier social critics, identifies "spiritual poverty," "alienation," and "the domination of man by things" as the illness of contemporary society. Like some of his predecessors, Fromm fears "the advent of the age of barbarism" and the "destruction of all civilization," which he believes can be averted if a "unifying spiritual principle underlying all reality assumed more developed expression" (Fromm, 1955: 185, 187, 307, 315).

Concern with a declining sense of relatedness and growing individualism goes at least as far back as Emilé Durkheim at the turn of the century. The French sociologist is widely regarded as the first person in modern times to have called attention to increasing detachment among people – a lack of significant attachment to cohesive groups, the tendency to pursue one's private interests without regard to the interest of others, breakdown of social controls, and spreading deviance. Durkheim characterized the phenomenon as *anomie* – a condition which he defines as personal and social confusion resulting from weak or conflicting norms of behavior and lack of effective guidelines for conduct. Perceiving the condition as a threat to social organization, Durkheim feared it could eventually lead to the disintegration of society (see, for example, Fromm, 1955: 191).

Different social analysts attribute what they see as a declining sense of community and relatedness to different factors. Some see it as a by-product of industrialization, the accompanying fragmentation of work, and the tendency to focus so much on one's specialization that one tends to ignore the contributions of others. Others attribute the phenomenon to urbanization and the growing sense of anonymity and independence with which city life has come to be associated. Mihaly Csikszentmihalyi, for example, attributes a declining sense of community and "increasing psychological isolation" to the enormous advances in geographical mobility brought about by cars, trains, and other self-propelled vehicles (Csikszentmihalyi, 1996: 318). Max Weber (1958) and some sociologists blame bureaucracy and the attendant "impersonality of the society" for the problem.

240

Every side has a point. What these writers sometimes seem to overlook, however, is the *personality* (i.e., beliefs, assumptions, attitudes, emotions, values, and behaviors) that individuals bring to their relationships with fellow human beings, as mediated, of course, by industrialization, urbanization, bureaucracy, and many other intrapersonal and extra-social factors. Personality, in this sense, is the extent to which the individual recognizes and accepts his unique abilities and feels accepted, valued, and respected by others.

To the extent that the notions of "self-actualization" and "healthy personality" are valid, only people who are able to develop and constructively engage their natural abilities, who recognize and accept their personal worth, and who feel accepted, valued, and respected by others can build genuine community. Conversely, to the extent that the notion of "psychic deprivation" is valid, we are unlikely to build a genuine community of people who feel inadequate and rejected and who have no personal sense of who they are, the talents that they possess, the work that they are particularly suited to do, how they are different from all other people, and how they could use their unique abilities to build their lives and to enrich the human experience (see, in particular, Moustakas, 1967: 7-8, 18-19).

Traditional notions of community and, more recently, "social capital" perceive the social phenomenon as an informal social support network that is based on such things as "geographical contiguity," "membership," "local identification," "reciprocity," "shared goals and values," "commitment," "trust," and "performance." *Geographical contiguity* refers to the territorial place that members perceive as their own, or as the physical context for their interaction and relationships. *Membership* is the biological, social, cultural, ideological, or professional characteristics that members perceive as defining and setting them apart from nonmembers. *Local identification* is the sense of belonging, concern with neighborhood issues, and time spent by members on neighborhood activities. *Reciprocity* is the pattern of relationships between members, including visits, exchanges, helping with small tasks, borrowing and lending things, and willingness to call on one another for help in emergencies. *Shared goals and values* are material and nonmaterial things and conditions that members perceive as beneficial to their group interests and worthy of their collective effort. *Commitment* is the collective orientation of members to their shared goals and values. *Trust* is the degree of dependability,

241

mutual understanding, and the extent to which residents rely on one another to promote their shared goals and values. *Performance* is the effectiveness of members and a record of their ability to discharge their local obligations and achieve goals. (For an extended review of "social capital," see, for example, Ahlbrandt, 1984; Cohen and Shinar, 1985; Coleman, 1988; Senge, 1990; Cortés, 1993; Putnan 1993; Fukuyama, 1995; and Wilson, 1997.)

Perceiving the community in largely territorial terms has been useful for many practical purposes: planning, mutual help, social control, conflict resolution, law enforcement, and other forms of social action. The problem with this perception, however, is the tendency to regard as a local phenomenon what is essentially infinite and universal. Those who perceive community as a unifying principle and the interrelatedness of all life criticize attempts to restrict the feeling to a particular geographical neighborhood or a particular set of local institutions such as families, churches, schools, mosques, synagogues, clubs, associations, or chambers of commerce. They agree that charity necessarily begins at home, but argue that genuine goodwill (community feeling), by definition, transcends place and, in the words of Erich Fromm, encompasses "fellow humans and all that exists."

Additional support for a more inclusive notion of community include: (a) its embeddedness in the human psyche and its necessity for human fulfillment; (b) the global (even "cosmic") significance of many of today's actions by people; and (c) the rapidly expanding spheres of human interactions and relationships. The central ideas of this notion of community are

- *relatedness* – our common humanity; the interconnectedness of all things; oneness with fellow humans and nature; overcoming separateness and alienation; "interexistence."

- *mutual dependence and mutual coexistence* – the common good; collective fate and "our common future"; individuals needing one another to be able to deal with the crises facing humanity; thinking, dreaming, and solving common problems together; sense of obligation for the welfare of others; "interexistence"; "interwoven destiny"; living in a way that allows other people to live as well; the win of one is the win of all; "man lives not for himself alone ... in others' good he finds his own."

- *mutual enhancement* – recognizing, respecting, and catalyzing the unique abilities of all people to "creatively confront the problems all of us now face in common."

242

• *environmental responsibility* – the realization that the choices and decisions that one makes generate consequences not only for oneself, but also for fellow human beings and, indeed, for all life; an appreciation of specific ways in which one's thoughts, feelings, and actions affect the well-being of other human beings and the natural environment; the integrity and equal value of each life; individual fulfillment in the context of other individuals and things.

(See, for example, Gardner, 1968: 114, 115; Charon, 1971: 31; Davidson, 1974: 375, 376, 402; Fromm, 1974: 425-426; The Club of Rome, 1979: 13; Theobald, 1981: 143; Harman and Hormann, 1990: 93; Covey 1992: 272; Laszlo, 1993: 107-140; Pinchot and Pinchot, 1993: 219; Peck, 1997: 167-173; Jaccaci and Gault, 1999: 7).

Evidently, not every one subscribes to the universalistic notion of community. Analysis of common perceptions and the conduct of economic, social, and political life identifies several attitudinal dispositions that make it difficult for some people to see the interconnectedness of all life and the community as a framework for personal growth and fulfillment. The following potentially anti-community dispositions are easily recognizable both in popular discourse and also in the arrangement of many economic, social, and political institutions:

• *pessimistic assumptions about human nature:* the perception of human society as a geographical aggregation of individuals pursuing their own private interests; the beliefs that: (a) human beings cannot organize their lives in ways that benefit others as well as themselves; (b) individual interests and societal goals are incompatible and mutually exclusive; (c) human nature is basically irrational and the human impulse, if not controlled, will develop antisocial tendencies.

• *"zero-sum mentality":* a view of the structure of human society and social relations in adversarial terms (e.g., "winners and losers," "predator and prey," "victor and vanquished"); the perception of human nature as inherently competitive and self-centered; the "I've-got-to-get-mine, get-yours-before-it-is-finished" mentality; the beliefs that: (a) private interests are inherently antagonistic, and must necessarily damage one another; (b) everyone acts only to benefit himself, without regard for others; and (c) the popularity of such clichés as: "cream rises to the top"; the only way to get ahead is to "beat 'em"; "the price of morality [is always] defeat"; "nice guys often finish last"; and "it hurts so much to be good."

- *masking:* pretenses, insincerity, and superficial politeness in social relations; the tendency to look and/or act as if one is in total control of one's life; the feeling that one is standing alone: independent, autonomous, and not needing anybody for anything; the tendency to keep one's personal problems to oneself – lest one reveal one's inadequacies.

- *cynicism:* the tendency to dismiss the notion of conscious, collaborative, humane, personally fulfilling, and mutually-beneficial human community as naive, utopian, or unrealistic; insistence on proofs that the new social order will be better than the present; contentment with the existing order of things and doubts that "the new society" is feasible.

- *despair:* the belief that what is variously described as "our sick society" and "our trouble-ridden world" cannot be healed or reconstructed; the inability to see ways in which one's thoughts, feelings, and actions can change the world.

(For a more detailed review some of those dispositions, see, for example, Rogers, 1961: 174-195; Moustakas, 1967: 8; Gardner, 1968: 69; Theobald, 1981: 130, 142-143; Heilbroner, 1986: 217; Peck, 1996: 167-178).

Contrary to beliefs that genuine community is utopian, that individual interests and societal goals are incompatible, and that human beings are inherently selfish and cannot organize their lives in ways that benefit others as well as themselves, the evidence suggests that community feeling is actually growing. Practical illustrations are (a) the large number of movements, programs, and projects that are being designed to forge linkages among people and (b) a growing desire among individuals to enter into deeply satisfying and more meaningful relationships with fellow human beings, to belong to something larger than themselves, and to participate in worthy and mutually-beneficial projects (see, for example, The Club of Rome, 1979: 36; Toffler, 1980: 345-352; Gardner, 1990; Harman and Hormann, 1990; Pinchot and Pinchot, 1993: 246-250).

Apparent revival of community feelings has given rise to several interpretations. Two of these – the embeddedness of humaneness and altruism in the human psyche, and inner longing for connectedness and collaboration – are particularly germane to this section.

With regard to humaneness and altruism, social analysts suggest that the human potential for brotherliness, for public-spiritedness, and for self-sacrifice probably outweighs the tendency for selfishness. Charlene Spretnak (1988: 39) defines this sense of community as "individual responsibility toward all beings." Ervin Lazslo characterizes humaneness and altruism variously as: "culture of interexistence"; "planetary consciousness"; living in a way that allows others to live as well; eating in a way that allows everyone to eat as well; and an arrangement in which "the win of one is also the win of all others" (Laszlo, 1994: 108, 125, 126, 128). Tom Thiss (1995: 108) describes the feeling as "responsibility to something higher than my family, my community, my country, my company, my success."

With regard to connectedness and collaboration, humanistic psychologists and social commentators characterize human beings as interdependent and "highly social animals," "biologically ordained" to communicate with, and care about, one another (Rogers, 1961: 194; Pinchot and Pinchot, 1992: 247, 248). They see community both as a framework for personal growth and fulfillment and also as a natural expression of our deep need for association with fellow human beings. John Gardner (1991: 9, 29), for example, simply describes human beings as "a community-building species." Scott Peck (1996: 178) calls attention to our personal inadequacies and incompleteness and the individual's inevitable dependence on others to overcome those limitations. Jaccaci and Gault (1999: 129, 133) describe community as the "web of life," and perceive "conscious, creative, collaborative, and compassionate community" as the inevitable destiny of humanity.

If, as suggested, community feeling is embedded in the human psyche, and collaboration is the natural order of social life, the question arises: Why are cooperation, altruism, selflessness, and related behaviors reportedly so rare?

Some people matter-of-factly attribute the perceived lack of community to "human nature" which they view as innately egocentric and competitive. Others suggest that just because community is "wired" into the human psyche does not necessarily mean that people will always exhibit humaneness and cooperation in their daily behaviors and activities. To be able to do so, they argue that people would need to perceive the economic, social, and political conditions of their existence as affirming their personhood and integrity as human beings, as recognizing and enhancing their natural abilities, and also as genuinely valuing and promoting altruism and collaborative behaviors. This view of community building is based on the assumptions that (a) the individual's complementary needs to be liked by others and to give affection to others is at least as strong as his self-interest; (b) self-regard and regard for other people go together, as do self-appreciation and appreciating others, self-acceptance and accepting other people, self-enhancement and enhancing others, self-valuing and valuing the integrity of others; and, (c) personal goals and societal interests are synergistic (rather that antagonistic).

The next subsection reviews the significance of these attributes for human progress and, specifically, for enhancing human capacity and building a more humane, more fulfilling, and more ecologically responsible human civilization.

Human Progress

There was a time when development and "progress" were measured almost exclusively by such things as gross national product, national budget, daily newspapers, health services, life expectancy, population per doctor, school enrollment, pupil-teacher ratio, literacy rate, nutrition, rate of employment, population density, telephones, international telephone calls, televisions, radios, tax revenue, current account balances, military expenditure, urbanization, energy consumption, cinema and museum attendance, letters posted, motor vehicles, scientists and technicians, reported crimes, etc. Countries and even regions of the world were measured, compared, and rank-ordered by the degree to which they rated on those variables (see, for example, UNDP, 1994). With national pride and international prestige based on their relative positions on those commonly accepted indicators of development, most countries, understandably, devoted the bulk of their resources to providing their citizens with more and better goods and services – to creating ever-higher standards of living. And, so, the trend continued until development virtually came to be regarded as the quantum of material goods consumed and/or available for consumption by a population.

The importance and, indeed, the necessity of food, clothing, shelter, education, jobs, income, health care, recreation, entertainment, national security, and so on, need no argument. The problem, as is beginning to be realized, is the tendency to concentrate on material things themselves and to ignore the ends that material things are meant to serve. "Ends" here refers to human potential and its fulfillment – the recognition, development, and actualization of people's capacities and the psychological well-being that the condition engenders. Humanistic psychologists and some existentialist thinkers remind us that providing people with all of the material comfort and all the sensual pleasures they can consume without corresponding opportunities for them to realize their creative potential is to deny their most fundamental need. Humanistic psychologists further describe inadequate, or lack of, opportunity to realize one's potential as "psychic deprivation" – a condition which they blame for a variety of psychological problems including, as indicated earlier, meaninglessness, worthlessness, emptiness, insecurity, and incompleteness, even among seemingly very successful people. John Gardner's instructive statement on the problem is worth repeating:

> "Having enough of everything" isn't enough. ... Comfort is not enough. ... If it were, [the rich and famous] who have been able to indulge their whims on a scale unprecedented in history would be deliriously happy. They would be telling one another of their unparalleled serenity and bliss instead of trading tranquilizer prescriptions" (Gardner, 1968: 115).

One of the most fundamental shifts in modern thinking is the growing realization that material things alone do not fulfill an individual, and that material standards of living alone do not necessarily define progress. Part of this shift can be traced to early social critics and reformers who, rejecting what they perceived as "the domination of man by things" and "the fettering of the human spirit," have called for a "more comprehensive notion of progress" and a different set of criteria for its measurement. *

A growing number of institutions and individuals support that view. The United Nations Development Program, for example, has proposed "a [new] paradigm of development [that] enables all individuals to enlarge their human capabilities to the full and to put those capabilities to their best use ..." (UNDP, 1994: 4). Erich Fromm (1955: 61) characterizes human progress as "a world based on human solidarity and justice." Key indicators of human progress and "the sane society," according to the

---

* For a more comprehensive review of this position, see, for example, Erich Fromm (1955: 185-204)

humanistic psychoanalyst, are "universal brotherliness" and the experience of oneness with all that exists. John Gardner (1968: 12, 69, 75, 138, 150, 172) defines human progress as the capacity to develop the talents and potentialities of people – to enable every individual to discover and fulfill the best that is in him, regardless of his gender, race, creed, social standing, or economic position. The social analyst and commentator sees as the "highest goals" of society the ability to provide every individual with "successive opportunities" and the particular kind of education and experiences that benefit him and that enable him to live his life with dignity.

Jaccaci and Gault (1999: 8, 130, 133, 134) describe human progress variously as "holistic all-win well-being"; a "new cosmology of love"; "ever-deepening compassion for the whole of life"; "conscious, creative, collaborative, and compassionate community"; "expanding grace and love among ourselves and all planetary life"; transforming our lives and affecting the direction of human evolution in ways that support all life; and defining prosperity and profit in a way that supports all life.

Alvin Toffler (1980: 339, 340, 347) characterizes human progress as "a practopian future," a term which he defines as:

> ... civilization that makes allowance for individual differences, and embraces (rather than suppresses) racial, regional, religious, and subcultural variety. A civilization built in considerable measure around the home. A civilization that is not frozen in amber but pulsating [sic] with innovation, yet which is also capable of providing enclaves of relative stability for those who need or want them. A civilization no longer required to pour its best energies into marketization. A civilization capable of directing great passions into art. A civilization facing unprecedented historical choices ... and inventing new ethical or moral standards to deal with such complex issues. A civilization ... that is at least potentially democratic and humane, in better balance with the biosphere and no longer dangerously dependent on exploitative subsidies from the rest of the world (Toffler, 1980: 339-340).

Influential global development reports, ecologists, postmodernists, and human potential advocates define human progress not so much in terms of the quantum of material things that are available for human consumption but, rather, by the extent to which people are able to realize their potential, to relate genuinely and responsibly with fellow human beings and the natural environment, to do the things that they are uniquely equipped to do, and, therefore, to find meaning and fulfillment in their lives. Advocates of this position see as the goal of every society, every institution, every economic and political arrangement, to provide the conditions in which:

- the integrity of every individual is recognized and respected.

- individuals are able to meet and relate with one another as persons of worth.

- people are able to find out what they are passionate about and to express their abilities in those things.

- people are able to participate meaningfully in socially and ecologically beneficial actions and to feel that their contributions really matter and are valued.

- the integrity of the natural environment is recognized and respected in every human action – private or collective, economic, social, or political.

(See for, example, Fromm, 1955: 242; Schumacher, 1975; The Club of Rome, 1979: 36; Theobald 1981: 147; Griffin, 1988; 1988a; Spretnak, 1988; Harman and Hormann, 1990: 93; Pinchot and Pinchot, 1993: 246-250).

The difficulty of achieving these ideals is widely recognized, and is the reason why some people dismiss them as utopian, unrealistic. But the "business-as-usual" alternative, as is becoming increasingly obvious, could be more costly. The challenge of human progress therefore is a case of doing the seemingly impossible in order to avoid the unthinkable.

Summary and Conclusion

This introductory synopsis has been motivated in part by the so-called "control versus freedom" controversy. The "control" viewpoint perceives human nature as inherently selfish and rebellious and believes that, for the stability of society, people must be shown the direction of growth and development and controlled by external authorities to do the right things. Fearing possible undesirable side effects of human creativity, supporters of this view maintain that to permit individuals to develop according to their nature is to invite chaos. The "freedom" viewpoint argues that every human being intuitively knows his "purpose"* in life and should be free to develop in ways that are most congenial to him. The one extreme argues for societal determination and control of the direction of individual growth; the other emphasizes personal choices. The former view attributes personal, interpersonal, and social problems to human depravity. The latter view attributes many antisocial behaviors to perceived or actual blockages of personal growth (i.e., inadequate opportunities for people to realize their potential).

Between proponents of control and supporters of freedom are advocates of *balance*. The central idea of balance, of course, is "freedom with responsibility" – freedom for people to actualize their creative potential and, *also*, the existence of a moral/ethical framework for channeling people's creative expressions to socially and ecologically beneficial ends. Social analysts suggest that achieving such a goal requires a unifying vision or compelling moral purpose that people perceive as worthy of their commitment and for which they are willing to invest themselves and their creativity (see, for example, Gardner, 1964: 119-129; Schumacher, 1975: 95, 101, 297; Laszlo, 1994: 121-140).

Advocates of balance perceive human creativity as a natural and irresistible force that will express itself one way or another, depending on the "channels" or opportunities that are available. Humanistic psychologists suggest that where recognized, nourished, and allowed to be expressed, human creativity often gives rise to socially and ecologically beneficial behaviors. Conversely, where undiscovered, blocked, or neglected, human capacities are said to create "pent-up energy" that at times erupts into antisocial behaviors.

Prognoses like these leave human societies with two options:

Option A:
• Create visions and purposes that inspire people to act in ways that benefit themselves, their societies, and the rest of nature; develop larger and more humane systems of values that enhance people's worth as human beings and that therefore compel their individual and collective allegiance; find synergistic, mutually-beneficial goals and formulate them in such a way that damaging other people's interests is perceived as simultaneously damaging one's own.

Option B:
• Develop more effective deterrents to prevent people from harming themselves and one another, and to apprehend and punish those who do; raise the fences; put up more gates; install more barricades; enact more private property laws; increase the size of the police force and other security agencies; build more prisons; enlist more vigilantes; focus more "eyes on the street"; post more "Residents Only" and "No Trespassing" signs; acquire more

personal security gadgets; and/or sleep with eyes open – all to keep out "undesirable elements," protect ourselves from "miscreants," "take back [our] threatened neighborhoods," and "reclaim [our] streets from criminals."

The first option is the thesis of this introductory overview and the reason why many of the remarks in this section were selected. It is also one of the principal reasons for this project.

Regarding the second alternative, we must not forget the probable reasons why people feel the need to protect themselves from one another or why security devices are necessary in the first place. Nor should we underestimate the effect of fortresses, barricades, mutual suspicion, and insecurity on the human psyche and personal functioning. Psychologists tell us that the path to emotional health and mental well-being lies not in fear but in security, not in mistrust but in mutual confidence, not in isolation but in community. Social analysts and futurists tell us that genuine progress in the emerging world order will be built on collaboration rather than rivalry, compassion rather than indifference. They warn, however, that human progress is not an inevitable end, but one that could be accelerated, retarded, blocked, or even reversed. The determining factor, according to them, is the extent to which people's creative potentials are recognized, valued, nourished, and allowed to complement one another in mutually and ecologically beneficial ways. That, they propose, is the challenge and the "central project" of every human society.

The significance of creativity in personality development, community building, and human progress derives from the assumptions that (a) only people who have been able to discover their own talents can be expected to encourage others to explore their own potentialities; (b) only people who genuinely accept themselves and value their own abilities can be expected to appreciate the worth of other people; (c) only people who recognize the relative significance of what they are doing can be expected to appreciate the contributions of others; and (d) only people who have been able to find something that they are passionate about can be expected to help others find meaning in their lives.

If, therefore, people are to be able to deal with one another humanely, to respect individual differences, and to value the integrity of each person, their own daily life experiences must implicitly validate (rather than deny or threaten) their worth as human beings and must unequivocally affirm the unity, the relatedness, and the interdependence of all life.

Selected Insights
on
Creativity, Personality, Community, and Human Progress

Not in solitary and selfish contemplation
But in doing things with other people,
Does one fulfill oneself.

— (Anonymous).

The time has come for us to stop tuning separate instruments
and, together, to create a symphony.

— (Anonymous).

Compassion and acceptance are contagious.

— (Anonymous).

It is by becoming persons ourselves that we discover the persons
of our fellow-men.

— (Anonymous).

It takes a village to raise a child.

— African Saying.

Lacking absolutes, we will have to encounter one another as
people with different information, different stories, different
visions — and trust the outcome.

— Walter Truett Anderson (1990: 183).

Gates and barricades that separate people from one another also
reduce people's potential to understand one another and
commit to any common or collective purpose.

— Edward J. Blakely and Mary Gail Snyder (1997: 13).

Because everything we do is affected by our habits of mind, a fundamental task across cultures is to prepare citizens who are capable of the higher order thinking patterns demanded by a complex, dynamic society.

— Berenice Bleedorn (1998: 219).

While the sense of community has atrophied in small towns, the anonymity and transience of urban existence has made life evanescent, rootless, and devalued.

— Harold H. Bloomfield *et al.,* (1975: 4-5).

There is to be found in these ... communes not only an underlying sense of community and of social renewal, but also, and of equal importance the adequate meeting of an external need: "the need of man to feel his own home as a room in some greater, all embracing structure in which he is at home, to feel that the other inhabitants of it with whom he lives and works [sic] are all acknowledging and confirming his individual existence.

— Martin Buber (1950: 139-140).

Parents must realize that before their own children can have the greatest benefit from community activities all children in the community must have the right sort of living conditions.

— Childcraft (1949: 56).

Age-old discriminations and dangerous practices of domination and superiority continue to haunt a densely populated world which is unable to develop the equitable re-distribution schemes, cooperation, and moral solidarity on which survival of the species may, for the first time in history, increasingly depend.

— The Club of Rome (1979: 7).

The greatest obstacles to cooperation are the short-term gains that might be obtained through confrontation. Even if these gains are short-lived and demonstrably lead to long-term losses, there is always a pressure to go after these gains.

—The Club of Rome (1974: 144).

The concept of total freedom of individuals to pursue whatever goals they wish (as long as they do not overtly break the system of liberal laws) [will have to] give way to an emphasis on the freedom *and responsibility* of individuals to pursue those enlightened self-interests [sic] which result in benefit both to themselves and to their society.

— The Club of Rome (1978: 334).

When you organize the global society primarily for the purpose of increasing production and consumption, you systematically destroy community (human and nonhuman).

— John Cobb (1999: 267).

Japan was devastated [by the Second World War] and left with few resources, except people. And they rapidly learned under those humbling circumstances that the only way they could survive and prosper was to get people to work hard and work together.

— Stephen R. Covey (1992: 281).

It may be possible, for a while, to barricade suburban streets against outsiders, but there are no walls that can block out the state of the world in a modern society.
— William Damon (1995: 15)

We talk about quality of product and service. But what about the quality of our relationships and the quality of our communications and the quality of our promises to each other?
— Max De Pree (991: 116)

[A]ll reforms which rest simply upon the enactment of law, or the threatening of certain penalties, or upon changes in mechanical or outward arrangements, are transitory and futile. ... Only by being true to the full growth of individuals who make it up, can society by any chance be true to itself.
— John Dewey, (1974: 95).

Are we living in a plastic and tinfoil society? Have the technological advances of the past decades [sic.] so dulled our human sensitivities that we are a machine-, rather than person-oriented, society? Perhaps. But so long as we are a society of individuals, there will be those among us who possess the inner freedom to pursue a creative life style.
— Elaine Donelson (1973: 600).

One of the fundamental freedoms of a democracy should be the right of every individual to his own creative expressions.
— Finley Eversole (1971: 59).

It is the greenness of every tree that makes the whole forest green.
— Jack Forem (1974: 236).

[The human] heart is restless unless he has found, and fulfilled, meaning and purpose in life.
— Viktor E. Frankl (1969: 55).

The naming of the world, which is an act of creation and re-creation, is not possible if it is not infused with love.
— Paulo Freire (1972: 78-79).

Attempting *to be more* human, individualistically, leads to *having more,* egotistically; a form of dehumanization. Not that it is not fundamental *to have* in order *to be* human. Precisely because it *is* necessary, some men's *having* must not be allowed to constitute an obstacle to others' *having.*
— Paulo Freire (1972: 73-74).

Mankind is on the threshold of a new stage in its development. We should not only promote the expansion of its material, scientific, and technical basis, but, what is most important, the formation of new value and humanistic aspirations in human psychology, since wisdom and humaneness are the "eternal truths" that make the basis of humanity.
— I. T. Frolov (1987: 39).

[W]hat we use is not ours simply because we use it. Ours is only that to which we are genuinely related by our creative activity, be it a person or an inanimate object.
— Erich Fromm (1941: 288).

The necessity to unite with other living things, to be related to them, is an imperative need on the fulfillment of which man's sanity depends.
— Erich Fromm (1941: 36).

[M]an is a social being with a deep need to share, to help, to feel as a member of a group. What has happened to this social strivings in man?
— Erich Fromm (1955: 127).

Just as love for one individual which excludes the love for others is not love, love for one's country which is not part of one's love for humanity is not love, but idolatrous worship.
— Erich Fromm (1955: 60).

Only when man succeeds in developing his reason and love further than he has done so far, only when he can build a world based on human solidarity and justice, only when he can feel rooted in the experience of universal brotherliness, will he have transformed his world into a truly human home.
— Erich Fromm (1955: 61).

Well-being means to be fully related to man and nature affectively, to overcome separateness and alienation, to arrive at the experience of oneness with all that exists – and yet to experience myself at the same time as the separate entity I am, as the individual.

Well-being means to be fully born, to become what one potentially is. It means ... to awake from the half-slumber the average man lives in, and to be fully awake. ... it means also to be creative; that is, to react and respond as the real, total man that I am to the reality of everybody and everything as he or it is.

— Erich Fromm (1974: 425).

It is of the utmost importance that we recognize and nurture all of the varied human intelligences, and all of the combinations of intelligences. We are all so different largely because we all have different combinations of intelligences. If we recognize this, I think we will have at least a better chance of dealing appropriately with the many problems that we face in the world. If we can mobilize the spectrum of human abilities, not only will people feel better about themselves and more competent; it is even possible that they will also feel more engaged and better able to join the rest of the world community in working for the broader good. Perhaps if we can mobilize the full range of human intelligences and ally them to an ethical sense, we can help to increase the likelihood of our survival on this planet, and perhaps even contribute to our thriving.

— Howard Gardner (1993: 12).

In a viable community, members recognize their differences and strive to be tolerant, while learning to talk constructively with one another and perennially searching for common ground.

— Howard Gardner (1993: 84).

No society will successfully resolve its internal conflicts if its only asset is cleverness in the management of these conflicts. It must also have compelling goals that are shared by the conflicting parties; and it must have a sense of movement toward these goals.

— John W. Gardner (1961: 117).

Individual fulfillment on a wide scale can occur only in a society which is designed to cherish the individual, which has the strength to protect him, the richness and diversity to stimulate and develop him and the system of values within which he can find himself — and lose himself! — as a person.

— John W. Gardner (1961: 145).

Those who suffer from the sense of anonymity would feel better if they could believe that their society needed them. And the irony is that their society needs them desperately. ... That is why our goal must be a society that is vital in all its parts ... a society in which every individual feels that there is a role for him in shaping his local institutions and local community.

— John W. Gardner (1968: 148).

If men wish to remain free, they had better look to the health, the vigor, the viability of their free society.
— John W. Gardner (1968: 149).

No society can properly define for any individual the purpose and meaning of his life. The good society will create conditions in which the individual can find his own purpose and meaning in life.
— John W. Gardner (1968: 152).

Humans are community-forming animals.
— John W. Gardner (1991: 9).

The members of a good community deal with one another humanely, respect individual differences and value the integrity of each person.
— John W. Gardner (1991: 18).

Because we are experiencing, purposive beings, who are ends in ourselves, not mere instruments for the ends of others, it can be argued that we should treat other human beings by analogy as ends in themselves.
— David Ray Griffin (1988: 5).

One task of postmodern thought is to create a consciousness in which the need to [actualize one's potentials and to make a contribution to others] is recognized to be as essential to the life of individuals, communities and nations as is the need to feel they are getting their fair share of [material and aesthetic goods].

— David Ray Griffin (1988a: 150).

It is precisely in our relations with other human beings … that our prophecies are most self-fulfilling. If we expect the worst from others and act accordingly, that is precisely what we will get.

— David Ray Griffin (1988a: 151).

There are … those who insist that the future must be a repetition of the past; that [new] ideas are dangerous, that ideals are freaks … Humanity has a long road to perfection, but we … can make sure progress if we will preserve our individualism, if we will preserve and stimulate initiative of our people … if we hold abiding faith in the intelligence, the initiative, the character, the courage, and the divine touch in the individual.

— Herbert Hoover (1963: 530).

By mutual confidence and mutual aid,
Great things are done, and great discoveries made.

— Homer.

Society is to be improved, not by forcing a program of social reform down its throat, through the schools or otherwise, but by the improvement of the individuals who compose it. ... The individual is the heart of society.
— Robert Hutchins (1974: 95).

The whole next stage of human evolution is the era of conscious evolution. It is the transformation of the scientific industrial era into a union of our present capabilities with the emergence of our already indwelling social and spiritual fulfillment, the flowering of higher-order unity of human values and intentions.
— August T. Jaccaci and Susan B. Gault (1999: 8).

Somehow in our current age we may have allowed ourselves to believe that doing well and doing good are antithetical.
— August T. Jaccaci and Susan B. Gault (1999: 72).

Our cosmological story has been unbalanced on the side of the physical and the material ... This unbalance is one of the causes of the excesses of our materialistic culture. It is now time to project all of ourselves, the fullest and deepest meanings of our humanity, into the universe to create our cosmological renaissance story.
— August T. Jaccaci and Susan B. Gault (1999: 156).

One thing I want you to know is that if every youth gets something to do, something legitimate [creative and self-fulfilling] to occupy his time, nobody will go [to] the street to kill or maim a fellow human being.

— Orji Uzor Kalu (2000).

We must learn to live together as brothers ... or perish as fools.

— Martin Luther King, Jr. (1992: 145).

In the last decade of the twentieth century, different people and different societies must do more than merely tolerate one another. [sic] They must learn to complete and complement one another.

— Ervin Laszlo (1994: 106).

But if rivalry and the status it yields provide some of the arpeggios of living, the more continuous melody is the craving of the personality for human mutuality, the sharing of purposes, feeling, and action with others. The personality craves to belong to others richly and confidently and to have them belong in turn to it. It craves the expression and the receipt of affection. It craves to be actively accepted and given secure status as a person, *for* the person that it is — as well as for the work it can do. Sympathy is normal to it. Conversely, it suffers when forced to live in physical or psychological isolation.

— Robert S. Lynd (1939: 196).

The chance of securing more coherent, constructive behavior from persons depends upon recognizing the large degree of irrationality that is natural to them and upon structuring the culture actively to support and encourage intelligent types of behavior, including inevitably opportunity for creative, spontaneous expression of emotion.

— Robert S. Lynd (1939: 234).

[C]ulture, if it is to be creative in the personalities of those who live it, needs to discover and to build prominently into its structure a core of richly evocative common purposes which have meaning in terms of the deep personality needs of the great mass of the people.

— Robert S. Lynd (1939: 239).

Destructiveness, sadism, cruelty, malice, etc., seem ... to be not intrinsic but rather ... violent reactions *against* frustration of our intrinsic needs, emotions and capacities.

— Abraham H. Maslow (1968: 3).

No psychological health is possible unless [the] essential core of the person is fundamentally accepted, loved and respected by others and by himself ...

— Abraham H. Maslow (1968: 196).

[A] society or any institution in it can be characterized as fostering or hindering the self-actualization of its individuals.
— Abraham H. Maslow (1968: 220).

What will startle many people is the clear indication, backed by a growing research literature, that under certain "synergic" conditions, ... the good of the individual [sic] and the good of the society can come closer and closer to being synonymous rather than antagonistic.
— Abraham H. Maslow (1968: 221).

[T]he ultimate disease of our time is valuelessness ... rootlessness, emptiness, helplessness, the lack of something to believe in and to be devoted to.
— Abraham Maslow (1970: 82).

Learning to live together is not simply a moral imperative; it is our only chance of survival.
— Federico Mayor (1993: 105).

Growth has no meaning unless it contributes to the fulfillment of individuals and of the community, unless it offers greater chances to be human and to create.
— Amadou-Mahtar M'Bow (1978: 158).

The challenge ahead is for us to transcend the self-interest of our respective nation-states so as to embrace a broader self-interest — the survival of the human species in a threatened world.

— Hon. Tom McMillan (987: 263).

Human society must not be based on economics. Economics must be based on human society. ... [I]t is not on economics that human societies must be based but on human relations.

— Ashley Montagu (1962: 60).

For every human being is born a co-operative creature and remains ineradicably so throughout life.

— Ashley Montagu (1962: 62).

Having the freedom to grow and to actualize one's self provides the best foundation for interacting with others within groups, and in society.

— Clark Moustakas (1967: 8).

To permit another person to be and become does not promote selfishness on his part. Rather it affirms his truly human self.

— Clark Moustakas (1967: 10).

There is no way to realize the full possibilities in group life as long as one person is rejected, minimized, ignored or treated as an inferior or outcast. To the extent that there is malice toward on person, ill-will and ill-feeling spread. Every person in the group is afflicted and is powerless to channel available resources into creative expression. One cannot carry evil thoughts, feelings, and intentions in his heart without at the same time deterring and restraining himself in his own purposes or directions. One, therefore, must live through and work out one's state of rejecting or being rejected before group life can contain a depth of spirit, devotion, and authentic community.

— Clark Moustakas (1967: 18-19).

The custom of our time is to think no change worth even discussing unless it can be … organized into a visible movement, [yet] only in one place can an immediate renewal begin: that is, within the person; and a remolding of the self … is an inescapable preliminary to the great changes that must be made throughout every community, in every part of the world.

— Lewis Mumford (1974: 226).

I look to future centuries of self-actualizing individuals, whose main purpose in life is self-actualizing themselves and helping others to do the same (children, families, students, employees, friends, colleagues, mentees) to ever higher levels of an infinite continuum of human potential development.
— Sidney J. Parnes (1992: 152).

The communication, knowledge, and information explosion augurs well for planet earth. The communication systems of the body share, coordinate, and promote the welfare of the individual, cell by cell. Improved, rapid and effective communication of information between each individual, community, and nation – the cells of mankind – will harmonize these cells into a healthy, vital, and mutually advantageous unity. The creative forces of each individual, community, and nation will be a necessary and integral part of this process.
— Sidney J. Parnes (1997: 161).

This is how the world is made: by the aggregate effect of all the decisions – major and minor – each of us makes as we go about our lives.
— Carol S. Pearson (1991: 167).

Each of us has a piece of the puzzle of solving the great world problems of our time and creating a more just, humane, and beautiful world.
— Carol S. Pearson (1991: 171-172).

[A]ll of us are component parts of the fabric of human society. We are just beginning to wake up to the fact that the whole of that society is connected to the waters, to the land, to forests, and the atmosphere: the "ecosystem."

— M. Scott Peck (1997: 171).

[T]here is no way that we can evolve into a more civil society until ever greater numbers of us are willing to make the choice not only to be personally conscious but also to think in terms of whole systems and expand our awareness ...

— M. Scott Peck (1997: 173).

Great inequality is the enemy of community. Inequality creates envy that can overwhelm the binding force of common interest and make achieving the status of the fortunate more important than contributing to the success of the whole.

— Gifford and Elizabeth Pinchot (1993: 241).

Of course, most organizations cannot pay everyone the same wage, and differences in power and influence are inevitable. What organizations can do is strive to create systems that allow everyone dignity, respect as whole human beings, and a voice in the processes and decisions that affect them – giant steps away from relationships of dominance and submission ...

— Gifford and Elizabeth Pinchot (1993: 242).

States are not made of stone or wood, but out of the character of their citizens: these turn the scale and draw everything after them.

— Plato, (1974: 95).

[A] society without any objective legal scale is a terrible one indeed. But a society with no other scale but the legal one is also less than worthy of man. A society based on the letter of the law and never reaching anything [sic.] higher fails to take advantage of the full range of human possibilities. The letter of the law is too cold and formal to have a beneficial influence on society.

— Aleksandr I. Solzhenitsyn (1978: 17).

Whenever the tissue of life is woven of legalistic relationships, this creates an atmosphere of spiritual mediocrity that paralyzes man's noblest impulses.

— Aleksandr I. Solzhenitsyn (1978: 17, 19).

We need to create new organizational, institutional, and societal contexts and processes in which people can be responsible within their time and energy levels.

— Richard J. Spady and Cecil H. Bell, Jr. (1997: 20).

The discovery of new, vital feedback communication techniques applicable in all human groups, communities, organizations, institutions, and societies in the world today holds the key to the release of a fabulous amount of human creativity. This social energy is currently being wasted by most organizations and institutions because they have adopted inefficient management styles of "control" which often repress rather than encourage human creativity.
— Richard J. Spady and Cecil H. Bell, Jr. (1997: 27).

To work most effectively, human organizations and institutions (from the smallest – a husband and wife, up to the civilization itself – the largest) require a functional feedback communication capability. This is best accomplished in most organizations by a democratic, open, participative, reliable, viable, anonymous, routine, and objective feedback communication system. Most organizations, institutions, and governments in the world today have no such system.
— Richard J. Spady and Cecil H. Bell, Jr. (1997: 79).

[Civilization is fundamentally spiritual, not material]. And the spiritual destiny of humanity is unity and love for each other!
— Richard J. Spady and Cecil H. Bell, Jr. (1997: 107).

How can we replace the cultural ethics of dominance and control with more cooperative ways of interacting? How can we encourage people to care about persons outside their own group?

— Charlene Spretnak (1988: 39).

As long as man himself does not go through a transformation, no amount of science and knowledge will improve the human situation.

— D. T. Suzuki (1974: 226).

Because creativity is so natural to human life, blocking the flow of creativity will result in pent-up energy and frustration.

— Terry Lynn Taylor and Mary Beth Crain (1994: November 5).

We cannot afford to reject the diversity that we have discovered, for we now know that a monoculture is as dangerous as a monocrop.

— Robert Theobald (1981: 75).

Instead of trying to create a society where we can effectively prevent people from doing wrong, I am suggesting that we create a system designed to facilitate human and intelligent behavior.

— Robert Theobald (1981: 75).

If we are to learn to live in the win-win world, which is essential in the future, we must become sensitive to the possibilities and the necessities of others as well as ourselves.

— Robert Theobald (1981: 140).

[E]ach of us must struggle to help those around us live their own lives more fully and successfully.

— Robert Theobald (1981: 141).

People with faces refuse to act in ways that please them at the cost of damage to others; rather they seek to organize their lives so that the actions they want to take also benefit those with whom they live, work, play, and worship.

— Robert Theobald (1981: 143).

If we are to deal with our situation, we must find ways to encourage people to wear faces and to destroy their masks.

— Robert Theobald (1981: 144).

Community is in short supply.

— Alvin Toffler (1980: 349).

I believe there is little question that prolonged, enforced repression of the creative desire may lead to actual breakdown of the personality.

— E. Paul Torrance (1962: 32).

Each of us does his best to hide behind a shield.

— Paul Tournier (1957: 143).

[Our] changing world requires a return to the values of "sharing," "being good trustees of what we have," "tolerance," "brotherly love," "a new society" ... where net human benefit would be the important thing rather than gross national product, where the good life would replace the life of 'more,' where the value of people would be judged by not what they owned but what they are and what they do.
— Pierre Trudeau (1978: 9).

Development must ... be aimed at the spiritual, moral and material fulfillment of man in his entirety, both as a member of society and as an individual ...
— UNESCO (1978: 158).

Working for equal justice is part of the process of being born; retreat from the challenge is being busy dying.
— Carl Weinberg (1971: 286).

The successful community is not a collection of atomistic individuals bumping into each other's self-interest, but rather is a network, a web of individuals-in-community ... The communities that successfully build or rebuild productive social capital will be those best positioned for prosperity and adaptability in the coming century.
— Patricia Wilson (1997: 756).

How are individuals in the real world to be persuaded or made to act in the common interest?
— The World Commission of Environment and Development (1987: 46).

I am, because we are.
— Zulu (South Africa) Saying.

274

VIII
The Tentativeness of Knowledge: Implications for Human Creativity

Our knowledge is vast and impressive ...
Our ignorance is boundless and overwhelming ...
— Karl Raimund Popper.

True or False?

What would happen if we found out tomorrow that much of what we accept as true today is actually false? What would happen if we discovered that many of our economic, social, and political arrangements and actions have been driven by invalid or untenable assumptions?

Typical reactions to these hypothetical situations would be: "Impossible!" "You must be joking!" "That will never happen!" "I wouldn't be surprised; it wouldn't be the first time or the last."

The reader might wish to read the following one-time expert conclusions before reaching his own.

Expert Conclusions

The story is told of a world-famous scientist who, in the belief that everything about the physical world had been discovered, declared physics a dead subject and advised aspiring physicists to find something else to do. The story is also told of the sage who thought he had figured out everything that could be known in his field, and all that was left to do was for his protégés and successors to work out the details that he could not finish (see Root-Bernstein, 1989: 242). There is, finally, the common students' joke of the proverbial professor who regularly reminded his students that there were only two ways of thinking in his course: "The wrong way, and my own way!"

Amusing and outlandish as they may sound, these stories and joke are not isolated cases of "finality" or attempts to represent knowledge as certain and settled. Consider, for example, the following au-

275

thoritative pronouncements from the best and brightest in their respective fields:

"Louis Pasteur's theory of germs is ridiculous fiction."
(a professor of physiology, 1872).

"The abdomen, the chest, and the brain will forever be shut from the intrusion of the ... surgeon."
(a nationally and internationally distinguished surgeon, 1873).

"[The telephone] has too many shortcomings to be seriously considered as a means of communication."
(internal memo in a leading telephone and telecommunications company, 1876).

"Heavier-than-air flying machines are impossible."
(president of a royal society, 1895).

"Everything that can be invented has been invented."
(commissioner of a national office of patents, 1899).

"Airplanes are interesting toys but of no military value."
(a professor of strategy in a national war college, circa 1910).

"The wireless music box [radio] has no imaginable commercial value."
(communications associates, 1920s).

"I think there is a world market for maybe five computers."
(chairman of a leading computer manufacturing company, 1943).

"There is no reason anyone would want a computer in their home."
(president, chairman and founder of a major computer manufacturing corporation, 1977).

"640K [computer hard drive] ought to be enough for anybody."
(a world famous computer giant, 1981).

These statements were selected from a widely-publicized list* of expert conclusions that turned out to be not so expert after all – pointed examples of today's truths that became tomorrow's errors and signal reminders that, in the realm of human knowledge, "all of the stories have *not* yet been told."

The Allure of Certitudes

The history of ideas is, in large part, a record of falsified postulates and collapsed or collapsing belief systems. Well-known casualties include: the flat Earth; the Earth-as-the-center view of the universe; the clockwork notion of the cosmos; the "machine" concept of organizations; scientific management; social Darwinism; the conquest-of-nature concept of development; the material-consumption notion of well-being; the *tabula-rasa* notion of the child; the philosopher-king concept of leadership; the wage-motive of work; gender and racial superiority; and, of course, the genius theory of creativity. Surprisingly, the persistent assault and frequent overthrow of so many one-time hallowed dogmas do not seem to have sufficiently diminished the human tendency to present ideas (even opinions!) as settled conclusions. If they did, there probably would be far fewer certainties and much more tentativeness in the conduct of inquiry, presentation of evidence, and statements of conclusion, as well as in economic, social, and political arrangements.

Historians of ideas attribute the allure of certitudes to deep-seated psychological and intellectual needs that "truth" presumably satisfies, including: (a) the urge to understand one's world and figure out how it works; (b) the comfort of knowing that one's world is finite, logical, orderly, and predictable; (c) the reassurance of knowing that what one knows is absolute, irrefutable, and complete, and that the idea that one espouses is part of a larger system of ideas that will last forever; (d) the desire to feel in control of things; and (f) the self-satisfaction of being part of the great and immortal achievements of one's era (see, for example, Popper, 1968; Whitehead, 1978).

---

* Compiled by David Raimondo of DSR Technologies Associates, Kitchener, Ontario, Canada, and shared on the internet under the subject: "Think Before You Speak."

Complacency and Transcendence

As tempting and comfortable as it has always been to regard an existing fund of knowledge as truth, historically not everybody has subscribed to the assumption that humanity has reached or could ever reach "the end of what can be known." Many of the discoveries that have transformed the human condition from the stone age to the information era are attributed to a few dissenting voices that kept on reminding humanity of how little it knows and how fragmentary that knowledge is (see, for example, Boorstin, 1985; Root-Bernstein, 1989). Illustrative examples are Isaac Newton and Albert Szent-Györgyi in science, Socrates and Karl Popper in philosophy.*

Newton's famous comparison of scientists to children playing by the edge of a vast unknown sea calls attention to the relative insignificance of existing bodies of knowledge *vis à vis* the infinite range of things that are yet to be discovered, explained, and understood. Newton's characterization of himself and his monumental achievements as "a child picking up a seashell from the shore of the great ocean of knowledge" signifies, among other things, his dissatisfaction with the paltry state of human knowledge and, also, his caution against the twin temptations of self-satisfaction and complacency. Szent-Györgyi's appeal to fellow scientists to rededicate themselves and, if need be, give their lives to filling the many "[blank] spots on the map of human knowledge" demonstrates his profound disappointment with the meager state of human knowledge (see Root-Bernstein, 1989: 329, 407).

Socrates' famous last words that he knew nothing (despite his immense contributions in the realm of ideas) typifies the old saw that the more one knows, the more one realizes how little one knows. Popper's characterization of the existing body of knowledge** as a "floating pile-work over a bottomless swamp of uncertainty" evidently is intended to portray both the superficiality and the scantiness of human knowledge (Popper, 1968: 111).

Philosophical analogies aside, there are practical, everyday reminders that our knowledge is still very limited. One signal indication of the rudimentary and formative state of human knowledge is the rate at which

---

* Whether documented or undocumented, practically every domain of human activity and every culture appears to have had its mavericks and revolutionary spirits.
** Popper (1968: 317) does not look upon science as a "body of knowledge" but rather as a "system of [falsifiable] hypotheses."

new discoveries are made – shattering hallowed dogmas, vitiating the great ideas of the past, and opening up hitherto unsuspected new possibilities. The astounding developments in science, engineering, medicine, technology, economics, and management in the past one hundred years illustrate the point. Another indication of the unsatisfactory condition of human knowledge is what the Club of Rome refers to as the "human gap." This is the "mismatch" between the tremendous advances that humanity has made in several domains and its "lagging understanding" or inability to translate those achievements into a qualitatively improved human condition (see The Club of Rome, 1979). Still another reminder of the paltry state of human knowledge is the large number of perennial problems (social, economic, political, scientific, and environmental) that continue to defy solution. Consider, for example, poverty, hunger, AIDS and similar hard-to-cure diseases, unemployment, disenchantment with work and dissatisfaction with worklife, social inequalities, frustration, depression, ethnic/racial conflicts, violence, wars, environmental degradation, and others. The persistence of so many crises despite all the resources that have been committed to their solution has given rise to the suggestion that either we still do not know enough or are not putting what we know to socially and environmentally beneficial ends (see, for example, Peccei, 1979; Laszlo, 1994).

Epistemological Limitations to Knowledge

The problem with human knowledge is not only its paucity. There are several other problems, some of which appear to directly affect human creativity. The focus here is on the metaphysical foundations of existing knowledge, knowing processes, and tools of inquiry, as they appear to influence the way we think, what we "know," and how we use that knowledge.

Metaphysical foundations of knowledge refer to the unifying systems of belief, including the fundamental assumptions, principles, and values, that explain how the world works and that also regulate the way people live and think. Alternatively referred to as "worldview," these belief systems not only provide the context within which life is organized but also determine the range of problems and issues that are considered important, delimit the kinds of questions that can be asked, set the directions of inquiry, specify the types of evidence that can be admitted, prescribe how data is to be interpreted, and define the range of solutions and conclusions that are acceptable (see for example, Cohen and Manion, 1994: 8; Crombie, 1989: 351; Root-Bernstein, 1989: 57, 60, 62, 351).

Among the many established belief systems are astrology, folklore, mysticism, science, and many other cultural and spiritual traditions. Ironically, the same metaphysical systems that inspire human knowledge sometimes tend to constrain that cultural heritage. The same intellectual traditions, principles, myths, and values upon which cultures and even civilizations are built often tend to circumscribe what a people can know, do, or become. The same theories and philosophies by which people try to apprehend their world and make sense of their experience also tend to blind their adherents to other possibilities, thereby preventing them from making certain observations (see, in particular, Root-Bernstein, 1989: 354-382).

It should be added that metaphysical limitations are not an anomaly, but simply the way things are. By its very nature, every belief system liberates and constrains at the same time.

Some of the ways in which worldviews tend to constrain human knowledge are (a) the tendency to mistake a particular belief system for the way the world works, or to assume that the way we see the world is the way that it really is; (b) the tendency to force-fit problems into an accepted worldview, regardless of its relevance; (c) the tendency to restrict inquiry to only those problems that can be tackled within a given framework and, therefore, to dismiss information and phenomena that seemingly lie outside an accepted tradition as bizarre or unimportant (see, for example, Root-Bernstein, 1989: 16, 351); (d) the tenacity of certain belief systems even when, as Confucius once observed, they no longer make any progress; and (e) inordinate faith in a particular belief system and reluctance to acknowledge the validity or the capabilities of other traditions, even when the problem at hand could be tackled more successfully by combining the strengths of different methodologies.

The second aspect of human knowledge that tends both to expand and to constrain its development is the processes by which knowledge is acquired, i.e., the procedures through which human beings come to "know" or to interpret and relate to their world. Several of these procedures have been identified and analyzed. They include: *empiricism* – by which knowledge is acquired through sense experience, by direct and independently verifiable observation; *rationalism* – by which knowledge is acquired by logical reasoning, typically involving observation of phenomena, analysis of individual cases, development and testing of a hypothesis (or hypotheses) and, finally, generalization; *pragmatism* – by which knowledge is acquired by proposing, testing, and/or adopting workable (successful) ideas; *existentialism* – by which knowledge is acquired through personal interpretation of phenomena (i.e., the way things appear in the individual's consciousness); *intuition* – by which knowledge is acquired through the individual's immediate insight, presumably unaided by any rational processes; *emotion* – by which knowledge is acquired through the individual's private feelings, needs, and desires; *dream, trance, divination, etc.* – by which knowledge is acquired through some kind of "revelation," without conscious personal effort.

Metaphysicists regard all of the paths to knowledge as potentially useful or productive, depending on the type of "information" that is being sought and the level of awareness that is desired. They observe, however, that some of the paths are not being used as much or as regularly as others. As evidence, they point to instances in which certain ways of knowing have been disparaged, actively repressed, or even proscribed, with incalculable loss to the human experience. They attribute the relative neglect of some knowledge processes to the same reasons that certain metaphysical foundations are preferred to others: (a) cultural and intellectual bias, or the reluctance to recognize the validity, relevance, or usefulness of other knowing processes; (b) the belief that a particular way of acquiring knowledge is the only reliable way of understanding the world; (c) selective capability of the various paths to knowledge and the tendency to consider only those phenomena that are accessible to a preferred tradition and, *ipso facto,* to exclude everything else that does not meet accepted "criteria of evidence"; and (d) the tendency to try to understand everything within one particular framework that has been found useful when applied to certain types of phenomena, thereby ignoring its domain limitations.

The third aspect of human knowledge with serious implications for human creativity is the tools of inquiry. These are the concepts, models, equations, theorems, and common-sense notions that different cultures and intellectual communities use to observe phenomena, analyze problems, formulate and evaluate hypotheses, perform experiments, collect data, record measurements, interpret results, and give meaning to events and things. Karl Popper (1995: 490) analogously describes these tools as "searchlights," the illumination (i.e., effectiveness in generating knowledge) of which depends on their position, direction, intensity, and color.

The problems with existing tools of inquiry, as with their methodological foundations, are a subject of considerable debate. Those that bear most directly on human creativity include: (a) the relatively small number of tools (i.e., concepts, models, equations, theorems) and, therefore, the potentially large number of phenomena that cannot be observed and problems that cannot be tackled or solved; (b) the limited accuracy of existing tools and techniques and, therefore, the probability of inaccurate observation, measurement, and conclusions; (c) the limited scope of existing concepts *vis à vis* the complexity of the phenomena that they purportedly represent; (d) the sociocultural embeddedness of concepts and other tools of analysis and, therefore, the tendency to perceive in fixed, culturally predefined ways and, at times, to assume that is the way things are; and (e) the tendency to try to understand all phenomena using a particular set of concepts, to limit inquiry to only those problems that are accessible to available tools and, therefore, to overlook much else (see, for example, Root-Bernstein, 1989: 342-382; Popper 1968; 1995).

The Tentativeness of Human Knowledge

Given the many limitations to human knowledge outlined in this overview and also highlighted in many of the selected remarks for this section, some metaphysicists have come to the conclusion that what we know (or claim we know) is, at best, "fragmentary," "uncertain," "unfinished," and "tentative." Proponents of this view compare various systems of human knowledge to the languages by which different cultures try to make sense of their world and to communicate their meanings. In this view, every system of knowledge (e.g., mysticism, folklore, mythology, science, or whatever) could be regarded as a "vocabulary." As such, the issue is not which language is "true," but which vocabulary works better than the others for the things that matter to a people or to a particular community.

Central to the tentative view of knowledge is the belief that no known system of knowledge represents objective and universal truth. This claim is based on the inherently falsifiable assumptions and subjective values upon which every system of knowledge is founded. Rejecting the view of the world as a given (i.e., something "out there" waiting to be discovered and mapped), proponents of the tentative view of knowledge argue that what is traditionally regarded as objective knowledge is essentially a social construction, reflecting the way things appear to members of a particular culture or intellectual community, as well as their goals, interests, values, and aspirations. Proponents of the tentative view of knowledge further suggest that meanings are not immanent in things themselves, but derive from the intentions of a particular culture or particular "community" and the interpretation that the culture or community gives to things (see, for example, Grenz, 1996: 55-56, 111-112).

Concern with the "tentativeness" of human knowledge (even if not widely shared) has a long history that goes back at least to ancient Greek civilization. Representative propositions include Socrates' "uncertainty"; Xenophane's "subjective certainty"; Bacon's "divinity-of-errors"; Peirce's "fallibilism"; Hume's "skepticism"; Nietzsche's "truth as self-contained set of illusions" and "knowledge as lies"; Heisenberg's "uncertainty principle"; William James' "altars to unknown gods"; Popper's "refutation of errors"; Csikszentmihalyi's "convenient simplifications" and "tried-and-true prejudices"; Mark Runco and Ruth Richards' "consensual delusion"; Rollo May's "parochial prejudice raised to the level of a scientific principle"; and Root-Bernstein's "answer that best fits one's needs." The point of these theses is not that human knowledge is "wrong," but that its usefulness, as significant as it has been, is only *for the time being, pending the development of still more successful ideas and more durable belief systems which, themselves, are also destined to refutation, revision, and replacement* (see, for example, Popper, 1968). Grenz's concise paraphrase of Kuhn summarizes this view:

> While possessing great interpretive power, no belief system or puzzle-solution is ever able to explain all the data. Researchers keep coming across anomalies or findings that the prevailing theory cannot explain. The anomalies compound. Then someone proposes a new explanatory system that more successfully accounts for the anomalies, and eventually this new system replaces the old one (Grenz, 1996: 55).

A seemingly unrelated comparison illustrates the provisional and uncertain state of human knowledge. It is a history teacher's description of one country's unwritten constitution. "The [national] constitution" he read or said, "is a somewhat rambling structure and, like a house which many successive owners have altered just so far as suited their immediate convenience or the needs of the times, it bears the marks of many hands and is convenient rather than symmetrical."*

Convenient, rather than finely honed; *experimental,* rather than settled; *tentative* rather than definitive – these terms may well summarize the current state of human knowledge.

Conclusion and Implications for Human Creativity

The large number of phenomena that cannot be explained by existing systems of knowledge suggests that, as yet, we do not know enough about the world in which we live. The successful overthrow of many previously hallowed belief systems reminds us that what we know today is, at best, tentative and subject to falsification.

A more durable system of knowledge probably would require: (i) a different metaphysical foundation; (ii) open and honest exploration of every available path to knowledge, and their eventual synthesis; (iii) a thoroughgoing review of the usefulness of existing tools, retiring those that tend to inhibit the exercise of people's imagination; and, (iv) society-wide participation in the knowledge-building enterprise, a recognition of the validity of everyone's unique insights and their indispensability for constructing a more complete system of knowledge.

For that project to succeed, however, human knowledge would have to be recognized for what it is: a social construction, rather than a "secret" to be discovered; a work in progress, rather than a finished product; evolutionary, rather than fixed; provisional, rather than certain. *Tentative*!

---

* From notes taken in a high school history class, many years ago.

Selected Insights
on
The Tentativeness of Knowledge:
Implications for Human Creativity

Nothing can be more disputed than an indisputable fact.
>   — (Anonymous)

The more a man knows, the more he realizes that the sum total of his knowledge is but an infinitesimal fraction of all knowledge.
>   — (Anonymous)

Everything passes, everything perishes, everything palls.
>   — French Saying.

All truth, even the highest, is accessible to test. By doubting we are led to inquire, and by inquiry we perceive the truth.
>   — Peter Abelard (1965: 45).

[A]s a rule, the philosopher becomes so convinced of the validity of his own system that he presents it to the world as the ultimate truth or as a way to proceed toward the ultimate truth. Were he to admit that his system is only a hypothesis – and most likely wrong ... — he would run the risk of being considered an artist ...
>   — Silvano Arieti (1976: 284).

[W]e must admit that we do not know the answers, in spite of many philosophical attempts to find them.

— Silvano Arieti (1976: 408).

Man alone is aware of his infinitude and of the infinite, and of his need to cope with both. When he tries to decrease the unknown with his creativity, he remains surrounded by transcendence, mystery, and God's creation. He runs and runs toward an ultimate goal, which always escapes.

— Silvano Arieti (1976: 413).

If a man will begin with certainties, he shall end in doubts; but if he will be content to begin with doubts, he shall end in certainties.

— Francis Bacon (1977: 24).

Those who have taken upon them to lay down the laws of nature as a thing already searched out and understood, whether they have spoken in simple assurance or professional affectation, have therein done philosophy and the sciences great injury. For as they have been successful in inducing belief, so they have been effective in quenching and stopping inquiry; and have done more harm by spoiling and putting an end to other men's efforts than good by their own.

— Francis Bacon (1982: 2).

The logic now in use serves rather to fix and give stability to the errors which have their foundation in commonly received notions than to help the search after truth. So it does more harm than good.

— Francis Bacon (1982: 9).

[A]ll theories should be steadily rejected and dismissed as obsolete.

— Francis Bacon (1982: 25).

Does not natural science presuppose mechanical causation, determinism and the reduction of all higher phenomena to lower ones, the complex to the simple, and do not the successes of that science in astronomy, physics, chemistry, and biology attest to the truth of its presuppositions?

— Allan Bloom (1987: 302).

How many people understand, even today, that the concepts of science are neither absolute nor everlasting?

— Jacob Bronowski (1965: 37).

There is no such source of error as the pursuit of absolute truth.
— Samuel Butler (1993: 926).

Our ideas. They are for the most part like bad sixpences and we spend our lives in trying to pass them on one another.
— Samuel Butler (1993: 926).

> Opinions are made to be changed
> - or how is truth to be got at?
> — Lord Byron (1993: 651).

I often wish ... that I could rid the world of the tyranny of facts. What are facts but compromises? A fact merely marks the point where we have agreed to let investigation cease.
— Bliss Carman (1992: 131).

All progress is experimental.
— John Jay Chapman (1993: 737).

[T]he knowledge we have, and the basis upon which we judge the world around us, is becoming obsolete at an ever increasing rate ...
— M. Cooley (1989: 61).

Dominant intellectual commitments have made certain kinds of questions appear cogent and have given certain kinds of explanation their power to convince, and have excluded others, because they have established, antecedent to any particular research, the kind of work that was supposed to exist and the appropriate methods of inquiry.
— A. C. Crombie (1989: 351).

The pursuit of science leads only to the insoluble.
— Benjamin Disraeli (1993: 807).

There are three kinds of lies: lies, dammed lies, and statistics.
— Benjamin Disraeli (Attributed).

All education is a continuous dialogue — questions and answers that pursue every problem to the horizon.
— William O. Douglas (1997: 65).

[Knowledge] constantly makes itself obsolete, with the result that today's advanced knowledge is tomorrow's ignorance.
— Peter F. Drucker (1997: 22).

Sixty years ago I knew everything; now I know nothing; education is a progressive discovery of our ignorance.
— Will Durant (1997: 5).

Concepts which have proved useful for ordering things easily assume so great an authority over us that we forget their terrestrial origin and accept them as unalterable facts. ... The road to scientific progress is frequently blocked for long periods by such errors.

— Albert Einstein (1989: 348).

The whole of science is nothing more than a refinement of everyday thinking.

— Albert Einstein (1993: 807).

What we call "progress" is the exchange of one nuisance for another nuisance.

— Havelock Ellis (1992: 341).

The idea of a method that contains firm, unchanging, and absolutely binding principles for conducting the business of science meets considerable difficulty when confronted with the results of historical research. We find then, that there is not a single rule, however plausible, and however firmly grounded in epistemology, that is not violated at some time or other. It becomes evident that such violations are not accidental events ... On the contrary, we see that they are necessary for progress.

— Paul Feyerabend (1992: 132).

Knowledge emerges only through invention and re-invention, through the restless, impatient, continuing, hopeful inquiry men pursue in the world, with the world, and with each other.

— Paulo Freire (1972: 58).

[N]othing can be seen in its totality.

— Erich Fromm (1955: 153).

Our thoughts and insights are at best partial truths, mixed with a great deal of error, not to speak of the unnecessary misinformation about life and society to which we are exposed almost from the day of birth.

— Erich Fromm (1955: 174).

The more we learn the more we realize how little we know.

— R. Buckminster Fuller (1997: 125).

[T]he horizon is the range of vision that includes everything that can be seen from a particular vantage point.

— H. C. Gadamer (1996: 136).

The enemy of the conventional wisdom is not ideas but the march of events.

— John Kenneth Galbraith (1993: 292).

The ever-renewing organization (or society) is not one which is convinced that it enjoys eternal truth.
— John W. Gardner (1964: 84).

We need to be aware, for example, of how often our role, status, or position in a social network can cut us off from certain classes of informative data.
— Thomas Gilovich (1991: 187).

The more science one learns, the more one becomes aware of what is *not* known, and the provisional nature of much of what is [known]. All of this contributes to a healthy skepticism toward claims about how things are or should be. This general intellectual outlook, this awareness of how hard it can be to really know something with certainty, while humbling, is an important side benefit of participating in the scientific enterprise.
— Thomas Gilovich (1991: 189).

No idea is so antiquated that it was not once modern. No idea is so modern that it will not someday be antiquated.
— Ellen Glasgow (1992: 211).

In fact, history can be viewed as a series of transitions from one defining myth to another; older narratives inevitably wane and are replaced by newer ones.
— Stanley Grenz (1996: 45).

Much of what we "know is true," perhaps even "scientifically true," is a false collective belief made difficult to check because everyone around us shares the same belief — and so their minds confirm the same view of reality.

— Willis Harman (1984: xvii).

More trouble is caused in this world by indiscreet answers than by indiscreet questions.

— Sydney J. Harris (1993: 345).

When a thing ceases to be a subject of controversy, it ceases to be a subject of interest.

— William Hazlitt (1993: 184).

Yesterday's avant-garde experience is today's chic and tomorrows' cliché.

— Richard Hofstadter (1990: 11).

Certainty generally is illusion, and repose is not the destiny of man.

— Oliver Wendell Holmes, Jr. (1992: 51).

Every day some beautiful theory is destroyed by cruel, harsh reality.

— Aldous Huxley (1989: 414).

So far, evolution has been nothing but staggering from one error to the other.
— Henrik Ibsen (1991: 116).

There is no worse lie than a truth misunderstood by those who hear it.
— William James (1992a: 363).

All the magnificent achievements of mathematical and physical science – our doctrines of evolution, of uniformity of law, and the rest – proceed from our indomitable desire to cast the world into a more rational shape in our minds than the crude order of our experience. The principle of causality, for example – what is it but a postulate, an empty name covering simply a demand that the sequence of events shall some day manifest a deeper kind of belonging of one thing with another than the mere arbitrary juxtaposition which now phenomenally appears. It is as much an altar to an unknown god as the one that Saint Paul found at Athens. All our scientific and philosophic ideals are altars to unknown gods.
— William James (1999: 173).

Any solution to a problem changes the problem.
— R. W. Johnson (1993: 734).

Round numbers are always false.
— Samuel Johnson (Attributed).

There are no pure perceptions.
— Immanuel Kant (Attributed).

In its empirical meaning, the term 'whole' is always only comparative.
— Immanuel Kant (1992: 222).

All progress is precarious, and the solution of one problem brings us face to face with another problem.
— Martin Luther King, Jr. (1993: 339).

To believe it is possible we may be in error is the first step toward getting out of it.
— Johann K. Lavater (1991: 116).

Life is one long struggle in the dark.
— Lucretius (1993: 212).

[W]e must be fully committed, but we must also be aware at the same time that we might possibly be wrong.
— Rollo May (1976: 12-13).

People who claim to be *absolutely* convinced that their stand is the only right one are dangerous. Such conviction is the essence not only of dogmatism, but of its more destructive cousin, fanaticism.
— Rollo May (1976: 13).

All genuine progress results from finding new facts.
— Wheeler McMillen (1991: 71).

Only absolute fools are absolutely certain.
— Ashley Montagu (1995: 110).

All truth is not to be found at home.
— Baron de la Brède et de Montesquieu (1955: 142).

We never stop investigating. We are never satisfied that we know enough to get by. Every question we answer leads on to another question. This has become the greatest survival trick of our species.
— Desmond Morris (1993: 209).

People ... need to have the ability to say to themselves that "what I believed yesterday may not be true today."
— Helen M. Moye (1993: 155).

The more ignorant the authority, the more dogmatic it is. In the fields where no real knowledge is even possible, the authorities are the fiercest and most assured and punish non-belief with the severest of penalties.
— Abraham Myerson (attributed).

What are man's truths ultimately? Merely his *irrefutable* errors.
— Friedrich Nietzsche (1992: 319).

Oh, how much is today hidden by science! Oh, how much it is expected to hide!
— Friedrich Nietzsche (1993: 809).

That no universal is a substance existing outside the mind can be evidently proved.
— William of Ockham (1992: 459).

Some of the most foolish ideas from five years ago are now a reality.
— Roger von Oech: (1983: 141).

Those who seek certainty, or who claim certainty in their knowledge, cannot tolerate ambiguity. The word "ambiguous" means "uncertain" or "doubtful," or "capable of being under-stood in more than one way." And because that means not knowing – perhaps not ever being able to know – we have great trouble with ambiguity... .
— M. Scott Peck (1987: 220).

Every step of progress the world has made has been from scaffold to scaffold, and from stake to stake.
— Wendell Phillips (1992: 341).

The only certainty is that nothing is certain.
— Pliny the Elder (1993: 128).

The game of science is, in principle, without end. He who decides one day that scientific statements do not call for any further test, and that they can be regarded as finally verified, retires from the game.

— Karl Raimund Popper (1968: 53).

The empirical basis of objective science has ... nothing 'absolute' about it. Science does not rest upon solid bedrock. The bold structure of its theories rises, as it were, above a swamp. It is like a building erected on piles. The piles are driven down from above into the swamp, but not down to any natural or 'given' base; and if we stop driving the piles deeper, it is not because we have reached firm ground. We simply stop when we are satisfied that the piles are firm enough to carry the structure, at least for the time being.

— Karl Raimund Popper (1968: 111)

Science is not a system of certain, or well-established, statements; nor is it a system which steadily advances towards a state of finality. Our science is not knowledge ... it can never claim to have attained truth ...

— Karl Raimund Popper (1968: 278).

We do not know; we can only guess.

— Karl Raimund Popper (1968: 278).

The old scientific ideal of *episteme* -- of absolutely certain, demonstrable knowledge -- has proved to be an idol. The demand for scientific objectivity makes it inevitable that every scientific statement must remain *tentative for ever* ... Only in our subjective experiences of conviction, in our subjective faith, can we be 'absolutely certain'.

— Karl. R. Popper (1975: 246).

All clues, no solutions. That's the way things are.

— Dennis Potter (1993: 345).

Isaac Newton's laws were considered final in their domain of application, somewhat the way quantum mechanics is now considered to be final by many physicists.

— Ilya Prigogine (1996: 2).

Mankind is at a turning point, the beginning of a new rationality in which science is no longer identified with certitude and probability with ignorance.

— Ilya Prigogine (1996: 7).

Chance, or probability, is no longer a convenient way of accepting ignorance, but rather part of a new, extended rationality.

— Ilya Prigogine (1996: 155).

The world was not created once and for all for each of us. In the course of life things that we never even imagined are added to it.

— Marcel Proust (1948: 87).

Everything that seems to us imperishable tends toward its destruction.

— Marcel Proust (1948: 105).

Each generation of critics does nothing but take the opposite of the truths accepted by their predecessors.

— Marcel Proust (1948: 185).

Theories and schools, like microbes and corpuscles, devour each other and by their struggle assure the continuity of life.

— Marcel Proust (1948: 205).

Gone is the ideal of a universe whose course follows strict rules, a predetermined cosmos that unwinds itself like an unwinding clock. Gone is the ideal of the scientist who knows the absolute truth. The happenings of nature are like rolling dice rather than like revolving stars; they are controlled by probability laws, not by causality.

— Hans Reichenbach (1992: 371).

There are more things in heaven and earth than are dreamt of in your philosophy, my dear logician.
— Hans Reichenbach (1992: 371).

The only good copies are those which make us see the absurdity of bad originals.
— François duc de La Rochefoucauld (1993: 445).

Experience has shown each of us that it is very easy to deceive ourselves, to believe something which later experience shows is not so.
— Carl R. Rogers (1961: 217).

Never, *never* accept anyone else's evaluation of the state of the art, including mine. I am going to show you the best way I know to do surgery. Fifty years from now, my techniques will be considered barbarous. But if I have my way, you — the students I'm training in this room — will be the ones who will make my techniques look barbarous. Then at least my teaching, if not my practices, will justify themselves. So never assume that what I show you is the best way to do anything. Never assume that any idea you may have has already been tried. Surgery will only advance when and if you look at what I and my colleagues do, and say to yourself, 'That's not so hot. I bet I could do it better.'
— (Anonymous Surgeon; see Robert Scott Root-Bernstein, 1989: 67).

[F]acts are context dependent, as much as it may hurt to hear it! ... [A]ny given set of data is compatible with a range of alternative explanations, each determined by the assumptions and the aesthetic criteria you employ in choosing, weighing, and organizing the data.
— Robert Scott Root-Bernstein (1989: 179).

What we consider to be the best solution depends on what our criteria are. And historically, these keep changing.
— Robert Scott Root-Bernstein (1989: 357).

Doubt most that which you would most believe.
— Robert Scott Root-Bernstein (1989: 419).

[I]t appears that sometimes problems are unsolvable because they are posed within the wrong methodological and episte-mological framework.
— Robert Scott Root-Bernstein (1989: 351-352).

If science were truth, then once an answer was obtained it would be *the* answer.
— Robert Scott Root-Bernstein (1989: 358).

It is sometimes well for a blatant error to draw attention to overmodest truths.
                                        — Jean Rostand (1993: 287).

It is sometimes important for science to know how to forget the things she is surest of.
                                        — Jean Rostand (1993: 809).

Nothing leads the scientist so astray as a premature truth.
                                        — Jean Rostand (1993: 813).

Science tells us what we can know, but what we can know is little, and if we forget how much we cannot know we become insensitive to many things of very great importance.
                                        — Bertrand Russell (1992: 369).

[O]ne must be prepared to consider the possibility that a body of ideas that might seem almost self-evident is, in fact, highly distorted and highly selective …
                                        — William Ryan (1971: 21).

For an idea ever to be fashionable is ominous, since it must afterwards be always old-fashioned.
                                        — George Santayana (1992: 212).

The chief cause of problems is solutions.
                              — Sevareid's Law (1986: 51).

Science becomes dangerous only when it imagines that it has
reached its goal.
                              — George Bernard Shaw (1993: 809).

The more we study the more we discover our ignorance.
                              — Percy Bysshe Shelley (1997: 124).

All poetry is experimental poetry.
                              — Wallace Stevens (1990: 11).

We must not suppose that the nature of reality is exhausted
by the kinds of knowledge which we have of it.
                              — P. F. Strawson (1992: 436).

The last thing we're supposed to realize is that we have been
lied to most of our lives.
                              — Charles Swindoll (1995: 24).

[A]ll knowledge is based on challengeable assumptions.
                              — Robert Theobald (1981: 122).

[Most students] leave college believing that what they have learned in economics, sociology, political science, and psychology rests on some rational theoretical base, rather than on a nineteenth-century set of assumptions that have long ago been shown to be special cases.

— Robert Theobald (1981: 123).

Your five senses detect only a very limited portion of what *is*. Without intuition as a sixth sense, you would have a very incomplete understanding of what *is*.

— Tom Thiss (1995: 118).

The universe is wider than our views of it.

— Henry David Thoreau (1987: 50).

[N]ew facts turn our old assumptions inside out.

— Alvin Toffler (1983: 21).

How easily do individuals as well as whole nations take their own so-called civilization as the true civilization ...

— L. Tolstoy (1955: 188).

Civilization is a movement and not a condition, a voyage and not a harbor.

— A. J. Toynbee (1993: 156).

Science is a cemetery of dead ideas.
                           —Miguel de Unamuno (1993: 809).

It is the spirit of the age to believe that any fact, no matter how suspect, is superior to any imaginative exercise, no matter how true.
                           — Gore Vidal (1992: 132).

Doubt is not a pleasant condition, but certainty is an absurd one.
                           — Voltaire (1992: 52).

Doubt grows with knowledge.
                           — Johann Wolfgang von Goethe (1992: 105).

There are no whole truths; all truths are half truths. It is trying to treat them as whole truths that plays the devil.
                           — Alfred North Whitehead (1992: 426).

Don't get involved in partial problems, but always take flight to where there is a free view over the whole *single* great problem, even if this view is still not a clear one.

Ludwig Wittgenstein (1993: 734).

Man has to awaken to wonder ... Science is a way of sending him to sleep again.

Ludwig Wittgenstein (1993: 810).

IX
Paradigm Shift and Human Creativity

[A] frog if put in cold water will not bestir itself if that water is heated up slowly and gradually and will in the end let itself be boiled alive, too comfortable with continuity to realize that continuous change at some point may become intolerable and demand a change in behavior. If we want to avoid the fate of ... the boiling frog we must learn to look for and embrace discontinuous change.

— Charles Handy

Mismatch

"Looking Where the Light Is" is a popular allegory in creative problem solving. This is the story of a drunk who lost his keys in a dark alley but came to look for them at a street corner where a street lamp glowed. A policeman, seeing the drunk groping on his hands and knees, asked, "What are you doing there?" "Looking for my keys," the drunk replied. "Where did you lose them?" the policeman asked. "In the alley," the drunk replied. "Then why are looking for them under the lamp?" the policeman further inquired. "Because it's too dark in the alley to see them," the drunk replied (see Harman and Rheingold, 1984: 67; Root-Bernstein, 1989: 411).

"Unthinkable!" "Ridiculous!" "How illogical!" are likely reactions to this story. But the drunk is probably not alone in his apparent "illogicality." Many human activities show similar inconsistencies:

- a preference for the easy, the obvious, or the convenient, even when such responses are not producing desired results.

- institutionalization of activities and goals far beyond the reasons for which those activities and goals were originally established.

- perpetuation of previously successful policies, programs, and procedures long after and far beyond the circumstances in which they were appropriate.

- excessive confidence in current principles and theories and, therefore, the tendency to continue to interpret the world within an existing framework, even when the evidence appears to contradict accepted beliefs and traditions.

Mismatch between desired human ends and the means employed to achieve them is a commonly observed phenomenon, but with different descriptions. "Culture shock" is the term that social anthropologists use to describe a situation in which another culture's practice clearly differs from one's own or in which another culture's practice does not seem to be producing what one perceives as the desired result. "Squabbling for the proverbial deck chairs on a sinking *Titanic*" is a metaphor that some social commentators use to refer to actions that are totally inconsistent with the needs of the time or are even producing disastrous results. "Unproductive" is the way that economists describe an activity or the use of a resource when the results achieved defy rational calculations, often in monetary terms. "Hampered by yesterday's myths in concentrating on today's needs" is the way that public policy analysts describe a society in which a previously successful policy or program is continued long after the time or the circumstances in which it was appropriate. "Resistance to change," "rigid maxims," "rule-of-thumb routines," "cast-iron particular doctrines," "driving into the future while looking out of the rearview mirror," "enslaved by the organizational arrangements we have designed to serve us," are some of the terms that management scholars use to describe what they see as organizational inertia (see, for example, Whitehead, 1964: 103; Gardner, 1964: xiii; Drucker, 1970: 32; Toffler, 1980: 11; Kanter, 1983: 62).

Creativity scholars attribute the difficulty of solving many problems largely to mismatch between the desired objectives (solutions) and the techniques (processes) used to achieve those objectives. In their view, one reason why many problems are not solved is not because they are impossible to solve, but because either the way that they are interpreted, or the strategies used in tackling them, are inappropriate. Inappropriate problem interpretation and solution strategies, creativity scholars further observe, are often due to false systems of belief, values, and assumptions that influence the way that a particular community, society, or generation perceives the world and tries to relate to its elements (see, for example, Root-Bernstein, 1989: 351).

Paradigms

Thomas Kuhn's (1970) widely-referenced work *Structure of Scientific Revolution* elucidates the influence of a "community's" belief system on the activities of members of that community. Focusing mainly on the scientific community, Kuhn argues that the problems scientists decide to solve, the means they consider appropriate for solving those problems, the evidence they regard as admissible, and the conclusions the community is willing to accept, are all influenced by the community's belief system. Kuhn characterizes those beliefs as "paradigms," which he defines as "the entire constellation of beliefs, values, techniques, [concepts, and theories] shared by the members of a given community" (Kuhn, 1970: 175).

"Paradigm," of course, is not an exclusively scientific concept. It is fundamental to every aspect of a culture and includes the (often unspoken) assumptions, myths, beliefs, theories, and values that are shared by the members of a society, that lie behind their actions, and that give direction to their economic philosophy, political structure, intellectual orientation, as well as their customs and traditions. Karl Marx's term "the ruling ideas of each age" aptly signifies the intellectual status and cultural influence of paradigms. Illustrative paradigms are:

- assumptions about the world, that define things and how they work and interrelate.

- assumptions about knowledge that specify what can be known, how inquiry is to be conducted, and how information is to be generated, managed, and transmitted.

- assumptions about the human species that define our place in the universe and our relationship with the rest of nature.

- assumptions about the individual human being that define personal identity and relationships with fellow human beings and other creatures.

- assumptions about social groups that, as Emilé Durkheim suggests, remind people of their common group membership, reaffirm their distinctiveness as well as their traditional values, maintain prohibitions and taboos, transmit their cultural heritage from one generation to the next and, generally, try to keep the people together as a social entity (see Robertson, 1987: 401).

- assumptions about culture that prescribe appropriate behavior in specific situations and also provide guidelines for actions.

Usefulness and Limitations

Paradigms fulfill two basic functions. First, they explain the world, or provide a framework within which people try to make sense of their experiences and the things around them. Second, they define the limits of human action as well as the principles (rules and procedures) by which a community, society, or civilization conducts its affairs.

The state of the world (or of a society) at any point in time, including the material, psychological, and spiritual condition of people, attest to the usefulness, success, or relevance of a prevailing paradigm.

A case in point is the Twentieth Century or, more accurately, the period between 1900 and now. With the dazzling achievements that have been made in practically every domain of human activity, the modern era, justifiably, has been regarded as the most successful human civilization. As has been reviewed earlier, more goods and services have been produced and consumed during this period than at any other period in recorded human history. People have been living longer and, presumably, feeling healthier, at least in some parts of the world. Some of the diseases that plagued previous generations have been eradicated or largely controlled. Many hitherto inaccessible parts of the universe have been discovered and probed. It has been possible to communicate with one another from practically anywhere in the world, and in real time. With the aid of an ever-exploding technology, people have been able to do things that were previously thought impossible. As a result, overall standards of living have been rising, at least in some parts of the world and some sections of society.

But, as "successful" as modern civilization has been, the fear exists that human and environmental conditions are actually deteriorating. Influential global development reports identify several crises that, the reports note, threaten the survival of the human species and could even wreck human civilization as we know it (see, for example, The Club of Rome, 1974; 1979; Worldwatch Institute, 1984; 1985; World Commission on Environment and Development, 1987; UNDP, 1994). Four crises of particular concern are

312

(a) *Unsustainable patterns of economic growth and a threatened future for humanity and planet Earth:*

• patterns of consumption that are depleting biodiversity and, therefore, undermining ecological balance.

• technologies that seek to maximize efficiency even at the expense of human potential and the integrity of human ingenuity.

• farming and industrial production methods that are degrading the physical environment - land, water, and air.

• population growth rates that are rapidly outstripping the world's stock of nonrenewable resources.

(b) *Deteriorating economic, social, psychological, and political conditions:*

• poverty, hunger, lack of health services, diseases, unemployment, and underemployment.

• social inequalities, mistrust, violence, conflicts, fear, anxiety, uncertainty.

• alienation, frustration, depression, meaningless jobs, disenchantment with work.

• family instability, community disintegration, crumbling social order.

(c) *The "human gap":* *

• apparent incongruity between human actions and human understanding of the psychological, social, economic, political, and environmental implications of those actions.

• lack of synchronicity among various aspects of the human experience (for example, the amazing success in material terms and abysmal failure in moral values).

• the growing complexity of modern life, which appears to be outstripping the human capacity to cope.

• new problems that are arising faster than the human capacity to solve them.

---

* The phrase is The Club of Rome's (1979).

(d) *The "great waste"* of human potentials:*

- the vast reservoir of human capacity (creativity) that largely goes unrecognized, undiscovered, repressed or, in more fortunate circumstances, is only partially developed.

- socialization processes that, in some cultures, require people to perceive, think, feel, and behave in a particular way and that therefore tend to inhibit originality and individual expressions.

- educational systems that, in many parts of the world, seem more interested in preparing learners for the job market than in enabling them to find out and to do what they are "naturally" good at.

- labor conditions that selectively recognize and engage only those human abilities that an employer perceives as "useful," and that therefore tend to reject other human attributes as "irrelevant."

- patterns of social organization that inadvertently tend to recognize and/or to nourish the creativity of some members of a society while, at the same time, ignoring (and even repressing) the abilities of others.

- the perception of gross national product, rather than human potential, as the central goal of development.

The seriousness of these and related conditions is widely recognized; some of them are already on the "global agenda for change." The general feeling is that "something is fundamentally wrong" and needs to be fixed. Beyond that notion, however, considerable disagreement exists regarding what to do and how to go about the needed changes. Two commonly observed positions deserve particular mention:

1. Those who believe that the problems facing humanity still can be resolved within the framework of existing ideas.

2. Those who argue that some of the central ideas upon which modern civilization has been built are no longer relevant and need to be revised or retired.

The first position reflects a commitment to the present order and the (often unstated) assumption that the ideas that have created and sustained "the most remarkable civilization in human history" must be

---

* The phrase is Edward Deming's (1992: 264).

right, that the principles that have worked so well in the past will continue to produce good results. In this view, perceived problems are due to faulty methods of implementation, rather than to the faulty assumptions that underlie those methods. Solutions and remedial actions therefore tend to focus on improving the methods of delivery (i.e., finding better or more efficient ways to achieve desired goals) rather than on changing the way that problems are perceived or understood.

The second position acknowledges the usefulness, but also the limitations, of some of the fundamental assumptions upon which modern civilization has been built. Proponents of this position call attention to the fragmentary state of human knowledge and, therefore, the pretentiousness of categorical statements. They also point to changing conditions and the changing configuration of issues that require corresponding changes in thinking and values. In particular, they observe the coming together of so many global crises that, they believe, are too complex to be expressed via traditional concepts. In this view, no significant improvement in the human or environmental condition can be expected until we (a) recognize the limitations of the fundamental assumptions, concepts, and logic upon which certain actions are based, and (b) start questioning and relinquishing irrelevant and unproductive assumptions.

Paradigm Shift

Identifying, questioning, and relinquishing irrelevant and unproductive assumptions and replacing them with more relevant and more productive worldviews is what this anthology means by "paradigm shift." The literature refers to the same concept variously as: "a change in direction"; "a break with tradition"; "thinking along new lines"; "deep value changes in individual and social attitudes"; "new ways of thinking and acting"; new patterns of relationship"; "a new mindset"; "a different map of reality"; "a new metaphor for understanding reality"; and "reassessment of the most basic assumptions underlying human society" (see, for example, Kuhn, 1962: x-xi; De Bono, 1971; The Club of Rome, 1979: xv; Toffler, 1980: 228, 229; Theobald, 1981: 19-25; McRobie, 1981:188; von Oech, 1983: 57; Root-Bernstein, 1989: 351; Blanchard, 1989: 237; Harman and Hormann, 1990: 68; Gilovich, 1991: 194; Thompson, 1992: 79; Sternberg and Lubart, 1995: 95; Barret, 1998).

Paradigm shifts come in different forms, depending on the "community" and what it is trying to achieve. Regarding human creativity and fulfillment, paradigm shifts of particular relevance would involve, among other things:

- the realization that prevailing worldviews (i.e., assumptions, beliefs, and theories), however successful in the past, are not necessarily right or even the best ways to understand reality.

- a thoroughgoing review of some of the values, beliefs, and assumptions that underlie our actions and behaviors.

- letting go of assumptions that tend to constrain human potentials or to undermine social and ecological well-being.

- a willingness to listen to, and consider, seemingly unconventional or unorthodox ideas.

- imagining, developing, and testing new assumptions, concepts, and theories that more adequately represent the complex problems currently facing humanity, and that also enhance the human capacity to deal with those problems.

Trends and Proposals

Paradigm shifts, though rare, are not a new phenomenon. They have been happening since the dawn of civilization and, indeed, have been the basis of all significant advances in the human condition. Frequently cited illustrations include: Columbus' and Magellan's redefinition of the shape of the earth; Copernicus', Galileo's, and Kepler's revolutionary maps of the heavenly bodies; Vesalius' and Harvey's groundbreaking anatomies of the human body; Darwin's revolutionary theory of the evolution of the species; Newton's, Faraday's, and Einstein's imaginative interpretations of the structure of the universe; plus so many other set-breaking ideas in music, painting, sculpture, literature, poetry, and other fields.

For a long time, noted paradigm shifts tended to concentrate almost exclusively on revolutionary new ideas about the physical universe and the material aspects of human culture. Only recently has attention been given to the less tangible but equally fundamental rethinking of the social values that inspired those great achievements and facilitated (or sometimes hindered) their adoption.

Table IX.1 presents ten key values in which significant change of direction in thought is beginning to be observed. The values are selected from a very large set of beliefs and assumptions about human nature, life, work, education, leadership, and social relations. The reason for focusing on this particular set of values is their potential influence on human creativity and, by implication, human fulfillment.

Table IX.1

TRADITIONAL VALUES AND EMERGING SHIFTS	
Traditional Beliefs and Values	**Emerging Shifts and Trends**
The Certainty and Universality of Knowledge • Reality is something out there, independent of the knowing individual. It consists mostly of the things we can see, touch, smell, taste, and hear. • Truth is absolute, timeless, and universally valid. Events and phenomena have objective, universal meaning for all people. • Shared human nature implies shared perception. Everybody looks at the world and sees the same things. • There is only one reliable method of obtaining knowledge. • The concepts by which phenomena are observed and explained are transcendental (i.e., value-free), universally valid, and capable of representing the world as it is.	**The Tentativeness of Knowledge** • Reality is a social construction, reflecting the perspective, language, needs, and interests of the observing individual, group, community, or culture. • Human knowledge is the subjective interpretation of phenomena by a people. Events and phenomena have different meanings for different people. • What is true for one group of people may not necessarily be true for another group. What is true at one time may not necessarily be true at another time. • There is no known method of inquiry that, alone, can explain all phenomena. Different methods are useful for different types of phenomena. • The languages, concepts, and categories by which human perceptions are organized do not have the capability to represent the world as it really is and, therefore, do not necessarily reflect reality. • Certain human experiences and phenomena are not accessible to currently available methods of inquiry. Other phenomena that are currently regarded as unimportant could eventually turn out to be critical.
Categorization of Issues • Events and issues are separate and distinct. The world is composed of independently existing phenomena, each separate and autonomous. • Explanation of an event is to be found within the immediate context in which it occurs or is observed.	**Creative Synthesis** • The universe is an interconnected whole in which everything is related to every other thing. Issues and events are interdependent, always influencing one another and acquiring their nature, or meaning, from their dynamic interactions.

Table IX.1., continued

Traditional Beliefs and Values	Emerging Shifts and Trends
Categorization of Issues, *continued* • For a deeper and fuller understanding of the world, it is necessary to divide knowledge into disciplines and sub-disciplines, each dealing with a separate issue. • To adequately address people's various needs, it is necessary to design a separate program for every need and issue. • Different problems have different origins that must be identified and dealt with individually.	**Creative Synthesis,** *continued* • Explanation of even the minutest event is to be found in the widest context, which takes into account the myriad of factors involved and their dynamic influences. • The interconnectedness of issues calls for integration (rather than compartmental-ization) of knowledge about those issues. • The holistic nature of human beings and the inseparability of their physical, emotional, and spiritual needs call for greater balance and more integrated human service programs and experiences. • Many of the problems currently facing humanity are symptoms of an underlying "cause"– unrecognized, underutilized, or unfulfilled human potential – and can most effectively and efficiently be dealt with at that level.

Individualism and Competitiveness
• The only way to resolve perennial problems of scarcity is by interpersonal and intergroup competition.
• Life is a constant struggle against others. Success is the ability to get to the top of the heap, regardless of the cost to other people.
• Human beings have the same abilities and can be measured and compared along whatever set of attributes a society happens to value at a particular time.
• Superiority in a given ability implies overall superior endowment.
• People are either "we" or "they," "insiders" or "outsiders," members of "in-groups" or "out-groups." Solidarity is the proper in-group behavior. Hostility toward perceived outsiders is normal.
•Dominant values and mindsets:
  • Fixed-pie view of resources.
  • Confrontation.
	Cooperation and Mutual Dependence
	• Life is a partnership in which the individual strives to fulfill himself with the active support of others. Genuine success is the ability to realize one's potential and to contribute one's talents to the common good.
	• It is not necessary to "be" better than others to feel fulfilled or successful. The goal of life is personal best, rather than the number and caliber of people defeated.
	• Other people are as significant, as necessary, and as worthy of appreciation as I am.
	• Dominant values and mindsets:
	  • Collaboration.
	  • "Interexistence" and collective survival.
	  • Mutual support.
	  • Networking.
	  • "The sky is big enough for every bird to fly."

Table IX.1., continued

Traditional Beliefs and Values	Emerging Shifts and Trends
Individualism ..., *continued* • Survival of the fittest. • Cream rises to the top. • Beat the competition. • Look after yourself and your family. • The ship is full.	**Cooperation ...,** *continued* • Win-win approach to issues. • Generalized reciprocity. • Expanded sense of relatedness. • Abundance.
Messianic Leadership • Leaders are endowed with superior abilities and wisdom; they know what is best for the people. • The leader is someone who knows the way and shows the way. • Most people are not capable of making intelligent decisions and, therefore, must be led and controlled. • Leadership is a responsibility to set the direction and enforce compliance by whatever means (e.g., threat of punishment or promise of reward).	**Creative Leadership.** • People are the best judge of what is good for them. • A leader is someone who can get people with fundamentally different perceptions and beliefs to think together and to decide the way they want to go and how to get there. • Decisions on matters affecting the people should be collective, in which all available viewpoints are considered. • If allowed, people are capable of making intelligent decisions and managing their lives. • Leadership is a responsibility to promote the conditions in which people are able to recognize their talents (including *leadership*) and reach their potential.
Traditional Education • Education is a process of transmitting and acquiring knowledge. • The purpose of education is to prepare learners for the job market – providing them with the skills to perform particular tasks and to earn a living. • Test scores measure educational success. The prestige of an educational institution depends on the quantity of facts taught, passes recorded, diplomas awarded, and recognitions received.	**Creative Education** • Education is a process of personal growth and development – finding out and actualizing one's talents. • The purpose of education is to unfold the unique abilities of the learner so that he can become happy and fulfilled as a person, productive and committed as an employee, and responsible as a national and global citizen. • As much as possible, educational materials should reflect the actual circumstances of the learner's life. • Methods of teaching and learning should be varied to suit different learning styles and needs.

Table IX.1., continued

Traditional Beliefs and Values	Emerging Shifts and Trends
Traditional Education, *continued* • The proper basis of the curriculum and materials taught in schools is the needs of the labor market. • The really important learning has to be intellect-based. • To expand, knowledge has to be divided into specialties.	**Creative Education,** *continued* • All talents are equally valid. Their development and actualization is, therefore, a legitimate and important educational goal. • Specialized knowledge is critically important. However, to provide learners with more holistic perspectives on issues, it is equally important to reintegrate the various branches of knowledge.
Structured Social Relationships • Human beings are either male or female and belong to one or the other economic, social, racial, ethnic, or professional group that also determines their worth. • Perceived similarities and differences are the natural basis of relationship between people. • Certain categories of people are economically, socially, politically, and/or intellectually insignificant and, therefore, lack the capacity to participate effectively in economic, social, and political affairs. • To be autonomous is to behave as if one is independent of other people and as if one does not need others for anything. • Sophistication means relating to others superficially (i.e., formally, officially, ritually) with set patterns of behavior, even where those responses belie the behaving individual's genuine desires and true feelings.	**Spontaneous Social Relationships** • People are, first and foremost, human beings. The gender, economic, social, racial, or ethnic group within which a person falls, or is assigned, has nothing to do with his natural abilities and intrinsic worth as a human being. • Meaningful relationships between people are generalized and oblivious of boundaries. • Every human being is innately endowed with a one-of-a-kind set of talents and is to be valued and cherished for the important and unique contributions he can make for the common good. • Autonomy does not imply "cocooning," but living out one's natural abilities (i.e., recognizing and actualizing one's potential in the context of other people). An essential part of autonomy is recognizing one's incompleteness, or vulnerability, and how much one depends on others for the things one needs and values. • Real (as opposed to phony) sophistication is responding to others spontaneously (directly and honestly), according to one's genuine feelings.

Table IX.1., continued

Traditional Beliefs and Values	Emerging Shifts and Trends

Bureaucratic Management
 • The corporation is an institution de signed to:
  • produce and distribute economic goods.
  • generate and satisfy market needs.
  • maximize profit for shareholders.
  • reward workers for their labor.
 • The proper organizational structure is departmental (divisional), with a hierarchical chain of command and supervision. Normal organizational processes include vertical communication, strict adherence to rules, impersonal relations, and standardized procedures, usually, in the form of rules and regulations.
 • Loyalty and commitment to the organization require generous pay and benefits, bonuses and tenure.
	Creative Management
	 • The corporation is a multipurpose institution, having both economic and trans-economic goals including:
	  • profit for shareholders.
	  • respect for the dignity of workers as human beings and opportunities for their personal growth and development.
	  • promotion of societal and environ-mental interests.
	  • good citizenship.
	 • A productive, fulfilling, and self-renewing organizational structure is characterized by initiative, "community," collaboration, inclusiveness, all-round communication, and creativity.
	 • Loyalty to the organization is an inevitable by-product of creative, challenging, meaningful, and fulfilling work.

Paid labor • Work is tedious, unpleasant, and tiring. • Labor is a commodity to be bought and sold. Work is a means to earn a living and, thereby, to be able to support oneself and one's family. • Workers are irresponsible and require some form of coercion or inducement to achieve required levels of productivity and responsibility.	**Creative Work** • Work is an integral and necessary part of life – a source of joy and fulfillment, meaningful and desirable in and of itself. • Work is primarily an opportunity to participate with fellow human beings in some important project, to do something that is useful to one's organization, community, or society. Material compensation is very important, but personal fulfillment is the ultimate goal of work. • Increased productivity is a natural concomitant of creative, challenging, and fulfilling work.

Table IX.1., continued

Traditional Beliefs and Values	Emerging Shifts and Trends

Socially-Ascribed Identity
• One is either male or female, and belongs to a specific racial, ethnic, professional, and social group.
• Material possession and consumption are the true measures of one's success and worth.
• What "they say" and what they think and expect of one is more important for one's sense of worth than how one perceives oneself.
 	
Self-Reflection:
        How am I doing in terms of what people in my position should be doing?
	Creative Selfhood
	• One is essentially a human being, endowed with unique abilities and, therefore, of intrinsic worth to one's society and the world.
	• Success consists in being able to actualize one's potential, to develop and express one's talents in something that is beneficial not only to oneself but also to one's society.
	• One's sense of worth depends primarily on how one perceives and regards oneself.
	Self-Reflection:
	        Who am I? Why am I here? Where am I going?
	        In what ways can my unique set of abilities benefit my society and the rest of nature?

Economic Development • Gross national product is the principal index of development. • Poverty and underdevelopment in some sections of society and in some parts of the world are a function of internal constraints, such as insufficient savings and investment, resource scarcity, lack of education and skills, inferior genetic inheritance, and lack of achievement motivation.	**Human Development** • The quality of people's lives – the extent to which they are able to realize their potential and to be happy with themselves and with one another – is the ultimate purpose of development. • Material deprivation in some sections of society and some parts of the world is not due to lack of ability or talent, but to long periods of neglect and/or gross underutilization of available human potential in those places.

Conclusion

Analysis of ongoing shifts in thinking indicates a definite trend toward a more creative, more humane, and more fulfilling human civilization. But, as hopeful as the signs appear, some snags can be expected. Human values, however questionable or unproductive, do not change overnight. Underlying their apparent tenacity are several pragmatic reasons including:

- the mystique or the sanctity of the origins of certain assumptions (e.g., legend, mythology, science, religion, ethics, etc.), some of which are hard to question.

- the amazing success of modern civilization and, therefore, the presumed validity of the assumptions upon which it has been built.

- the prestige, comfort, and security (financial, intellectual, social, and emotional) that some of the beliefs are providing for those who hold them.

- coherence with preexisting theories and other widely accepted values.

- the convenience of clinging to what has always been "true" or what has "worked" over the years (e.g., "the words of our elders" or the "faith of our fathers").

- the heavy investment of time, energy, money, and other resources in the existing order of things and, therefore, the potentially high costs of having to dismantle and redo them.

- natural human reluctance to upset the *status quo,* particularly when the present condition is perceived as satisfactory.

- fear that abandoning current beliefs might create other problems that are more serious than the current situation.

However strong the reasons for their persistence, some of the assumptions and values by which we live are simply not promoting human creativity or, for that matter, the prospects of finding imaginative, more humane, and more durable solutions to the increasingly complex problems that many societies and, indeed, the whole world are facing. Some of these values may actually be responsible for some of the problems. Leaving them unexamined will only perpetuate or even exacerbate present crises. Averting possible catastrophe and building a more sustainable and more fulfilling human civilization call for a fundamental change in direction.

The difficulty of such a "shift" should not be minimized. The alternative – waiting for crises to reveal the shortcomings of some of our beliefs and values – could be disastrous. As the Club of Rome (1979: 10, 118) fears, "the shock could be fatal" and no one might survive to make use of "the lessons." This is not a cause for despair but, rather, a call to action at all levels of society to make the necessary value adjustments on which further progress depends.

Fortunately, a large and growing number of people are recognizing both the challenge and the need for action, and they are rising to the occasion. Already, three groups of people and actions can be discerned:

- The first group – realizing that building a more humanly fulfilling civilization calls for a different perception of people and their capabilities – is questioning some of the assumptions upon which modern economic, social, and political arrangements are based and is proposing more liberating, more humane, and more collaborative alternatives.

- The second group – realizing that our collective survival and social well-being ultimately depend on the extent to which everyone's creative potential is developed and expressed in their daily activities – is working to humanize the way that children are reared, the way that students are taught or enabled to learn, the way that work is organized and workers are managed, and the way people are perceived, governed, or led.

- The third group – realizing that to regain our humanity (creativity) and restore meaning to our lives, we can no longer afford to let a few "gifted" individuals do the thinking for us – is working to make their families, communities, organizations, governments, and other social institutions more creativity-friendly and more participatory.

The indications are that these transforming efforts will intensify, leading to a more fulfilling and more durable human civilization which is everyone's dream.

Selected Insights
on
Paradigm Shift and Human Creativity

Old ways are not necessarily the best ways.

— (Anonymous).

If you always do what you've always done, you'll always get what you already have.

— (Saying).

The limits of our language mean the limits of our world. A new world is the beginning of a new language. A new language is the seed of a new world.

— (Anonymous).

If you cannot find a solution, enlarge the problem.

— (saying; see Michael Sherraden, 1991: 13).

We fail more often because we solve the wrong problem than because we get the wrong solution to the right problem.

— R. L. Ackoff (1974: 8).

It would be an unsound fancy and self-contradictory to expect that things which have never yet been done can be done except by means which have never yet been tried.

— Francis Bacon (1982: 8).

It is idle to expect any great advancement in science from the superinducing and engrafting of new things upon old.

— Francis Bacon (1982: 14).

A paradigm is a set of rules and regulations that defines boundaries and helps us be successful within those boundaries, where success is measured by the problems solved using these rules and regulations.
— Joel Barker (1993: 21).

It is long past the time when labels, absolute numbers, and strict categorizations can be allowed to totally define anyone or anything.
— Berenice Bleedorn (1998: 219).

To deal with crime, we must identify its roots. ... The failure of all current methods in widespread use indicates either that treatment programs do not resolve the problems to which they are addressed or else that the analyses of the crime problem have failed to identify its real root.
— Harold H. Bloomfield *et al.,* (1975: 194).

[B]efore searching for new ideas it is useful to examine current ideas and identify the major influences giving shape to them.
— Edward de Bono (Attributed).

The future is the only part of our lives that we can change.
— Ben Bova, (1983: 13).

[T]he problems of our time will *not* be solved in the routine course of events.
— The Club of Rome (1974: 10).

Today it seems that the basic values, which are ingrained in human societies of all ideologies and religious persuasions, are ultimately responsible for many of our troubles. But if future crises are to be avoided, how then should these values be readjusted?

— The Club of Rome (1974: 11).

For the first time in man's life on earth, he is being asked to refrain from doing what he can do; he is being asked to restrain his economic and technological advancement, or at least to direct it differently from before; he is being asked by all the future generations of the earth to share his good fortune with the unfortunate — not in a spirit of charity, but in a spirit of necessity. He is being asked to concentrate now on the organic growth of the total world system. Can he, in good conscience, say no?

— The Club of Rome (1974: 142).

In industrialized countries, more and more people are re-thinking such basic concepts as those concerning the nature of self-interest, efficiency, the distribution of wealth, the value of specialists, and the role of values and beliefs.

— The Club of Rome (1978: 180).

[D]evelopment can no longer be defined in terms of economic growth [increasing gross national product] alone.
— The Club of Rome (1979: 6).

Learning by shock often follows a period of overconfidence in solutions created solely with expert knowledge or technical competence and perpetuated beyond the conditions for which they were appropriate.
— The Club of Rome (1979: 11).

The deep, fundamental problems we face cannot be solved on the superficial level on which they were created. We need a new level of thinking ... to solve these deep concerns.
— Stephen R. Covey (1992: 63).

Often we can't embrace a new paradigm until we let go of the old one. Likewise, until we drop unwarranted assumptions about people, we can't expect to bring about lasting improvements in our organizations.
— Stephen R. Covey (1992: 69).

In our attempt to improve the world, have we been fighting the smoke instead of the fire - the symptoms instead of the disease?
— Jack Forem (1974: 223).

Henry Ford invented the assembly line by changing the question from "How do we get the people to the work?" to "How do we get the work to the people?" Edward Jenner discovered the vaccine for smallpox simply by changing the question from "Why do people get smallpox?" to "Why *don't* milkmaids get smallpox?"

— Jack Foster (1996: 129).

The underlying causes of faulty reasoning and erroneous beliefs will never be eliminated. People will always prefer black-and-white over shades of grey, and so there will always be the temptation to hold overly-simplified beliefs and to hold them with excessive confidence.

— Thomas Gilovich (1991: 186).

Our beliefs ... appear to receive too much support from equivocal evidence, and they are too seldom discredited by truly antagonistic results.

— Thomas Gilovich (1991: 188).

We will not overcome the present disastrous ways of ordering our individual and communal lives until we reject the view of the world upon which they were based. And we cannot reject this old view until we have a new view that seems more convincing. The modern paradigm will die only as a postmodern paradigm begins to emerge.

— David Ray Griffin (1988a: 144).

[N]o ethic that will reverse the exploitative and war-creating tendencies of modernity will be developed until a postmodern vision of the world becomes prevalent, one in which nothing [and no person] is mere object to be exploited with impunity, in which all people and all things are seen as embodying the Holy.

— David Ray Griffin (1988a: 147-148).

The self-destructive path on which the world has been set, as it has been increasingly dominated by the paradigm of [material and aesthetic satisfaction] can only be altered by developing a new worldview and thereby a new ethic.

— David Ray Griffin (1988a: 148).

Theories are made to be destroyed. Theories give birth to new knowledge which cannot be encompassed by the parents. New theories are then needed to give this knowledge form and meaning. A theory is useful to a researcher because it gives him a benchmark from which to start, not a mooring against which to rest.

— Daniel E. Griffiths (1997: 105).

[A] frog if put in cold water will not bestir itself if that water is heated up slowly and gradually and will in the end let itself be boiled alive, too comfortable with continuity to realize that continuous change at some point may become intolerable and demand a change in behavior. If we want to avoid the fate of ... the boiling frog we must learn to look for and embrace discontinuous change.

— Charles Handy (1989: 9).

Our use of old words to describe new things can often hide the emerging future from our eyes.
— Charles Handy (1997: 26).

Practice by no means makes perfect - for without development, practice simply reinforces, intensifies and perpetuates early mistakes.
— Sydney Harris (1986: 171).

It is impossible to create a well-working society on the basis of a view of reality which is fundamentally inadequate, seriously incomplete, and mistaken in basic assumptions. Yet this is precisely what the modern world has been attempting to do.
— Willis Harman and John Hormann (1990: 141).

Some men look at constitutions with sanctimonious reverence and deem them like the ark of the covenant, too sacred to be touched. They ascribe to the men of the preceding age a wisdom more than human, and suppose what they did to be beyond amendment. ... I am certainly not an advocate for frequent and untried changes in laws and constitutions. But I also know that laws and institutions must go hand in hand with the progress of the human mind. ... As new discoveries are made, new truths disclosed, and manners and opinions change with the change of circumstances, institutions must advance also, and keep pace with the times.
— Thomas Jefferson (1980: 396-397)

[O]ur transforming era requires not only that we change our practices in response but also that we change the way we *think* about what we do.

— Rosabeth Moss Kanter (1983: 61).

There are two ways of escaping our more or less automatized routines of thinking and behaving. The first is the plunge into dreaming or dream-like states, where the rules of rational thinking are suspended. The other way is also an escape — from boredom, stagnation, intellectual predicaments and emotional frustrations — but an escape in the opposite direction; it is signaled by the spontaneous flash of insight which shows a familiar situation or event in a new light.

— Arthur Koestler (1975: iii).

New facts alone do not make a new theory; and new facts alone do not destroy an outlived theory ... [It] requires creative originality to achieve the task.

— Arthur Koestler (1975: 235).

The measure of an artist's originality, put into the simplest terms, is the extent to which his selective emphasis deviates from the conventional norm and establishes new standards of relevance. All great innovations, which inaugurate a new era, movement, or school, consist in such sudden shifts of attention and displacements of emphasis onto some previously neglected aspect of experience, some blacked-out range of the existential spectrum.

— Arthur Koestler (1975: 334).

The decisive turning points in the history of every art-form
are discoveries which ... uncover what has always been there;
they are 'revolutionary', that is, destructive and constructive;
they compel us to revalue our values and impose a new set of
rules on the eternal game.

— Arthur Koestler (1975: 334-335).

Failure of existing rules is the prelude to a search for new
ones.

— Thomas Kuhn (1962: 68).

No great improvements in the lot of mankind are possible,
until a great change takes place in the fundamental constitution of their modes of thought.

— John Stuart Mill (1992: 460).

When society requires to be rebuilt, there is no use in attempting to rebuild it on the old plan.

— John Stuart Mill (1992: 460).

It is highly important, indeed urgently so, that we consider
the possibility that our traditional ideas concerning the innate
nature of man may be wrong and damaging, for I am convinced that underlying much of man's malfunctioning ... is
this unsound conception of human nature.

— Ashley Montagu (1962: 11).

Can the rational choice paradigm, as currently practiced in the various disciplines of economics, philosophy, political science, and law, offer an account of ... man's decision and his behavior?
— Jennifer Roback Morse (1997: 179).

Without an appreciation of the larger shifts that are restructuring our society, we act on assumptions that are out of date. Out of touch with the present, we are doomed to fail in the unfolding future.
— John Naisbitt (1982: 13).

The problem is that our thinking, our attitudes, and consequently our decision making have not caught up with the reality of things. ... [T]he level of change involved is so fundamental yet so subtle that we tend not to see it, or if we see it, we tend to dismiss it as overly simplistic, and then we ignore it.
— John Naisbitt (1982: 13).

How can we improve our learning, i.e., change the posture of learning; learn to re-examine, to re-perceive, to re-formulate, and to re-learn; create new alternatives and change patterns of thinking and frames of reference?
— Participants of the Salzburg Conference on Learning (1979: 137).

Creative thinking is not only constructive, it is also destructive. Often, you have to break out of one pattern to discover another one.

— Roger von Oech (1983: 66).

Problems may be solved only when the appropriate techniques, data, theories, or concepts are invented to solve them.

— Robert Scott Root-Bernstein (1991: 62).

We have to ask whether ... problems are unsolved because they are too difficult to solve, or because we have not yet developed the right philosophy of science for dealing with them.

— Robert Scott Root-Bernstein (1991: 351).

[I]t appears that sometimes problems are unsolvable because they are posed within the wrong methodological and epistemological framework.

— Robert Scott Root-Bernstein (1991: 352).

[M]ountains can often be reduced to molehills by asking the right questions.

— Robert Scott Root-Bernstein (1989: 410).

When the problem-solving process becomes bogged down, it may be time to step back and examine which thinking language is being employed and consider the use of an alternative.

— Martin B. Ross (1981: 130).

Despite years of marches, commissions, judicial decisions, and endless legislative remedies, we are confronted with unchanging or even widening racial differences in achievement.

— William Ryan (1971: 9).

We are dealing, it would seem, not so much with culturally deprived children as with culturally depriving schools. And the task to be accomplished is not to revise, and amend, and repair deficient children but to alter and transform the atmosphere and operations of the schools to which we commit these children. Only by changing the nature of the educational experience can we change its product.

— William Ryan (1971: 60).

[W]e have social engineers who think up ways of "strengthen-ing" [poor families] rather than methods of eradicating [injustices and inequalities].
— William Ryan (1971: 8).

There are increasing indications that the chaos we are experi-encing is the result of trying to navigate the 20th-century world using a 17th-century map and, most important, not being able to distinguish between the map and the world.
— Carol Sanford (1992: 196).

The leading ideas of the nineteenth century, which claimed to do away with metaphysics, are themselves a bad, vicious, life-destroying type of metaphysics. We are suffering from them as from a fatal disease. It is not true that knowledge is sorrow. But poisonous errors bring unlimited sorrow... The errors are not in science but in the philosophy put forward in the name of science. ... [A]ll we got was bad metaphysics and appalling ethics.
— E. F. Schumacher (1975: 91-92).

The great ideas of the nineteenth century may fill our minds in one way or another, but our hearts do not believe in them all the same. Mind and heart are at war with one another, not, as is commonly asserted, reason and faith. Our reason has become beclouded by an extraordinary, blind and unreason-able faith in a set of fantastic and life-destroying ideas inher-ited from the nineteenth century. It is the foremost task of our reason to recover a truer faith than that.
— E. F. Schumacher (1975: 93).

We shrink back from the truth if we believe that the destructive forces of the modern world can be "brought under control" simply by mobilizing more resources - of wealth, education, and research - to fight pollution, to preserve wildlife, to discover new sources of energy, and to arrive at more effective agreements on peaceful coexistence. Needless to say, wealth, education, research, and many other things are needed for any civilization, but what is most needed today is a revision of the ends which these means are meant to serve. And this implies, above all else, the development of a life-style which accords to material things their proper, legitimate place, which is secondary and not primary.

— E. F. Schumacher (1975: 294).

Ninety-nine percent of Athenians could be wrong about something.

— Socrates (attributed).

[T]he mistake must be at the root, at the very foundation of thought in modern times ... at the prevailing ... view of the world ...

— Aleksandr I. Solzhenitsyn (1978: 47).

Bureaucratic, technocratic solutions will not work for many of the problems now facing humanity.

— Bruce Stokes (1981: 15).

The central organizing principles of the communications era can already be distinguished. We need to replace the concept of equality of results with those of diversity and pluralism. We need to change the drive for growth into an acceptance of the reality of finiteness and enoughness. We need to recognize that decision-making from the top down must be replaced by widespread opportunities for participation. We need to abandon our present competitive "we-they," "win-lose" models of the world and replace them with cooperative "win-win" understandings.

— Robert Theobald (1981: xviii).

We need to understand that the competitive model of the last two centuries — striving against others, trying to get to the top of the heap whatever the cost — is no longer feasible or desirable. The persistence of this model is now the prime reason why we cannot develop our own lives in sensible, valuable ways.

— Robert Theobald (1981: 20).

If we are to deal with our developing crises, we need to change our fundamental styles of thinking and action. We will have to reexamine the patterns within which we want to live our lives and the directions in which we want our society to move. It will require a basic change in priorities and perceptions, not a minimal policy shift. ... [We will] need to alter the myths by which we live, to recognize that our industrial-era styles are now obsolete, and that we must develop new patterns of understanding and action more appropriate to the conditions that we have ourselves created.

— Robert Theobald (1981: 126).

Our past history causes us to accept certain ideas and directions without question. [We need to] recognize that we shall either change our myths completely or we shall not survive.
— Robert Theobald (1981: 156).

[W]e need to revise our fundamental understandings, if we are to break out of oue win-lose patterns of thinking.
— Robert Theobald (1981: 99).

[W] e must now examine our very basic patterns of thinking and determine the rock on which we can build an effective social order in the future.
— Robert Theobald (1981: 129).

We are engaged ... in a process with no parallel in human history — an attempt to change the whole of a culture through a conscious process. The difficulty of such a sweeping approach becomes apparent when we realize that it is impossible to change one element in a culture without altering all elements.
— Robert Theobald (1981: 156).

Never solve a problem from its original perspective.
— Charles "Chic" Thompson (1992: 79).

Like many machines of the smokestack era, our intellectual tools, too, are ready for the museum.
— Alvin Toffler (1980: 189).

Second Wave [industrial] societies have attempted to cope with unemployment, for example, by resisting technology, closing off immigration, creating labor exchanges, increasing exports, decreasing imports, setting up public works programs, cutting back on work hours, attempting to increase labor mobility, deporting whole populations, and even waging war to stimulate the economy. Yet the problem becomes more complex and difficult every day.

Can it be that the problems of labor supply - both gluts and shortages - can *never* be satisfactorily solved within the framework of a Second Wave society, whether capitalist or socialist? By looking at the economy as a whole, rather than focusing exclusively on one part of it, can we frame the problem in a new way that helps us solve it?

— Alvin Toffler (1980: 267-268).

The super-ideology of the Second Wave [industrial civilization] will be seen, from the vantage point of tomorrow, to have been as provincial as it was self-serving.

— Alvin Toffler (1980: 267-293).

It would be a mistake to assume that the present-day educational system is unchanging. On the contrary, it is undergoing rapid change. But much of this change is no more than an attempt to refine the existent machinery, making it ever more efficient in pursuit of obsolete goals.

— Alvin Toffler (1997: 98).

[T]ill society be differently constituted, much cannot be
expected from education.
> — Mary Wollstonecraft (1997: 98).

The time has come to break out of past patterns. Attempts to
maintain social and ecological stability through old approaches to development and environmental protection will
increase instability. Security must be sought through change.
> — The World Commission on Environment
> and Development (1987: 309).

Scientific revolutions are forced upon us by the discovery of
phenomena that are not comprehensible in terms of the old
theories. Old theories die hard. Much more is at stake than
the theories themselves. To give up our privileged position at
the center of the universe, as Copernicus asked, was an
enormous psychological task. To accept that nature is fundamentally irrational ... which is the essential statement of
quantum mechanics, is a powerful blow to the intellect.
Nonetheless, as new theories demonstrate superior utility,
their adversaries, however reluctantly, have little choice but to
accept them. In doing so, they also must grant a measure of
recognition to the world views that accompany them.
> — Gary Zukav (1979: 192).

The way that we pose our questions often illusorily limits our
responses.
> — Gary Zukav (1979: 271).

X
Summary:
Toward a Global Creativity-Consciousness

Lacking absolutes, we will have to encounter one another as people with different information, different stories, different visions — and trust the outcome.
— Walter Truett Anderson.

Further Progress

Humans have come a long way in a relatively short period of time. We have transformed our condition from the stone age to the information era. We have progressed from fruit gathering to mechanized agriculture, from cave dwelling to climate-controlled skyscrapers, from apparent terrestrial confinement to space travel, and from isolated local settlements to the emerging global village. Practically every one of the advances that have brought about these transformations has been the product of human ingenuity and creativity. Here again, mention must be made of the great men and women in history – the Bacons, the Copernicuses, the Galileos, the Newtons, the Faradays, the Pasteurs, the Edisons, the Einsteins, and their undocumented counterparts in non-Western cultures. The cumulative result of the work of these "heroes of the imagination"* is the highly successful civilization of modern times.

However, as successful as modern civilization has been, there are growing signs of dissatisfaction. Even as technology is churning out an endless variety of consumer products, even as people are becoming physically healthier and living longer in some parts of the world, and even as it is becoming possible to communicate with one another in real time between any two points on the globe, modern civilization is still being criticized, particularly for environmental degradation and a colossal waste of human potential. Ecologists and other "friends of the earth" deplore what they see as devastation of the ecosystem and

---

* The phrase is Daniel J. Boorstin's (1992:xv).

threats to the global life support system: rapid destruction of vegetation, species loss, water pollution, soil erosion, desertification, ozone depletion, climate change, etc. Human potential advocates lament what they see as gross underdevelopment and underutilization of people's natural abilities and, in particular, the inability of large sections of the human population to realize their creative potential, to contribute their unique talents to their societies and organizations and, therefore, to find meaning and fulfillment in their lives.

With regard to the latter situation, human potential advocates point to the relatively disadvantaged economic, social, and political situations of women, minorities, citizens of Third World countries, and other underprivileged groups as indication that large segments of the human population are still living well below their natural capacities – a condition that advocates perceive as giving rise to the plethora of "liberation" and "personal growth" movements. Reviewing the shifting values in workplaces, schools, and the larger society, human potential advocates conclude that, more than ever before, people want to be more, and to do more, than is traditionally expected of them.

To illustrate (as has been reviewed earlier): Workers want not just to make money but also to do something important, meaningful, personally satisfying, and emotionally rewarding. A growing number of students in institutions of higher education no longer want knowledge for the sake of knowledge, but the opportunity to discover their natural abilities and to be able to apply mathematics, reading, writing, and other academic skills to areas of their greatest potential in order to achieve high levels of competence in those areas. Women, minorities, and the "forgotten four-fifths" of the human population want not only food, shelter, and clothing, but also identity, participation and, in Paulo Freire's famous words (highlighted in a number of places earlier), a chance to speak their word, to name their world, and to participate in changing it. More and more constituents no longer want "leaders" in the traditional, messianic sense, but people, visions, policies, and programs that enable them to discover their natural abilities and to develop their own leadership abilities in those areas.

The coming together of so many demands is significant in itself. Happening in the midst of what has been described as "the most brilliant civilization in human history" raises fundamental questions of values, reminiscent of Erich Fromm's opposed concepts: civilization of objects versus civilization of persons (Fromm, 1955: 270). The fear exists that in the (understandably) large-scale pursuit of material progress, humanity has tended to rely too much on a relatively small segment of its population (i.e., the gifted and talented, the best and brightest) to do the thinking, planning, inventing, and discovering – with the result that the creative potential of the vast majority of people has largely gone unrecognized, underdeveloped, or underutilized. As Oliver Goldsmith observes, wealth continues to accumulate, while the most distinctive human quality – creativity – atrophies or "decays."*

Analysis of the themes underlying some of the protest actions of feminists, ethnic minorities, labor unions, students, former colonials, and other social action groups identifies two recurring notions. First, people want to be recognized as creative human beings and be given the opportunity to maximize their abilities. Second, they want to contribute their insights to the decisions that affect their lives and their future. Underlying these two demands is the growing realization that, as successful as modern civilization has been, further progress depends on everyone's creative participation.

Recent developments in several areas of the human experience (especially business and politics) indicate that making everyone's creative participation the guiding principle of social organization is not just another nice thing to do, but an increasingly important condition for our collective survival.

The importance of the creative participation of all members of society is based on the belief that it is the only way that people can exist more fully and realize more of their human potential.** The statements upon which this project is based suggest that human beings are inherently creative and naturally driven to actualize that potential – that they function best as human beings, as committed and productive employees, and as responsible national and planetary citizens, only when they are able to do so. The second reason why the creative participation of all members of society is so crucial is the absolute necessity of everyone's contribution in order for an organic whole to be realized. Two statements, one by Leo F. Buscaglia and the other by Clark Moustakas, illustrate the point. According to Buscaglia:

---

* See "The Deserted Village" by Oliver Goldsmith.
** The words of Henry David Thoreau, and the central theme of this anthology.

Existence is like an intricate tapestry on which no part can remain unrealized if we are to experience the sublime totality. ... [N]o one life is of more or less significance than another nor is any one of us more or less responsible, for in each of us lies a vital part of the wholeness (Buscaglia, 1982: ix).

In a powerfully persuasive argument for diversity, mutual acceptance, and social inclusiveness, Clark Moustakas writes:

There is no way to realize the full possibilities in group life as long as one person is rejected, minimized, ignored or treated as an inferior or outcast. To the extent that there is malice toward one person, ill-will and ill-feeling spread. Every person in the group is afflicted and is powerless to channel available resources into creative expression. One cannot carry evil thoughts, feelings, and intentions in his heart without at the same time deterring and restraining himself in his own purposes or directions. One, therefore, must live through and work out one's state of rejecting or being rejected before group life can contain a depth of spirit, devotion, and authentic community (Moustakas, 1967: 18-19).

More practical reasons why everybody's creativity and participation in societal affairs is so crucial are

• clinically-observed behaviors of "self-actualized" (better, self-actualizing) individuals, such as mental health, self-acceptance, identification with fellow human beings, acceptance of nature, altruism, collaboration, democratic disposition, etc. in contradistinction to the mental illness, destructiveness, sadism, cruelty, purposelessness, feelings of inferiority or unworthiness, delinquency, and criminal tendencies that humanistic psychologists frequently associate with neglected, repressed, denied, or otherwise unfulfilled human talents (see, for example, Fromm, 1955: 111-49; Rogers, 1961: 36; Maslow, 1962: 3-4, 22, 25-26): The practical contributions of self-actualizing individuals to society, on the one hand, and so many psychological and social problems associated with unrealized human potential, on the other, suggest that it is in everybody's overall interest that every one's creative potential be recognized, nourished, and allowed expression (in constructive ways).

• increasing dependence of organizations and institutions on the insights and contributions of all their members: The success stories of organizations that are experimenting with such participatory management principles as empowerment, self-management teams, "intrapreneuring," Total Quality, leadership by consultation, and decentralized decision-making in contradistinction to their traditional command-and-control, problem-ridden counterparts illustrate the vitality and resilience of collective wisdom (see, for example, Pinchot III, 1985; Senge, 1990; Boyett *et al.*, 1993; Miller, 1993; Pinchot and Pinchot, 1993; Creech, 1994; Ghoshal and Bartlett, 1997).

• reported excitement, personal involvement, enthusiasm, and satisfaction in classrooms where learning grows out of, or is driven by, the children's interests and experiences: The reported success and growing popularity of the Reggio Emilia "community-of-learners" model of education* and its theoretical underpinning ("constructivism") underscore the importance of collaboration and participation in the human enterprise, even in teaching and learning (see, for example, Genishi, McCarrier, and Nussbaun, 1988: 190; Fosnot, 1996; Municipality of Reggio Emilia, 1996).

• growing dissatisfaction with conditions that people perceive as limiting their ability to reach their potential or to contribute their talents to societal and environmental ends: The current wave of "liberation" movements and related social protest actions, particularly in workplaces and in the political arena, indicate not only increased popular awareness of the most fundamental human need (creativity), but also conscious and, in some places, determined efforts to satisfy that need.

Given the psychological, economic, social, and political necessity of the creative participation of all members of a society, *the challenge* is to find ways to translate that principle into practical action or, in Ervin Laszlo's words, to "catalyze the capability in contemporary people to creatively confront the problems all of us now face in common" (Laszlo, 1994: 118). Action is needed in four critical areas: First, realizing, as Peter Drucker (1999: 45) observes, that "no society can function as a society unless it gives the individual member social status and function," every society and culture will need to recognize and respect the integrity of all of its members as human beings and, in particular, their unique and incomparable abilities – things that they are naturally good at and/or passionate about. Second, the role of society will need to be seen as facilitating human creativity – inspiring policies, programs, and goals that make constructive use of the talents

---

* This is a view of education as an individual meaning-making process in which both teacher and learners present, discuss, and share their personal interpretations of the matter of interest, during which process each expands his understanding. The classroom constitutes a learning community, a cooperative where members help one another to succeed (rather than a competition in which only a few can win).

of *all* their members and, to that end, providing the moral, economic, social, or political framework within which people can express and harmonize their individual abilities. Third, every society and culture will need to provide the context as well as the opportunity for individuals and groups to talk with one another and to work together to formulate mutually beneficial and environmentally responsible goals (see, for example, Gardner 1999: 45; Spady and Bell, 1999). Finally, we need to rethink and, in particular, to humanize some of our social, cultural, economic, and political institutions – making them more creativity-friendly and, therefore, more humanly fulfilling, more ecologically responsible and, ultimately, more durable. This project is intended to facilitate actions in these areas.

Rationale

The twin motivations of this project are (a) the colossal waste of human talents around the world, and (b) the urgent need for mass salvage action. The former motivation refers to gross underdevelopment and underutilization of human creativity and its impact on people's lives, including, among other things, widespread self-devaluation, disillusionment, depression, alienation, frustration, anger, hatred, poverty, low productivity as employees, crime, mutual suspicion, social and environmental irresponsibility (to the extent that these psychological and social problems can be attributed to that cause). The latter motivation is the perceived importance of human creativity in building the more durable human civilization that is everyone's dream and, therefore, what each of us can do in our respective areas of responsibility to realize that dream – to make our world more creativity-friendly and, therefore, a more fulfilling home for ourselves and posterity.

(a) Evidence of the current state of underdevelopment and under-tilization of human creativity and its impact on people and society:

• vast segments of the human population who live and die without ever finding themselves – without ever recognizing what they are particularly good at and, therefore, not able to fulfill what might have been their life's unique purpose.

- the large number of economic, social, cultural, and political arrangements, activities, and conditions that tend to inhibit, rather than facilitate, human development and self-actualization – to "demean and depreciate human dignity and fulfillment." *

- the growing incidence of stress, boredom, and burnout in workplaces that, in many cases, has been associated with unimaginative routines.

- the emotional devastation that has come to be associated with "competitive status seeking" and excessive preoccupation with material success and, therefore, the phenomenon of "Working Wounded" – outwardly successful yet emotionally troubled professionals ** who are resorting to psychotherapy and a variety of transcendental practices to restore balance in their lives.

- the large number of academic programs that are based on the assumption that education is about transmitting knowledge and preparing learners for the job market, rather than helping the individual learner to find his special abilities and to see how the three R's and other academic skills can enhance those talents.

- the millions of young people who drop out of school and, in many cases, go on to live lives of mediocrity not because they are not talented, but because their particular talents are not currently recognized in academe or are not yet socially valued.

- the vast majority of young people who are being made to believe that the ultimate goal in life is to be better than everybody else and who, therefore, base their sense of self-worth on competition and interpersonal rivalry, rather than on maximizing their unique and incomparable potential.

- the misleading assumption that wealth, consumption, fame, and power are the highest human values and the ultimate purpose of existence and, therefore, the gradual reduction of human life to material well-being.

- myths of unequal distribution of the creative potential and the rarity of genius that are keeping large segments of the human population performing well below their naturally endowed capacities.

---

* The phrase is Philo Pritzkau's (1970: 61).
** The description is Douglas LaBier's (1986: vi, vii, 144, 147).

- the growing number of unsolved economic, social, and environmental problems that require a fundamental rethinking of the assumptions upon which the present civilization has been built.

- rapid change that is still accelerating, making more and more people and ideas obsolete.

(b) *The bases of our individual and collective responsibility for the promotion of creativity:*

- the embeddedness of creativity in human nature, its centrality in every aspect of our life, and the necessity of its actualization for meaningful and fulfilling existence, for increased productivity as workers, and for social and environmental responsibility as national and planetary citizens.

- a global civilization that critically depends on everyone's creative insights (including those of women, minorities, ex-colonials, the poor or materially deprived, and the "forgotten four-fifths") for further progress.

- the potential richness and vitality of a civilization that is built on the diversity of available talents, ideas, perspectives, interests, and goals.

- the faith in human creativity as the best hope for a viable global future – a future that is good for the individual, good for institutions and corporations, good for customers and shareholders, good for society, and good for the natural environment.

- the growing realization that a world in which every human being is able to realize his unique capabilities and contribute them for the common good is no longer a utopian dream but a practical and attainable goal and, indeed, an absolute necessity for our collective survival.

- the small but growing number of individuals who are facilitating the creativity of vulnerable and underprivileged groups and who, therefore, might benefit from the conceptual tools of their self-selected mission. These individuals include: (a) constructivist educators who are turning their classrooms into learning communities in which both teacher and learners develop together and expand their individual understanding of the world by listening to others' interpretations and perspectives; (b) creative leaders and creative managers who are helping individuals to discover and express their special abilities in ways that are beneficial to themselves, their organizations, and the larger society; (c) managers, trainers, and mentors who are struggling to bring out the best both in themselves in others for whom they are responsible; and (d) human potential advocates who are working to repair some of the damage that a predominantly "one-sided view of human nature"* (i.e., the preoccupation with material well-being) has done to the human psyche.

• many more parents, educators, students, leaders, managers, consultants, public officials, and concerned individuals whose participation needs to be enlisted in the urgent task of making our world more creativity-friendly and, therefore, more humanly fulfilling.

Visions of a Viable Global Future

Dissatisfaction with the current state of the world and, in particular, fears of possible human-induced disaster have prompted the search for a more viable global future and for fundamental system changes necessary to bring about that future. Visionaries and world-order thinkers interested in more durable principles of global development reject many of the "symptomatic solutions"** that, so far, have failed to produce the desired "results." Of interest to many of these thinkers are deep-level ideals that are powerful enough to shape the values and actions of people and beneficial enough to enlist their voluntary commitment. Widely discussed proposals include war prevention, poverty eradication, green thinking, ecological balance, full employment, globalization, human-scale technology, a just world order, interexistence, nonviolent communication, "practopia," and collaborative, compassionate communities.

The absolute necessity of each of these visionary goals and proposals is universally recognized. Their successful implementation, however, will depend on the collective insights of all concerned. Recent developments in neighborhoods, schools, workplaces, national and the international political arena, as reviewed above (pages 346-350), suggest that building a viable global future of the type that is envisaged in the foregoing proposals cannot be left to the insights of a few (however talented). To endure, as already suggested, the new world order will have to be built on the creative participation of all men and women, majorities and minorities,

---

* The phrase is David Ray Griffin's (1988a: 149).
** The phrase is Peter Senge's (1990: 104).

teachers and students, employers and employees, First-, Second-, Third-, and Fourth-World nationals (see, for example, Harman and Horman, 1990: 61-95; Laszlo, 1994: 117-118, 191-193).

However, in order for people to participate effectively and meaningfully in global civilization building, they will need to be enabled to recognize their special abilities and, also, to appreciate the indispensability of their talents for that task.

The necessity of everyone's creative participation is based on the beliefs that:

• only to the extent that people are able to discover, to develop, and to express their natural abilities in things that are important to them and that they perceive as beneficial to their societies and the natural environment are they likely to find meaning, purpose, and fulfillment in their lives.

• only to the extent that people are able to find meaning, purpose, and fulfillment in their lives are they likely to genuinely love themselves and feel satisfied with their lives.

• only to the extent that people genuinely love themselves and feel satisfied with their lives are they likely to be maximally productive and genuinely humane, compassionate, cooperative, civic minded, socially and environmentally responsible.

Robert Theobald (1981: 19) has suggested that people always act in terms of their perceived self-interest. To the extent that Theobald's suggestion is valid, a global future that people can believe in and willingly work to bring about will be one that they themselves have helped to design and that they also perceive as enhancing their most important attributes and as producing benefits for their society and the natural environment.

Translating Vision into Action

How, then, can we bring about a viable global future that allows people to realize their special abilities and, at the same time, achieves a productive workforce for business and industry, high standards of living for all people, academic excellence, scientific and technological advances, compassionate and collaborative communities, a humane and civic-minded national and planetary citizens, and environmentally responsible behaviors?

The answer to that question depends on how we see our place in the planetary (indeed, cosmic) scheme of things and what we regard as the purpose of human existence.

The cumulative experience of the past few hundred years suggests that to achieve a viable global future, we will need to recognize human fulfillment as the ultimate purpose of our existence and environmental sustainability as the basis of every human activity. Accordingly, we will need to reexamine some of the assumptions upon which we base many of our activities, including the way we rear our children, teach our students, organize our work, manage our institutions, perceive and lead our constituents, use and manage the earth's resources. We will need to be courageous enough to revise or to retire those assumptions that we find to be unproductive or false. Finally, we will need to redesign our educational, economic, social, and political institutions and/or reorganize their activities in ways that respect the integrity of every human ability and that also promote and channel those abilities to socially desirable and environmentally responsible ends. To explain:

- Child rearing needs to focus more on determining and respecting the integrity of each child's unique abilities, aptitudes, and interests as indicated by the things that the child likes to do or to talk about, the way in which the child responds to situations, how the child manipulates symbols, and his unique way of looking at the world and interpreting events and things. The concept and practice of parenting needs to shift from molding and shaping the child to facilitating his growth and development according to the qualities and inclinations that he manifests.

- Our aim in educating our children and youth needs to shift from providing them with prepackaged information and knowledge as ends in themselves. We need to help each learner to "find out" the things that he is passionate about, and to realize how competence in various academic disciplines can practically enhance his performance in those areas. In this connection:

  - More teachers need to act as facilitators of learning rather than as purveyors of knowledge.

  - Learners need to be recognized and facilitated as people with different goals, different interests, different needs, different styles of learning, different modes of understanding the world, and different methods of representing what they learn and know.

- The classroom needs to be organized as a "collaborative community of learners"* engaged in dialogue, discourse, and reflection, in which participants (students and the teacher) share their unique perspectives and at the end of which everyone develops a more complete understanding of the matter.

- Work needs to be (re)designed as a meaningful, intrinsically satisfying, and self-actualizing experience – a means of earning a living and achieving results for one's employer as well as an opportunity to nourish and express one's unique abilities in an important and worthy economic, social, political, or cultural enterprise.

- The management of an institution or organization needs to concern itself less with enticing or coercing people to work harder for anticipated rewards or avoidance of punishment, and more with inspiring goals that people perceive as enabling them to become the kinds of people that they deeply desire to be, thereby encouraging their willing commitment. Employers of labor and corporate managers need to regard themselves as facilitators to be consulted, rather than old-style masters to be pleased or feared.

- Leaders need to recognize and respect the creative potential and, therefore, the intrinsic worth of every one of their constituents. Leadership needs to be seen as a responsibility to enhance constituents and subordinates as human beings and to facilitate their own leadership abilities in things that they are naturally good at, rather than as an opportunity to think for other people.

- Society needs to recognize the unique pattern of interests that its members represent (i.e., things that people intuitively feel that they must do in order for their lives to be "complete" or fulfilled) and, therefore, needs to be concerned more with finding a framework within which all interests can be constructively expressed and harmonized for the common good, and less with shaping people to think and see in the same ways.

- The goal of life needs to be defined primarily in terms of actualizing one's latent potentialities and contributing them for the common good, and only secondarily in terms of possession and power, or the prestige that has come to be

---

* See, for example, Theobald (1981: 99), Fosnot, (1996) and Municipality of Reggio Emilia (1996) for detailed discussion of this "constructivist" approach to education.

associated with those things. The concept of "success" needs to be redefined and considerably broadened to include performance on the infinite range of talents that members of a society possess. People should be able to achieve distinction, or even greatness, whatever their calling or their special interests. Here, again, we recall Carol Pearson's instructive words:

> If everyone who loved to create beauty did so, we would live in a beautiful world. If everyone who loved cleanliness and order, cleaned up, we would live in a clean and orderly world. If everyone who yearned to heal the sick did so, we would live in a healthier world. If everyone who cared about world hunger shared his or her creative ideas and acted to alleviate the problem, people would all be fed (Pearson, 1991: 172).

• Finally, we need to recognize that there is enough *useful* work for every ability and interest. Very importantly, we need to realize that someone's life; some group's economic, social, political, or spiritual well-being; and, indeed, the future of our civilization might just depend on each of us being able to find and to do our particular "work."

Toward a Global Creativity-Consciousness

A reconceptualization of the purpose and conduct of life of the scope that is suggested in the foregoing paragraphs clearly requires everyone's understanding and the widest possible participation. Fortunately, the signs are pointing in that direction. To illustrate:

• The increasing frequency with which people write and talk about "creative parenting," "creative aging," "creative education," "creative work," "creative management," "creative leadership," and "the creative organization" suggests that we are on the threshold of making human fulfillment part of our everyday activities and, thus, restoring meaning to our lives.

• The growing realization in national and international development circles that development is not all about goods and things but about people suggests that we are entering a period in history when human fulfillment or the realization of human potential will be recognized as the ultimate goal of human existence, the driving force all human activities and, indeed, the context within which other important human values acquire their meaning (see, for example, The Club of Rome, 1974: 69; Schumacher, 1975: 163-170; Parker, 1977: 178;

McRobie, 1981: 262; World Commission on Environment and Development, 1987: 309; Soedjatmoko, 1989: 62).

- The growing popularity of simpler and more collaborative life-styles in preference to the traditional competitive, success-at-all-costs paradigm indicates people's eagerness to transform their world from a civilization of things to a civilization of people – from a civilization of material well-being to a civilization of human fulfillment (see, for example, Fromm, 1955; Simple Living Collective, 1977; LaBier, 1986; Laszlo, 1994; Nouwen *et al.*, 1999; Jaccaci and Gault, 1999; Jaccaci, 2000).

It would be naïve to expect universal acceptance of the central ideas of this anthology. Understandably, not everyone would agree that every human being is inherently creative, or that human fulfillment should be the defining criterion and the organizing principle of all human activities, or that promoting creativity in every area of human activity is a feasible or even desirable proposition. Resistance can be expected from those who have acquired their fame, wealth, power, or position by promoting other "competing" values as the primary purpose of human existence. Resistance can also be expected from those whose means of livelihood depends on the continued division of humanity into the creative benefactors of the species and their grateful, sometimes unknowing, beneficiaries.* Also, given the long history of status differentials and social inequalities based on a presumed unequal distribution of abilities, it is understandable if some people are reluctant to believe that, in terms of creative potential, all people are born equal – regardless of gender, class, race, ethnicity, or nationality.

But, as convenient as it often is to continue to divide humanity into the creative and the uncreative, social philosophers keep reminding us that "reality" rarely, if ever, corresponds to our ideas of what is. With respect to the creative potential, humanistic psychologists argue that because we think that some individuals or groups of people are not creative does not make them inherently less creative than they naturally are. What this type of thinking frequently does is set off a negative self-fulfilling prophecy: That is, by believing that a person or group of people is not creative and relating to that person or to that group of people as if he/they were not creative, we inadvertently get the person or group to behave as expected. But, as so many great thinkers have

---

* The expression is Robert Weisberg's (1986).

observed, the creative force, whether explicitly recognized or not, always finds expression, and does so either in beneficial or in harmful ways. Dan Millman's words (quoted earlier in this work) summarize this observation:

> We create in constructive ways,
> or we create in destructive ways;
> either way, creative energy finds expression.
> (Millman,1993: 330).

Concerns about unrecognized or underutilized human potential, and fears of probable relationships between that condition and certain social and psychological problems, have been expressed by such great thinkers as Abraham Maslow, Mihaly Csikszentmihalyi, David Ray Griffin, and Philo Pritzkau. Abraham Maslow (already referenced), elaborating his famous "capacities clamor to be used, and cease their clamor only when they are well used," reminds us that unused human potential frequently gives rise to psychological and social problems. Mihaly Csikszentmihalyi, reviewing the experiences and achievements of some men and women who invented new paradigms and changed their respective fields, warns against undiscovered or underutilized human abilities. In the words of the psychologist:

> "… it is dangerous to ignore the spiritual needs of people; *it is dangerous to underutilize human potentialities"* (Csikszentmihalyi, 1996: 315; emphasis added).

David Ray Griffin (1988a), in obvious reference to the natural and universal human urge to "create," calls attention to the dangers of continuing to perceive some individuals and groups of people as "not creative" and, based on that assumption, continuing to deny them the opportunity to develop and express their natural abilities – to *exist more fully and realize more of their human potential.* Here are Griffin's words:

> The failure to recognize the essential creativity of all human beings and the correlative assumption that the receptive values [passively receiving and consuming other people's creative achievements] are alone essential leads those with political and economic power to form unrealistic policies. In establishing factories, for example, the modern assumption has been that, as long as the workers made enough money and did not have to work too hard, they would be content. A

postmodern orientation would have told them what some have been discovering only recently – that the workers are not just "workers"; they are people, and as such they want to get some satisfaction from their job, to do something creative, to feel they are making a worthwhile contribution to something, and to participate in the decision making processes of the company. Powerful nations, in relation to less powerful ones, have likewise ignored these other nations' desires to take pride in their own nation, to see it making its own decisions, and to see it as making important contributions to the world community.

World peace is endangered just as much by actions and attitudes that wound the pride of other nations and thwart their desires to exercise their creativity as it is by actions that threaten receptive values. One task of postmodern thought is to create a consciousness in which the need to experience self-actualizing and contributory values is recognized to be as essential to the life of individuals, communities and nations as is the need to feel they are getting their fair share of essential receptive values (Griffin, 1988a: 149-150).

Philo Pritzkau, also commenting on human potentialities and the necessity of their actualization, posits that:

All men have the capability of creating their own form, not simply using that of others (Pritzkau, 1970: 11).

The sum total of these statements is that, contrary to the conventional wisdom, human beings are not just passive consumers of the creative products of other people: Each person has both the ability to achieve something unique and important, and the desire to contribute his creative achievements to others. As the old saying goes: Human beings don't live just to eat; rather, they eat to *live*. And "living," in the deepest sense of the word, consists in being able to realize one's unique potential and to contribute it to fellow human beings (just as one receives the contributions of other people).

Finally, concerning global problems and the deteriorating human condition that are popularly referred to as the human predicament or world *problematique* (including poverty, unemployment, hunger, racism, tribalism, hatred, mutual suspicion, social inequality, conflicts, environmental degradation, threats of a nuclear war, fear, dissatisfaction with life, etc.), the general tendency has been to attribute these problems to such things as culture deficiency, lack of resources, bad governance, poor leadership, avarice, greed, not-enough-aid, and other such explanations. Depending on what has been perceived as the "cause" of specific problems, a variety of solution strategies have been proposed and tried: mass literacy, job training, administrative reforms, technical assistance, population control, income redistribution, national and regional security, a just world order, and others. With regard to economic prosperity and material well-being, for example, the assumption has been that "a rising tide lifts all boats" – that the prosperity and material well-being of a few would eventually trickle down and translate into the prosperity and material well-being of all. The persistence and increasing complexity of many social and environmental problems, despite all the resources that have been committed to their solution and despite the phenomenal increase in the aggregate quantity of goods and services available, suggest that we may have been targeting the "wrong problem" – the symptom, rather than the underlying "cause." As E. F. Schumacher suggests:

> We shrink back from the truth if we believe that the destructive forces of the modern world can be "brought under control" simply by mobilizing more resources – of wealth, education, and research – to fight pollution, to preserve wildlife, to discover new sources of energy, and to arrive at more effective agreements on peaceful coexistence. Needless to say, wealth, education, research, and many other things are needed for any civilization, but what is most needed today is a revision of the ends which these means are meant to serve. And this implies, above all else, the development of a life-style which accords to material things their proper, legitimate place, which is secondary and not primary (Schumacher, 1975: 294).

This takes us back to the ideas with which we began this work and, indeed, the central theme of this project: the principle of individual endowment – the inherence of creativity in human nature, the inner urge to actualize (develop and express) one's talents, and the necessity of the latter condition for emotional and spiritual well-being, increased productivity as employee, responsibility as a national and planetary citizen, and humaneness in relationships with fellow human beings and the rest of nature. To the extent that these ideas are valid, it is doubtful whether current global crises can be solved by governments "pumping in more money," or by replacing one set of leaders with another, or by producing and consuming ever more goods and services, or by more technical assistance, etc., essential as some of these strategies are. The accumulated wisdom of the ages reminds us that what will make people happy with themselves and willing to behave responsibly, humanely, and collaboratively is if they could be enabled to *become all that they were created capable of being*, that is, to recognize, to develop, and to practically express their natural abilities in important and beneficial ways and, therefore, to find meaning and purpose in their lives. That, of course, presupposes more creativity-friendly families, schools, organizations, governments, national and international organizations. The hope is that the insights brought together in this anthology will inspire more parents, educators, students, leaders, public officials, corporate executives, employees, consultants, and concerned individuals to try to translate applicable ideas into their everyday actions and, therefore, to participate in making our world a more fulfilling place for all to live.

Postcript

Great Insights on Human Creativity is a five-volume anthology of some of the profoundest commentaries on human nature and human creativity. The 7,000-plus statements, selected for their wisdom and relevance to the present human situation, are arranged thematically and synthesized for the guidance they provide for meeting some of the most pressing challenges of our time and restoring meaning and purpose to human life.

Volume one, *The Essence and Significance of Human Creativity,* provides a general overview of creativity: its inherence in human nature, its significance in every sphere of human activity, and the necessity of its actualization for mental and emotional well-being, economic productivity, social and environmental responsibility.

Volume two, *The Social Context of Human Creativity,* identifies major sociocultural influences on human creativity. The focus is on the larger economic, social, intellectual, and political patterns as they tend to determine who creates and who does not, as well as the content and direction of the creative expressions of a people or an era.

Volume three, *The Individual and Creativity,* focuses on the psychological dimensions of human creativity as well as the growing significance of creativity for personal well-being. The concern in this volume is with the individual's creative functioning (i.e., his ability to learn and commit himself to learning, his productivity as a worker or employee, his responsibility as a national or planetary citizen, his political, social, and economic behavior, and his contribution to the human heritage), as mediated by internal conditions, such as self-concept, aptitude, attitude, habit, values, and personal outlook.

Volume four, *Theoretical Issues,* features leading "theories of creativity" and related conceptual issues, including: creativity distribution; presumed origins of creative ideas; creative process(es); creativity measurement, training, and development; and criteria for assessing creative ideas and products.

Volume five, *Facilitating and Channeling Human Creativity to Humane and Environmentally Responsible Ends,* is devoted to practical issues of daily significance, such as: (a) making our families, business organizations, governments, and other social institutions more creativity-friendly; (b) facilitating and promoting creativity across activities, across social strata, and across the life-span; (c) dismantling existing roadblocks to human creativity; and (d) channeling human creativity to desirable social and ecological ends.

Following is the outline of themes for the five volumes in the series:

Great Insights on Human Creativity is a work in progress. Readers who have published statements of their own or who know of other published ideas that they would like to be included in this collection should, please, send them to me at:

globecreativity@cs.com

Suggested ideas should be brief one- or two-line statements: witty, easy to understand, memorable, and relevant to modern conditions. National sayings and local or tribal adages (translated into English) are particularly welcome. Every contribution will be gratefully received and considered. Those selected will be duly acknowledged. I appreciate the growing interest in this project.

References

Abelard, Peter, 1965. Quoted in Jacob Bronowski, *Science and Human Values*. (New York: Harper and Row, Publishers).

Ackoff, Russell L., 1974. *Redesigning the Future: A Systems Approach to Societal Problems*. (New York: Wiley).

Ackoff, Russell L., 1981. *Creating the Corporate Future: Plan or Be Planned For.* (New York: John Wiley and Sons, Inc.).

Ackoff, Russel L., 1991. *Ackoff's Fables: Irrelevant Reflections on Business and Bureaucracy.* (New York: John Wiley & Sons, Inc.).

Ahlbrandt, Roger S., 1984. *Neighborhoods, People, and Community.* (New York: Plenum Press).

Aldiss, Brian, 1993. "Apéritif," *Bury My Heart at W. H. Smith's.* In Robert Andrews (ed.), *The Columbia Dictionary of Quotations*. (New York: Columbia UniversityPress).

Ali, Muhammad. 1997. Quoted in *Readers Digest*, June.

Allen, Dwight W., 1970. "Youth Education: Promises," Youth Education. 1968 Yearbook of the Association for Curriculum Development. (Washington, D.C.: National Education Association), p. 120. Quoted in Philo T. Pritzkau, *On Education for the Authentic*. (Scranton, Pennsylvania: International Textbook Company).

Amabile, Teresa M., 1983. The Social Psychology of Creativity. (New York: Springer-Verlag).

Amabile, Teresa M., 1989. *Growing Up Creative: Nurturing a Lifetime of Creativity.* (New York: Crown Publishers, Inc.).

Amabile, Teresa M., 1996. *Creativity in Context: Update to the Social Psychology of Creativity.* (Boulder, Colorado: Westview Press).

Anderson, Lucy, 1977. "Work." In Simple Living Collective, American Friends Service Committee (ed.), Taking Charge: Personal and Political Change Through Simple Living. (New York: Bantam Books), pp. 149-167.

Anderson, Walter Truett, 1990. *Reality Isn't What It Used to Be: Theatrical Politics, Ready-to-Wear Religion, Global Myths, Primitive Chic, and Other Wonders of the Postmodern World.* (San Francisco: Harper & Row).

Anouilh, Jean, 1993. In Margaret Miner and Hugh Rawson (selected and annotated), *The New International Dictionary of Quotations*. Second Edition. (New York: Penguin Books).

Applegath, John, 1982. *Working Free: Practical Alternatives to the 9 to 5 Job.* (New York: Ballantine Books).

Arieti, Silvano, 1976. *Creativity: The Magic Synthesis.* (New York: Basic Books, Inc.).

Aristotle, 1974. Reviewed in Robert F. Davidson, *Philosophies Men Live By.* Second Edition. (New York: Holt, Rinehart and Winston, Inc.), pp. 197-200.

Aristotle, 1993. *Poetics.* In Margaret Miner and Hugh Rawson (selected and annotated), *The New International Dictionary of Quotations*. Second Edition. (New York: Penguin Books).

Aronovici, David, 1995. Quoted in James M. Kouzes and Barry Z. Posner, *The Leadership Challenge: How to Keep Getting Extraordinary Things Done in Organizations* (San Francisco, California: Josey-Brass Publishers).

Aronowitz, Stanley and Henry A. Giroux, 1985. *Education Under Siege: The Conservative, Liberal and Radical Debate Over Schooling.* (South Hadley, Massachusetts: Bergin & Garvey Publishers, Inc.).

Aristotle, 1993. *Poetics.* In Margaret Miner and Hugh Rawson (selected and annotated), *The New International Dictionary of Quotations.* Second Edition. (New York: Penguin Books).

Auden, W. H., 1993. In Robert Andrews (ed.), *The Columbia Dictionary of Quotations.* (New York: Columbia University Press).

Bacon, Francis, 1977. Quoted in *The Oxford Dictionary of Quotations.* Second Edition. (Oxford: Oxford University Press).

Bacon, Francis, 1982. *The New Organon: Aphorisms, Book One,* Aphorism XII. Reproduced in Lynchburg College Symposium Readings, *Classical Selections on Great Issues.* Series Two, Volume I. *Man and the Universe.* (Lanham, Maryland: University Press of America).

Badawy, Michael, 1988. "How to Prevent Creativity Mismanagement." *Research Management.* Quoted in Winston Fletcher, *Creative People: How to Manage Them and Maximize Their Creativity.* ((London: Basic Books Limited).

Barany, George, 1985. Quoted in Connie C. Schmitz and Judy Galbraith, *Managing the Social and Emotional Needs of the Gifted: A Teachers Survival Guide.* (Minneapolis, Minnesota: Free Spirit Publishing, Inc.).

Barrett, Derm , 1998. *The Paradox Process: Creative Business Solutions ... Where You Least Expect to Find Them.* (New York: American Management Association).

Barron, F., 1969. *Creative Person and Creative Process.* (New York: Holt, Rinehart and Winston).

Becker, Mary Lamberton, 1992. Quoted in Gloria Steinem, *Revolution from Within.* (Boston: Little, Brown and Company).

Beckett, Samuel, 1993. Quoted in Deirdre Bair, *Samuel Beckett, a Biography*, Chapter 21. In Robert Andrews (ed.), *The Columbia Dictionary of Quotations.* (New York: Columbia University Press).

Bell, Daniel, 1973. *The Coming of Postindustrial Society.* (New York: Basic Books).

Bennis, Warren, 1976. *The Unconscious Conspiracy: Why Leaders Can't Lead.* (New York: American Management Association, 1976).

Bennis, Warren, 1989. *Why Leaders Can't Lead: The Unconscious Conspiracy Continues.* (San Francisco, California: Jossey-Bass Publishers).

Bennis, Warren, 1992. Quoted in John W. Thompson, "Corporate Leadership in the 21st Century." In John Renesch (ed.), *New Traditions in Business: Spirit and Leadership in the 21st Century.* (San Francisco: Berret-Koehler Publishers), pp. 209-222.

Bennis, Warren and Burt Nanus, 1987. Quoted in Tom Peters, *Thriving on Chaos: Handbook for a Management Revolution.* (New York: Harper Perennial).

Berger, Peter L. and Thomas Luckmann, 1980. *Social Construction of Reality: A Treatise in the Sociology of Knowledge.* (New York: Irvington Publishers, Inc.).

Berlo, David, 1979. Quoted in Michael LeBoeuf, *Working Smart: How to Accomplish More in Half the Time.* (New York: Warner Books.

Biondi, Angelo M., 1972. *The Creative Process.* (Buffalo, New York: D. O. K. Publishers).

Blakely, Edward J. and Mary Gail Snyder, "Putting Up the Gates," *Shelter Force,* May/June, 1997.

Blanchard, Francis, 1989. Quoted in Michael P. Todaro, *Economic Development in the Third World.* Fourth Edition. (New York: Longman, Inc.).

Blanchard, Ken, John P. Carlos, and Alan Randolph, 1996. *Empowerment Takes More Than a Minute.* (San Francisco, California: Berrett-Koehler Publishers).

Blau, P. M., 1955. *The Dynamics of Bureaucracy.* (Chicago: University of Chicago Press).

Bleedorn, Berenice, 1998. *The Creative Force in Education, Business, and Beyond: An Urgent Message.* (Lakeville, Minnesota: Galde Press, Inc.).

Bloom, Allan, 1987. *The Closing of the American Mind: How Higher Education Has Failed Democracy and Impoverished the Souls of Today's Students.* (New York: Simon and Schuster).

Boden, Margaret A., 1992. *The Creative Mind: Myths & Mechanisms.* (New York: Basic Books).

Boorstin, Daniel J., 1985. *The Discoverers: A History of Man's Search to Know His World and Himself.* First Vintage Books Edition. (New York: Vintage Books).

Boorstin, Daniel J., 1992. *The Creators.* (New York: Random House).

Boorstin, Daniel J., 1995. Quoted in *Reader's Digest,* December.

Borges, Jorge Luis, 1993. In Margaret Miner and Hugh Rawson (selected and annotated), *The New International Dictionary of Quotations.* Second Edition. (New York: Penguin Books).

Boss, Medard, 1987. *Psychoanalysis and Daseinanalysis.* Translated by Ludwig B. Lefebre (New York: Basic Books). Reviewed in Jeffrey Steele, *The Representation of the Self in the American Renaissance.* (Chapel Hill, North Carolina: The university of North Carolina Press).

Bova, Ben, 1983. "Preface." *The Omni Future Almanac.* (New York: World Almanac Publications).

Boyett, Joseph, Stephen Schwartz, Laurence Osterwise, and Roy Bauer, 1993. *The Quality Journey: How Winning the Baldrige Sparked the Remaking of IBM.* (New York: Dutton).

Bramnick, Lea and Anita Simon, 1983. *The Parents' Solution Book: Your Child From Five to Twelve.* (New York: The Putnam Publishing Group).

Brecht, Bertolt, 1993. *Galileo.* In Margaret Miner and Hugh Rawson (selected and annotated), *The New International Dictionary of Quotations.* Second Edition. (New York: Penguin Books).

Bredekamp, Sue, 1993. "Reflections on Reggio Emila," *Young Children,* November.

Briggs, Dorothy Corkille, 1975. *Your Child's Self-Esteem: Step-by-Step Guidelines for Raising Responsible, Productive, Happy Children.* Dolphin Books Edition. (New York: Doubleday and Company, Inc.).

Bronowski, Jacob, 1965. *Science and Human Values.* (New York: Harper and Row, Publishers).

Brockmeyer, Steve, 1993. Quoted in Edward and Monika Lumsdaine, *Creative Problem Solving: Thinking Skills for a Changing World.* Second Edition. (New York: McGraw-Hill, Inc.).

Bronowski, Jacob, 1965. *Science and Human Values.* (New York: Harper and Row, Publishers).

Bronowski, Jacob, 1973. *The Ascent of Man*, Chapter 4. In Robert Andrews (ed.), *The Columbia Dictionary of Quotations.* (New York: Columbia University Press).

Bloomfield et al., Harold H., 1975. *Transcendental Meditation: Discovering Inner Energy and Overcoming Stress.* (New York: Delacorte Press).

Brown, Lester R. and Edward C. Wolf, 1985. "Getting Back on Tract." In Lester R. Brown, *et al., State of the World, 1985: A Worldwatch Institute Report on Progress Toward a Sustainable Society.* (New York: W. W. Norton & Company).

Buber, Martin, 1950. *Paths in Utopia.* (New York: Macmillan).

Buber, Martin, 1958. *Hasidism and Modern Man.* Edited and translated by Maurice Friedman. (New York: Horizon Press).

Bühler, Charlotte, and Melanie Allen, 1972. *Introduction to Humanistic Psychology.* (Belmont, California: Brooks/Cole Publishing Company).

Bultmann, Rudolph, 1950. *Essays: Philosophical and Theological.* James C. G. Greig (trans.). (New York: Macmillan). Quoted in Jeffrey Steele, *The Representation of the Self in the American Renaissance.* (Chapel Hill, North Carolina: The university of North Carolina Press).

Burk, Edmund, 1977. *A Letter to a Noble Lord.* Quoted in *The Oxford Dictionary of Quotations.* Second Edition. (Oxford: Oxford University Press).

Burns, James MacGregor, 1978. *Leadership.* (New York: HarperCollins).

Burns, Tom and G. M. Stalker, 1961. *The Management of Innovation.* (London: Tavistock Publications).

Buscaglia, Leo F., 1982. *Personhood: The Art of Being Fully Human.* First Ballantine Books Edition. (New York: Ballantine Books).

Bussis, Anne M., Edward A. Chittenden, Marianne Amarel, and Edith Klauser, 1985. *Inquiry into Meaning: An Investigation of Learning to Read.* (Hillsdale, New Jersey: Lawrence Erlbaum Associates, Inc., Publishers).

Butler, Samuel, 1993. In Robert Andrews (ed.), *The Columbia Dictionary of Quotations.* (New York: Columbia University Press).

Byron (Lord), 1993. In Robert Andrews (ed.), *The Columbia Dictionary of Quotations.* (New York: Columbia University Press).

Camus, Albert, 1996. Quoted in Bernard Haldane, *Career Satisfaction and Success: A Guide to Job and Personal Freedom.* (Indianapolis, Indiana: JIST Works, Inc.).

Canetti, Elias, 1993. In Robert Andrews (ed.), *The Columbia Dictionary of Quotations.* (New York: Columbia University Press).

Carman, Bliss (Attributed), 1992. In Merriam-Webster, Inc., *The Merriam-Webster Dictionary of Quotations.* (Springfield, Massachusetts: Merriam-Webster, Inc.).

Carr, Clay, 1994. *The Competitive Power of Constant Creativity.* (New York: American Management Association).

Carrigan, Patricia M. 1987. Quoted in James M. Kouzes and Barry Z. Posner, *The Leadership Challenge: How to Keep Getting Extraordinary Things Done in Organizations.* First Edition. (San Francisco, California: Josey-Brass Publishers).

Cassels, William, 1971. "Countdown to Excellence." In John Curtis and E. Paul Torrance (eds.), *Educating the Ablest: A Book of Readings on the Education of Gifted Children.* (Itasca, Illinois: F. E. Peacock Publishers, Inc.), pp. 276-280.

Castell, Alburey, 1946. *An Introduction to Modern Philosophy in Six Philosophical Problems.* (New York: The Macmillan Company).

Chambers, J. A., 1983. "College Teachers: Their Effect on Creativity of Students," *Journal of Educational Psychology,* 65, pp. 326-334. In Teresa M. Amabile, *The Social Psychology* of Creativity. (New York: Springer-Verlag).

Channing, William Ellery, 1987. Quoted in Jeffrey Steele, *The Representation of the Self in the American Renaissance.* (Chapel Hill, North Carolina: The University of North Carolina Press).

Chapman, John Jay, 1993. In Robert Andrews (ed.), *The Columbia Dictionary of Quotations.* (New York: Columbia University Press).

Charon, Jean E., 1971."Physics Reveals that Evolution Has a Goal," *Main Currents in Modern Though.,* Quoted in Don Fabun with Kathy Hyland and Robert Conover, *Dimensions of Change.* (Beverly Hills, California: Glencoe Press).

Chenery, Hollis and Moises Syrquin, 1989. *Patterns of Development,* (London: Oxford University Press, 1950). Reviewed in Michael P. Todaro, *Economic Development in the Third World.* Fourth Edition. (New York: Longman, Inc.).

Chesterton, Gilbert Keith, 1992. In Merriam-Webster, Inc., *The Merriam-Webster Dictionary of Quotations.* (Springfield, Massachusetts: Merriam-Webster, Inc.).

Chesterton, Gilbert Keith, 1997. In Rosalie Maggio, *Quotations on Education.* (Paramus, New Jersey: Prentice Hall).

Childcraft. 1949. Volume 12. (Chicago: Field Enterprises, Inc.).

Churchill, Sir Winston, 1993. Address at Harvard University, Sept. 6, 1943. In Margaret Miner and Hugh Rawson (selected and annotated), *The New International Dictionary of Quotations.* Second Edition. (New York: Penguin Books).

Cicero, 1992. In Merriam-Webster, Inc., *The Merriam-Webster Dictionary of Quotations.* (Springfield, Massachusetts: Merriam-Webster, Inc., 1992).

Clark. James F., 1991. In Charles Robert Lightfoot, *Handbook of Business Quotations: Choice Words of Wisdom for Successful Speeches, Reports, Letters, and Papers.* (Houston, Texas: Gulf Publishing Company).

Clifford, Jr., Donald K. and Richard E. Cavanagh, 1985. *The Winning Performance: How America's High-Growth Midsize Companies Succeed.* (Toronto: Bantam Books).

Club of Rome (The), 1974. *Mankind at the Turning Point:* The Second Report to the Club of Rome by Mihajlo Mesarovic and Eduard Pestel. (New York: A Signet Book).

Club of Rome (The), 1979. *No Limits to Learning: Bridging the Human Gap.* Report by James Botkin, Mahdi Elmandjra, and Mircea Malitza. (Oxford, England: Pergamon Press).

Cobb, John, 1999. Quoted In Henri Nouwen et al., *Simpler Living: Compassionate Life.* (Denver, Colorado: Living the Good News).

Cohen, Yehoshua S. and Amnon Shinar, 1985. *Neighborhoods and Friendship Networks: A study of Three Residential Neighborhoods in Jerusalem.* (Chicago: The University of Chicago Press).

Colemen, J., 1988. "Social Capital in the Creation of Human Capital." *American Journal of Sociology,* 94 (Supplement), pp. S95-S120.

Confucius, 1991. In Charles Robert Lightfoot, *Handbook of Business Quotations: Choice Words of Wisdom for Successful Speeches, Reports, Letters, and Papers.* (Houston, Texas: Gulf Publishing Company).

Considine, Daniel, 1991. In Charles Robert Lightfoot, *Handbook of Business Quotations: Choice Words of Wisdom for Successful Speeches, Reports, Letters, and Papers.* (Houston, Texas: Gulf Publishing Company).

Conwell, Russell H., 1915. *Acres of Diamonds.* (New York: Harper & Brothers).

Cooley, M., 1989. "Computers and the Mechanization of Intellectual Work," *Architect or Bee? The Human-Technology Relationship.* (Slough, England: Langley Technical Services). Excerpted in Gareth Morgan (ed.), *Creative Organization Theory: A Resourcebook.* (Newbury Park, California: Sage Publications).

Cortés, Ernesto, Jr., 1993. "Reweaving the Fabric: The Iron Rule and the IAF Strategy for Power and Politics." In Henry G. Cisneros (ed.), *Interwoven Destinies: Cities and the Nation.* (New York: W. W. Norton & Company).

Covey, Stephen R., 1992. *Principle-Centered Leadership.* First Fireside Edition. (New York: Simon & Schuster).

Creech, Bill, 1994. *The Five Pillars of TQM: How to Make Total Quality Management Work for You.* (New York: Truman Talley Books/Plume).

Crocker, Lester G., 1968. *Rousseau's Social Contract: An Interpretive Essay.* (Cleveland, Ohio: The Press of Case Western Reserve University).

Crombie, A. C., 1989. Quoted in Robert Scott Root-Bernstein, *Discovering: Inventing and Solving Problems at the Frontiers of Scientific Knowledge.* (Cambridge, Massachusetts: Harvard University Press).

Csikszentmihalyi, Mihaly, 1996. *Creativity: Flow and the Psychology of Discovery and Invention.* (New York: Harper Collins Publishers).

Cuatrecasas, Pedro, 1995. "Corporate America: Creativity Held Hostage." In Cameron M. Ford and Dennis A. Gioia (eds.), *Creative Action in Organizations: Ivory Tower Visions and Real World Voices.* (Thousand Oaks, California: Sage Publications, Inc.).

Cummings, ee., 1995. Quoted in Charles Swindoll, *Living Above the Level of Mediocrity.* In *The Collected Works of Charles Swindoll.* (New York: Inspirational Press, 1995).

Dacey, John S., 1989. *Fundamentals of Creativity.* (Lexington, Massachusetts: D. C. Heath and Company).

Damon, William, 1995. *Greater Expectations: Overcoming the Culture of Indulgence in America's Homes and Schools.* (New York: The Free Press).

de Bono, Edward, 1970. *Lateral Thinking: Creativity Step by Step.* (New York: Harper & Row, Publishers).

de Bono, Edward, 1971. *Lateral Thinking for Management: A Handbook.* (Maidenhead, Berkshire, England: McGraw-Hill Book Company Ltd.).

de Montesquieu, Baron de la Brède et (Attributed), 1995. In George R. Havens, *The Age of Ideas: From Reaction to Revolution in Eighteenth-Century France.* (New York: Collier Books).

de Pree, Max, 1991. Quoted in J. W. McLean and William Weitzel, *Leadership — Magic, Myth, or Method?* (New York: American Management Association).

DeVries, Rheta and Betty Zan, 1996. "A Constructivist Perspective on the Role of the Sociomoral Atmosphere in Promoting Children's Development." In Catherine

Twomey Fosnot (ed.), *Constructivism: Theory, Perspectives, and Practice.* (New York: Teachers College Press), pp. 103-119.

Dewey, John, 1964. *The School and Society.* (Chicago: 1899), pp. 23-24. Quoted in Lawrence A Cremin, *The Transformation of the School: Progressivism in American Education 1876-1957.* (New York: Vintage Books).

Dewey, John, 1974. "My Pedagogic Creed." Quoted in Wade Baskin (ed.), *Classics in Education.* (New York: Philosophical Library, 1966), p. 186, 189. Quoted in Jack Forem, *Transcendental Meditation: Maharishi Mahesh Yogi and the Science of Creative Intelligence.* (New York: E. P. Dutton & Co., Inc.).

Dinkmeyer, Don and Gary D. McKay, 1973. *Raising a Responsible Child: Practical Steps to Successful Family Relationships.* (New York: Simon and Schuster).

Disraeli, Benjamin, 1993. In Robert Andrews (ed.), *The Columbia Dictionary of Quotations.* (New York: Columbia University Press).

Donelson, Elaine, 1973. *Personality: A Scientific Approach.* (New York: Appleton-Century-Crofts).

Douglas, William O., 1997. In Rosalie Maggio, *Quotations on Education.* (Paramus, New Jersey: Prentice Hall).

Doyle, Arthur Conan, 1992. *The Sign of Four.* In Merriam-Webster, Inc., *The Merriam-Webster Dictionary of Quotations.* (Springfield, Massachusetts: Merriam-Webster, Inc.).

Drucker, Peter F., 1955. *Concept of the Corporation.* (New York: The John Day Company, 1946), p. 179. Quoted in Erich Fromm, *The Sane Society.* (New York: Fawcett World Library).

Drucker, Peter F., 1970. *The Age of Discontinuity.* (London: William Heinemann Ltd.).

Drucker, Peter F., 1982. *The Changing World of the Executive.* (London: William Heinemann Ltd.).

Drucker, Peter F., 1997. "The Future That Has Already Happened," *Harvard Business Review,* September - October, pp. 20, 22, 24.

Drucker, Peter F., 1999. Quoted in John J. Tarrant, Drucker: The Man Who Invented the Corporate Society. (New York: Warner Books, 1976), p. 50. Quoted in Richard J. Spady and Cecil H. Bell, Jr., *The Search for Enlightened Leadership.* Volume 2: *Many-to-Many Communication. A Breakthrough in Social Science.* (Olympia, Washington: Panpress Publishers).

Dubois, Charles, 1976. Quoted in John Adams, John Hayes, and Barrie Hopson (eds.), *Transition: Understanding and Managing Personal Change.* (London: Martin Robertson & Co.).

Durant, Will, 1997. In Rosalie Maggio, *Quotations on Education.* (Paramus, New Jersey: Prentice Hall).

Dykstra, Jr., Dewey, 1996. "Teaching Introductory Physics to College Students." In Catherine Twomey Fosnot (ed.), *Constructivism: Theory, Perspectives, and Practice.* (New York: Teachers College Press).

Eckstein, George R., 1962. Quoted in Sidney J. Parnes, "The Creative Problem-solving Course and Institute at the University of Buffalo." In Sidney J. Parnes and Harold F. Harding, (eds.), *A Source Book for Creative Thinking.* (New York: Charles Scribner's Sons).

Eckstein, George R., 1972. "Pleasure for the Creative Mind." In Angelo M. Biondi (ed.), *The Creative Process*. (Buffalo, New York: D. O. K. Publishers).

Edelhart, Michael, Owen Davis, Paul Hills, and Robert Malone, 1983. "Science and Technology." In Robert Well (ed.), *The Omni Future Almanac*. (New York: World Almanac Publications, 1983), pp. 17-53.

Egon Zehnder International, 1990. Quoted in John Naisbitt and Patricia Aburdene, *Megatrends: 2000: Ten New Directions for the 1990's*. (New York: William Morrow and Company, Inc.).

Einstein, Albert. and L. Infeld, 1938. *The Evolution of Physics*. (New York: Simon & Schuster). Quoted in Robert J.Sternberg, and Todd I. Lubart, *Defying the Crowd: Cultivating Creativity in a Culture of Conformity*. (New York: The Free Press).

Einstein, Albert, 1969. Quoted in Viktor E. Frankl, *The Will to Meaning*. (New York: The World Publishing Company).

Einstein, Albert, 1989. Quoted in Robert Scott Root-Bernstein, *Discovering: Inventing and Solving Problems at the Frontiers of Scientific Knowledge*. (Cambridge, Massachusetts: Harvard University Press).

Einstein, Albert, 1993. In Robert Andrews (ed.), *The Columbia Dictionary of Quotations*. (New York: Columbia University Press, 1993).

Eitzen, D. Stanley and Maxine Bacca Zinn, 1997. *Social Problems*. Seventh Edition. (Boston: Allyn and Bacon).

Eliot, George, 1993. Quoted in Dan Millman, *The Life You Were Born to Live: A Guide to Finding Your Life Purpose*. (Tiburon, California: H. J. Kramer, Inc.).

Ellis, Havelock, 1992. In Merriam-Webster, Inc., 1992. *The Merriam-Webster Dictionary of Quotations*. (Springfield, Massachusetts: Merriam-Webster, Inc.).

Emerson, Ralph Waldo, 1991. In Charles Robert Lightfoot, *Handbook of Business Quotations: Choice Words of Wisdom for Successful Speeches, Reports, Letters, and Papers*. (Houston, Texas: Gulf Publishing Company).

Emerson, Ralph Waldo, 1992. *Society and Solitude*. In Merriam-Webster, Inc., *The Merriam-Webster Dictionary of Quotations*. (Springfield, Massachusetts: Merriam-Webster, Inc.).

Emerson, Ralph Waldo, 1993. In Margaret Miner and Hugh Rawson (selected and annotated), *The New International Dictionary of Quotations*. Second Edition. (New York: Penguin Books).

Emshoff, James R. with Teri E. Denlinger, 1991. *The New Rules of the Game: The Four Key Experiences Managers Must Have to Thrive in the Non-Hierarchical 90s and Beyond*. (New York: HarperBusiness).

Erickson, Joan, 1992. Quoted in Gloria Steinem, *Revolution from Within*.(Boston: Little, Brown and Company).

Eversole, Finley, 1971. "The Politics of Creativity," *Journal of the Creative Society*, June 1969. Quoted in Elizabeth O'Connor, *Eighth Day of Creation: Discovering Your Gifts*. (Washington, DC: The Servant Leadership School).

Fabun, Don with Kathy Hyland and Robert Conover, 1971. *Dimensions of Change*. (Beverly Hills, California: Glencoe Press).

Farber, Jerry, 1972. Quoted in Charlotte Bûhler and Melanie Allen, *Introduction to Humanistic Psychology*. (Belmont, California: Brooks/Cole Publishing Company).

Feldman, Ruth Duskin, 1985. "The Promise and Pain of Growing Up Gifted" *Gifted/ Creative/Talented*, May/June, 1985, p.1. Quoted in Connie C. Schmitz and Judy

Galbraith, *Managing the Social and Emotional Needs of the Gifted: A Teachers Survival Guide.* (Minneapolis, Minnesota: Free Spirit Publishing, Inc.).

Ferguson, Marilyn, 1997. In Rosalie Maggio, *Quotations on Education.* (Paramus, New Jersey: Prentice Hall).

Feyerabend, Paul, 1992. In A. J. Ayer and Jane O'Grady (eds.), *A Dictionary of Philosophical Quotations.* (Oxford, Blackwell Publishers).

Fichte, J. G., 1992. In P. Heath and J. Lachs (trans.), *Science of Knowledge.* In A. J. Ayer and Jane O'Grady (eds.), *A Dictionary of Philosophical Quotations.* (Oxford, UK: Blackwell Publishers).

Fiedler, Fred E., 1971. "Validation and Extension of the Contingency Model of Leadership Effectiveness: A Review of Empirical Findings," *Psychological Bulletin,* 76(2), pp. 128-148.

Filippini, Tiziana, 1990. Lecture. National Association for the Education of Young Children, Washington, DC, November 16.

Fine, T. L., 1992. In A. J. Ayer and Jane O'Grady (eds.), *A Dictionary of Philosophical Quotations.* (Oxford, UK: Blackwell Publishers).

Fitz-Gibbon, Bernice, 1991. In Charles Robert Lightfoot, *Handbook of Business Quotations: Choice Words of Business Wisdom for Successful Speeches, Reports, Letters, and Papers.* (Houston, Texas: Gulf Publishing Company).

Fitzgerald, F. Scott, 1991. In Charles Robert Lightfoot, *Handbook of Business Quotations: Choice Words of Wisdom for Successful Speeches, Reports, Letters, and Papers.* (Houston, Texas: Gulf Publishing Company).

Flesch, Rudolf, 1991. In Charles Robert Lightfoot, *Handbook of Business Quotations: Choice Words of Business Wisdom for Successful Speeches, Reports, Letters, and Papers.* (Houston, Texas: Gulf Publishing Company).

Forem, Jack, 1974. *Transcendental Meditation: Maharishi Mahesh Yogi and the Science of Creative Intelligence.* (New York: E. P. Dutton & Co., Inc.).

Forman, George, 1996. "The Project Approach in Reggio Emilia." In Catherine Twomey Fosnot (ed.), 1996.*Constructivism: Theory, Perspectives, and Practice.* (Columbia University, New York: Teachers University Press), pp. 172-181.

Fosnot, Catherine Twomey (ed.), 1996.*Constructivism: Theory, Perspectives, and Practice.* (Columbia University, New York: Teachers University Press).

Foster, Jack, 1996. *How to Get Ideas.* (San Francisco:Berret-Koehler Publishers).

Frankl, Viktor Emil, 1992. *Man's Search for meaning: An Introduction to Logotherapy.* Fourth Edition. (Boston, Massachusetts: Beacon Press).

Freire, Paulo, 1972. *Pedagogy of the Oppressed.* (London: Sheed and Ward Ltd.).

Friedman, Maurice S., 1976. *Martin Buber, The Life of Dialogue.* (Chicago: The University of Chicago Press)

Frolov, I. T., 1987. Statement at the World Commission on Environment and Development Public Hearing, Moscow, 8 December, 1986. Quoted in The World Commission on Environment and Development, *Our Common Future.* (New York: Oxford University Press).

Fromm, Erich, 1941. *Escape from Freedom.* (New York: Avon Books).

Fromm, Erich, 1955. *The Sane Society.* (New York: Fawcett World Library).

Fromm, Erich, 1974. *Marx's Concept of Man.* (New York: Ungar, 1961). Quoted in Robert Davidson, *Philosophies Men Live By.* Second Edition. (New York: Holt, Rinehart and Winston, Inc.).

Fukuyama, F., 1995. *Trust: The Social Virtues and the Creation of Prosperity.* (New York: Free Press).

Fuller, Margaret, 1987. *Woman in the Nineteenth Century: A Facsimile of the 1845 Edition.* Edited by Joel Myerson and Introduced by Madeline B. Stern. (Columbis, South Carolina: University of South Carolina Press, 1980), p. 26. Quoted in Jeffrey Steele, *The Representation of the Self in the American Renaissance.* (Chapel Hill, North Carolina: The university of North Carolina Press, 1987).

Fuller, R. Buckminster, 1997. In Rosalie Maggio, *Quotations on Education.* (Paramus, New Jersey: Prentice Hall).

Gadamer, H. C., 1996. *Truth and Method.* (New York: Crossroads, 1989), p. 269. Quoted in Maxine Greene, "A Constructivist Perspective on Teaching and Learning in the Arts." In Catherine Twomey Fosnot, *Constructivism: Theory, Perspectives, and Practice.* (Columbia University, New York: Teachers University Press).

Galbraith, John Kenneth, 1974. *Economics and the Public Purpose.* (London: Andre Deutsch).

Galbraith, John Kenneth, 1993. In Robert Andrews (ed.), *The Columbia Dictionary of Quotations.* (New York: Columbia University Press).

Galileo, Galilei, 1977. Quoted in Muriel James and Dorothy Jongeward, *Born to Win: Transactional Analysis with Gestalt Experiments.* Thirty-seventh Printing. (Reading, Massachusetts: Addison-Wesley Publishing Company).

Gardner, Howard, 1983. *Frames of Mind: The Theory of Multiple Intelligences.* (New York: Basic Books).

Gardner, Howard, 1993. *Multiple Intelligences: The Theory in Practice.* A Reader. (New York: Basic Books).

Gardner, John W. 1961. *Excellence: Can We be Equal and Excellent Too?* (New York: Harper & Row Publishers).

Gardner, John 1964. *Self-Renewal: The Individual and the Innovative Society.* (New York: Harper & Row, Publishers).

Gardner, John 1968. *No Easy Victories.* (New York: Harper and Row Publishers).

Gardner, John W., 1996. Quoted in Mihaly Csikszentmihalyi. *Creativity: Flow and the Psychology of Discovery and Invention.* (New York: Harper Collins Publishers).

Gardner, John W., 1999. Godkin Lectures, Harvard University Lectures. Reported in *Christian Science Monitor,* April 16, 1969. Quoted in Richard J. Spady and Cecil H. Bell, Jr., *The Search for Enlightened Leadership.* Volume 2: *Many-to-Many Communication. A Breakthrough in Social Science.* (Olympia, Washington: Panpress Publishers).

Gates, James E., 1962. Quoted in Sidney J. Parnes, "The Creative Problem-solving Course and Institute at the University of Buffalo." In Sidney J. Parnes and Harold F. Harding, (eds.), *A Source Book for Creative Thinking.* (New York: Charles Scribner's Sons).

Gawain, Shakti, 1982. *Creative Visualization.* (Toronto: Bantam Books, Inc).

Geneen, Harold S., 1991. In Charles Robert Lightfoot, *Handbook of Business Quotations: Choice Words of Wisdom for Successful Speeches, Reports, Letters, and Papers.* (Houston, Texas: Gulf Publishing Company).

Genishi, C., A. McCarrier, and R.N. Nussbaum, 1988. "Research Currents: Dialogue as a Context for Teaching and Learning," *Language Arts,* 65, pp. 182 - 190. Quoted in Maxine Greene, "A Constructivist Perspective on Teaching and Learning in the Arts." In Catherine Twomey Fosnot (ed.), *Constructivism: Theory, Perspectives, and Practice.* (Columbia University, New York: Teachers University Press), pp. 120-141.

Ghoshal, Sumantra and Christopher A. Bartlett, 1997. *The Individualized Corporation: A Fundamentally New Approach to Management.* (New York: HarperCollins Publishers, Inc.).

Gibb, C. A., 1947. "The Principles and Traits of Leadership," *Journal of Abnormal Social Psychology,* 3, 267-284.

Gibran, Kahlil, 1973. *The Prophet.* (New York: Alfred A Knopf).

Gide, Andre, 1987. Quoted in Marsha Sinetar, *Do What You Love, The Money Will Follow: Discovering Your Right Livelihood.* (New York: Dell Publishing).

Gillespie, J. J., 1955. *Free Expression in Industry.* (London: The Pilot Press, Ltd, 1948). Quoted in Erich Fromm, *The Sane Society.* (New York: Fawcett World Library).

Gillespie, Robert J., 1972. "Roadblocks to Creativity." In Angelo M. Biondi (ed.), *The Creative Process.* (Buffalo, New York: D.O.K. Publishers).

Gilovich, Thomas, 1991. *How We know What Isn't So: The Fallibility of Human Reason in Everyday Life.* (New York: The Free Press).

Glasgow, Ellen, 1992. In Merriam-Webster, Inc., 1992. *The Merriam-Webster Dictionary of Quotations.* (Springfield, Massachusetts: Merriam-Webster, Inc.).

Glasow, Arnold H., 1991. In Charles Robert Lightfoot, *Handbook of Business Quotations: Choice Words of Wisdom for Successful Speeches, Reports, Letters, and Papers.* (Houston, Texas: Gulf Publishing Company).

Goldman, Emma, 1992. Quoted in Alix Kates Shulman, *Red Emma Speaks: Selected Speeches of Emma Goldman.* (New York: Random House, 1972), p.133. Quoted in Gloria Steinem, *Revolution from Within: A Book of Self-Esteem.* (Boston, Massachusetts: Little, Brown and Company).

Goldsmith, Edward, *et al.,* 1974. *Blueprint for Survival.* First Signet Printing. (New York: The New American Library, Inc.).

Goulner, A., 1950. *Studies in Leadership.* (New York: Harper).

Gouldner, Alvin, 1989. "The Not-Enough World of Work." In Gareth Morgan (ed.), *Creative Organization Theory: A Resourcebook.* (Newbury Park, California: Sage Publications), pp. 260-263.

Gournay, 1995. *Financial Times* of London, 30 May.

Gowan, J. C., 1978. "The Facilitation of Creativity Through Meditational Procedures," *Journal of Creative Behavior,* 12, pp. 156-160.

Gozdz, Kazimierz, 1993. Quoted in Gifford and Elizabeth Pinchot, *The End of Bureaucracy and the Rise of the Intelligent Organization.* (San Francisco, California: Berrett-Koehler Publishers).

Gragg, Charles I., 1940. "... Because Wisdom Can't be Told." *Harvard Alumni Bulletin.* October 19. Reprinted in *The Case Method at the Harvard Business School.* (New York: McGraw-Hill Book Company, Inc., 1954), pp. 6-14.

Gramsci, Antonio, 1985. *Selections from Prison Notebooks.* Edited and translated by Quinten Hoare and Geoffrey Smith. (New York: International Publishers, 1971),

p. 33. Quoted in Stanley Aronowitz and Henry A. Giroux, *Education Under Siege: The Conservative, Liberal and Radical Debate Over Schooling.* (South Hadley, Massachusetts: Bergin & Garvey Publishers, Inc.).

Gravely, Samuel I., 1994. In Dennis Kimbro, *Daily Motivations for African-American Success.* First Mass Market Edition. May. 6. (New York: Fawcett Crest).

Greenber, J., 1993. "The Social Side of Fairness: Interpersonal and Informational Classes of Organizational Justice." In R. Cropaanzano (ed.), *Justice in the Workplace.* (Hillside, New Jersey: Elbaum), pp. 79-103.

Greenber, J., 1993a. "Stealing in the name of Justice: Informational and Interpersonal Moderators of Theft Reactions to Underpayment Inequity," *Organizational Behavior and Human Decision Processes,* 54, 81-103.

Greenber, J., and K. S. Scott, 1995. "Why do Workers Bite the Hands that Feed Them? Employee Theft as a Social Exchange Process." In B. M. Staw and L. L. Cumming (eds.), *Research in Organizational Behavior,* 18, (Greenwich, Connecticut: JAI Press).

Greene, Maxine, 1996. "A Constructivist Perspective on Teaching and Learning in the Arts." In Catherine Twomey Fosnot (ed.), *Constructivism: Theory, Perspectives, and Practice.* (Columbia University, New York: Teachers University Press). pp.120-141.

Greenleaf, Robert K., 1977. *Teacher as Servant.* (New York: Paulist Press).

Greenleaf, Robert K., 1997. "The Servant as Leader." In Robert P. Vecchio (ed.), *Leadership: Understanding the Dynamics of Power and Influence in Organizations.* (Notre Dame, Indiana: University of Notre Dame Press), pp. 429-438.

Grenz, Stanley, 1996. *A Primer on Postmodernism.* (Grand Rapids, Michigan: William B. Eerdmans Publishing Company).

Griffin, David Ray, 1988. "Introduction: Postmodern Spirituality and Society." In David Ray Griffin (ed.), *Spirituality and Society: Postmodern Visions.* (Albany, New York: State University of New York Press), pp. 1-31.

Griffin, David Ray, 1988a. "Peace and the Modern Paradigm." In David Ray Griffin (ed.), *Spirituality and Society: Postmodern Visions.* (Albany, New York: State University of New York Press), pp. 143-154.

Griffiths, Daniel E., 1997. "Administrative Performance and System Theory." Paper presented at An Interdisciplinary Seminar on Administrative Theory, Austin Texas, March 20-21, 1961, p. 5. Quoted in Richard J. Spady and Cecil H. Bell, Jr., *The Search for Enlightened Leadership.* Volume One: Applying New Administrative Theory. (Olympia, Washington: Panpress Publishers).

Guba, Egon G. and Virginia S. Lincoln, 1994. "Competing Paradigms in Qualitative Research." In Norman K. Denzin and Yvonna S. Lincoln (eds.) *Handbook of Qualitative Research.* (London: Sage Publications), pp. 104-117.

Guetzkow, Harold, 1965. "The Creative Person in Organizations." In Gary A. Steiner (ed.), *The Creative Organization.* (Chicago: University of Chicago Press, 1965).

Guilford, J. P., 962. "Creativity: Its Measurement and Development." In Sidney J. Parnes and Harold F. Harding (eds.), *A Source Book for Creative Thinking.* (New York: Charles Scribner's Sons).

Hadamard, J., 1975. *The Psychology of Invention in the Modern Mathematical Field.* (Princeton: Princeton University Press, 1949). Quoted in Arthur Koestler, *The Act of Creation.* Picador Edition. (London: Pan Books).

Hadrian (Roman Emperor, AD 76-138), 1996. Quoted in Bernard Haldane, *Career Satisfaction and Success: A guide to Job and Personal Freedom.* (Indianapolis, Indiana: JIST Works, Inc.).

Haldane, Bernard, 1996. *Career Satisfaction and Success: A guide to Job and Personal Freedom.* (Indianapolis, Indiana: JIST Works, Inc.).

Halsey, George, 1994. Quoted in Dennis Kimbro, *Daily Motivations forAfrican-American Success.* First Mass Market Edition. (New York: Fawcett Crest), May. 19.

Hammer, Michael and James Champy, 1993. *Reengineering the Corporation: A Manifesto for Business Revolution.* (New York: Harper Business).

Handy, Charles, 1989. *The Age of Unreason.* (Boston, Massachusetts: Harvard Business School Press).

Handy, Charles, 1997. "The Citizen Corporation," *Harvard Business Review,* September - October, pp. 26, 28.

Harman, Willis, 1984. "Introduction: The Cat Who Wasn't There." In Willis Harman and Howard Rheingold, *Higher Creativity: Liberating the Unconscious for Breakthrough Insights.* (Los Angeles, California: Jeremy Tharcher, Inc.).

Harman, Willis and Howard Rheingold, 1984. *Higher Creativity: Liberating the Unconscious for Breakthrough Insights.* (Los Angeles, California: Jeremy Tharcher, Inc.).

Harman, Willis and John Hormann, 1990. *Creative Work: The Constructive Role of Business in a Transforming Society.* (Indianapolis, Indiana: Knowledge Systems, Inc.).

Harmon, Frederick G., 1989. *The Executive Odyssey: Secrets for a Career Without Limits.* (New York: John Wiley & Sons).

Harrington, H. James, Glen D. Hoffher, and Robert P. Reid, 1998. *The Creativity Toolkit: Provoking Creativity in Individuals and Organizations.* (New York: McGraw-Hill Companies, Inc.)

Harris, Philip R. and Robert T. Moran, 2000. *Managing Cultural Differences: Leadership Strategies for a New World of Business.* Fifth Edition. (Houston, Texas: Gulf Publishing Company).

Harris, Sydney, 1986. Quoted in George W. Downs and Patrick D. Larkey, *The Search for Government Efficiency: From Hubris to Helplessness.* (New York: Random House).

Harris, Sydney J., 1993. In Margaret Miner and Hugh Rawson (eds.), *The New International Dictionary of Quotations,* Second Edition. (New York: Penguin Books).

Hauchler, Ingomar and Paul M. Kennedy (eds.), 1994. *Global Trends: The World Almanac of Development and Peace.* (New York: The Continuum Publishing Company).

Hayes, John and Patricia Hough, 1976. "Career Transitions as a Source of Identity Strain." In John Adams, John Hayes, and Barrie Hopson (eds.), Transition: Understanding and Managing Personal Change. (London: Martin Robertson & Company.

Hayes, Roger and Reginald Watts, 1986. *Corporate Revolution: New Strategies for Executive Leadership.* (London: William Heinemann Ltd.).

Hazlitt, William, 1991. In Charles Robert Lightfoot, *Handbook of Business Quotations: Choice Words of Wisdom for Successful Speeches, Reports, Letters, and Papers.* (Houston, Texas: Gulf Publishing Company).

Hazlitt, William, 1993. In Robert Andrews (ed.), *The Columbia Dictionary of Quotations.* (New York: Columbia University Press).

Heilbroner, Robert L., 1975. *An Inquiry into the Human Prospect.* (New York: W. W. Norton and Company, Inc.).

Heilbroner, Robert L., 1986. *The Worldly Philosophers: The lives, Times and Ideas of the Great Economic Thinkers.* (New York: Simon and Schuster).

Heisenberg, W., 1996. Quoted in Stanley Grenz, *A Primer on Postmodernism.* (Grand Rapids, Michigan: William B. Eerdmans Publishing Company).

Helmstetter, Shad, 1982. *What to Say When You Talk to Your Self.* (New York: Pocket Books).

Henderson, C. William, 1975. *Awakening: Ways to Psycho-Spiritual Growth.* (Englewood Cliffs, New Jersey: Prentice Hall, Inc.).

Henwood, M., 1991. "No Sense of Urgency: Age Discrimination in Health Care," *Critical Public Health*, 2, pp. 4-14.

Heron, A. R., 1955. *Why Men Work,* (Stanford, California: Stanford University Press, 1948), pp. 121, 122. Quoted in Erich Fromm, *The Sane Society.* (New York: Fawcett World Library).

Heschel, Abraham, 1986. Quoted in Michael Ray and Rochelle Myers, *Creativity in Business.* (New York: Doubleday and Company, Inc.).

Hicks, Herbert G. and C. Ray Gullet, 1976. *The Management of Organizations.* (New York: McGraw-Hill Book Company).

Higgins, James M., 1994. *101 Creative Problem Solving Techniques: The Handbook of New Ideas for Business.* (Winter Park, Florida: New Management Publishing Company, Inc.)

Hofstadter, Richard, 1990. In Meic Stephens (compiled), *A Dictionary of Literary Quotations.* (London: Routledge).

Holmes, Sr., Oliver Wendell, 1992. *The Professor at the Breakfast-Table.* In Merriam-Webster, Inc., *The Merriam-Webster Dictionary of Quotations.* (Springfield, Massachusetts: Merriam-Webster, Inc).

Holt, John, 1976. *How Children Fail.* (New York: Dell Publishing Co., Inc)

Holt, John, 1992. Quoted in Gloria Steinem, *Revolution from Within.* (Boston: Little, Brown and Company).

Hoover, Herbert, 1963. "The Future." From Herbert Hoover, *American Individualism.* Reprinted in Marvin Laser, Robert S. Cathcart, and Fred H. Marcus (eds.), *Ideas and Issues: Readings for Analysis and Evaluation.* (New York: The Ronald Press Company).

Howe, II, Harold, 1996. "The Systemic Epidemic," *Education Week,* July 13, 1994, p. 40. Quoted in Robert Evans, *The Human Side of School Change: Reform, Resistance, and the Real-Life Problems of Innovation.* (San Francisco: Jossey-Brass Publishers).

Howell, James, 1991. In Charles Robert Lightfoot, *Handbook of Business Quotations: Choice Words of Wisdom for Successful Speeches, Reports, Letters, and Papers.* (Houston, Texas: Gulf Publishing Company).

Hubbard, Elbert, 1967. *Epigrams.* In Burton Stevenson (ed.), *The Home Book of Quotations.* (New York: Dodd, Mead and Company).

Hubbard, Elbert, 1997. In Rosalie Maggio, *Quotations on Education.* (Paramus, New Jersey: Prentice Hall).

Hughes, Robert, 1987. *The Shock of the New.* (New York: Alfred A. Knopf).

Humphrey, Hubert H., 1993. Speech, 10 Oct., 1966, Gainesville, Florida. In Robert Andrews (ed.), *The Columbia Dictionary of Quotations.* (New York: Columbia University Press).

Hutchins, Robert M., 1974. *The Conflict in Education in a Democratic Society.* (New York: Harper, 1953). Quoted in Jack Forem, *Transcendental Meditation: Maharishi Mahesh Yogi and the Science of Creative Intelligence.* (New York: E. P. Dutton & Co., Inc.).

Huxley, Aldous (Attributed), 1989. In Robert Scott Root-Bernstein, *Discovering: Inventing and Solving Problems at the Frontiers of Scientific Knowledge.* (Cambridge, Massachusetts: Harvard University Press).

Huxley, T. H., 1975. Quoted in Arthur Koestler, *The Act of Creation.* Picador Edition. (London: Pan Books Ltd.).

Hybels, Bill, 1987. *Who You Are When No One's Looking.* (Downers Grove, Illinois: InterVarsity Press).

Ibsen, Henrik, 1991. In Charles Robert Lightfoot, *Handbook of Business Quotations: Choice Words of Wisdom for Successful Speeches, Reports, Letters, and Papers.* (Houston, Texas: Gulf Publishing Company).

Ijiri, Yuji, 1993. Quoted in Robert Lawrence Kuhn, "A Personal Summary." In Robert Lawrence Kuhn (ed.), *Generating Creativity and Innovation in Large Bureaucracies.* (Westport, Connecticut: Quorum Books).

Innes, Judith E., 1996. "Planning Through Consensus Building: A New View of the Comprehensive Planning Ideal," *APA Journal,* Autumn, pp. 460-472.

Jaccaci, August T. and Susan B. Gault, 1999. *Chief Evolutionary Officer: Leaders Mapping the Future.* (Boston, Massachusetts: Butterworth-Heinemann).

Jaccaci, August T., 2000. *General Periodicity: Nature's Creative Dynamics.* (Kearney, Nebrske: Morris Publishing).

Jackson, Jesse, 1988. Quoted in *Daily Mail.* London. (9 March).

Jackson, K. F., 1975. *The Art of Solving Problems.* (London: William Heinemann Ltd.).

James, William, 1964. Quoted in John Gardner, *Self-Renewal: The Individual and the Innovative Society.* (New York: Harper & Row, Publishers).

James, William, 1992. *The Principles of Psychology.* In Merriam-Webster, Inc., *The Merriam-Webster Dictionary of Quotations.* (Springfield, Massachusetts: Merriam-Webster, Inc.).

James, William, 1992a. In Angela Partington (ed.), *The Oxford Dictionary of Quotations.* Fourth Edition. (Oxford: Oxford University Press).

James, William, 1999. Quoted Timothy C. Weiskel, "Some Notes from Belshaz'zar's Feast." In Henri Nouwen et al., (eds.), *Simpler Living: Compassionate Life.* (Denver, Colorado: Living the Good News), pp. 161-174.

Jay, Antony, 1980. Quoted in Brian C. Twiss, *Managing Technological Innovation.* Second Edition. (London: Longman Group Ltd).

Jefferson, Thomas, 1980. Quoted in Alvin Toffler, *The Third Wave.* (New York: William Morrow and Company, Inc.).

Jennings, H. H., 1943. *Leadership and Isolation.* (New York: Longman).

Jewkes, J., D. Sawer, and R. Stillerman, 1961. *The Sources of Invention.* (London: Macmillan, 1957), pp. 94-95. Quoted in Tom Burns and G. M. Stalker, *The Management of Innovation.* (London: Tavistock Publications).

Joad, Cyril E. M., 1962. "What Eastern Religion Has to Offer to Western Civilization," *The Aryan Path,* vol. 1, 1930, pp. 16-19. Quoted in Ashley Montagu, *The Humanization of Man: Our Changing Conception of Human Nature.* (New York: Grove Press, Inc.).

Johnson, Allan G., 1989. *Human Arrangements: An Introduction to Sociology.* Second Edition. (San Diego, California: Harcourt Brace and Jovanovich, Publishers).

Johnson, R. W., 1993. In Robert Andrews (ed.), *The Columbia Dictionary of Quotations.* (New York: Columbia University Press).

Johnson, Samuel, 1997. In Rosalie Maggio, *Quotations on Education.* (Paramus, New Jersey: Prentice Hall).

Johnson, Samuel, 1990. In Meic Stephens (compiled), *A Dictionary of Literary Quotations.* (London: Routledge).

Joyce, James, 1992. In Merriam-Webster, Inc., *The Merriam-Webster Dictionary of Quotations.* (Springfield, Massachusetts: Merriam-Webster, Inc.).

Jung, Carl, 1993. In Robert Andrews (ed.), *The Columbia Dictionary of Quotations.* (New York: Columbia University Press).

Kabat-Zinn, Jon, 1994. *Wherever You Go There You Are: Mindfulness Meditation in Everyday Life.* (New York: Hyperion).

Kalu, Orji Uzor, 2000. Press interview. Minna, Nigeria. Reported in Naija-news@egroups.com, October, 30.

Kant, Immanuel, 1974. Quoted in Wade Baskin (ed.), *Classics in Education.* (New York: Philosophical Library, 1966), p. 327. Quoted in Jack Forem, *Transcendental Meditation: Maharishi Mahesh Yogi and the Science of Creative Intelligence.* (New York: E. P. Dutton & Co., Inc.).

Kant, Immanuel, 1992. In A. J. Ayer and Jane O'Grady (eds.), *A Dictionary of Philosophical Quotations.* (Oxford, Blackwell Publishers).

Kanter, Rosabeth Moss, 1983. *The Change Masters: Innovation and Entrepreneurship in the American Corporation.* (New York: Simon and Schuster, Inc.).

Kaufman, Bel, 1997. In Rosalie Maggio, *Quotations on Education.* (Paramus, New Jersey: Prentice Hall).

Kennedy, John F., 1997. In Rosalie Maggio, *Quotations on Education.* (Paramus, New Jersey: Prentice Hall).

Kiefer, Charles F., 1992. "Leadership in Metanoic Organizations." In John Renesch (ed.), *New Traditions in Business: Spirit and Leadership in the 21st Century.* (San Francisco: Berret-Koehler Publishers), pp. 175-191.

Kierkegaard, Søren, 1961. Quoted in Carl R. Rogers, *On Becoming a Person: A Therapist's View of Psychotherapy.* (Boston, Massachusetts: Houghton Mifflin Company).

Kierkegaard, Søren, 1992. In A. J. Ayer and Jane O'Grady (eds.), *A Dictionary of Philosophical Quotations.* (Oxford, UK: Blackwell Publishers.

Kilpatrick, William Heard, 1964. *Foundations of Method.* (New York: 1925).
Quoted in Lawrence A Cremin, *The Transformation of the School: Progressivism in American Education 1876-1957.* (New York: Vintage Books).

King, Jr., Martin Luther, 1992. In Susan Winebrenner, *Teaching Gifted Kids in the Regular Classroom: Strategies and Techniques Every Teacher Can Use to Meet the Academic Needs of the Gifted and Talented.* (Minneapolis, Minnesota: Free Spirit Publishing).

King, Jr., Martin Luther, 1993. In Margaret Miner and Hugh Rawson (selected and annotated), *The New International Dictionary of Quotations.* Second Edition. (New York: Penguin Books).

Kingsolver, Barbara. 1995. *Animal Dreams.* (Harper Collins). Quoted in *Reader's Digest,* September.

Koestler, Arthur, 1975. *The Act of Creation.* Picador Edition. (London: Pan Books Ltd.).

Koontz, Elizabeth Duncan, 1975."Women as a Minority Group." In Mary Lou Thompson (ed.), *Voices of the New Feminism.* (Boston, Massachusettes: Beacon Press), pp. 77-86.

Kotter, John P., 1990. *The Leadership Factor.* Quoted in John Naisbitt and Patricia Aburdene,: 218. *The New Directions for the 1990's: Megatrends 2000.* (New York: William Morrow and Company, Inc.).

Kouzes, James M. and Barry Z. Posner, 1987; 1995. *The Leadership Challenge: How to Keep Getting Extraordinary Things Done in Organizations.* First Edition. (San Francisco: Jossey-Brass Publishers).

Krech, D. and R. S. Crutchfield, 1948.*Theory and Problems of Social Psychology.* (New York: McGraw Hill).

Krishnamurti, Jiddu, 1964. *Think on These Things.* (New York: Harper & Row).

Krishnamurti, Jiddu, 1997. In Rosalie Maggio, *Quotations on Education.* (Paramus, New Jersey: Prentice Hall).

Kuhn, Thomas, 1962. *The Structure of Scientific Revolutions,* Vol. I. Foundations of the Unity of Science. (Chicago: University of Chicago Press).

Kuhn, Thomas S., 1970. *The Logic of Scientific Revolution.* Second Edition. (Chicago: University of Chicago Press).

Kuhn, Robert Lawrence, 1993. "A Personal Summary." In Robert Lawrence Kuhn (ed.), *Generating Creativity and Innovation in Large Bureaucracies.* (Westport, Connecticut: Quorum Books).

Labier, Douglas, 1986. *Modern Madness: The Emotional Fallout of Success.* (Reading, Massachusetts: Addison-Wesley Publishing Company, Inc.).

Landau, Ralph 1982. "The Innovative Milieu." In Sven B. Lundstedt and E. W. Colglazier, Jr. (eds.), *Managing Innovation.* (New York: Pergamon Press).

La Rochefoucauld, François duc de, 1993. In Robert Andrews (ed.), *The Columbia Dictionary of Quotations.* (New York: Columbia University Press).

Lao-tsu, 1991. In Charles Robert Lightfoot, *Handbook of Business Quotations: Choice Words of Wisdom for Successful Speeches, Reports, Letters, and Papers.* (Houston, Texas: Gulf Publishing Company).

Laszlo, et al., Ervin, 1978. *Goals for Mankind: A Report to the Club Of Rome on the New Horizons of Global Community.* (New York: Signet).

Laszlo, Ervin, 1994. *The Choice: Evolution or Extinction? A Thinking Person's Guide to Global Issues.* (New York: G. P. Putnam's Sons).

Laurie, Sanders G., and Melvin J. Tucker, 1978. *Centering: Your Guide to Inner Growth.* (New York: Warner/Destiny Books).

Lavater, Johann K., 1991. In Charles Robert Lightfoot, *Handbook of Business Quotations: Choice Words of Wisdom for Successful Speeches, Reports, Letters, and Papers.* (Houston, Texas: Gulf Publishing Company).

Lavelle, Robert, et. al. (eds.), 1995. *America's New War on Poverty: A Reader for Action.* (San Francisco: KQED Books and Tapes).

Law, Vernon, 1997. In Rosalie Maggio, *Quotations on Education.* (Paramus, New Jersey: Prentice Hall).

Lawton, George, 1963. Quoted in Alex Osborn, *Applied Imagination: Principles and Procedures of Creative Problem-Solving.* Third Edition. (New York: Charles Scribner's Sons).

Lay-Dopyera, Margaret and John Dopyera, 1987. *Becoming a Teacher of Young Children.* Third Edition. (New York: Random House).

LeBoeuf, Michael, 1979. *Working Smart: How to Accomplish More in Half the Time.* (New York: Warner Books).

Lefevre, Mike, 1974. Reported in Studs Terkel, *Working: People Talk about What They do All Day and How They Feel about What They Do.* (New York: Pantheon Books).

L'Engle, Madeleine, 1997. In Rosalie Maggio, *Quotations on Education.* (Paramus, New Jersey: Prentice Hall).

LeShan, Eda J., 1997. In Rosalie Maggio, *Quotations on Education.* (Paramus, New Jersey: Prentice Hall).

Lichtenberg, G. C., 1995. Quoted in *Reader's Digest,* February.

Lightfoot, Charles Robert, 1991. *Handbook of Business Quotations: Choice Words of Wisdom for Successful Speeches, Reports, Letters, and Papers.* (Houston, Texas: Gulf Publishing Company).

Lincoln, J. F., 1955. (Paraphrased). In Erich Fromm, *The Sane Society.* (New York: Fawcett World Library).

Lindsay, John V., 1974. Graduation address at Manhattanville College, Purchase, New York. Reported in *New York Times,* June 1, 1969. Quoted in Jack Forem, *Transcendental Meditation: Maharishi Mahesh Yogi and the Science of Creative Intelligence.* (New York: E. P. Dutton & Co., Inc.).

Lowell, James Russell, 1991. In Charles Robert Lightfoot, *Handbook of Business Quotations: Choice Words of Business Wisdom for Successful Speeches, Reports, Letters, and Papers. (Houston,* Texas: Gulf Publishing Company).

Lowell, James Russell, 1992. In Merriam-Webster, Inc., *The Merriam-Webster Dictionary of Quotations.* (Springfield, Massachusetts: Merriam-Webster, Inc.).

Lucretius, 1993. In Margaret Miner and Hugh Rawson (selected and annotated), *The New International Dictionary of Quotations.* Second Edition. (New York: Penguin Books).

Lumsdaine, Edward and Monika Lumsdaine, 1993. *Creative Problem Solving: Thinking Skills for a Changing World.* Second Edition. (New York: McGraw-Hill, Inc.).

Lundy, James L., 1991. Quoted in J. W. McLean and William Weitzel, *Leadership — Magic, Myth, or Method?* (New York: American Management Association).

Luthe, Wolfgang, 1976. *Creativity Mobilization Techniques.* (New York: Grune and Stratton).

Lynd, Robert S., 1939. *Knowledge for What? The Place of Social Science in American Culture.* (Princeton: Princeton University Press).

MacArthur, Douglas (General), 1975. Quoted in Robert H. Schuller, *Move Ahead with Possibility Thinking.* (Old Tappan, New Jersey: Pillar Books).

Maccoby, Michael, 1987. *Challenge: How to Keep Getting Extraordinary Things Done in Organizations.* First Edition. (San Francisco: Jossey-Brass Publishers).

Machado, Luis Alberto, 1980. *The Right to Be Intelligent.* (Oxford: Pergamon Press).

Machiavelli, Niccolo, 1976. Quoted in Herbert G. Hicks and C. Ray Gullet, *The Management of Organizations.* (New York: McGraw-Hill Book Company).

Mackay, Harvey, 2000. "Be a Believer to be an Achiever," *Connections: The Inflight Magazine of ASA,* September/October.

Mackenzie, Robert, 1956. *The Nineteenth Century — A History.* Quoted in R. G. Collingwood, *The Idea of History.* (New York: Oxford University Press, 1956).

MacKinnon, D. W., 1995. "The Personality Correlates of Creativity: A Study of American Architects." In G. S. Nielson (ed.), *Proceedings of the SIV International Congress of Applied Psychology, 2. 11-33.* Quoted in Craig C. Lundberg, "Creativity Training and Hemispheric Function: Bringing the Left Brain Back In." In Cameron M. Ford and Dennis A. Gioia (eds.), *Creative Action in Organizations: Ivory Tower Visions and Real World Voices.* (Thousand Oaks, California: Sage Publications, Inc., 1995).

MacLean, Malcolm S., 1964. Quoted is Lawrence A. Cremin, *The Transformation of the School: Progressivism in American Education 1876-1957.* (New York: Vintage Books, 1964).

McRobie, George, 1981. *Small is Possible.* (New York: Harper & Row Publishers, 1981).

Malaguzzi, Loris, 1994. "Your Image of The Child," *Exchange,* 3.

Malaguzzi, Loris, 1996. "No Way. The Hundred is There," Quoted in Municipality of Reggio Emilia, *The Hundred Languages of Children.* (Reggio Emilia, Italy: Reggio Children).

Mann, R. D., 1959. "A Review of the Relationship Between Personality and Performance in Small Groups," *Psychological Bulletin,* 56, pp. 241-270.

Martin, Jack and Jeff Sugarman, 1999. *The Psychology of Human Possibility and Constraint.* (Albany, New York: State University of New York Press).

Marx, Karl, 1955. Quoted in Erich Fromm, *The Sane Society.* (New York: Fawcett World Library, 1955).

Marx, Karl, 1964. *Early Writings.* Translated by T. B. Bottomore. (New York: McGraw-Hill).

Maslow, Abraham H., 1959. *Psychological Data and Value Theory.* In Abraham Maslow (ed.), *New Knowledge in Human Values.* (New York: Harper).

Maslow, Abraham H., 1962. *Toward a Psychology of Being.* (Princeton, New Jersey: Nostrand).

Maslow, Abraham H., 1970. *Motivation and Personality.* Second Edition. (New York: Harper & Row).

Matt (Anonymous "Gifted" Student), 1985. Quoted in Connie C. Schmitz and Judy Galbraith, *Managing the Social and Emotional Needs of the Gifted: A Teachers Survival Guide.* (Minneapolis, Minnesota: Free Spirit Publishing, Inc.).

Maugham, W. Somerset, 1963. *Quoted in Alex F. Osborn,* Applied Imagination: Principles and Procedures of Creative Problem-Solving. *Third Edition. (New York: Charles Scribner's Sons).*

Maugham, W. Somerset, 1991. In Charles Robert Lightfoot, *Handbook of Business Quotations: Choice Words of Business Wisdom for Successful Speeches, Reports, Letters, and Papers.* (Houston, Texas: Gulf Publishing Company).

Maurois, André, 1993. In Robert Andrews (ed.), *The Columbia Dictionary of Quotations.* (New York: Columbia University Press).

May, Rollo, 1972. Quoted in Charlotte Bühler and Melanie Allen, *Introduction to Humanistic Psychology.* (Belmont, California: Brooks/Cole Publishing Company).

May, Rollo, 1976. *The Courage to Create.* Bantam Edition. (New York: W. W. Norton and Company, Inc.).

Mayor, Federico, 1993. Quoted in Ervin Laszlo, *The Choice: Evolution or Extinction? A Thinking Person's Guide to Global Issues.* (New York: G. P. Putnam's Sons).

M'Bow, Amadou-Mahtar, 1978. *Quoted in Ervin Laszlo, et al.,* Goals for Mankind: A Report to the Club Of Rome on the New Horizons of Global Community. *(New York: Signet).*

McCarthy, Mary, 1992. In Angela Partington (ed.), *The Oxford Dictionary of Quotations.* Fourth Edition. (Oxford: Oxford University Press, 1992).

McLean, J. W. and William Weitzel, 1991. *Leadership — Magic, Myth, or Method?* (New York: American Management Association).

McLuhan, Marshall (Attributed), 1970. Quoted in Philo T. Pritzkau, *On Education for the Authentic.* (Scranton, Pennsylvania: International Textbook Company).

McMillan (Hon.), Tom, 1987. Statement at the World Commission on Environment and Development Public Hearing, Ottawa, 26-27 May, 1986. Quoted in The World Commission on Environment and Development, *Our Common Future.* (New York: Oxford University Press).

McMillen, Wheeler, 1991. In Charles Robert Lightfoot, *Handbook of Business Quotations: Choice Words of Wisdom for Successful Speeches, Reports, Letters, and Papers.* (Houston, Texas: Gulf Publishing Company).

McPherson, J. H., 1967. The People, the Problems and Problem Solving Methods. (Pendell, Midland, Michigan).

Mearns, Hughes, 1958. *Creative Power: The Education of Youth in the Creative Arts.* (New York: Dover Publications, Inc.).

Melvile, Herman, 1993. In Margaret Miner and Hugh Rawson (selected and annotated), *The New International Dictionary of Quotations.* Second Edition. (New York: Penguin Books). Menninger, Karl, 1996. Quoted in Bernard Haldane, *Career Satisfaction and Success: A guide to Job and Personal Freedom.* (Indianapolis, Indiana: JIST Works, Inc.).

Meredith, Owen, 1992. "Last Words of a Sensitive Second-Rate Poet." In Merriam-Webster, Inc., *The Merriam-Webster Dictionary of Quotations.* (Springfield, Massachusetts: Merriam-Webster, Inc.).

Merton, Thomas, 1996. *No Man Is an Island.* Quoted in *Reader's Digest,* December.

Meyerhoff, M. K. and B. L. White, 1986. "Making the Grade as Parents," *Psychology Today,* (September), pp. 38-45.

Middi, S. R. and P. Costa, 1972. *Humanism in Personology.* (Chicago: Aldine and Atherton).

Mill, John Stuart, 1992. In Angela Partington (ed.), *The Oxford Dictionary of Quotations.* Fourth Edition. (Oxford: Oxford University Press).

Miller, B. C. and D. Gerard, 1983. "Family Influences on the Development of Creativity in Children: An Integrated Review," *Family Coordinator,* 1979, 28, pp. 295-312. Quoted in Teresa M. Amabile, *The Social Psychology of Creativity.* (New York: Springer-Verlag).

Miller, Henry, 1993. In Robert Andrews (ed.), *The Columbia Dictionary of Quotations.* (New York: Columbia University Press).

Miller, James B. with Paul B. Brown, 1993. *The Corporate Coach: How to Build a Team of Loyal Customers and happy Employees.* (New York: HarperBusiness).

Milton, John, 1993. *Paradise Lost.* In Margaret Miner and Hugh Rawson (selected and annotated), *The New International Dictionary of Quotations.* Second Edition. (New York: Penguin Books).

Mitin, Mark, 1972. "The Concept of Man in Marxist Thought." In S. Radhakrishnan and P. T. Raju (eds.), *The Concept of Man: A Study in Comparative Philosophy.* Third Printing. (Lincoln, Nevraska: Johnsen Publishing Company), pp. 477-535.

Montagu, Ashley, 1962. The Humanization of Man: Our Changing Conception of Human Nature. *(New York: Grove Press, Inc.).*

Montagu, Ashley, 1974. *The Direction of Human Development.* Revised Edition. (New York: Hawthorn Books, 1970), p. 300. Quoted in Jack Forem, *Transcendental Meditation: Maharishi Mahesh Yogi and the Science of Creative Intelligence.* (New York: E. P. Dutton & Co., Inc.).

Montagu, Ashley (Attributed), 1995. Quoted in Tom Thiss, *The Wizard of Is.* (Minneapolis, Minnesota: Fairview Press).

Moore, Leo B., 1962. "Creative Action — The Evaluation, Development, and Use of Ideas." In Sidney J. Parnes and Harold F. Harding, (eds.), *A Source Book for Creative Thinking.* (New York: Charles Scribner's Sons).

Morgan, Gareth (ed.), 1989. *Creative Organization Theory: A Resourcebook.* (Newbury Park, California: Sage Publications).

Morris, Desmond, 1993. In Robert Andrews (ed.), *The Columbia Dictionary of Quotations.* (New York: Columbia University Press).

Morris, Richard, 1983. *Dismantling the Universe: The Nature of Scientific Discovery.* (New York: Simon & Schuster, Inc.).

Morse, Jennifer Roback, 1997. "Who is Rational Economic Man?" *Social Philosophy & Policy,* 14(1), Winter, pp. 179-206.

Mosenthal, Peter B., 1999. "Critical Issues: Forging Conceptual Unum in the Literacy Field of Pluribus: An Agenda - Analytic Perspective," *Journal of Literacy Research,* 31(2), pp. 213-254.

Moshman, David and Leslie E. Lukin, 1989. "The Creative Construction of Rationality: A Paradox?" In John A. Glover, Royce R. Ronning, and Cecil R.

Reynolds (eds.), *Handbook of Creativity*. (New York: Plenum Press), pp. 183-197.

Moustakas, Clark, 1967. *Creativity and Conformity*. (New York: D. Van Nostrand Company).

Moustakas, Clark E., 1973. "Awareness and Freedom in Learning." In Clark E. Moustakas and Cereta Perry, *Learning to Be Free*. (Englewood Cliffs, New Jersey: Prentice-Hall, Inc.), pp. 1-20.

Moye, Helen M., 1993. "Reassuring Human Resources in Large-Scale Bureaucracies." In Robert L. Kuhn (ed.), *Generating Creativity and Innovation in Large Bureaucracies*. (Westport, Connecticut: Quorum Books).

Mumford, Lewis, 1974. *The Condition of Man*. (New York: Harcourt, Brace, 1944), p. 421. Quoted in Jack Forem, *Transcendental Meditation: Maharishi Mahesh Yogi and the Science of Creative Intelligence*. (New York: E. P. Dutton & Co., Inc.).

Muggeridge, Malcolm, 1995. Quoted in Charles Swindoll. *The Collected Works of Charles Swindol: Living on the Ragged Edge & Living Above the Level of Mediocrity*. (New York: Inspirational Press).

Muir, John, 1993. *John of the Mountains*. In Margaret Miner and Hugh Rawson (selected and annotated), *The New International Dictionary of Quotations*. Second Edition. (New York: Penguin Books).

Municipality of Reggio Emilia, 1996. *The Hundred Languages of Children*. (Reggio Emilia, Italy: Reggio Children).

Murray, Pauli, 1975. "The Liberation of Black Women." In Mary Lou Thompson (ed.), *Voices of the New Feminism*. (Boston, Massachusetts: Beacon Press), pp. 87-102.

Mussen, Paul Henry, et al., 1984. John J. Conger, Jerome Kagan, and Aletha Carol Husson, *Child Development and Personality*. (New York: Harper and Row, Publishers).

Naisbitt, John, 1982. *Megatrends: Ten New Directions Transforming Our Lives*. (New York: Warner Books).

Naisbitt, John, 1991. In Charles Robert Lightfoot, *Handbook of Business Quotations: Choice Words of Wisdom for Successful Speeches, Reports, Letters, and Papers*. (Houston, Texas: Gulf Publishing Company).

Naisbitt, John and Patricia Aburdene, 1986. *Re-inventing the Corporation: Transforming Your Job and Your Company for the New Information Society*. (New York: Warner Books, Inc.).

Naisbitt, John and Patricia Aburdene, 1990. *The New Directions for the 1990's: Megatrends 2000*. (New York: William Morrow and Company, Inc., 1990).

Nanus, Burt, 1992. *Visionary Leadership*. (San Francisco: Jossey-Brass Publishers).

Naumburg, Margaret, 1928. Quoted in Lawrence A. Cremin, *The Transformation of the School: Progressivism in American Education 1876-1957*. (New York: Vintage Books, 1964).

Nietzsche, Friedrich, 1992. *The Gay Science*, S. 261. Translated by Walter Kaufmann. In A. J. Ayer and Jane O'Grady (eds.), *A Dictionary of Philosophical Quotations*. (Oxford, UK: Blackwell Publishers).

Nietzsche, Friedrich, 1993. In Robert Andrews (ed.), *The Columbia Dictionary of Quotations*. (New York: Columbia University Press).

Nouwen, Henri, et al., 1999. *Simpler Living: Compassionate Life.* (Denver, Colorado: Living the Good News).

Ockham, William of, 1992. In A. J. Ayer and Jane O'Grady (eds.), *A Dictionary of Philosophical Quotations.* (Oxford: Blackswell Publishers).

O'Connor, Elizabeth, 1971. *Eighth Day of Creation: Discovering Your Gifts.* (Washington, DC: The Servant Leadership School).

Orwell, George, 1995. Quoted in *Reader's Digest,* April.

Osborn, Alex F., 1963. *Applied Imagination: Principles and Procedures of Creative Problem-Solving.* Third Edition. (New York: Charles Scribner's Sons).

Osborne, David and Ted Gaebler, 1993. *Reinventing Government: How the Entrepreneurial Spirit is Transforming the Public Sector.* (New York: Penguin Books).

Palmer, Parker J., 1997. Quoted in Diana Chapman Walsh, "Cultivating Inner Resources for Leadership." In Frances Hesselbein, Marshall Goldsmith, and Richard Beckhard (eds.), *The Organization of the Future.* (San Francisco: Jossey-Bass Publishers), pp. 295-302.

Palmer, Russell E. 1990. Quoted in John Naisbitt and Patricia Aburdene, *The New Directions for the 1990's: Megatrends 2000.* (New York: William Morrow and Company, Inc.).

Papalia, Diane and Sally Wendkos Olds, 1978. *Human Development.* (New York: McGraw-Hill Book Company).

Parker, Jeffrey, 1977. "Adding Human Potential to Urban Economic Development." In Subcommittee on the City of the Committee on Banking, Finance and Urban Affairs, US House of Representatives, 95th Congress, First Session, *How Cities Can Grow Old Gracefully.* (Washington, D.C: US Government Printing Office), pp. 171-180.

Parker, R. C., 1982. *The Management of Innovation.* (New York: John Wiley & Sons, Ltd.).

Participants of the Salzburg Conference on Learning, 1979. "Summary of Workshop III: Learning and Global Issues," (June, 1979). In The Club of Rome, *No Limits to Learning: Bridging the Human Gap.* Report by James Botkin, Mahdi Elmandjra, and Mircea Malitza. (Oxford, England: Pergamon Press).

Parnes, Sidney J., 1988. *Visionizing: State-of-the-Art Processes for Encouraging Innovative Excellence.* (Buffalo, New York: Creative Education Foundation Press).

Parnes, Sidney J. (ed.), 1992. *Source Book for Creative Problem Solving.* (Buffalo, New York: Creative Education Foundation Press).

Parnes, Sidney J., 1997. *Optimize: The Magic of Your Mind.* (Buffalo, New York: Bearly Limited).

Parnes, Sidney J. and Harold F. Harding (eds.), 1962. *A Source Book for Creative Thinking.* (New York: Charles Scribner's Sons).

Pascarella, Perry, 1990. *The New Achievers.* (New York: Free Press, 1984). Quoted In Willis Harman and John Hormann, *Creative Work: The Constructive Role of Business in a Transforming Society.* (Indianapolis, Indiana: Knowledge Systems, Inc.).

Pasteur, Louis 1975. Quoted in Arthur Koestler, *The Act of Creation.* Picador Edition. (London: Pan Books Ltd).

Patridge, Robert A., 1997. "Epilogue." In Sidney J. Parnes, *Optimize: The magic of Your Mind.* (Buffalo, New York: Bearly Limited, 1997), pp. 155-161.

Patton (General), George S., 1993. Quoted in David Osborne and Ted Gaebler, *Reinventing Government: How the Entrepreneurial Spirit is Transforming the Public Sector.* (New York: Penguin Books).

Pearson, Carol S., 1991. *Awakening the Heroes Within: Twelve Archetypes to Help Us Find Ourselves and Transform Our World.* (San Francisco: HarperCollins).

Peck, M. Scott, 1987. *The Different Drum: Community Making and Peace.* (New York: Simon & Schuster, Inc.).

Peck, M. Scott, 1997. *The Road Less Traveled and Beyond: Spiritual Growth in an Age of Anxiety.* (New York: Simon & Schuster).

Perrow, Charles, 1989. "The Short and Glorious History of Organization Theory." In Gareth Morgan (ed.), *Creative Organization Theory: A Resourcebook.* (Newbury Park, California: Sage Publications, 1989), pp. 41- 48.

Perry, Cereta, 1973. "Extending the Invitation to Others." In Clark E. Moustakas and Cereta Perry, *Learning to Be Free.* (Englewood Cliffs, New Jersey: Prentice-Hall, Inc.), pp. 146-166.

Peterson, Peter G., 1965. "Some Approaches to Innovation in Industry." In Gary A. Steiner (ed.), *The Creative Organization.* (Chicago: University of Chicago Press).

Peterson, Severin, 1971. *A Catalog of the Ways People Grow.* (New York: Ballantine Books, Inc.).

Petrocorp Department Philosophy, 1983. Quoted in Rosabeth Moss Kanter, *The Change Masters.* (New York: Simon and Schuster, Inc.).

Phillips, Wendell, 1992. Speech, 1851. In Merriam-Webster, Inc., *The Merriam-Webster Dictionary of Quotations.* (Springfield, Massachusetts: Merriam-Webster, Inc.).

Piaget, Jean, 1998. Quoted in Berenice Bleedorn, *The Creative Force in Education, Business, and Beyond: An Urgent Message.* (Lakeville, Minnesota: Galde Press, Inc.).

Picard, Eileen, 1979. *The Development of Creativity.* (Berkshire, England: NFER Publishing Company Ltd.).

Pinchot III, Gifford, 1985. *Intrapreneuring: Why You Don't Have to Leave the Corporation to Become an Entrepreneur.* (New York: Harper & Row, Publishers).

Pinchot III, Gifford and Elizabeth Pinchot, 1993. *The End of Bureaucracy and the Rise of the Intelligent Organization.* (San Francisco, California: Berrett-Koehler Publishers).

Plato, 1974. *The Republic,* VII, § 536E, 537A. Quoted in Robert F. Davidson, *Philosophies Men Live By.* Second Edition. (New York: Holt, Rinehart and Winston, Inc.).

Plato, 1974. Quoted in Robert M. Hutchins, *The Conflict in Education in a Democratic Society.* (New York: Harper, 1953). Quoted in Jack Forem, *Transcendental Meditation: Maharishi Mahesh Yogi and the Science of Creative Intelligence.* (New York: E. P. Dutton & Co., Inc.).

Pliny the Elder, 1993. In Robert Andrews (ed.), *The Columbia Dictionary of Quotations.* (New York: Columbia University Press).

Popper, Karl Raimund, 1963. *Conjectures and Refutations: The Growth of Scientific Knowledge.* (London: Routledge and Kegan Paul).

Popper, Karl Raimund, 1968. *The Logic of Scientific Discovery.* (London: Hutchinson & Co Publishers Ltd.).

Popper, Karl Raimund, 1985. *Postscript to the Logic of Scientific Discovery, Vol. 1: Realism and the Aim of Science.* (London: Routledge).

Popper, Karl R. and John Eccles, 1993. *The Self and Its Brain.* (London: Routledge).

Popper, Karl Raimund, 1997. *Die Zukunft ist offen. Das Altenberger Gespräch. Mit den Texten des Wiener Popper-Symposiums, Piper, Munich, 1985,* P. 52. Quoted In Roberta Corvi, *An Introduction to the Thought of Karl Popper.* (London: Routledge).

Potter, Dennis, 1993. In Margaret Miner and Hugh Rawson (eds.), *The New International Dictionary of Quotations,* Second Edition. (New York: Penguin Books).

Pound, Ezra, 1992. *The ABC of Reading.* Chapter 8. (1934). In Angela Partington (ed.), *The Oxford Dictionary of Quotations.* Fourth Edition. (Oxford: Oxford University Press).

Prigogine, Ilya, 1996. *The End of Certainty: Time, Chaos, and the New Laws of Nature.* (New York: The Free Press).

Pritzkau, Philo T., 1970. *On Education for the Authentic.* (Scranton, Pennsylvania: International Textbook Company).

Proust, Marcel, 1948. *The Maxims of Marcel Proust.* (Translated by Justin O'Brien). (New York: Columbia University Press).

Putnam, R. D., 1993. "The Prosperous Community: Social Capital and Economic Growth." *The American Prospect,* Spring, pp. 35-42.

Rabbin, Robert, 1992. Quoted in John W. Thompson, "Corporate Leadership in the 21st Century." In John Renesch (ed.), *New Traditions in Business: Spirit and Leadership in the 21st Century.* (San Francisco: Berret-Koehler Publishers), pp. 209-222.

Rainbolt, Ricky, 2000. "The Magic of a work Force that is Ready, Willing and Energized," *Connections: The Inflight Magazine of ASA,* September/October, pp. 11, 33.

Rawlinson, J. G., 1978. *Creative Thinking and Brainstorming.* (London: BIM Foundation).

Ray, Michael, and Rochelle Myers, 1886. *Creativity in Business.* (New York: Doubleday and Company, Inc.).

(Reactions of an East Orange, New Jersey, high school class to the evaluative system, 1973). Reproduced in Gerald Weinstein and Mario D. Fantini (eds.), *Toward Humanistic Education.* (New York: Harper & Row, 1969), p. 154. Quoted in Clark Moustakas, *Learning to be Free.* (Englewood Cliffs, New Jersey: Prentice Hall, Inc.).

Redfield, James and Carol Adrienne, 1995. *The Celestine Prophecy: An Experiential Guide.* (New York: Warner Books).

Reichenbach, Hans, 1992. In A. J. Ayer and Jane O'Grady (eds.), *A Dictionary of Philosophical Quotations.* (Oxford, Blackwell Publishers).

Reynolds, Sir Joshua, 1975. Quoted in P. R. Whitfield, *Creativity in Industry.* (Harmondsworth, Middlesex, England: Penguin Books).

Rickards, Tudor, 1988. *Creativity at Work.* (Aldershot, England: Gower Publishing Company, Ltd.).

Rickover (Admiral), 1962. Quoted in E. Paul Torrance, "Creative Thinking Through School Experience." In Sidney J. Parnes and Harold F. Harding (eds.), *A Source Book for Creative Thinking.* (New York: Charles Scribner's Sons).

Ritzer, George, 1993. *The MacDonalization of Society: An Investigation into the Changing Character of Contemporary Social Life.* Revised Edition. (Newbury Park, California: Pine Forge Press).

Robertson, Ian, 1987. *Sociology.* Third Edition. (New York: Worth Publishing, Inc.).

Robertson, James, 1976. *Power, Money and Sex: Towards a New Social Balance.* (London: Marion Boyars).

Robertson, James, 1974. *Profit or People? The New Social Role of Money.* (London: Calder and Boyars).

Robinson, Allan G. and Sam Stern, 1997. *Corporate Creativity: How Innovation and Improvement Actually Happen.* (San Francisco: Berrett-Koehler Publishers, Inc.).

Rockefeller, Sr., John D., 1991. In Charles Robert Lightfoot, *Handbook of Business Quotations: Choice Words of Wisdom for Successful Speeches, Reports, Letters, and Papers.* (Houston, Texas: Gulf Publishing Company).

Rodin, Judith and Ellen Langer, 1980. "Aging Labels: The Decline of Control and the fall of Self-Esteem," *Journal of Social Issues.* 36(2), pp. 12 - 29.

Roe, Anne, 1965. Quoted in Milton Rokeach, "In Pursuit of the Creative Process." In Gary A. Steiner (ed.), *The Creative Organization.* (Chicago: University of Chicago Press).

Rogers, Carl R., 1961. *On Becoming a Person: A Therapist's View of Psychotherapy.* (Boston, Massachusetts: Houghton Mifflin Company).

Rogers, Carl R., 1962. "Toward a Theory of Creativity." In Sidney J. Parnes and Harold F. Harding, (eds.), *A Source Book for Creative Thinking.* (New York: Charles Scribner's Sons).

Rogers, Raymond, 1967. *Coming Into Existence: The Struggle to Become an Individual.* (Cleveland, Ohio: World Publishing Co.).

Roosevelt, Theodore, 1993. Speech, 24 October, 1910, Binghamton, New York. In Robert Andrews (ed.), *The Columbia Dictionary of Quotations.* (New York: Columbia University Press).

Root-Bernstein, Robert Scott, 1989. *Discovering: Inventing and Solving Problems at the Frontiers of Scientific Knowledge.* (Cambridge, Massachusetts: Harvard University Press).

Rosen, Robert H., 1997. "Learning to Lead." In Frances Hesselbein, Marshall Goldsmith, and Richard Beckhard (eds.), *The Organization of the Future.* (San Francisco: Jossey-Bass Publishers), pp. 303-312.

Roskos-Ewoldsen, Berverly, M. J. Intons-Peterson, and R. E. Anderson, 1993. "Imagery, Creativity, Discovery: Conclusions and Implementation." In Roskos-Ewoldsen, Berverly, Margaret J. Intons-Peterson, and Rita E. Anderson (eds.), *Imagery, Creativity, Discovery: A Cognitive Perspective.* (North Holland: Elsecier Science Publishers), pp. 313-327.

Ross, Martin B., 1981. "Creativity and Creative Problem Solving." In John E. Jones and J. W. Pfeiffer (eds.), *The 1981 Annual Handbook for Group Facilitators.* (San Diego, California: University Associates, Inc.).

Rostand, Jean, 1993. In Robert Andrews (ed.), *The Columbia Dictionary of Quotations.* (New York: Columbia University Press).

Rousseau, Jean-Jacques, 1716. *The Social Contract, Book I, Chapter I.*

Rowan, Helen, 1969. "The Creative People: How to Spot Them," *Think,* 28, November-December 1962. In George A. Steiner, *Top Management Planning.* (New York: Macmillan Publishing Company, Inc.).

Ruskin, John, 1993. *Stones of Venice.* In Margaret Miner and Hugh Rawson (selected and annotated), *The New International Dictionary of Quotations.* Second Edition. (New York: Penguin Books).

Russell, Bertrand 1992. In Merriam-Webster, Inc. *The Merriam-Webster Dictionary of Quotations.* (Springfield, Massachusetts: Merriam-Webster, Inc).

Ryan, William, 1971. *Blaming the Victim.* (New York: Vintage Books).

Ryerson, Alice Judson and Wendy Coppedge Sanford, 1978. "Being Parents of Grownups." In The Boston Women's Health Book Collective, *Ourselves and Our Children: A Book by and for Parents.* (New York: Random House, Inc.).

Salk, Jonas, 1989. Quoted in Robert Scott Root-Bernstein, *Discovering: Inventing and Solving Problems at the Frontiers of Scientific Knowledge.* (Cambridge, Massachusetts: Harvard University Press).

Salk, Jonas, 1996. Quoted in Jack Foster, *How to Get Ideas.* (San Francisco:Berret-Koehler Publishers).

Sanford, Carol, 1992. "A Self-Organizing Leadership View of Paradigms." In John Renesch (ed.), *New Traditions in Business: Spirit and Leadership in the 21st Century.* (San Francisco: Berret-Koehler Publishers), pp. 193-206.

Santayana, George, 1992. *Winds of Doctrine.* In Merriam-Webster, Inc., *The Merriam-Webster Dictionary of Quotations.* (Springfield, Massachusetts: Merriam-Webster, Inc.).

Sevareid's Law, 1986. Quoted in George W. Downs and Patrick D. Larkey, *The Search for Government Efficiency: From Hubris to Helplessness.* (New York: Random House).

Schaef, Anne Wilson and Diane Fassel, 1989. "Hooked on Work." In Gareth Morgan (ed.), *Creative Organization Theory: A Resourcebook.* (Newbury Park, California: Sage Publications, 1989), pp. 241-244.

Schifter, Deborah, 1996. "A Constructivist Perspective on Teaching and Learning Mathematics." In Catherine Twomey Fosnot (ed.), *Constructivism: Theory, Perspectives, and Practice.* (Columbia University, New York: Teachers University Press). pp. 73-91.

Schuller, Robert H., 1975. *Move Ahead with Possibility Thinking.* (Old Tappan, New Jersey: Pillar Books).

Schulman, M., 1991. *The Passionate Mind: Bringing up an Intelligent and Creative Child.* (New York: Free Press).

Schumacher, E. F., 1973. *Small is Beautiful: A Study of Economics as if People Mattered.* (London: Blond and Brigs, Ltd.).

Schumacher, E. F., 1992. Quoted in David Osborne and Ted Gaebler, *Reinventing Government: How the Entrepreneurial Spirit is Transforming the Public Sector.* (New York: Penguin Books USA Inc.).

Schwebel, M., C. A. Maher, and N. S. Fagley (eds.), 1990. *Promoting Cognitive Growth Over the Life Span.* (Hillsdale, New Jersey: Erlbaum).

Scott, Sir Walter, 1997. Quoted in *Reader's Digest,* September.

Seidel, George J., 1978. Quoted in J. G. Rawlinson *Creative Thinking and Brainstorming.* (London: BIM Foundation).

Seneca, 1969. In Bergen Evans, *Dictionary of Quotations.* (New Jersey: Wings Books).

Senge, Peter M., 1990. *The Fifth Discipline: The Art and Practice of the Learning Organization.* (New York: Doubleday Currency).

Senge, Peter M., 1992. "The Leader's New Work: Building Learning Organizations." In John Renesch (ed.), *New Traditions in Business: Spirit and Leadership in the 21st Century.* (San Francisco: Berret-Koehler Publishers), pp. 81-93.

Shah, Idries, 1971. *Thinkers of the East: Teachings of the Dervishes.* (Baltimore, Maryland: Penguin Books, Inc.).

Shakespeare, William, 1993. *King Lear,* I, I. In Margaret Miner and Hugh Rawson (selected and annotated), *The New International Dictionary of Quotations.* Second Edition. (New York: Penguin Books).

Shahn, Ben, 1971. *The Shape of Content.* (Cambridge, Massachesettes: Harvard University Press, 1957). Quoted in Elizabeth O'Connor, *Eighth Day of Creation: Discovering Your Gifts.* (Washington, DC: The Servant Leadership School).

Shapero, Albert, 1985. *Managing Professional People: Understanding Creative Performance.* (New York: The Free Press).

Shapiro, E. J., 1966. "The Identification of Creative Research Scientists," *Psychologia Africana,* II, 99-132.

Shaull, Richard, 1972. "Foreword." In Paulo Freire, *Pedagogy of the Oppressed.* (London: Sheed and Ward Ltd.).

Shaw, George Bernard, 1993. In Robert Andrews (ed.), *The Columbia Dictionary of Quotations.* (New York: Columbia University Press).

Shelley, Percy Bysshe, 1997. In Rosalie Maggio, *Quotations on Education.* (Paramus, New Jersey: Prentice Hall).

Siks, Geraldine Brain, 1958. "Preface to the Second Edition." In Hughes Mearns, *Creative Power: The Education of Youth in the Creative Arts.* (New York: Dover Publications, Inc.).

Simeon, 1991. In Charles Robert Lightfoot, *Handbook of Business Quotations: Choice Words of Wisdom for Successful Speeches, Reports, Letters, and Papers.* (Houston, Texas: Gulf Publishing Company).

Simon, Herbert A., 1986. "What We Know About the Creative Process." In Robert L. Kuhn (ed.), *Frontiers in Creative and Innovative Management.* (Cambridge, Massachusetts: Ballinger Publishing Company).

Simple Living Collective, American Friends Service Committee (ed.), 1977. *Taking Charge: Personal and Political Change Through Simple Living.* (New York: Bantam Books).

Smith, Cyril Stanley, 1989. Quoted in Robert Scott Root-Bernstein, *Discovering: Inventing and Solving Problems at the Frontiers of Scientific Knowledge.* (Cambridge, Massachusetts: Harvard University Press).

Smith, Logan Pearsall, 1969. *Afterthoughts.* In Bergen Evans, *Dictionary of Quotations.* (New Jersey: Wing Books).

Smith, Logan Pearsall, 1986. Quoted in Michael L. Ray and Rochelle Myers, *Creativity in Business.* (New York: Doubleday).

Snyder, C. R. and Howard L. Fromkin, 1980. *Uniqueness: The Pursuit of Difference.* (New York: Plenum Press).

Soedjatmoko, Ambassador, 1989. Quoted in Michael P. Todaro, *Economic Development in the Third World.* Fourth Edititon. (New York: Longman, Inc.).

Solzhenitsyn, Aleksandr I., 1978. *A World Split Apart.* Commencement Address Delivered at Harvard University, June 8. (New York: Harper & Row, Publishers).

Sontag, Susan, 1993. In Robert Andrews (ed.), *The Columbia Dictionary of Quotations.* (New York: Columbia University Press).

Seymour, Daniel T., 1993. *Causing Quality in Higher Education.* (Phoenix, Arizona: The Oryx Press).

Spady, Richard J. and Cecil H. Bell, Jr., 1996. *The Search for Enlightened Leadership.* Volume One: Applying New Administrative Theory. (Olympia, Washington: Panpress Publishers).

Spady, Richard J. and Cecil H. Bell, Jr., 1999. *The Search for Enlightened Leadership.* Volume Two: Many-to-Many Communication. A Breakthrough in Social Science. (Olympia, Washington: Panpress Publishers).

Spretnak, Charlene, 1988. "Postmodern Directions." In David Ray Griffin (ed.), *Spirituality and Society: Postmodern Visions.* (New York: State University of New York Press, 1988), pp. 33 - 40.

Stata, Ray, 1990. Quoted in Peter M. Senge, *The Fifth Discipline: The Art and Practice of the Learning Organization.* (New York: Doubleday/ Currency).

Staw, Barry M., 1995. "Why No One Really Wants Creativity." In Cameron M. Ford and Dennis A. Gioia (eds.), *Creative Action in Organizations: Ivory Tower Visions and Real World Voices.* (Thousand Oaks, California: Sage Publications, Inc).

Steele, Jeffrey, 1987. *The Representation of the Self in the American Renaissance.* (Chapel Hill, North Carolina: The university of North Carolina Press).

Stein, Morris I., 1992. "Creativity Programs in Sociohistorical Context." In Sidney J. Parnes (ed.), *Source Book for Creative Problem Solving.* (Buffalo, New York: Creative Education Foundation Press), pp. 85-88.

Steinem, Gloria, 1992. *Revolution from Within: A Book of Self-Esteem.* (Boston, Massachusetts: Little Brown and Company).

Steiner, Gary A., 1965a. "Summary." In Gary A. Steiner (ed.), *The Creative Organization.* (Chicago: University of Chicago Press), pp. 104-105.

Steiner, Gary A., 1965b. "Introduction." In Gary A. Steiner (ed.), *The Creative Organization.* (Chicago: University of Chicago Press), pp. 1-24.

Stern, Philip Van Doren (ed.), 1960. *The Annotated Walden,* by Henry D. Thoreau. (New York: Bramhall House).

Sternberg, Robert J. and Todd I. Lubart, 1995. *Defying the Crowd: Cultivating Creativity in a Culture of Conformity.* (New York: The Free Press).

Stevens, Wallace, 1993. In Margaret Miner and Hugh Rawson (selected and annotated), *The New International Dictionary of Quotations.* Second Edition. (New York: Penguin Books).

Stevens, Wallace, 1990. In Meic Stephens (compiled), *A Dictionary of Literary Quotations.* (London: Routledge).

Stone, Joseph and Joseph Church, 1982. Quoted in Leo F. Buscaglia, *Personhood: The Art of Being Fully Human.* (New York: Ballantine Books).

Strawson, P. F., 1992. In A. J. Ayer and Jane O'Grady (eds.), *A Dictionary of Philosophical Quotations.* (Oxford, Blackwell Publishers).

Sullivan, Edmund, 1985. Quoted in Stanley Aronowitz and Henry A. Giroux, *Education Under Siege: The Conservative, Liberal and Radical Debate Over Schooling.* (South Hadley, Massachusetts: Bergin & Garvey Publishers, Inc.).

Suzuki, D. T., 1974. Quoted in Erich Fromm, *Marx's Concept of Man.* (New York: Ungar, 1961). Quoted in Robert Davidson, *Philosophies Men Live By.* Second Edition. (New York: Holt, Rinehart and Winston, Inc.).

Suzuki, D. T., 1974. "Human Values in Zen." Quoted in Abraham Maslow (ed.), *New Knowledge in Human Values.* (New York: Harper, 1959), pp. 100-105. Quoted in Jack Forem, *Transcendental Meditation: Maharishi Mahesh Yogi and the Science of Creative Intelligence.* (New York: E. P. Dutton & Co., Inc.).

Swetchine, Anne-Sophie, 1997. In Rosalie Maggio, *Quotations on Education.* (Paramus, New Jersey: Prentice Hall).

Swindoll, Charles, 1995. *Living Above the Level of Mediocrity.* In Charles Swindoll, *The Collected Works of Charles Swindoll.* (New York: Inspirational Press).

Syrus, Publilius, 1991. In Charles Robert Lightfoot, *Handbook of Business Quotations: Choice Words of Business Wisdom for Successful Speeches, Reports, Letters, and Papers. (Houston,* Texas: Gulf Publishing Company).

Szekely, Edmond Boreaux, 1987. Quoted in Marsha Sinetar, *Do What You Love, The Money Will Follow: Discovering Your Right Livelihood.* (New York: Dell Publishing).

Tannenbaum, Robert and H. Schmidt, 1958. "How to Choose a Leadership Pattern," *Harvard Business Review,* March-April, pp. 95-101.

Tart, Charles T., 1976. "Discrete Stages of Consciousness." In Philip Lee *et al., Symposium on Consciousness.* Presented at the annual meeting of the American Association for the Advancement of Science, February, 1974. (New York: The Viking Press), pp. 91-175.

Taylor, Terry Lynn and Mary Beth Crain, 1994. *Angel Wisdom.* (New York: HarperCollins Publishers).

Terkel, Studs, 1974. *Working: People Talk about What They do All Day and How They Feel about What They Do.* (New York: Pantheon Books).

Theobald, Robert, 1962. *The Challenge of Abundance.* (New York: The New American Library of World Literature, Inc.).

Theobald, Robert, 1981. *Beyond Despair: A Policy Guide to the Communications Era.* Revised Edition. (Cabin John, Maryland: Seven Locks Press, Inc.).

Thiss, Tom, 1995. *The Wizard of Is.* (Minneapolis, Minnesota: Fairview Press).

Thomas, David A., 1991. In Charles Robert Lightfoot, *Handbook of Business Quotations: Choice Words of Wisdom for Successful Speeches, Reports, Letters, and Papers.* (Houston, Texas: Gulf Publishing Company).

Thomas, Jr., R. Roosevelt, 1997. "Diversity and Organizations of the Future." In Frances Hesselbein, Marshall Goldsmith, and Richard Beckhard (eds.), *The Organization of the Future.* (San Francisco: Jossey-Bass Publishers), pp. 329-339.

Thomas, Jr., R. Roosevelt, 1997. "Diversity and Organizations of the Future." In Frances Hesselbein, Marshall Goldsmith, and Richard Beckhard (eds.), *The Organization of the Future.* (San Francisco: Jossey-Bass Publishers), pp. 329-339.

Thompson, Charles "Chic," 1992. *What a Great Idea: Key Steps Creative People Take.* (New York: Harper Perennial).

Thompson, John W., 1992. "Corporate Leadership in the 21st Century." In John Renesch (ed.), *New Traditions in Business: Spirit and Leadership in the 21st Century.* (San Francisco: Berret-Koehler Publishers), pp. 209-222.

Thoreau, Henry, 1955. "Life Without Principles." In Carl Bode (ed.), *The Portable Thoreau.* (New York: The Viking Press, 1947), pp. 631-655. Quoted in Erich Fromm, *The Sane Society.* (New York: Fawcett World Library).

Thoreau, Henry David, 1957. *The Annotated Walden: Walden; or, Life in the Woods.* Edited by Philip van Doren Stern. (New York: Bramhall House).

Thoreau, Henry David, 1987. Quoted in Jeffrey Steele, *The Representation of the Self in the American Renaissance.* (Chapel Hill, North Carolina: The university of North Carolina Press).

Tillich, Paul, 1952. *The Courage to Be.* (New Haven, Connecticut: Yale University Press).

Todaro, Michael P., 1989. *Economic Development in the Third World.* Fourth Edititon. (New York: Longman, Inc.).

Toffler, Alvin, 1983. *Previews and Premises.* (New York: William Morrow and Company, Inc.).

Toffler, Alvin, 1980. *The Third Wave.* (New York: William Morrow and Company, Inc.).

Toffler, Alvin, 1985. Quoted in John Naisbitt and Patricia Aburdene, *Re-inventing the Corporation: Transforming Your Job and Your Company for the New Information Society.* (New York: Warner Books, Inc.).

Toffler, Alvin, 1997. In Rosalie Maggio, *Quotations on Education.* (Paramus, New Jersey: Prentice Hall).

Tolstoy, L., 1955. Quoted in Erich Fromm, *The Sane Society.* (New York: Fawcett World Library).

Torrance, E. Paul, 1962. "Creative Thinking Through School Experiences." In Sidney J. Parnes and Harold F. Harding, (eds.), *A Source Book for Creative Thinking.* (New York: Charles Scribner's Sons).

Torrance, E. Paul, 1979. *The Search for Satori and Creativity.* (Buffalo, NewYork: Creative Education Foundation).

Touraine, Alan, 1971. *The Post-Industrial Society.* (New York: Random House).

Tournier, Paul, 1957. *The Meaning of Persons.* (New York: Harper and Row).

Toynbee, A. J., 1958. Quoted in *The Reader's Digest,* October. In Robert Andrews (ed.), *The Columbia Dictionary of Quotations.* (New York: Columbia University Press).

Trevelyan, G. M., 1990. In Meic Stephens (compiled), *A Dictionary of Literary Quotations.* (London: Routledge).

Trudeau, Pierre, 1978. Quoted in Ervin Laszlo, et al., *Goals for Mankind: A Report to the Club Of Rome on the New Horizons of Global Community.* (New York: Signet, 1978).

397

Tumin, Melvin, 1992. "Obstacles to Creativity." In Sidney J. Parnes (ed.), *Source Book for Creative Problem Solving*. (Buffalo, New York: Creative Education Foundation Press), pp. 105-113.

Twain, Mark, 1997. In Rosalie Maggio, *Quotations on Education*. (Paramus, New Jersey: Prentice Hall).

Twiss, Brian C., 1980. *Managing Technological Innovation*. Second Edition. (London: Longman Group Limited, 1980).

Unamuno, 1993. In Robert Andrews (ed.), *The Columbia Dictionary of Quotations*. (New York: Columbia University Press).

United Nations Development Program (UNDP), 1994. *Human Development Report 1994*. (New York: Oxford University Press).

United Nations Educational, Scientific, and Cultural Organization (UNESCO), 1978. *Medium Term Plan (1977-1982)*. Quoted in Ervin Laszlo, et al., *Goals for Mankind: A Report to the Club Of Rome on the New Horizons of Global Community*. (New York: Signet).

Updike, John, 1998. Quoted in *Readers Digest*, July.

van der Rohe, Ludwig Mies, 1993. "Motto." In Margaret Miner and Hugh Rawson (selected and annotated), *The New International Dictionary of Quotations*. Second Edition. (New York: Penguin Books).

Vaizey, John, 1967. *Education in the Modern World*. (New York: McGraw-Hill Book Company).

VanGundy, Arthur B., 1988. *Techniques of Structured Problem Solving*. Second Edition. (New York: Van Nostrand Reinhold Company).

Varse, Edgard, 1985. Quoted by Martha Graham, Interview, *The New York Times*, March 31.

Varse, Edgard, 1993. Quoted by Martha Graham, Interview, *The New York Times*, March 31, 1985. In Margaret Miner and Hugh Rawson (selected and annotated), *The New International Dictionary of Quotations*. Second Edition. (New York: Penguin Books).

Vasconcellos, John, 1974. "Foreword." In Robert E. Alberti and Michael L. Emmons, *Your Perfect Right: A Guide to Assertive Behavior*. (San Luis Obispo, California: IMPACT).

Vaughan, Alan, 1982. *The Edge of Tomorrow: How to Foresee & Fulfill Your Future*. (New York: Coward, McCann & Geoghegan).

Vidal, Gore, 1992. In Merriam-Webster, Inc., *The Merriam-Webster Dictionary of Quotations*. (Springfield, Massachusetts: Merriam-Webster, Inc.).

Viscott, David, 1984. *The Viscott Method*. (New York: Pocket Books).

Viscott, David, 1987. *Language of Feelings*. (New York: Pocket Books, 1976), p. 127. Quoted in Marsha Sinetar, *Do What You Love, the Money Will Follow: Discovering Your Right Livelihood*. (New York: Dell Publishing).

Viteles, M. S., 1955. *Motivation and Morale in Industry*. (New York: W. W. Norton and Company, 1947), pp. 49, 50. Quoted in Erich Fromm, *The Sane Society*. (New York: Fawcett World Library).

Voltaire, 1992. In Merriam-Webster, Inc. *The Merriam-Webster Dictionary of Quotations*. (Springfield, Massachusetts: Merriam-Webster, Inc.).

von Goethe, Johann Wolfgang, 1991. In Charles Robert Lightfoot, *Handbook of Business Quotations: Choice Words of Wisdom for Successful Speeches, Reports, Letters, and Papers*. (Houston, Texas: Gulf Publishing Company).

von Oech, Roger, 1983. *A Whack on the Side of the Head: How You Can be More Creative*. (New York: Warner Books).

Von Schiller, Friedrich 1966. *Naïve and Sentimental Poetry and On the Sublime*. Trans. Julius A. Elias. (New York: Friedrich Ungar: 1966), pp. 34 - 35, 58. Quoted in Jeffrey Steele, *The Representation of the Self in the American Renaissance*. (Chapel Hill, North Carolina: The university of North Carolina Press, 1987).

Walker, Alice, 1992. Quoted in Gloria Steinem, *Revolution from Within*.(Boston: Little, Brown and Company).

Walsh, Diana Chapman, 1997. "Cultivating Inner Resources for Leadership." In Frances Hesselbein, Marshall Goldsmith, and Richard Beckhard (eds.), *The Organization of the Future*. (San Francisco: Jossey-Bass Publishers), pp. 295-302.

Washington, Booker T., 1994. Quoted in Dennis Kimbro, *Daily Motivations for African-American Success*. First Mass Market Edition. (New York: Fawcett Crest), Jan. 20.

Watson, Nora, 1974. Comments. In Studs Terkel, *Working: People Talk About What They Do All Day and How They Feel About What They Do*. (New York: Pantheon Books), pp. 521-524.

Watts, Glenn and Lou Gerber, 1982. "Organized Labor: 'Busy Being Born,'" In US Association for the Club of Rome, *Making It Happen: A Positive Guide to the Future*. (Washington, DC: US Association for the Club of Rome), pp. 158-165.

Weber, Max, 1958. *The Protestant Ethic and the Spirit of Capitalism*. (New York: Scribner's).

Weber, Max, 1987. Quoted in Ian Robertson, *Sociology*. Third Edition. (New York: Worth Publishing, Inc., 1987).

Webber, Ross, 1979. *Management: Basic Elements of Managing Organizations*. (Homewood, Illinois: Richard D. Irwin).

Weinberg, Carl, 1971. *Education and Social Problems*. (New York: The Free Press).

Weinstein, Gerarld and Mario D. Fantini (eds.), 1970. *Toward Humanistic Education*. (New York: Praeger, 1970), p. 154. In Clark E. Moustakas, "Awareness and Freedom in Learning." In Clark E. Moustakas and Cereta Perry, *Learning to Be Free*. (Englewood Cliffs, New Jersey: Prentice-Hall, Inc.), p. 1-20.

Weisberg, Robert W., 1986. *Creativity: Genius and Other Myths*. (New York: W. H. Freeman and Company).

Weisberg, Robert W., 1993. *Creativity: Beyond the Myth of Genius*. (New York: W. H. Freeman and Company).

Welch, Jr., John F., 1985. Quoted in Donald K. Clifford, Jr. and Richard E. Cavanagh, *The Winning Performance: How America's High-Growth Midsize Companies Succeed*. (Toronto: Bantam Books).

Weldon, Fay, 1997. In Rosalie Maggio, *Quotations on Education*. (Paramus, New Jersey: Prentice Hall).

White, L. A., (Attributed), 1976. In Silvano Arieti, *Creativity: The Magic Synthesis*. (New York: Basic Books, Inc.).

Whitehead, Alfred North, 1961. *Science and the Modern World.* Seventh Impression. (London: Cambridge University Press, 1933). Quoted in Tom Burns & G. M. Stalker, *The Management of Innovation.* (London: Tavistock Publications).

Whitehead, Alfred North, 1978. *Process and Reality.* Edited by D. Griffin and D. Sherborne. (New York: Macmillan).

Whitehead, Alfred North, 1992. In Merriam-Webster, Inc. *The Merriam-Webster Dictionary of Quotations.* (Springfield, Massachusetts: Merriam-Webster, Inc.).

Whitman, Walt, 1987. Quoted in Jeffrey Steele, *The Representation of the Self in the American Renaissance.* (Chapel Hill, North Carolina: The university of North Carolina Press).

Wiesner, Jerome, 1989. Quoted in Robert Scott Root-Bernstein, *Discovering: Inventing and Solving Problems at the Frontiers of Scientific Knowledge.* (Cambridge, Massachusetts: Harvard University Press).

Wilde, Oscar, 1992. *The Decay of Lying,* p. 235. In A. J. Ayer and Jane O'Grady (eds.), *A Dictionary of Philosophical Quotations.* (Oxford, UK: Blackwell Publishers).

Williams, Michele, 1982. Quoted in John Applegath, *Working Free: Practical Alternatives to the 9 to 5 Job.* (New York: Ballantine Books).

Wilson, Patricia, 1997. "Building Social Capital: A Learning Agenda for the Twenty-first Century." *Urban Studies,* 34(5/6), pp. 745-760.

Wittgenstein, Ludwig, 1993. In Robert Andrews (ed.), *The Columbia Dictionary of Quotations.* (New York: Columbia University Press).

Wolcott, Harry F., 1994. *Transforming Qualitative Data: Description, Analysis, and Interpretation.* (Thousand Oaks, California: Sage Publications).

Wolf, Susan, 1997. "Happiness and Meaning: Two Aspects of the Good Life," *Social Philosophy and Policy,* 14(1), Winter, pp. 207-225.

Wollstonecraft, Mary, 1997. In Rosalie Maggio, *Quotations on Education.* (Paramus, New Jersey: Prentice Hall).

Woodcock, Mike and Dave Francis, 1979. *Unblocking Your Organization.* (La Jolla, California: University Associates, Inc.).

Wordsworth, William, 1977. *Miscellaneous Sonnets. To B. R. Haydon: High is our Calling, Friend.* In The Oxford *Dictionary of Quotations.* Second Edition. (Oxford: Oxford University Press).

World Commission on Environment and Development (The), 1987. *Our Common Future.* (Oxford, England: Oxford University Press).

Worldwatch Institute, 1984. *State of the World: 1984.* (New York: W. W. Norton & Company).

Worldwatch Institute, 1985. *State of the World: 1985.* (New York: W. W. Norton & Company).

Wriston, Walter, 1992. Quoted in Peter M. Senge, "The Leader's New Work: Building Learning Organizations." In John Renesch (ed.), *New Traditions in Business: Spirit and Leadership in the 21st Century.* (San Francisco: Berret-Koehler Publishers). pp. 81 - 93.

Zukav. Gary, 1979. *The Dancing Wu Li Masters: An Overview of the New Physics.* (Toronto: Bantam Books).

Index

H

N

O

P

R